THE FIRST MOROCCAN CRISIS
1904–1906

THE FIRST
MOROCCAN CRISIS
1904·1906

By

EUGENE N. ANDERSON

ARCHON BOOKS

HAMDEN, CONNECTICUT

1966

LIBRARY OF CONGRESS CATALOG CARD NUMBER: 66-12325
PRINTED IN THE UNITED STATES OF AMERICA

DEDICATED
TO
MY MOTHER

PREFACE

The fall of Morocco under European control marks the nadir in the annals of Islam. The land was the last important Mohammedan territory to be taken by the Christians. Thereafter began the Islamic revival which is still in course. This volume, however, deals not with that subject but with the history of a conflict in European diplomacy, referring to Morocco proper only when necessary to explain the moves of the Powers.

The Moroccan crisis of 1904–6 contained all those elements that were present at the other crises on the road to the great war —desire for colonial acquisition, trade and investment rivalries, national honor, diplomacy which contained the threat of war, the principle of the balance of power, fears, and counterfears. The special interest of this episode lies in the fact that, as the first of the series, it shows the Powers choosing sides and fixing their opinions and policies. It determined the mental attitude of the players in the subsequent struggles and gave direction and mind, so to speak, to the later events.

In the history of the Moroccan affair from approximately 1898 to 1906, when the first crisis ended, are mirrored almost all the important movements of the Powers with reference to one another. The grouping of the Powers around France, the development of Anglo-German rivalry, the failure of Germany's policy of playing between Great Britain and the Dual Alliance, Germany's *riposte* and attempts to restore her position—all are either intimately connected with the Moroccan question or can be explained in the light of it. The Moroccan problem was the political barometer of Europe.

In making this study I have relied chiefly upon the official documents contained in *Die Grosse Politik der Europäischen Kabinette, 1871–1914,* in *British Documents on the Origins of the War, 1898–1914,* and in the two *Livres jaunes* concerning the

vii

Moroccan affair from 1901–1906. The presence of so much new material has rendered antiquated most of the older accounts of the subject. I have therefore not cited all of this secondary literature, preferring to give source references.

In spite of this rich material, there are still obstacles to a complete, impartial, and balanced account of this episode. The outstanding one is the absence of adequate French documents. The French policy has practically to be studied through British or German eyes and on the basis of the accomplished fact. The British and the German policies are thus treated with more understanding and detail. But even here difficulties arise. History cannot be written alone on the basis of the official diplomatic documents of today. The variety and amount of information which Ranke found condensed in the reports of the Venetian ambassadors of the sixteenth century is now scattered in a hundred places. The improved facilities for communication and transportation have limited and specialized the correspondence of governments and their foreign representatives. Information is now obtained as well from personal interviews, newspapers, and all those means which create governmental as well as public opinion. Much of great importance is never written down at all. Foreign secretaries often give orders to their ambassadors without explaining their reasons. This is particularly true of the British, less true of the Germans. Moreover, statesmen are at times inclined for reasons of policy to write down how they wish a certain event to be viewed, not how they actually view it. To check and supplement the official documents, therefore, the intimate and more personal information in biographies, autobiographies, and memoirs has been especially valuable, although neither the number of those works, particularly on the French side, nor the material in them is complete.

While international relations were more complex in the prewar days than ever before in history, the study of them is facilitated by the fact that diplomacy was still secret, that a relatively few individuals guided it. By focusing attention upon these individuals, one can interpret the motives which consciously or unconsciously determined foreign policy. These men sublimated and represented the diplomatic mind of the nations. A new actor had also made its appearance in their midst, that combination of Proteus and Fata Morgana, public opinion; but even it was given tangible shape in the minds of the responsible statesmen who had to interpret it and respond to its demands. I have tried to test these interpretations by checking them against the opinions of contemporaries and by reading in the contemporary newspapers, magazines, speeches, and letters.

Diplomatic policies and situations cannot be explained in a formula. Statesmen are all more or less opportunists; they usually keep several alternatives in mind. To assert that one country is bent on war and another on peace, one on revenge and aggression and another on defense, is to give an incomplete view. In handling the fluid and shifting materials of diplomacy, one must avoid both oversimplicity and historical fatalism. Further information will probably add or change many details in this study, but I believe that the main lines of the history of this crisis are herein explained.

I wish especially to express my appreciation to Professor Bernadotte E. Schmitt, Professor Ferdinand Schevill, Associate Professor Arthur P. Scott, and Associate Professor Louis R. Gottschalk—all of the University of Chicago—for much beneficial advice and criticism in reading this work in manuscript, and to thank my sister, Dr. Jesse May McFadyen, of the University of Minnesota, for many hours of help in searching for the right phrase.

Eugene N. Anderson

Chicago, 1929

TABLE OF CONTENTS

CHAPTER I

FRANCE AND MOROCCO, 1898–1904

I. THE DECADENT MOROCCO

Morocco was one of the last of the "backward" countries to be taken under control by a European state. It was a historic land with a long record of wars against the Christians; but, like many another, it had never adapted itself to the course of European civilization, and by the end of the nineteenth century had consequently become consigned by statesmen interested in colonial conquest to the category of "dying states." Hence it was qualified for acquisition, division, or control.

The execution of this work was beset with unusually grave difficulties. Several centuries of more or less regular diplomatic and commercial relations with European Powers had assured Morocco international recognition as a sovereign and independent land. Moreover, the rival interests of the Powers there were so firmly established and so conflicting that they seemed irreconcilable. Down to 1900 these Powers had jealously blocked each other from a special position, and, in case of necessity, as in 1880, had settled common problems concerning Morocco by means of an international conference.[1] And while this disunion obtained, that country of eight million fanatical and warlike souls able to play one potential enemy against the other was secure.

At the opening of the twentieth century Morocco was one of the least-known lands of the world. Insecurity of life, absence of roads and means of transportation and communication of any but the most primitive sort, undeveloped harbors poor by nature, and a governmental policy designed to prevent any Power from gaining a foothold in the land by the acquisition of property,

---

[1] This was the Conference of Madrid.

mining or other concessions had excluded the "Christian dogs" and maintained Mohammedan purity.[2]

Nevertheless, the country was reputed by Europeans to be rich in natural resources, the "pearl of North Africa."[3] The plains and valleys, if irrigated and cultivated by modern methods, would, it was held, produce vast supplies of foodstuffs and would become one of the granaries of Europe. Other regions were declared to be admirably suited for grazing; while the mountains, those bulwarks against the encroachments of the desert, were envisaged as teeming with minerals. Popular imagination glorified Morocco into another Promised Land.[4]

However that might be, Europeans were doing very little business there. Official French statistics reckoned the total amount of foreign trade with Morocco in 1903 as 109,495,888 francs. Of this small sum France and Algeria enjoyed 31 per cent; Great Britain, 41.6 per cent; Germany, 9 per cent; Spain, 8.4 per cent; and the other Powers insignificant amounts.[5] The contrast between economic fact and economic possibility acted as a spur to the groups desirous of political acquisition; but the smallness of these economic interests and their substantial equality for a number of the Powers made it difficult to determine which had the dominant claim to develop Morocco.

A conflict of strategic interests added to this complication.

[2] See among the numerous works on Morocco: Albert Salmon, *Le Maroc. Son état économique et commercial* (Paris, 1906); René Pinon, *L'empire de la Méditerranée* (Paris, 1904), p. 96; Eugène Aubin, *Morocco of To-Day* (London, 1906), p. 119.

[3] Victor Piquet, *La colonisation française dans l'Afrique du Nord: Algérie, Tunisie, Maroc* (Paris, 1912), p. 15.

[4] For typical reactions see Pinon, *L'empire de la Médit.;* M. Aflalo, *The Truth about Morocco. An Indictment of the Policy of the British Foreign Office with Regard to the Anglo-French Agreement* (London, 1904); *Zwanzig Jahre alldeutscher Arbeit und Kämpfe* (Leipzig, 1910), pp. 219 ff. For a more scientific discussion see Piquet, pp. 514 ff.

[5] The statistics about Morocco are all unreliable. They vary according to the persons taking them. The Moroccan government took none itself. Those given above are quoted in André Tardieu, *La conférence d'Algésiras. Histoire diplomatique de la crise marocaine (15 Janvier–7 Avril, 1906)* (Paris, 1909), pp. 499 ff.

Morocco's geographic situation on the Straits of Gibraltar and on the route to South Africa, her proximity to the French and Spanish possessions in North Africa and to Spain, made the Sherifian Empire a land coveted by all Powers with Western Mediterranean interests, in particular Great Britain, Germany, France, Spain, and Italy. Since each state suspected that any rival would abuse its advantages if it gained ascendancy, disagreement over the future of Morocco persisted. However, in an era which was coming to be more and more dominated by the urge for colonial control, this problem would not long remain unsolved. At the close of the century a favorable turn in international affairs and an accentuation of the chronic state of anarchy in the land itself brought the question to the fore.

The period of strong rule in Morocco under Sultan Mulai-el-Hassan (1873–94) and the grand vizier, Ba-Ahmed, came to an end with the death of the latter in May, 1900, when the young, inexperienced, and incompetent sultan, Abd-el-Aziz, assumed authority in person. By his preference for foreign goods and society he soon not only exhausted his treasury but also estranged his subjects. He acquired a fantastic collection in which figured cameras, coaches, bicycles, dolls, pianos by the dozen, and animals for a menagerie. He amused himself lavishly with his European friends. He listened to the advice of his two intimates, Kaid Ṣir Harry Maclean, a former English soldier from Gibraltar who had been in Moroccan service for almost two decades, and Mr. W. B. Harris, correspondent in Morocco of the *London Times;* and by promulgating a program of fiscal reform sought to replenish his resources and reorganize his country in time to prevent the intervention of the Powers, particularly of France, and the consequent loss of his independence. But, while his intentions were good, his actions proved disastrous for himself and his land.[6] Scandalized by the tales of his antics with the Chris-

[6] On the new sultan see Pinon, *L'empire de la Médit.*, pp. 150 ff.; Aubin, pp. 137 ff., 178; Walter B. Harris, *Morocco That Was* (Edinburgh and London, 1921), esp. pp. 65 ff.

tians and outraged by the new taxes that violated the Koran, the natives revolted in 1900.[7] The rebellions in the north and north-east constituted a double menace since they might lead to attacks on the French and Spanish possessions and bring on an intervention of those two Powers.[8] The Sultan had no money, therefore no army; and without an army he could collect no taxes. The rumor spread that he had actually turned Christian and sold the land to the English. The political and religious ties with his people were everywhere breaking.[9] By 1903 his precarious authority was confined to a few towns; and his capital, Fez, was itself threatened by the rebels.[10]

As this situation was nothing unusual in Moroccan annals, the natives were not greatly disturbed. If events had been permitted to take their normal course, a revolution would probably have replaced Abd-el-Aziz by some stronger man, and the country would have returned to its usual condition of semianarchy. The tragedy for Morocco lay in the fact that this disorder gave the opportunity for the interested Powers to intervene. The increasing insecurity of foreigners and the Sultan's need for loans foreshadowed the end of Moroccan independence. In 1899 Lord Salisbury, British prime minister, had declared that Morocco was decaying and might collapse at any moment.[11] Politicians elsewhere began to turn their attention toward this corner of Africa. Among them the French assumed the lead and solved the problem.

[7] See Aubin, pp. 203 ff.; Auguste Lombard, *La banque d'état du Maroc* (Montpellier, 1911), pp. 14 ff.

[8] On this disorder see Victor Bérard, *L'affaire marocaine* (Paris, 1906), p. 82; Ministère des Affaires Etrangères, *Documents diplomatiques. Affaires du Maroc, 1901–1905* (Paris, 1905), Nos. 33 ff., 42 ff., 61 ff., 90, 98 ff. (This *Livre jaune* is hereafter cited as *L.j., 1901–5.*) See also *Bulletin du comité de l'Afrique française, Supplément,* 1901, pp. 193 ff. (This magazine is hereafter cited as *Bulletin.*)

[9] Aubin, p. 109.   [10] *Ibid.,* pp. 320–21.

[11] Hatzfeldt to Bülow, Feb. 8, 1899, *Die Grosse Politik der Europäischen Kabinette, 1871–1914. Sammlung der diplomatischen Akten des Auswärtigen Amtes* (im Auftrage des Auswärtigen Amtes herausgegeben von Johannes Lepsius, Albrecht Mendelssohn-Bartholdy, Friedrich Thimme; Berlin, 1922–27), XVII, 295 f., No. 5152 (hereafter cited as *G.P.*).

II. FRANCE AND THE MOROCCAN PROBLEM, 1898–1904

By the end of the nineteenth century France's North African empire was assuming definitive form. In the 1890's agreements with Great Britain, Germany, and Spain (1900) consolidated France's possession and left only Morocco, a country almost inclosed on the land side by French territory, as an object whose acquisition was coming to be regarded by Frenchmen as essential to the completion of their ambitions in that region.[12]

To aid in the achievement of this goal a Comité de l'Afrique française had been organized in 1889 to popularize African questions with the French people, to exert pressure upon the government, and to carry on a unified and consistent activity for colonial expansion which the French cabinets could not do. Its membership was relatively small—about seventy in all—but very select. With the Prince d'Arenberg as its president, it numbered in its ranks deputies, senators, military and naval officers, officials in the government (although no cabinet members, of course), members of the Academy, newspaper editors and owners, members of the Institute, members of various geographical societies, colonial societies, chambers of commerce—men such as M. Gabriel Hanotaux, former minister of foreign affairs; M. Jules Siegfried, who resigned temporarily when he became minister of commerce in 1893; M. Paul Révoil, governor-general of Algeria; General Joseph Galliéni, governor-general of Madagascar; M. Eugène Etienne, former undersecretary of state for the colonies and future cabinet member; M. Antoine Guillain, vice-president of the Chamber for a time and former minister of the colonies; M. Paul Deschanel, president of the committee for foreign and colonial affairs in the Chamber. Through common membership and close co-operation the Comité was assured of the active support of the other colonial, geographical, and commercial organizations. The character and position of its members in state affairs gave it an undeniably great influence

---

[12] See Pinon, *Empire de la Médit.*; speech by M. Etienne on June 16, 1903, reprinted in *Bulletin, Supplément*, 1903, p. 179.

upon the government as well as upon the nation. This influence was enhanced by the organization of groups favoring colonial acquisition in both the Chamber (1892) and Senate (1898), the former of which under the presidency of M. Etienne boasted in 1902 almost two hundred members.[13]

During the 1890's the French advocated a policy of *status quo* with reference to Morocco. They opposed permitting any Power to gain undue influence there or allowing Morocco to reform herself. They were suspicious of any individual or collective intervention by the Powers, and wanted to hold the future completely free. But the defeats of Italy by Abyssinia in 1896 and of Spain by the United States in 1898 dampened the ardor of those two rivals. Then, when British attention was claimed by the Boer War and when the internal disintegration of Morocco increased the possibilities of intervention, the proponents of aggression demanded that France should act.

Late in 1899 the official publication of the Comité declared that the Moroccan question was of paramount importance in French foreign policy.[14] It promoted the campaign for the acquisition of Morocco so successfully that by the end of 1903 almost all parties in France, including even the Socialists under M. Jaurès, had come to consider the French claims to predominance in Morocco as superior to those of any other Power.[15] The popular arguments, based largely upon the proximity of Algeria to Morocco, ranged from the theory of the "natural frontier" to economic and strategic contentions. In Morocco rebellions and religious wars could easily start, it was claimed, spreading thence over the whole of North Africa and endangering France's possessions. If any other European Power established itself in that land, it could utilize the native resources in troubling France. On the other hand, by virtue of her experience in handling and

---

[13] *Bulletin,* July, 1902, p. 267.   [14] *Ibid.,* Dec., 1899, pp. 412, 429.

[15] See the debates in the Chamber on this subject, Nov., 1903, *Journal officiel de la République française. Débats parlementaires* (Chambre des Députés, Nov., 1903); Tardieu, pp. 17 ff.

employing Mohammedans, France was better fitted to perform this work of civilization than anyone else. These were, of course, the stock arguments of all parties advocating the establishment of European control over "backward" areas.

The Comité formulated a policy for handling both the internal and the international aspects of the question—a policy which M. Delcassé, minister of foreign affairs from 1898 to 1905, was actually to follow. It was the popular solution, and, for France, the only possible one.[16] As the Fashoda affair had taught the French that the approval of the Powers was necessary for the acquisition of colonial territory, the first requisite was to make agreements with the interested states, among whom the *Bulletin* included Germany. Moreover, the nature of the problem demanded this approach. For Morocco's international status, the interests of the Powers there, the military strength of the fanatical population, and the consequent need of having French hands completely free from the danger of complications before attempting to reform Morocco made this preliminary international understanding imperative. The program contained four essential points. The sovereignty of the sultan and the independence and integrity of his land should be assured. Adequate guaranties for the freedom of the straits should be provided. The legitimate interests of the Powers, considered to be chiefly economic, should be satisfied through the acceptance of the principle of full commercial liberty. Lastly, Spain's territorial claims should be satisfied. By this course the Comité and its followers thought to dispose of the international aspect.

At the same time Morocco itself had to be won. The *Bulletin* believed that a policy of "pacific penetration" carried on through the agency of the sultan would solve this task. The sultan was the sole source of authority, religious as well as political, that

[16] See *Bulletin*, Dec., 1899, pp. 412, 429; Jan., 1900, p. 2; April, 1900, p. 140; June, 1901, p. 182; March, 1902, p. 107; Oct., 1902, pp. 347, 350; Oct., 1903, pp. 301, 305; Jan., 1904, p. 3, etc. Also speech by M. Etienne, June 16, 1903, in *ibid.*, *Supplément*, 1903, p. 179.

France could properly utilize. By working through him she might further her own interests and might introduce reforms without provoking the natives to war. The sovereignty of the Sultan would not be touched nor the independence and integrity of his land be violated. The "pacific" aspect would prevent the other Powers from taking offence and would satisfy the French people. The "penetrating" aspect would give satisfactory reality. It was a masterful combination, with an air of superficial plausibility so long as one did not attempt to reconcile the phrases "pacific penetration" and "preponderant influence" with those of "sovereignty of the sultan" and "independence and integrity of the land."[17]

The French minister of foreign affairs from 1898 to 1905 was, as already said, M. Théophile Delcassé. Born in 1852, he was at a very impressionable age when the Franco-Prussian War occurred. He became so ardent a disciple of Gambetta that he could never speak afterward of their friendship without emotion. Journalist, deputy, colonial undersecretary, colonial minister— such was the course of his rise. Uncommunicative by nature, he avoided Parliament as much as possible. He was on intimate terms with M. Waldeck-Rousseau, premier from 1899 to 1901; but with the latter's successors, MM. Combes and Rouvier, his relations were cool, and he asserted his entire independence in the conduct of his office. In a short and caustic sketch, November, 1900, Sir Edmund Monson, British ambassador at Paris, wrote of him:

Delcassé is an unsatisfactory Minister to us diplomatists in Paris. He is extremely uncommunicative, not to say secretive. Consequently it is very rare that any one of us succeeds in extracting information from him. He has plenty of commonplace conversation, which flows glibly enough, and he will talk eloquently in an academical fashion. But he hardly ever tells one anything in the way of political news, and he has an adroit way of feigning ignorance which took me in at first, until I convinced myself that it was all shamming. He always urges that he is not a diplomatist by profession, but he carries the practice of subterfuge to an extent which I have hardly ever

[17] See *ibid.*, July, 1900, p. 257; Aug., 1901, pp. 259 f.; April, 1903, p. 120; Pinon, *Empire de la Médit.*, p. 182.

met before in a Minister of Foreign Affairs. On the other hand, he does not tell lies systematically, as X did.[18]

His long tenure in office and the free scope given him by the cabinet and Parliament, both engrossed in internal affairs,[19] enabled him to put his own impress upon French foreign policy and to give it a positive, constructive content. Although a member of radical cabinets that reduced the military and naval budgets and neglected the defenses of the land, he openly disapproved of that policy and advocated rearing a virile, patriotic generation of fighters. He courted and received the support of all parties. He took as the sole objective in his foreign policy the maintenance and development of French interests, and avowed himself an opportunist in his method of diplomacy. He was a *Realpolitiker* at a moment when the French people seemed to be turning toward internationalism and pacifism. His policy unfolded itself gradually, and, in the absence of adequate documentary material, it has to be explained largely upon the basis of its accomplishments.[20]

The new elements introduced into French policy by this minister were associated almost altogether with the Moroccan question. He seems from the start to have coveted that country.[21] He thought that since the Dual Alliance was firmly established,

[18] Lord Newton, *Lord Lansdowne, A Biography* (London, 1929), p. 209.

[19] Such as the Dreyfus case, the law of the Congregations, the separation of church and state.

[20] On Delcassé see Christian Schefer, *D'une guerre à l'autre. Essai sur la politique extérieure de la Troisième République (1871–1914)* (Paris, 1920), pp. 221 f.; Georges Reynald, *La diplomatie française. L'œuvre de Delcassé* (Paris, 1915); René Millet, *Notre politique extérieure de 1898 à 1905* (Paris, 1905), p. 2; Robert Dell, *My Second Country* (New York, 1920), p. 176; René Pinon, *France et Allemagne, 1870–1913* (Paris, 1913), pp. 116 ff.; Delcassé's speeches; Monson to Lansdowne, Nov. 15, 1904, *British Documents on the Origins of the War, 1898–1914* (ed. by G. P. Gooch and Harold Temperley; London, 1927——), III, 14 f., No. 11 (hereafter cited as *B.D.*).

[21] See his speeches, *Journal officiel, Debats parlem.*, Sénat, April 3, 1900, pp. 299 f.; Chambre, Jan. 21, 1902, quoted in *Bulletin, Supplément*, 1902, pp. 46 f.; Chambre, March 11, 1903, *Journal officiel, Debats parlem.*, p. 1356; especially his speech on Nov. 10, 1904, in the Chambre, *ibid.*, pp. 2381, 2386; Sénat, Dec. 7, 1904, pp. 1048 ff.; Reynald, p. 11.

France as well as Russia ought to reap some benefits therefrom. But, as Russia was turning her energies more and more to the Far East and was thereby weakening the effectiveness of the Alliance, he desired some means of re-establishing the equilibrium of forces in Europe. Particularly was this necessary since Germany had inaugurated her *Weltpolitik;* for, with German power increasing at so fast a pace, France had to seek new friends for the protection of herself, her colonies, her interests, and for the realization of her ambitions toward Morocco before it was too late.[22] This triple aim of better defense, of increased prestige, and of colonial acquisition in Northwest Africa he saw could be realized by the settlement of the international aspect of the Moroccan question. Italy and Spain as Mediterranean neighbors and Great Britain as a formidable colonial rival should be won to the French plan by agreements which at the same time should create friendships between them and fortify and aggrandize the French position in Europe. Moreover, M. Delcassé hoped to reconcile Russia with Great Britain, above all to prevent them from actual conflict. And, depending upon circumstances, he was apparently willing to treat with Germany. A colonial acquisition and a rearrangement in international relations were to be achieved together, and the Moroccan problem came to signify both.[23]

[22] André Mévil, *De la Paix de Francfort à la Conférence d'Algésiras* (Paris, 1909), pp. 117 f. Mévil's book contains the official apology for Delcassé's work.

[23] See Mévil, pp. 120 f., and Delcassé's speeches. On Dec. 7, 1904, in the Senate and on Nov. 10, in the Chamber, he spoke as follows: "The problem, in effect, was this: to establish the preponderance of France in Morocco, thereby to augment her power in the Mediterranean, not by alienating but rather by conciliating the Powers whose position in the Mediterranean brings them to our attention. . . . . In considering the positions occupied not only by England, but by Italy and by Spain in the Mediterranean, it is evident that if diplomacy succeeds in resolving this problem [of Morocco] it will have at one blow fortified and aggrandized the situation of France in Europe by the friendships which it will have procured and by the *rapprochements* of interests of which it will have been the creator."
He further declared that this had been his conscious policy during his six years of residency at the Quai d'Orsay (see *Journal officiel, Debats parlem.*, Sénat, Dec. 7, 1904, pp. 1048 ff.; Chambre, Nov. 10, 1904, p. 386).

The basis of the Franco-Moroccan relations was laid by the treaty of 1845 regulating the boundary between Algeria and her western neighbor.[24] However, the frontier remained in part indefinite; border raids recurred; the possession of the oases, Touat, Gourara, and Tidikelt, discovered after the treaty was made, remained unsettled.[25] The consequence was chronic trouble, which France tried to eliminate by occupying these oases late in 1899 and in 1900 and by beginning to construct railroads toward them.

Alarmed by this activity, the Sultan asked Queen Victoria in the autumn of 1900 to obtain assurances from France which would tranquilize his fears. Realizing that this would be impossible, the British government refused, and Sir Edmund Monson, the British ambassador at Paris, merely mentioned the Sultan's anxieties to the French Foreign Minister (October 17).[26] The Italian, Spanish, and German governments also showed some concern over this action at Touat.[27] M. Delcassé replied to them all with the statement which he had made in the French Senate on April 3, that in Africa France would honor all treaties signed by her, that she would respect the frontiers of neighboring states, and that she had no intention of changing the *status quo* in the

[24] See Augustin Bernard, *Les confins algéro-marocaine* (Paris, 1911). Treaty given in De Clercq, *Recueil des traités de la France*, pp. 271 ff.

[25] See various articles in the *Bulletin;* also Pinon, *Empire de la Médit.;* Bérard, *L'affaire marocaine;* speech of Waldeck-Rousseau in the Chamber, July 2, 1900, *Journal officiel, Debats parlem.*, pp. 1739 f.

[26] Exactly what the Sultan requested is not known. Count Bülow, the German foreign minister, heard in June, 1900, from an Italian source that the Grand Vizier of Morocco just before his death had proposed to Salisbury, the British premier, that the Powers guarantee a new boundary to be made between Algeria and Morocco, but that the British Minister had refused to consider the matter. See Bülow to Tschirschky, June 5, 1900, *G.P.*, XVII, 318, No. 5167. On the Sultan's proposal of October see Monson to Salisbury, Oct. 12, 17, 1900, *B.D.*, II, 259, Nos. 312 f.

[27] We have positive evidence that the Spanish and German governments did so; and as Italy was then in negotiation with France over the question of Morocco (see below), it is safe to say that her government did also. See Bülow to Münster, April 27, 1900, *G.P.*, XVII, 299 ff., No. 5156; Münster to Hohenlohe, May 9, 1900, *ibid.*, 301 f., No. 5157.

Mediterranean. She was merely occupying territory manifestly belonging to her.[28]

The number of attacks of the Moroccans upon Algeria increased. After several particularly bold raids had occurred early in 1901, the French government sent a sharply worded note to the Sultan which he interpreted as threatening action against his ancestral home, Tafilelt.[29] He appealed to the British government for protection,[30] and in June and July sent an embassy headed by the minister of war, el-Menebhi, to London and Berlin to obtain aid against France and to negotiate a loan.[31] As the question of an alliance was then engrossing the attentions of both the British and the German governments, neither felt inclined to give the Moroccans anything but innocuous advice, and this mission was a failure.[32]

The dispatch of that embassy just at the time when Anglo-German relations were so cordial alarmed the French Foreign Minister.[33] Through M. Révoil, governor-general of Algeria, he

[28] See *Journal officiel, Debats parlem.*, Sénat, April 3, 1900, p. 299. He also said in private that France had no intention of attacking Morocco. Münster to Hohenlohe, May 9, 1900, *G.P.*, XVII, 301 f., No. 5157; Monson to Salisbury, Oct. 17, 1900, *B.D.*, II, 259, No. 313.

[29] See Bérard, p. 68; Aubin, p. 178; *Bulletin*, Aug., 1901, p. 279; *L.j., 1901–5*, Nos. 1, 3, 4, 6. For the note see Révoil to Delcassé, March 23, 1901, Révoil to Si Mohamméd Torres and Ben Sliman, March 18, *ibid.*, No. 2 and annexe.

[30] So the British Minister at Tangier stated to his German colleague (Richthofen to Hatzfeldt, April 13, 1901, *G.P.*, XVII, 326 f., No. 5173).

[31] Richthofen to Hatzfeldt, April 13, 20, 1900, *ibid.*, 326 f., No. 5173; 328, No. 5174.

[32] See Cambon to Delcassé, July 4, 1901, *L.j., 1901–5*, 13 ff., No. 19 and annexe; Hatzfeldt to foreign office, June 19, 1901, *G.P.*, XVII, 332 f., No. 5177 and note; Holstein to Eckardstein, July 8, 1901, *ibid.*, 333, No. 5178; memorandum by Mentzingen concerning the conversations between Richthofen and the Moroccan Ambassador, *ibid.*, 334 ff., No. 5179, undated though handed in to the foreign office on July 19, 1901; Mühlberg to Mentzingen, July 19, 1901, *ibid.*, 336 f., No. 5180; Eckardstein to F. O., July 29, 1901, *ibid.*, 338 f., No. 5182.

[33] On the cordiality of their relations see below. Late in 1899 Joseph Chamberlain, the British colonial secretary, had made a speech at Leicester advocating an Anglo-German–American alliance; an accord over China had been made between them in 1900, and the Emperor had in January, 1901, hurried to the bedside of the dying Queen Victoria.

warned the Moroccan government against signing any political
or commercial agreement without French approval, and exacted
a promise from a Moroccan embassy then in Paris concerning the
execution of any accord which might be signed.[34] Among the
Powers, M. Delcassé had little to fear from Spain, with whom he
was on intimate terms, or from Italy, with whom in the previous
December he had made an agreement about Morocco.[35] He assured the British government that France had no intention of
raising "serious questions in Morocco." The Marquess of Lansdowne, British foreign secretary, responded with a frank account
of his conversations with the Moroccan embassy.[36] It was Germany of whose reactions M. Delcassé was most uncertain. In
June, through his friend M. Leon y Castillo, the Spanish ambassador, he suggested to Prince Radolin, the German ambassador
in Paris, that if the German government, as the victor in 1870,
would take the initiative, he would like to discuss various matters with a view to arriving at an entente.[37] The German response
to the Spanish Ambassador was that before Germany could enter into an arrangement with France whereby the hostility of a
third Power might be incurred the two countries must make a
mutual guaranty of each other's territorial integrity. Since
France would thereby have to guarantee the German possession

---

[34] Delcassé to Saint-René Taillandier, July 27, 1901, *L.j., 1901–5*, 20, No. 21.
What the promise was is not related. Also editor's note, *G.P.*, XVII, 332 f., No.
5177; Eckardstein to F. O., July 29, 1901, *ibid.*, 338 f., No. 5182; Richthofen to
Hatzfeldt, July 5, 1901, *ibid.*, XVIII, 781 f., No. 5872.

[35] See below.

[36] Lansdowne to Monson, July 3, 1901, *B.D.*, II, 261, No. 318; Cambon to Delcassé, July 4, 1901, *L.j., 1901–5*, 13 ff., No. 19.

[37] On these conversations see Radolin to Bülow, June 5, 1901, *G.P.*, XVIII,
772 ff., No. 5868; June 15, *ibid.*, 775 ff., No. 5869; *ibid.*, 777 f., No. 5870. Leon y
Castillo declared that Delcassé had said to him that "he wished for nothing better
than to converse with the German Ambassador on different points, that he would
be very desirous of arriving at an entente with him" (*ibid.*, 775 ff., No. 5869). At
the same time leading articles appeared in *Temps* and *Figaro,* papers in close touch
with the foreign office, to the effect that Germany had the opportunity in the Moroccan affair to prove her good will toward France (Richthofen to Hatzfeldt, July
5, 1901, *ibid.*, 781, No. 5872).

of Alsace-Lorraine, the proposed negotiation was crushed.[38]
None the less, in a conversation with Prince Radolin on June 23,
1901, M. Delcassé made and received an important statement
about Morocco. When the Ambassador mentioned the discussion in the French newspapers of a French protectorate over that
land, the Foreign Minister replied:

"If by that word protectorate one means that France, mistress of Algeria
and Tunis, has and must conserve toward Morocco an unique situation [*une
situation absolument à part*], it seems to me that it is self-evident [*il me
semble que c'est l'évidence même*]." "Nothing is more just, every one takes
account of that situation [*tout le mond se rend compte de cette situation*],"
answered Prince Radolin.[39]

Much or little could be read into either remark; but together
with the general diplomatic situation they enabled M. Delcassé
in the Senate on July 5 to declare that

if France, mistress of Algeria and through Algeria neighbor of Morocco
along an immense frontier, is forced to follow what occurs there with a singular interest,—our vigilance does not aim at other than the tranquillity,
prosperity, and integrity of the Sherifian empire. . . . .[40]

The presence of an embassy in Paris simultaneously with the
one in London and Berlin[41] gave the French Minister an opportunity for taking the first steps toward "pacific penetration."
The mission came to Paris to seek an agreement with the French
government upon a definite boundary line between Algeria and
Morocco which would assure Moroccan isolation. M. Delcassé,
however, aimed, by leaving the frontier line indefinite, to utilize
this geographic proximity as a means of creating a community

[38] Bülow to Radolin, June 19, 1901, *ibid.*, 778 ff., No. 5871; Richthofen to Hatzfeldt, July 5, 1901, *ibid.*, 781 f., No. 5872; Mühlberg to Mentzingen, July 19, 1901,
ibid., XVII, 336 f., No. 5180.

[39] Delcassé to Noailles, June 23, 1901, *L.j., 1901–5*, 13, No. 18. No account of
the conversation is given in *G.P.*

[40] *Journal officiel, Debats parlem.*, Sénat, July 5, 1901, p. 1207.

[41] The British government might have prevented the sending of that mission.
See Richthofen to Hatzfeldt, April 20, 1901, *G.P.*, XVII, 328, No. 5174. The German Minister at Tangier reported that the Sultan had asked Mr. Nicolson, British
minister there, whether he should also send a mission to Paris and St. Petersburg.

of interests with the Sultan and his people and of familiarizing them with things European.

The French Minister succeeded partially in incorporating this plan in an agreement with the Moroccan embassy in July, 1901, supplementing that of 1845. Drawn "to consolidate the bonds of amity existing between them [France and Morocco] and to develop their reciprocal good relations," the treaty provided that the boundary should remain uncertain, but that France and Morocco should each have the right to set up a line of posts for purposes of defense and customs collection in the desert region on soil which unquestionably belonged to them. The tribes living in the territory between those two lines should be permitted to choose which authority they preferred to reside under. Moroccans and Algerians could enter that territory freely for commercial or other purposes. Moroccan tribes who owned pastures in Algeria could continue to use them, and vice versa. For the preservation of amicable relations between the two countries each government agreed to appoint two commissioners annually to settle future border disputes.[42]

To Ben Sliman, the leader of the embassy to Paris, M. Delcassé offered French friendship and aid, but added a veiled threat of the trouble which France would make for Morocco if his offers were not accepted. While the French Minister showed a nice regard for Moroccan sensitiveness toward innovations, he voiced the expectation that when the land should decide to "enter into new ways" it would give France the preference for furnishing it with the needed resources. In an important dispatch of July 27, 1901, M. Delcassé instructed M. Saint-René Taillandier, the French representative at Tangier, concerning his future conduct. The French Minister was to assure the Sultan of French respect for the integrity of his land and for his own sovereignty, to af-

---

[42] On these negotiations see Révoil to Delcassé, April 27, 1901, *L.j., 1901-5*, 5, No. 5; Delcassé to Martiniére, July 20, 1901, *ibid.*, 15 ff., No. 20 and annexe; Delcassé to Saint-René Taillandier, July 27, 1901, *ibid.*, 18 ff., No. 21; Saint-René Taillandier to Delcassé, Sept. 19, 1901, *ibid.*, 22, No. 22.

firm France's desire to give him friendly aid, and to point out the benefit which the Sultan, as ruler, might derive therefrom. He was to warn the latter against foreign innovations which might imperil the security of Algeria.[43] Lastly he was to support all enterprises, commercial, industrial, and philanthropic, calculated to increase French influence in the land.[44]

Thus the French government could note with satisfaction that whereas the Moroccan mission to London and Berlin had accomplished nothing, the one to Paris had enabled France to feel out the Powers on this question, to proclaim publicly her special interests, and to begin the actual execution of her program. M. Delcassé was now started upon a conscious policy of establishing French predominance in the Sherifian Empire.

When the French and Moroccan commissioners appointed to execute the agreement of 1901 set to work, they found that its terms were impracticable. The assassination of two French captains by Moroccans in January, 1902, also showed that if order were ever to obtain along the frontier, French power would have to strengthen the Sultan's efforts.[45] The commissioners therefore negotiated in April and May, 1902, two further treaties, the content of which was much more in harmony with the French objective of loosening the boundary instead of tightening it, of providing a complete program of military, economic, and political co-operation between the two governments as follows: In case of need the two states should concert in pacifying and policing the frontier from Teniet-Sassi to Figuig, but no guard or customs posts should be established between those two points. In lieu of these customs duties, France agreed to pay Morocco a lump sum annually. In the other frontier area the two governments should establish markets and customs posts at specified

[43] Such, for instance, as the recent tax reforms.

[44] Delcassé to Saint-René Taillandier, July 27, 1901, *L.j.*, *1901–5*, 18 ff., No. 21.

[45] Révoil to Delcassé, Feb. 22, 1902, *ibid.*, 31, No. 25.

points in order to develop commerce between Algeria and Morocco.[46]

It became impossible to carry out the commercial clauses of the treaty because of anarchy on the Moroccan side of the border. But the Sultan made immediate use of the military articles by requesting permission of the French government to send Moroccan troops and munitions to the frontier by way of Algeria, and by asking it in July to furnish military instructors for these troops. M. Delcassé readily agreed.[47]

Notwithstanding these requests, the Sultan was dissatisfied with the course of affairs, and in September, 1902, sent Kaid Maclean to Europe to seek aid in stemming the tide of the French advance. Carrying personal letters from the Sultan to King Edward and to the German Emperor, the Kaid went first to London. He proposed to the King and to Lord Lansdowne that the integrity of Morocco be guaranteed by Great Britain, or, failing that, by Great Britain and Germany, for a period of seven years, and that, if at the end of this period Morocco had not thoroughly reformed her government and developed her natural resources, the guaranty should lapse. He proposed also that a Moorish loan be made in England, France, and Germany, and that all railway concessions be divided between those three countries. The British government approved the method of handling the project for a loan and for railroad construction; but, as it was already in conversation with the French government over the future of Morocco and was disinclined to tie its hands, it refused to consider the other measure. Thus the mission was a failure.[48]

[46] Révoil to Delcassé, Jan. 18, April 26, May 17, 1902, *ibid.*, 26 ff., No. 24; 33 ff., Nos. 27 f.; Graham H. Stuart, *French Foreign Policy from Fashoda to Serajevo (1898–1914)* (New York, 1921), p. 144.

[47] See especially Saint-René Taillandier to Delcassé, July 22, Aug. 6, 1902, *L.j., 1901–5*, 44 ff., Nos. 29 f.

[48] See memo. for Maclean, Oct. 24, 1902, by Lansdowne, *B.D.*, II, 272 f., No. 328; Sir Sidney Lee, *King Edward VII. A Biography* (London, 1925, 1927), II, 220 f. Apparently Maclean did not go to Berlin at all, although he threatened to do so if the British government refused his proposal. See Lee, II, 220 f.

In 1903 the Sultan was in dire straits. While the whole country was more or less in rebellion, the main center of danger lay in the northeast near Taza where the pretender to the throne, Bu-Hamara, "Father of the She-Ass," had acquired a large following late in 1902. He was in a position to attack the French along the border or the Sultan in Fez, and did so. His defeat of the Sherifian army endangered Fez itself. Even in his capital the Sultan angered his subjects by summarily executing the murderers of a British missionary. In this plight, he turned to the obliging French for further aid. He received permission for his troops and the loyal border tribes to seek refuge in Algeria. After M. Delcassé had officially intervened in his behalf, he was able to obtain a loan of 7,500,000 francs from the French banking-house of Gautsch. By the time the Anglo-French agreement of April 8, 1904, was made, the Sultan seemed to be falling in line with the French policy of "pacific penetration."[49]

[49] For instances of this co-operation see *L.j., 1901–5*, Nos. 33, 39, 44–46, 57, 60, 68, 70–72, 77–79, 81–84, 86, 89, 91–107, 110–11, 119–26, 132; for Delcassé's part in assuring the loan see Delcassé to Saint-René Taillandier, Jan. 5, 1903, *ibid.,* 53 ff., No. 39. The Sultan obtained similar loans in Spain and in England.

CHAPTER II

THE FRANCO-ITALIAN ENTENTE, 1900-1902

When M. Delcassé assumed office in 1898, the Bismarckian system of agreements which had isolated France in Europe had already crumbled away. The formation of the Franco-Russian alliance had been followed by the lapse in 1896 of the ententes between Austria-Hungary, Great Britain, Italy, and Spain for the maintenance of the *status quo* in the Mediterranean.[1] The way was clear for the enterprising French Foreign Minister gradually to win the friendship of the last three Powers, previously joined in enmity against France. The first of these *rapprochements* to bear fruit was the one with Italy.

During the nineties, Italian dissatisfaction with the foreign policy had been steadily growing. Italian leaders complained that Italy had suffered from a tariff war with France, that she had been unable to restrain France from denouncing Italian treaty rights in Tunis or from fortifying Bizerta, that she had failed to secure colonial territory in North Africa, especially in Tripoli, and in Abyssinia. They regarded the Triple Alliance and the good will of Great Britain as inadequate to Italian needs. They asserted that their country was the victim of the Triple Alliance, made to suffer by France because of membership in it, and not even protected against that Power, much less given compensatory benefits for these undeserved injuries. The anger directed at Great Britain was hardly less than that at Germany and Austria-Hungary.[2]

[1] Hatzfeldt to Hohenlohe, Feb. 8, 1896, *G.P.*, XI, 99 ff., No. 2664; Alfred Franzis Pribram (ed.), *The Secret Treaties of Austria-Hungary, 1879-1914* (Eng. ed. by Archibald Carey Coolidge; Cambridge, 1920-21), I, 124 ff., 142 ff.

[2] For manifestations of this feeling see Pribram, II, 104, 106; *Memoirs of Francesco Crispi* (ed. by Thomas Palamenghi-Crispi; trans. by Mary Prichard-Agnetti; London, 1914), III, 330 ff.; Hohenlohe to Bülow, Feb. 15, 1896, *G.P.*, XI, 230 ff., No. 2766; Bülow to Hohenlohe, Feb. 5, 1896, *ibid.*, 89, No. 2657; Bülow to Hohen-

To meet these difficulties, the Marquis de Rudini, premier from 1896 to 1898, inaugurated a policy of friendship toward France which his successors in office continued. While remaining loyal to her alliances, the Marquis said, Italy would henceforth endeavor to prevent trouble with other Powers and to restore normal relations with France.[3]

In 1896 Italy and France settled their difficulties over Tunis. In 1898 a commercial treaty put an end to ten years of tariff warfare between them and opened the way to the flow of French capital into Italy.[4] In the same year the two countries made a settlement of the boundary line between their possessions on the Red Sea. So when M. Delcassé visited Rome in 1898, he found that both he and the Italian foreign minister, Marquis Visconti Venosta (1896–98), thought necessary a durable entente between their two countries which would respect the French possession of Tunis and the Italian membership in the Triple Alliance; and they agreed that the Mediterranean, which had previously divided their states, should become the means of their *rapprochement*.[5] The Italian Minister was overthrown before any further steps could be taken; but under his successor, Admiral Canevaro (1898–99), an opportunity was offered to initiate the negotiations which finally led to the consummation of the entente.

---

lohe, Feb. 18, 1896, *ibid.*, 89 ff., No. 2658; and in general the documents in *ibid.*, chaps. lxviii, lxix. Currie to Lansdowne, Jan. 15, 1902, *B.D.*, I, 285, No. 355; 286, No. 356; Currie to Lansdowne, Nov. 27, 1900, Lansdowne to Currie, Dec. 12, 1900, Newton, *Lord Lansdowne*, pp. 211 ff.

[3] Bülow to Hohenlohe, Nov. 26, 1896, *G.P.*, XI, 285 f., No. 2813; Pückler to Hohenlohe, July 19, 1897, *ibid.*, 286, No. 2814; Bülow to Hohenlohe, March 17, 1896, *ibid.*, 293, No. 2819; Bülow to Hohenlohe, July 22, 1896, *ibid.*, 296 ff., No. 2821; Bülow to Hohenlohe, Oct. 23, 1896, *ibid.*, 299 f., No. 2823.

[4] *Politica èstera italiana* (1916), p. 499; André Tardieu, *La France et les alliances* (Paris, 1910), pp. 97 ff.; Radolin to Bülow, April 19, 1901, *G.P.*, XVIII, 716, No. 5833; Pinon, *Empire de la Médit.*, pp. 39, 44 f., 48.

[5] Mévil, *De la Paix de Francfort à la Conférence d'Algésiras* (Paris, 1909), p. 121; André Tardieu, *Questions diplomatiques de l'année, 1904* (Paris, 1905), p. 14.

In March, 1899, France and Great Britain settled the differences growing out of the Fashoda affair by an agreement which assigned to the former the hinterland of Tripoli. Since Italian leaders regarded the eventual possession of Tripoli as vital to the welfare of their state, they felt that Italy had been betrayed by her supposed friend, Great Britain, and the Italian government appealed to its German ally for advice.[6] The latter remained noncommittal, Lord Salisbury equally so.[7] It was France, the supposed enemy, who applied balm to the wound. The French ambassador, M. Barrère, assured Admiral Canevaro that Italy "need in no way fear that she will find France in her path if she should ever have ambitions toward Tripoli." When the Italian Minister asked for a written statement to that effect, M. Barrère replied that, although Tripoli was Turkish territory, M. Delcassé would "under conditions" attempt to find some way in which to satisfy this desire. Those conditions, of course, had to do with Italy's relations to Morocco. The materials were thus at hand for an agreement.[8]

[6] Canevaro called it an act of "perfidy," of "dishonesty," a "sharp slap in the face." See Saurma to F. O., March 29, 1899, *G.P.*, XIV, 429, No. 3946; Saurma to F. O., April 1, 1899, *ibid.*, 429 f., No. 3947; Saurma to Hohenlohe, March 29, 1899, *ibid.*, 430 f., No. 3948; Marschall to Hohenlohe, April 14, 1899, *ibid.*, 434 f., No. 3952; Bernhard Schwertfeger (ed.), *Zur europäischen Politik* (Berlin, 1919), I, No. 12; Rumbold to Salisbury, March 31, 1899, *B.D.*, I, 203, No. 246; Currie to Salisbury, April 4, 1899, *ibid.*, 203, No. 247.

[7] Hatzfeldt to Hohenlohe, April 4, 1899, *G.P.*, XIV, 432 f., No. 3950; Saurma to F. O., April 28, 1899, *ibid.*, 435, No. 3953; Bülow to Romberg, April 29, 1899, *ibid.*, 436, No. 3954; Romberg to F. O., April 30, 1899, *ibid.*, 436 f., No. 3955; Bülow to Saurma, April 30, 1899, *ibid.*, 437, No. 3956; Currie to Salisbury, Nov. 4, 1898, *B.D.*, I, 194, No. 236; Currie to Salisbury, April 4, 1899, *ibid.*, 204, No. 247; Currie to Salisbury, April 10, 1899, *ibid.*, 204 f., Nos. 248 f.; Salisbury to Currie, April 25, 1899, *ibid.*, 206, No. 251; Salisbury to Currie, May 13, 1899, *ibid.*, 207, No. 252; Salisbury to Currie, Oct. 12, 1900, *ibid.*, 282, No. 350. In Sept., 1900, Currie, apparently on his own initiative, appealed to his government to give the Lateran "some proof of our determination to stand by Italy in the event of her being attacked." Lansdowne refused (Newton, pp. 211 ff.).

[8] Saurma to F. O., April 28, 1899, *G.P.*, XIV, 435, No. 3953; Currie to Salisbury, April 4, 1899, *B.D.*, I, 204, No. 247. See also Canevaro's declaration in the Italian Senate, April 24, 1899, Senato, *Discussioni, XX Legislatura* (2d sess.), p. 946, quoted by G. Salvemini, "La Triple Alliance," *Revue des nationes latines,*

The negotiations were long drawn out; for, as France had Italy at her mercy, she drove a hard bargain. On December 14, 1900, Marquis Visconti Venosta, Italian foreign minister (1899–1901), and M. Barrère reached a secret agreement.[9] By its terms Italy received in writing a purely negative assurance that France harbored no designs upon Tripoli. The *quid pro quo* for France was more valuable.

> In that which concerns Morocco particularly, it is agreed . . . . that the action of France has for its object to exercise and safeguard the rights which result for her from the proximity of her territory to that empire. Thus defined, I [Marquis Visconti Venosta] have recognized that such action is not in our view of a nature to prejudice the interests of Italy as a Mediterranean Power. It has been likewise agreed that if there must result therefrom a modification of the political or territorial status of Morocco, Italy will reserve for herself, as a reciprocal measure, the right of eventually developing her influence in the Cyrenaic Tripolitaine.[10]

Oct., 1916, p. 250. Also see the interview between Delcassé and Ojetta in *Giornale d'Italia*, Jan. 3, 1902, reprinted in the *London Times*, Jan. 4, 1902.

Italy had formerly thought that she had vital interests in Morocco, and her hope to acquire the land had received expression in a clause concerning its future in the treaty of the Triple Alliance of 1891 (Pribram, I, 150 ff.; Vol. II, chap. iii). But the Moroccan vogue had passed; her wishes had become more modest. To be sure, the French occupation of Touat caused the Italian government in April, 1900, to declare excitedly to its German ally that the Moroccan question could become a reef upon which the House of Savoy might suffer shipwreck; but, as M. Prinetti later explained, what his predecessor in office had feared was that a French occupation of Morocco might force Italy to seize Tripoli in order to maintain the equilibrium of interests in the Mediterranean (Bülow to Münster, April 27, 1900, *G.P.*, XVII, 300, No. 5156; Bülow to Hatzfeldt, May 14, 1900, *ibid.*, 302 f., No. 5158; Wedel to Bülow, Dec. 12, 1901, *ibid.*, 718, No. 5834.

[9] On these negotiations, about which very little is known, see Barrère to Delcassé, Jan. 10, 1901, Ministère des Affaires Etrangères, *Documents diplomatiques. Les accords franco-italiens, 1900–1902* (Paris, 1919), 1 f., No. 1. (This *Livre jaune* is hereafter cited as *L.j., 1900–2.*) Salvemini, Oct., 1916, p. 249; Wedel to Bülow, March 31, 1901, *G.P.*, XVIII, 712 ff., No. 5831; Metternich to F. O., Dec. 21, 1901, *ibid.*, 726 f., No. 5840; Wedel to Bülow, Jan. 5, 1902, *ibid.*, 738 f., No. 5845; Wedel to Bülow, Jan. 19, 1902, *ibid.*, 747 f., No. 5851; Diplomaticus, "The Shifting Foundations of European Peace," *Fortnightly Review*, LXXVIII (Sept. 1, 1902), 370 f.; Anonymous, "The Marquis of Salisbury," *Quarterly Review*, CXCVI (Oct., 1902), 664 ff.

[10] Terms of the accord given in *L.j., 1900–2*, 3 f., No. 1, Annexes I and II. See also Wedel to Bülow, Jan. 19, 1902, *G.P.*, XVIII, 747 ff., No. 5851.

So vague a statement could be variously interpreted. M. Barrère thought that Italy had given France a free hand in dealing with Morocco so long as her action did not modify the political or territorial integrity of the land. Marquis Visconti Venosta declared later to the German Ambassador that the accord had only permitted France to take measures necessary for the defense of her frontier.[11] As either meaning could be read into the documents, the future course of Franco-Italian relations would determine which one would obtain.

The *rapprochement*, attested by M. Delcassé in the French Senate on February 11, 1901, and affirmed by a visit to Italian waters of the French fleet in April, had been facilitated by a number of circumstances. On the one hand, the Italian government was angry with Austria-Hungary for having excluded it, in violation of Article VII of their treaty of alliance, from the negotiation in 1897 of an agreement with Russia over Balkan affairs. Tariff difficulties with both allies were looming up, and an occasional irredentist voice was being heard. On the other hand, an anticlerical government in France made certain that in the near future at least the republic would not attempt to restore Rome to the pope. Moreover, King Victor Emmanuel, possibly influenced by his Montenegrin wife, leaned decidedly away from his father's policy of strict adherence to the Triple Alliance toward one of closer friendship with France, and, if possible, with Russia.[12] Italian public opinion was likewise showing itself markedly pro-French, a tendency which M. Barrère's courting of press and public helped to develop;[13] and when in 1901 the King chose the

[11] Barrère to Delcassé, Jan. 10, 1901, *L.j.*, *1900–2*, 1 f., No. 1; Wedel to Bülow, Jan. 19, 1902, *G.P.*, XVIII, 747 f., No. 5851.

[12] See Bülow to Wedel, Nov. 30, 1900, *G.P.*, XVIII, 502 f., No. 5704. The King made his first state visit to St. Petersburg in 1902 (A. Savinsky, *Recollections of a Russian Diplomat* [London, ——], pp. 25 f.).

[13] On Barrère's activity see Currie to Salisbury, Jan. 18, 1899, *B.D.*, I, 281, No. 347; Currie to Salisbury, April 24, 1899, *ibid.*, 205, No. 250; memo. by Richthofen, Dec. 17, 1901, *G.P.*, XVIII, 507 f., No. 5708.

pro-French M. Zanardelli to form a cabinet, the Italians applauded.[14]

The affinity for France of the new cabinet and the greater defiance toward Italy's allies were foreseen from the political past of some of its members. M. Zanardelli was a native of the Trentino, and would have been foreign minister in 1893 if the Austrian government had not objected.[15] M. Prinetti, the new foreign minister (1901–3), had spoken energetically in 1891 against the renewal of the Triple Alliance. M. de Martino, his undersecretary, had asked in the Italian Chamber, December, 1899, "how this Triple Alliance is able to serve Italy."[16] The attitude of these men was soon manifested. Toward the end of the year the Premier was making veiled threats of a tariff war with his allies;[17] while M. Prinetti, ambitious, inflammatory, and unreliable, was engaged in negotiations with France which radically transformed the nature of Italy's international obligations.

One of M. Prinetti's first undertakings was to gain better terms for Italy with reference to Tripoli. He proposed to France that "each of the two Powers be able freely to develop its sphere of influence in the regions Tripoli and Morocco at the moment that it judges opportune and without the action of the one of them being subordinated to that of the other."[18] The French government was willing to accept his overture for the sake of obtaining a freer hand in Morocco; it also saw an opportunity to win an even greater advantage. As the Triple Alliance was to be renewed

[14] Salvemini, Jan., 1917, p. 12; *London Times,* Dec. 16, 1901, p. 5; *G.P.,* Vol. XVIII, chap. xxii.

[15] Salvemini, Jan., 1917, p. 12 f., quoting Un Bresciano, "L'intervènto e le pressióni dell Austria nella crisi ministeriale de 1893" (*Nuova antologia,* Oct. 16, 1915).

[16] Salvemini, Jan., 1917, pp. 13 f.; Prinetti's explanation of this speech in the Chamber, June 14, 1901, is quoted in *Politica èstera italiana,* pp. 536 f. See also Zanardelli's interview in the *New York World,* quoted in *London Times,* March 27, 1901, p. 5.

[17] Dispatch of Jan. 24, 1902, *Zur europ. Politik,* I, 91.

[18] Barrère to Poincaré, March 10, 1912, *L.j., 1900–2,* 11 ff., No. 11.

in 1902, it determined to repeat its former endeavor to nullify the clauses in that treaty referring to France.[19]

M. Barrère argued the French case to the Italian government as follows: Italy had joined the Triple Alliance because of quarrels with France about the Mediterranean. As the two countries were now friends, with their difficulties already harmonized or capable of becoming so, should not their friendship be assured for the future by the removal of any aggressive point against France which the Triple Alliance might contain? Were the clauses of that treaty compatible with Franco-Italian friendship? "The alliance remains defensive," so he summarized his arguments later to his government. "But it permits a very broad interpretation of the duties of the allies; if France, openly provoked, should declare war, could Italy regard this declaration as a defensive step on our part? It is doubtful." So he concluded that "under defensive appearances, the Triple Alliance implied an eventually offensive character which ought to be eliminated in the interest of our security and of the relations of friendship between the two countries." Above all, the French government desired to bring about the suppression of the anti-French military conventions or protocols between Italy and her allies.[20]

M. Prinetti acknowledged the force of these remarks. In June, 1901—that is, before Great Britain had turned away from Germany to France, and while Austria-Hungary and Italy were still

---

[19] It had attempted to do this or to break the alliance in 1891 and 1896. See *G.P.*, Vol. XI, chap. lxix; *ibid.*, Vol. VIII, chap. lxv.

[20] These arguments are contained in Barrère to Poincaré, March 10, 1912, *L.j.*, *1900–2*, 11 ff., No. 11. One other argument, which, however, M. Barrère probably did not use with Prinetti, he formulated as follows: "What is more, nothing prevented her [Italy] from going beyond the actual text of the treaty, if she should judge that her political interests demanded it of her." See also Salvemini, Feb., 1917, p. 197. The military agreement of 1887 beween the allies had become known to the French government soon after its signing. See Salvemini, Feb., 1917, p. 198; also Jules Hansen, *L'alliance franco-russe* (Paris, 1897), p. 42. In March, 1901, *Matin* published a version of it and demanded its annulment (quoted in the *London Times*, March 27, 1901).

on passable terms—he made a verbal agreement with M. Barrère by which the rights of Italy toward Tripoli were put on a par with those of France toward Morocco. In return he promised that the renewed treaty of the Triple Alliance should contain "nothing hostile" to France.[21]

The problem of adjusting Italy's alliance obligations to her new international situation growing out of the Franco-Italian entente was taken up at the end of the year when negotiations for the renewal of the Triple Alliance were begun.[22] To strengthen Italy's hand, MM. Prinetti, Delcassé, and Barrère all attested publicly in December, 1901, and January, 1902, to the complete harmony of Franco-Italian interests in the Mediterranean; M. Delcassé referred pointedly to Tripoli and Morocco.[23] And the *Tribuna* gave bold notice, January 2, that "Italy counts for something and can with her weight turn the scale one way or the other."[24] In spite of his promises to France, however, M. Prinetti made very feeble efforts to change the Triple Alliance in accordance therewith. He said nothing to the German government about revising or omitting Articles II, IX, X, and the protocol[25] which Italy herself had had incorporated in the treaty.

[21] According to other reports from the German Ambassador in Rome, Prinetti promised "nothing aggressive" (Wedel to Bülow, Jan. 5, June 27, 1902, *G.P.*, XVIII, 512, No. 5711; 757, No. 5858).

[22] See Salvemini, Feb., 1917, p. 197.

[23] The occasion for these statements was the French occupation of Mytilene, which alarmed Italian public opinion. See Prinetti's speech in the Italian Chamber, Dec. 14, 1901, Cámera dei Depitatio, *Discussioni*, p. 6747; Delcassé's interview in *Giornale d'Italia*, Jan. 3, 1902, quoted in the *London Times*, Jan. 4, 14, 1902; Barrère's speech on Jan. 1, 1902, before the French colony in Rome, quoted in *ibid.*, Jan. 2, 1902; Delcassé's speech before the French Senate, March 20, 1902, *Journal officiel, Debats parlem.*, p. 605.

[24] *London Times*, Jan. 4, 1902.

[25] Article II of the Triple Alliance read as follows: "In case Italy, without direct provocation on her part, is attacked by France for any reason whatsoever, the two other contracting parties will furnish to the party attacked aid and assistance with all their forces. The same obligation is incumbent upon Italy in case of an aggression not directly provoked by France against Germany." Articles IX, X, XI, and

His sole proposal to Count Bülow, to whom he repeated his promise to M. Barrère, was that an introductory statement, intended for publication or for communication to France, should be included affirming the purely defensive character of the alliance. Other matters concerning Italy and her two allies were of far more importance to the Italian Foreign Minister in these negotiations. He wanted the allies officially to affirm Italy's preponderant rights in Tripoli; he wished for them to have a more binding understanding about the Balkans; above all, he sought to make the renewal of the alliance contingent upon the negotiation of tariff treaties with Germany and Austria-Hungary favorable to Italy. In discussing these questions with the German government he grew excited, wept, threatened to resign or not to renew the alliance. About those which concerned France he was more or less apologetic.[26]

German public opinion regarded the Franco-Italian *rapprochement* with misgivings. But the Chancellor assumed a nonchalant attitude, stating in the Reichstag, January 8, 1902:

The Triple Alliance still enjoys the best of health. . . . . The Triple Alliance is not a society for acquisition but an insurance company. It is not offensive but defensive; it is not aggressive but peaceful to a high degree. The Triple Alliance does not bar good relations between its members and other Powers, and I would not consider it proper if even a small part of the German press should show any uneasiness over Franco-Italian agreements. In a happy marriage the husband must not become jealous if his wife dances an innocent extra round with some one else. The main thing is that she does not run away from him, and she will not do so if she is best situated with him. . . . . The Franco-Italian agreements over certain Mediterranean questions do not violate the Triple Alliance. . . . . The goals of the present day *Weltpolitik* extend to areas and objects which lie far from Germany's

the protocol provided for the maintenance of the *status quo* in the Cyrenaic, Tripoli, Tunis, and Morocco, and, in certain eventualities, for an aggressive attack by Italy aided by her allies, upon France. See the document given in *G.P.*, VII, 99 ff., No. 1426.

[26] On these negotiations see *ibid.*, Vol. XVIII, chaps. cxxii, cxxv.

boundaries. I name in this connection, for example, the north coast of Africa, Persia, the Far East.[27]

That speech, however, did not reflect the Chancellor's actual feeling. He still assumed that, should any important change be made in the Mediterranean area, for instance in Morocco, Germany would be consulted;[28] but he relied upon Russia's retarding influence, Great Britain's hostility, and fear of Germany to prevent France from taking action in that land.[29] He was dissatisfied with the turn of affairs, and blamed Great Britain for having forced Italy into French arms by ignoring her interests.[30] He suspected that the Franco-Italian understanding contained more than M. Prinetti admitted.[31] He recognized the improvement in Italy's international relations, and realized that her antagonism to Austria would thenceforth become sharper, and that her Tripolitan ambitions would be so zealous as possibly to cause trouble with Germany's friend, the Turkish Sultan.[32] As to renewing the alliance, which he strongly desired, the Chancellor believed that self-interest and the known antagonism of Great Britain to the Dual Alliance would prevent Italy from changing camps.[33] Under other circumstances he might have been willing to make some further concessions to Italy in return for the re-

[27] Bernhard von Bülow, *Reden* (hrsg. von Johannes Penzler; Leipzig, 1903), I, 243 ff.

[28] Bülow to Metternich, Dec. 18, 1901, *G.P.*, XVIII, 721, No. 5835.

[29] Alvensleben to F. O., Dec. 26, 1901, *ibid.*, 727 f., No. 5841; Bülow to Wedel, Dec. 17, 1901, *ibid.*, 508 ff., No. 5709.

[30] Bülow to Metternich, Dec. 18, 1901, *ibid.*, 720 f., No. 5835.

[31] Memo. by Bülow, Jan. 12, 1902, *ibid.*, 524, No. 5715; Mühlberg to Bülow, April 25, 1902, *ibid.*, 589, No. 5754; Bülow to F. O., April 26, 1902, *ibid.*, 590 f., No. 5755; Wedel to Bülow, Dec. 26, 1901, *ibid.*, 728 ff., No. 5852; memo. by Holstein, Dec. 31, 1901, *ibid.*, 735, No. 5844.

[32] Bülow to Wedel, Dec. 17, 1901, *ibid.*, 508 ff., No. 5709.

[33] Memo. by Bülow, Jan. 12, 1902, *ibid.*, 523 ff., No. 5715; Wedel to Bülow, April 10, Dec. 17, 1901, *ibid.*, 715 f., No. 5832; 723, No. 5836; Bülow to Wedel, Dec. 17, 1901, *ibid.*, 509 f., No. 5709.

newal.[34] In the previous March he had relieved her from any obligations under the German-Italian military convention, although permitting the military conversations to continue as before.[35] But the Franco-Italian entente, the lever with which M. Prinetti expected to pry loose those concessions, was the very cause for Count Bülow's refusing to permit any change whatever in the treaty. As the alliance was already defensive, he said, there was no need for an introductory statement to that effect. Pointing to the expectation voiced by the French press that anti-French clauses would be dropped, he declared that any modification would permit the French to draw the desired conclusion and thereby to belie the true nature of the alliance. Before he would renew the Triple Alliance he demanded of M. Prinetti an assurance that Italy had made no agreements with other states which could diminish its defensive forces. He even expressed his willingness to drop the alliance rather than make any changes in it, remarking that Italy's adherence to it was of no fundamental importance. The Chancellor's adamantine attitude was effective. By May, 1902, M. Prinetti agreed to the renewal.[36]

In March, 1902, M. Prinetti had reported to M. Barrère the probability of his failure. He had refused to communicate the text of the treaty to the Ambassador, but had declared that the protocols thereto must be abolished,[37] and that he was ready, so M. Barrère reported, to give France "assurances of a nature to leave no doubt in our mind as to the character and scope of this document" (the treaty of the Triple Alliance).[38] On May 7, M. Prinetti informed the French Ambassador that "it will be neces-

[34] Bülow to Wedel, Feb. 24, 1902, *ibid.,* 545, No. 5727.

[35] *Ibid.,* chap. cxxiv.

[36] See the documents in *ibid.,* chaps. cxxii, cxxiv, esp. Nos. 5712, 5727, 5749, 5755.

[37] This was easily said since the German government had in the previous year released Italy from her obligations under the military convention (see above). Prinetti made it appear as a special favor yet to be performed.

[38] Barrère to Poincaré, March 10, 1912, *L.j., 1900–2,* 12, No. 11.

sary for us to discuss the future of our relations in regard to that treaty." Under French pressure, he agreed that "thenceforth it was in a direct understanding with us [France] that he should find the means of fixing the interpretation with regard to us which Italy intended to give to her obligations as an ally." He was willing to put this understanding into writing.[39]

Before the proper negotiations were well under way, the actual renewal of the alliance forced M. Prinetti to declare in the Italian Chamber, May 22, 1902, as follows:

> The Triple Alliance as it is and as it will be, completely and uniquely pacific and defensive, will remain in the future what it has been for years: the most solid rampart in the cause of peace. . . . . The Triple Alliance, containing nothing aggressive, either directly or indirectly against France, nothing which menaces her surety or tranquillity may not in any manner constitute an obstacle to the conservation and development of cordial relations with our Latin sister with whom we are and wish to remain friends. . . . . And since it has been said that there exists between certain Central Powers conventions and protocols adjoined to the Triple Alliance which modify its pacific character and would even be aggressive toward France, I hereby solemnly declare that there is no convention and no protocol of that nature.[40]

Presumably even prior to this statement, which was repeated in a formal note to the French government on June 4, M. Prinetti began negotiations with M. Barrère over the written agreement. It was the Ambassador's intention that that agreement

> would contain the engagement not to attack, not to join in any aggression on the part of one or several Powers against one of the contracting parties; not to consider as aggressive on the part of the contracting Powers the obligation to declare war in consequence of a manifest provocation [this was "the capital point" of the project, wrote M. Delcassé]; finally to abandon the military protocols and other dispositions of the same sort concerning us and envisaging war with us. If we are able to arrive at that result [wrote M. Barrère to his chief], we shall have obtained all that we could hope and desire.[41]

[39] Barrère to Delcassé, May 8, 1902, *ibid.*, 4 f., No. 3; Barrère to Poincaré, March 10, 1912, *ibid.*, 12 f., No. 11.

[40] Quoted in Salvemini, July, 1917, p. 321.

[41] Barrère to Delcassé, May 8, 1902, *L.j., 1900–2*, 5, No. 3; Delcassé to Barrère, June 18, 1902, *ibid.*, 6, No. 5.

The negotiations were far enough along to permit M. Delcassé to declare in the French Chamber, July 3, as follows:

The declarations which have thus been made to us [by the Italian government] have permitted us to feel assured that the policy of Italy by virtue of her alliances is not aimed either directly or indirectly against France; that she will not in any case be a menace to us, either in a diplomatic form or through protocols or in international military stipulations; and that in no case and in no form will Italy become either the instrument or the auxiliary of an aggression against our country.[42]

That statement was stronger and more inclusive than the one by M. Prinetti on May 22. It indicated the existence of a fuller understanding than the public knew of. It caused M. Prinetti some embarrassment when the German Ambassador brought up the subject. The Foreign Minister declared himself "somewhat astonished" at the speech; but after a feeble explanation in which he betrayed nothing, he remarked that "so far as he was concerned, he regarded the question as settled."[43]

Meanwhile the Franco-Italian negotiations continued. On November 1, in an exchange of notes an understanding was reached by which Italy was given a free hand to develop her "sphere of influence" in Tripoli, and France the same right with reference to Morocco. Nor should the action of the one be necessarily subordinated to that of the other. Then followed a clause which M. Delcassé was particularly eager to have incorporated:[44]

In case France [Italy] shall be the object of a direct or indirect aggression on the part of one or several Powers, Italy [France] will preserve a strict neutrality. The same will hold in case France [Italy] as a result of direct provocation is forced to take, for the defence of her honor or security, the initiative of a declaration of war.

A conditioning clause was added:

In that eventuality the government of the Republic [the Royal government] must communicate beforehand its intention to the Royal government

[42] *Journal officiel, Debats parlem.*, Chambre, July 3, 1902, pp. 444 f.

[43] Wedel to Bülow, July 6, 1902, *G.P.*, XVIII, 758 f., No. 5859.

[44] Barrère to Delcassé, May 8, 1902, *L.j., 1900–2*, 4 f., No. 3; Delcassé to Barrère, June 18, 1902, *ibid.*, 6, No. 5.

[the government of the Republic], so that the latter may verify that it is a case of direct provocation . . . . I am authorized to confirm to you that there does not exist on the part of Italy [France] and that there will not be concluded by her any protocol or military disposition of an international contractual order which will be in disagreement with the present declarations.

The Italian government asserted that these declarations were in "complete harmony" with its existing international engagements. The agreement was to be secret and to obtain until the Italian government abrogated it. A supplementary statement by M. Prinetti defined the term "direct provocation" to mean one which concerned the "direct relations between the Power provoking and the Power provoked."[45]

Was this accord compatible with the renewed and unchanged treaty of the Triple Alliance? With Article II it could be made to agree. Articles IX and X and the protocol it merely nullified but left standing.[46] It broke completely not the letter, but the spirit of the alliance. The dishonesty of the Italian Foreign Minister lay in three directions; toward the German government by permitting it to continue in the belief that the old relations as established in their treaty still obtained; toward the French government by informing it that this treaty contained nothing either directly or indirectly hostile to France, although Articles II, IX, X, and XI and the protocol of that treaty had been retained without any attempt to abolish them; toward Italy by not clarifying the situation.[47] The matter was so arranged that in the future the

[45] Terms given in *ibid.*, 7 ff., Nos. 7 and 8. On July 20 Barrère reported that Prinetti regarded the following cases as examples of direct provocation:

"1. The publication of sharpened dispatches [*dépêches maquillées*] by Prince Bismarck in 1870; King William's refusal to receive M. Benedetti.

"2. The Schnaebele incident."

As examples of indirect provocation, Prinetti cited "Prince Hohenzollern's candidacy to the throne of Spain, and such indirect initiative in Far Eastern affairs which do not aim at one of the contracting Powers, although that initiative may displease it and appear contrary to its direct interest" (Barrère to Delcassé, July 20, 1902, *ibid.*, 7, No. 6). The choice of examples is significant.

[46] See above.

[47] For a severer criticism of his actions see G. Lowes Dickinson, *The International Anarchy, 1904-1914* (New York, 1926), pp. 94 ff. Dickinson asserts that

Italian foreign ministers would be able to determine whether or not the agreement with France would be abrogated and the clauses of the Triple Alliance, temporarily in abeyance, would again be called into action. The Italian government was safeguarding its country on both sides and giving up none of its securities, although its policy looked toward two different international orientations. This was the equivocal position between France and the Triple Alliance, later between the Triple Entente and the Triple Alliance, which Italy was to occupy until she entered the World War.[48] The advantages of it lay in the fact that it gave greater mobility to Italian policy, that it caused Great Britain to iron out her differences with Italy early in 1902,[49] that

---

the Italian Minister broke both the letter and the spirit of the Triple Alliance. The analogy of this agreement to that of Bismarck's reinsurance treaty with Russia of 1887 was remarked upon by Italian statesmen at the time (see Lansdowne to Currie, Dec. 17, 1901, B.D., I, 284, No. 353). Bismarck's pacific attitude toward Russia was well known, however, and he was not responsible for the inclusion of the anti-Russian clauses in the Austro-German treaty of the Alliance. See Trützschler v. Falkenstein, *Bismarck und die Kriegsgefahr von 1887* (Berlin, 1924), chap. v., and *G.P.*, Vol. V. The Italian government, on the other hand, had not only pursued an anti-French policy, but had been responsible for including the clauses antagonistic to France in the treaty of the Triple Alliance.

[48] For analyses of the Italian policy see Rodd to Lansdowne, July 9, 1902, B.D., I, 292 ff., No. 364; Bertie to Lansdowne, Oct. 20, 1903, *ibid.*, 295, No. 366. For the German discussion see below. Mr. Bertie in October, 1903, formulated his conception of the Italian King's foreign policy as follows: "His aim, I believe, is that Italy should be a link between the several Powers of Europe and at the same time remain a partner in the Triple Alliance: that France should have hopes of drawing Italy away from Austria and Germany, and that those two Powers should be made to feel that an understanding between Italy and France and perhaps even with Russia also is possible. As to England the King probably feels pretty sure that her interests will not seriously clash with those of Italy, and he relies on England standing in the way of French supremacy in the Mediterranean" (Bertie to Lansdowne, Oct. 20, 1903, *ibid.*, 295, No. 366).

[49] On the renewal of the Anglo-Italian entente see Lansdowne to Currie, Dec. 17, 1901, *ibid.*, 284, No. 353; Currie to Lansdowne, Jan. 1, 1902, *ibid.*, 285, No. 355; Currie to Lansdowne, Jan. 5, 1902, *ibid.*, 286, No. 356; Lansdowne to Currie, Feb. 3, 1902, *ibid.*, 287, No. 359; Lansdowne to Currie, March 7, 1902, *ibid.*, 291, No. 361; Plunkett to Lansdowne, April 10, 1902, *ibid.*, 291, No. 362.

it opened up a future of closer relations with Russia, and that it assured Italy of the future possession of Tripoli. The French government profited most from these negotiations. M. Delcassé had won his initial victory in the execution of his policy.[50] He had, at least for the time being, nullified the anti-French clauses of the Triple Alliance and drawn Italy out of that group into a middle position.[51] He had also settled the important question of Morocco with the most jealous of the Mediterranean Powers, and had begun the process of pulling the Powers away from Germany and drawing them around France.

[50] This he realized. See *L.j.*, *1900–2*, 4 f., Nos. 2 f.

[51] Cf. Barrère to Poincaré, March 10, 1912, *ibid.*, 13, No. 11.

CHAPTER III

THE FRANCO-SPANISH ENTENTE, 1898–1903

The close of the nineteenth century found Spain at one of the lowest points in her history. She was disorganized, isolated, defeated in 1898 by the United States; her navy was destroyed; her colonial empire was shattered. Spain was particularly embittered toward Great Britain, whose Premier had openly spoken of "moribund nations" with direct reference to her, and whose attitude during the recent war had been strongly pro-American.[1] Fearful that the British might seize a Spanish port,[2] M. Silvela, head of the Conservative government, with the approval of the Liberal leaders, early in 1899 determined upon a change of policy by which Spain would seek to bring about a secret defensive alliance with France, Germany, and Russia.[3]

[1] In 1898 Chamberlain publicly advocated an alliance with the United States. See Jerónimo Becker, *Historia de Marruecos* (Madrid, 1915), pp. 414 f.; Wolff to Salisbury, May 15, 1898, *B.D.*, II, 253, No. 300.

[2] Early in 1899 Silvela asserted to the ambassadors of Germany, France, and Russia that if Great Britain and France had gone to war in the previous year, the former had intended to occupy Vigo (*G.P.*, XV, Vol. Nos. 4205–8). When this fear was brought to the attention of the British government, by an exchange of notes with the Spanish government it denied any such intention. See Wolff to Salisbury, March 10, 1899, *B.D.*, II, 255 f., No. 305; Salisbury to Wolff, March 16, 1899, *ibid.*, 256, No. 306; Conde de Romanones, *Las responsabilidades políticas del antique régimen de 1875 á 1923* (Madrid, ——), p. 36; Becker, pp. 415 f. The British and Spanish governments also found by an exchange of views in January, 1899, that they both wished to maintain the *status quo* in Morocco. The Spanish diplomat and historian, Becker, has written that they were about to make an agreement to that effect when the Liberal government in Spain fell from power (March, 1899) (*op. cit.*, p. 415; Salisbury to Wolff, Jan. 11, 1899, *B.D.*, II, 255, No. 304).

[3] The plan was approved by Sagasta, leader of the Liberals, by Leon y Castillo, the Liberal ambassador at Paris, and by the Queen Regent. See Alberto Mousset, *La política exterior de España, 1873–1918* (Madrid, 1918), chap. v; Radowitz to Hohenlohe, April 15, 1899, *G.P.*, XV, 115 ff., No. 4205; Bülow to Radowitz, April 27, 1899, *ibid.*, 119 ff., No. 4206; Radowitz to Hohenlohe, May 28, 1899, *ibid.*, 125 ff., No. 4210; and others in *ibid.*, chap. ic. Cf. F. de Leon y Castillo, *Mis tiempos* (Madrid, 1921), II, 255, written after the World War.

The sympathy of those Powers had been on the side of Spain during the recent war. But when the Premier laid the plan before them,[4] the German government was encouraging but skeptical; the French government, dilatory; the Russian government seemed not to favor it and advised Spain instead to hold closely to France.[5] Nevertheless, during the next few years the Spanish government continued its effort to realize this program, particularly a Franco-German *rapprochement*.

One of the main objects of this grouping was the defense of Spanish interests in Morocco. In spite of Spain's colonial losses in the war of 1898, her concern over the future of that Islamic land remained active. Spain claimed a special position with reference to it, just as France did   Economic interests, the number of her subjects resident in Morocco (larger than that of any other foreign nation), geographic proximity, historical attempts at conquest, and Spanish pride were all advanced in support of this claim. Strategic reasons, reinforced by her actual possession of small bits of territory in Northern Morocco, also prompted Spain to seek control of at least the northern part of the land and above all to prevent that area from falling into the hands of France or Great Britain.[6] The Spanish leaders recognized the French interests in Morocco and the British right to participate in any settlement of the problem of the straits. But, conscious of their weakness in dealing with other Powers, they preferred to main-

---

[4] Radowitz to Hohenlohe, May 28, 1899, *G.P.*, XV, 125 ff., No. 4210; Radowitz to Hohenlohe, Aug. 12, 1899, *ibid.*, 127 ff., No. 4211.

[5] Bülow to Radowitz, April 27, 1899, *ibid.*, 119 ff., No. 4206; Bülow to Radowitz, May 16, 1899, *ibid.*, 124 f., No. 4209; Radowitz to Hohenlohe, Oct. 5, 1899, *ibid.*, 130 ff., No. 4214; Tschirschky to Hohenlohe, Oct. 24, 1899, *ibid.*, 133 f., No. 4213; Radowitz to Hohenlohe, Feb. 4, 1900, *ibid.*, 134 f., No. 4214.

[6] Romanones, pp. 34 f.; Gabriel Maura, *La question du Maroc au point de vue espagnol* (Paris, 1911), pp. 1 ff.; Becker, pp. 446 ff., esp. chap. lxi; Pinon, *L'empire de la Médit.*, pp. 123 ff.; Emile Vidal, *La politique de l'Espagne au Maroc* (Montpellier, 1913), pp. 1 ff.; M. Ribera, "L'Espagne et la question du Maroc," *Questions diplomatiques et coloniales*, Jan. 1, 1902, pp. 46 ff.

tain the *status quo* as long as possible unless the larger Continental grouping was consummated.

In 1899 and 1900, when M. Delcassé showed a willingness to negotiate an accord over Morocco, the Spanish government evaded the overture,[7] and settled with him only the long standing dispute over the boundary of Rio de Oro.[8] During 1901 events moved faster. In March a Liberal ministry under M. Sagasta with the Duke of Almodovar as foreign minister came into office. It saw France, unchecked by Great Britain, pushing her frontier steadily forward in the desert region back of Morocco. So it suspected the existence of a secret accord between those two Powers. The British government denied it,[9] but Spain feared that an accord might be made to her exclusion and injury. The Franco-Italian entente also aroused her alarm. In this uncertainty the Spanish government endeavored to use the presence of the Moroccan missions in Europe in June and July to bring about a *rapprochement* between France and Germany.[10] The move failed. In August, M. Silvela published an article in *La Lectura* advocating a solution of the Moroccan problem by agreement with France. Encouraged by this expression and urged on by M. Leon y Castillo, Spanish ambassador in Paris, the Spanish government determined to open direct negotiations with M. Delcassé on the subject.[11] And that minister was ready to listen. The ne-

[7] This is asserted by Becker although he does not cite his authority. See Becker, pp. 414, 419; Radowitz to Hohenlohe, May 10, 1899, *G.P.*, XV, 123 f., No. 4208; Radowitz to Hohenlohe, Oct. 5, 1899, *ibid.*, 130 ff., No. 4212; Tschirschky to Hohenlohe, Oct. 23, 1899, *ibid.*, 133 f., No. 4213; Münster to Hohenlohe, May 9, 1900, *ibid.*, XVIII, 301 f., No. 5157; Wolff to Salisbury, Oct. 11, 1900, *B.D.*, II, 258, No. 311; Becker, p. 426; Romanones, p. 39.

[8] Schefer, *D'une guerre à l'autre, etc.*, p. 237; Mousset, pp. 121 ff.; Romanones, p. 38; Delcassé's statement in the French Senate, Feb. 11, 1901, *Journal officiel, Debats parlem.*, p. 295; Leon y Castillo, II, 143 ff.

[9] Durand to Lansdowne, April 13, 1901, *B.D.*, II, 259 f., No. 314; Lansdowne to Durand, April 16, 1901, *ibid.*, 260, No. 315.

[10] See below.

[11] Romanones, pp. 40 ff.; Mousset, pp. 132 ff.; Becker, pp. 425 ff.; Vidal, p. 138; Leon y Castillo, II, 173 ff., 122 ff. See also a speech of the Duke of Almodovar in

gotiations progressed slowly, not only because M. Delcassé was disinclined to concede to Spain the territory which she desired,[12] but also because he was treating with Italy and, to the disgust of the Spanish Ambassador, with Great Britain at the same time.[13] By September, 1902, the main lines of the accord were agreed upon. Then came further discussion over details; and, after a last effort (October, 1902) by M. Leon y Castillo to bring France and Germany together had failed, the accord was ready for signing early in December.

By the terms of the agreement Spain was to receive the region of the Sus in the south and almost all of the old kingdom of Fez, including the capital and Tangier in the north, as her sphere of influence, while the rest was to constitute that of France. The two governments agreed upon a policy of pacific penetration of the land, and the French government promised its diplomatic support to Spain in the execution of the treaty.[14]

The failure of this agreement was an accident. On December

---

the Spanish Chamber, June 8, 1904, *Diario de la sesiónes de Cortes, Legislatura de 1903* (Congreso de los Diputados), pp. 4919 ff.; speech by Romanones in the same, June 7, 1904, *ibid.*, p. 4883; Radolin to Bülow, June 15, 1901, *G.P.*, XVIII, 777 f., No. 5870.

[12] Romanones, p. 41.

[13] *G.P.*, XVII, 343, editor's note; Becker, p. 427.

[14] Leon y Castillo was allowed a free hand in those negotiations. See Romanones, pp. 41 f.; Becker, pp. 427 f.; Mousset, p. 135; speeches by Almodovar and Romanones in the Spanish Chamber, June 7, 8, 1904, *Sesiones del Congreso, Legislatura*, pp. 4883, 4944 f., 4917 ff.; exchange of letters between Silvela and Almodovar published in *L'Imparcial*, June, 1904, and reprinted in Leon y Castillo, II, 185 ff. The result was shown to Silvela early in September, 1902, and received his entire approval, "provided one treats of a work of peace and concord guaranteed against all suspicion and opposition of friendly Powers." The exact terms of the proposed accord are not known, only the main points. See R. Gay de Montella, *España ante el problema del Mediterráneo* (Barcelona, 1917), pp. 40 ff., quoting an article by Leon y Castillo in *Mercurio*, May 27, 1917; André Tardieu, "France et Espagne, 1902–1912," *Revue des deux mondes*, Dec. 1, 1912, pp. 635 f.; Durand to Lansdowne, Feb. 14, 1903, *B.D.*, II, 279, No. 336; Lansdowne to Monson, Aug. 5, 1903, April 29, May 13, 1904, *ibid.*, 306 ff., No. 364; III, 33, No. 34; 35, No. 37; Monson to Lansdowne, May 20, 1904, *ibid.*, 37, No. 41; Lansdowne to Egerton, April 27, 1904, *ibid.*, 31 f., No. 32; Leon y Castillo, II, 177 ff.

1 the Duke of Almodovar was called away from Madrid. Before he could return and issue instructions to sign the treaty, his government unexpectedly fell (December 3).[15] The incoming Conservative ministry under M. Silvela with M. Abarzuza at the foreign office refused to complete the accord. Although they recognized its advantages to Spain, they feared the possible attitude of Great Britain and decided to sound her out before completing the treaty. Upon doing so they were informed by Lord Lansdowne, early in January, 1903, that in case of a break-up of Morocco, Spain "would be entitled to a voice in any new international arrangements" over that land, but that the British government was strongly opposed to any discussion of such an eventuality at that moment.[16] In February, 1903, M. Abarzuza revealed the nature of the Franco-Spanish negotiations to the British Ambassador, and asked for an official British objection to it so that he (M. Abarzuza) would be in a firmer position to refuse his signature.[17] Lord Lansdowne replied as follows:

We regard it, as of the utmost importance that Spain and Great Britain should act together in regard to Morocco. . . . . I have more than once informed French Ambassador here that we deprecated attempts to bring about a virtual partition of Morocco. . . . . We should certainly not tolerate an attempt to deal with Morocco without regard to British interests.[18]

[15] Mousset, p. 135; Leon y Castillo, II, 128.

[16] On this question see a speech by Maura, minister of foreign affairs, in the Spanish Chamber, June 9, 1904, *Sesiones del Congreso, Legislatura,* p. 4959; Becker, pp. 429 f.; Tardieu, p. 635; Durand to Lansdowne, Jan. 3, 1903, *B.D.,* II, 276 f., No. 332; Lansdowne to Durand, Jan. 5, 1903, *ibid.,* 277, No. 333; Durand to Lansdowne, Jan. 17, 1903, *ibid.,* 278, No. 335; Metternich to F. O., Dec. 31, 1902, *G.P.,* XVII, 247 f., No. 5192; Groeben to F. O., Sept. 17, 1903, *ibid.,* 353 f., No. 5198 and note; Monson to Lansdowne, April 22, 1904, *B.D.,* III, 30, No. 30; Leon y Castillo, II, 179 f. There is a story that Silvela tried to change the basis of the accord in such a way as also to obtain Russian support for Spain against Great Britain and that he was willing to enter the anti-British camp. His proposal to spend eight hundred million *pesetas* in the building of a navy pointed in this direction; but that there is anything to the tale seems doubtful. See Mousset, pp. 137 ff.; Tardieu, pp. 635 f.; Anonymous, "Una nouva alleanza," *Nouva antologia,* Aug. 1, 1903, pp. 511 f.

[17] Durand to Lansdowne, Feb. 14, 1903, *B.D.,* II, 279, No. 336.

[18] Lansdowne to Durand, Feb. 16, 21, 1903, *ibid.,* 279 f., No. 337; 280, No. 339.

Thus while M. Delcassé was assuring the Spanish government that their agreement could be concluded without fear since Great Britain was interested only in Tangier,[19] the Spanish Foreign Minister was being informed to the contrary by Lord Lansdowne himself. As M. Abarzuza did not believe in the possibility of an Anglo-French agreement over Morocco, he let the negotiations with France fall through.[20]

Immediately thereafter, however, arose a report of Anglo-French conversations for that very purpose. In alarm the Spanish government questioned the British Foreign Secretary and received the following assurance: "We are quite willing to enter into an agreement with the Spanish Government that neither will commit itself to any settlement of Moorish question without previously consulting the other."[21]

As it developed later, Spain lost by relying upon Great Britain and not concluding this accord. For the British promise was too general to be of much value, and after the Anglo-French agreement was made, Spain had to accept the territory which the two Powers had reserved for her. Her portion was naturally not as large as before, nor were the terms as favorable. For France and M. Delcassé, on the other hand, it was fortunate that the project failed. The resulting agreement would have been strongly opposed by the French as too advantageous to Spain.[22] France obtained better terms by first arriving at a settlement with Great Britain. But the *rapprochement* between the two Latin Powers was an actuality, and that had been one of M. Delcassé's main objects.

---

[19] Durand to Lansdowne, Feb. 21, 1903, *ibid.*, 280, No. 338.

[20] See Tardieu, p. 635; Leon y Castillo, II, 179 f.

[21] Durand to Lansdowne, Feb. 21, 1903, *B.D.*, II, 280, No. 338; Lansdowne to Durand, Feb. 21, 1903, *ibid.*, 280, No. 339; Lansdowne to Durand, March 29, 1903, *ibid.*, 282, No. 334; Leon y Castillo, II, 180.

[22] Maura, p. 88; speeches by Ribot and Deschanel in the French Chamber, March 11, Nov. 19, 1903, *Journal officiel, Debats parlem.*, pp. 793, 1111 f.; Millet, *Notre politique extérieure*, pp. 193 ff.; Pinon, *France et Allemagne*, pp. 143 f.

CHAPTER IV

DELCASSÉ'S POLICY TOWARD GREAT BRITAIN AND GERMANY, 1898–1902

M. Delcassé assumed office at a most unpropitious time for the success of his policy with reference to Great Britain. On September 1, 1898, he remarked to Sir Edmund Monson, the British ambassador, that "he had always . . . . regarded as eminently desirable a cordial understanding between England, France, and Russia," and offered his service "in soothing the way both at St. Petersburgh and Paris for the attainment of this object."[1] From then until March of the next year he repeatedly urged Lord Salisbury, British premier and foreign minister, to agree to a general understanding on all matters at issue, so that Great Britain and France could exchange the old relation of hostility for one of friendship.[2] But in spite of the French Minister's cordiality the Fashoda crisis in the autumn and early winter of 1898 brought the two countries perilously close to war.[3] Anglo-Russian difficulties in China and elsewhere also remained acute.[4] Furthermore, Lord Salisbury replied to M. Delcassé that French ministries were too unstable to deal with.[5] Hence, instead of improving, relations between the two countries became more strained. In the late winter and early spring of 1899, the belli-

[1] Monson to Salisbury, Sept. 1, 1899, B.D., I, 216, No. 262.

[2] Monson to Salisbury, Sept. 8, 1898, ibid., 163, No. 188, and other documents in chaps. iv, v. Delcassé went so far as to state to Monson on Sept. 28, 1898, that "he would much prefer an Anglo-French to a Franco-Russian alliance." See Monson to Salisbury, Sept. 28, 1898, ibid., 171, No. 198.

[3] Monson to Salisbury, Sept. 22, 1898, ibid., 169, No. 196, and other documents in the same chapter.

[4] Monson to Salisbury, Sept. 8, 1898, ibid., 37, No. 58; and others in ibid., chap. i.

[5] So stated by Paul Cambon in an interview in the London Times, Dec. 22, 1920.

cose stand on the Fashoda affair taken by the British government and press aroused a general fear in France of a British attack.[6] By August, the French Foreign Minister complained bitterly to the British Ambassador that "the conduct of her Majesty's Government seemed to show a deliberate intention of being unfriendly to France in every possible way," and added that "he began to believe that the politicians who argue that there is nothing to be done with England are right."[7]

During the period of the Boer War, the presence of Lord Salisbury at the foreign office, the bitter feeling of the French against the British, the continued Anglo-Russian trouble in China, and the British attempt to align with Germany prevented M. Delcassé from obtaining any results.[8] In fact, conditions were more favorable for the pursuance of a directly anti-British policy. The Russian government wished it, and worked for closer concert against Great Britain among the Continental Powers.[9] The Spanish government had the more far-reaching ambition of bringing about a definite Continental union against Great Britain.[10] Italy was at odds with the latter. The German Emperor and his government had been wooing France and making veiled proposals for co-operation since 1890.[11] And French feeling

[6] Monson to Salisbury, Jan. 13, 1899, *B.D.*, I, 199, No. 241.

[7] Monson to Salisbury, Aug. 14, 1899, *ibid.*, 212, No. 259. Cambon had in March made similar complaints to Salisbury (Salisbury to Monson, March 15, 1899, *ibid.*, 211, No. 257).

[8] For expression of French public opinion against Great Britain see two articles by Ernst Lavisse in the *Revue de Paris*, Feb. 1, 1899, and Jan. 1, 1900. See also Monson to Salisbury, Feb. 3, 1899, *B.D.*, I, 200 f., No. 242; Mévil, *De la paix de Francfort, etc.*, pp. 128 f.; Sir Thomas Barclay, *Thirty Years; Anglo-French Reminiscences, 1876–1906* (London, 1914), pp. 193 f., 209 f.; J. A. Spender, *Life, Journalism, and Politics* (London, 1927), I, 183 ff.; Newton, *Lord Lansdowne*, p. 209.

[9] Romanones, *Las responsabilidades políticas, etc.*, pp. 27, 36; Monson to Salisbury, Oct. 27, 1899, *B.D.*, I, 234 f., No. 287; Rumbold to Salisbury, Nov. 3, 1899, *ibid.*, 237, No. 291; *G.P.*, Vol. XV, chaps. ic, ci, ciii.

[10] See above, chap. iii; also Emil Bourgeois et Georges Pagès, *Les origines et les responsabilités de la grande guerre* (Paris, 1922), p. 276.

[11] The German Emperor made a special endeavor to win France; hence his numerous telegrams of congratulations or condolence to French leaders, his toasts

toward Germany had become more amicable than at any time since 1870.

The French Foreign Minister did not deviate from his original purpose,[12] but tried rather to be friendly to both Great Britain and Germany, to play between them for the advantage of France; and, warned by Mr. Chamberlain's[13] open advocacy in November, 1899, of an alliance with Germany and the United States and by the signs of an Anglo-German *rapprochement*, he sought to eliminate the occasion for this alliance.[14] This policy had been foreshadowed during the Fashoda crisis.

In December, 1898, immediately after France had retreated before the British demands, M. Delcassé in a conversation with Herr Arthur von Huhn, correspondent of the *Kölnische Zeitung*,

---

and decorations for French officers, etc. The French called him the "new Lohengrin." Both he and Bülow made repeated hints to the French representatives for a *rapprochement;* and one of the Emperor's favorite schemes to form a Continental grouping against Great Britain and the United States was well known from his frequent references to it. See Theodor Wolff, *Das Vorspiel* (Munich, 1924), pp. 110, 114, 117, 123 f.; *G.P.*, Vol. XVIII, Nos. 5860–71; Bourgeois et Pagès, pp. 277 ff., 256 f.; William II to Bülow, Oct. 29, 1899, *G.P.*, XV, 406 ff., No. 4394; and the editor's long note thereto, pp. 406 ff. On June 4, 1899, the French Ambassador reported a conversation between the French naval attaché, Buchard, and the Emperor in which the latter said: "The hour is certainly come when the Continent must defend itself against England and America, and I think that it is necessary for Germany and France to rely upon each other [*s'appuient l'une sur l'autre*]." And Buchard added, "The Emperor is very desirous of establishing good relations with you" (Bourgeois et Pagès, p. 279). See also Spring Rice to Villiers, April 24, 1900, Stephen Gwynn (ed.), *The Letters and Friendships of Sir Cecil Spring Rice. A Record* (Boston and New York, 1929), I, 220.

[12] How entirely alien to Delcassé's mind was the idea of a Continental alliance with Germany was shown by the fact that in August, 1899, at his instigation the phrase "the maintenance of the equilibrium between the forces of Europe" was introduced into the Dual Alliance. See Ministère des Affaires Etrangères, *Documents diplomatiques. L'alliance franco-russe* (Paris, 1918), pp. 94 f.; Dickinson, *The International Anarchy, 1904–1914* (New York, 1926), p. 108; Georges Michon, *L'alliance franco-russe, 1891–1917* (Paris, 1927), pp. 87 ff.

[13] Chamberlain was Colonial minister in the Unionist cabinet.

[14] In September, 1898, Delcassé had spoken to Monson of the rumors of an "alliance" between Great Britain and Germany (Monson to Salisbury, Sept. 8, 1898, *B.D.*, I, 162, No. 187).

had bitterly denounced the brutal threats of Great Britain against France, had expressed his fear that that Power was seeking war in order to have an excuse for destroying the French fleet, and had proposed a *rapprochement* with Germany for pursuing a common policy against British encroachments and for making colonial accords.[15] Simultaneously with this indirect overture, which had never been followed up by either government, the French Minister had threatened the British government with the acceptance of indirect proposals from Germany for co-operation against it if Great Britain did not change her attitude toward France and assent to his offer of a general accord.[16]

During 1899 M. Delcassé had turned farther away from Great Britain and had sought means of holding her in check.[17] But when the Boer War broke out, he held aloof from any movements for intervention, even risked unpopularity by publicly denouncing the expressions of rabid anti-British sentiment on the part of the French people.[18] Upon the retirement of Lord Salisbury from the foreign office in November, 1900, he again suggested a

[15] Memo. by Huhn, Dec. 5, 1898, *G.P.*, XIII, 247 ff., No. 3558.

[16] Monson to Salisbury, Oct. 28, 1898, *B.D.*, I, 185, No. 221; Monson to Salisbury, Dec. 9, 1898, *ibid.*, 196, No. 238.

[17] Count Witte writes in his *Memoirs* (New York, 1921), p. 178, that when Delcassé came to St. Petersburg in August, 1899, he sought means of accomplishing this end, and urged the Russian government to push the construction of the Orenburg-Tashkent Railway so that in emergency Russia could threaten India. Leon y Castillo, Spanish ambassador at Paris and an intimate friend of the Minister, likewise stated in round terms to Radowitz, German ambassador at Madrid, in May, 1899, that Delcassé belonged to the party desirous of a closer understanding with Germany (Radowitz to Hohenlohe, May 28, 1899, *G.P.*, XV, 125 ff., No. 4210. On the other hand, Sir Thomas Barclay records that upon Delcassé's departure for St. Petersburg in August, 1899, the latter said to him that "there was nothing he [Delcassé] personally would welcome more warmly than a state of feeling which would permit the two Governments [French and British] to negotiate a solution of their outstanding difficulties in a friendly give-and-take spirit" (Barclay, p. 170).

[18] Barclay, pp. 169 f.; Monson to Salisbury, Dec. 1, 1899, *B.D.*, I, 242, No. 300; Monson to Salisbury, Nov. 7, 1899, *ibid.*, 239, No. 294; Wolff to Salisbury, June 9, 1900, *ibid.*, II, 258, No. 210.

general understanding to the British government.[19] He was accused of being Anglophile to the detriment of French interests, particularly in Morocco;[20] for many of the French writers advocated a policy of co-operation with Germany for the settlement of colonial questions (among which, of course, would be included the Moroccan), while Great Britain could not effectively object.[21] But M. Delcassé was willing merely to occupy the Saharan oases back of Algeria during the war and to initiate the French policy for the eventual acquisition of the Sherifian Empire.

Not that the French Foreign Minister was averse to any accord with Germany. As already seen, he made an indirect overture to the German government for an agreement while the Moroccan missions were in Europe in 1901. Although rebuffed on that occasion, he made another attempt in October of the same year at the urging of the Spanish and the Russian governments.[22] At this time M. Jules Hansen, a French agent, stated to the Ger-

[19] Lee, *King Edward VII*, II, 214.

[20] According to an anonymous article, "Quatre ans de politique extérieure," *Revue politique et parlementaire*, Oct., 1902, pp. 24 f., 31, on one occasion during the Boer War when a deputy asked Delcassé if he did not think this an opportune time to settle the Moroccan affair with Great Britain, the Minister replied, "How do you wish me to speak with the English Government? It is so occupied that it has no time to reply."

[21] Robert de Caix, writing in the *Bulletin*, was one of these. Moreover, in March, 1901, not long after the German Emperor's visit to England, Delcassé took advantage of the opportunity offered by the presence of the British mission in Paris for announcing the accession of King Edward VII to the throne, to let the British know that the French government wanted a "good understanding" with them (Lee, II, 14 f.).

[22] It must be remembered that Delcassé was then discussing the Moroccan problem with the Spanish Ambassador, who sought to use that question as the means for paving the way to the new Continental combination. Moreover, the Czar and the German Emperor, together with their foreign ministers, had an interview at Danzig in September at which the Russian Minister openly advocated a Russo-German alliance. From Danzig the Czar journeyed to France, and a short time thereafter occurred Delcassé's indirect overture to Radolin. On the meeting at Danzig see Bülow's account of the conversations on Sept. 12, 14, 1901, in *G.P.*, XVIII, 28 ff., Nos. 5393–95; Savinsky, *Recollections of a Russian Diplomat*, pp. 17 ff.

man Ambassador in Paris that M. Delcassé had recently expressed to him the earnest wish to meet Count Bülow personally. The problem was where and how to meet. The French Minister had said that if the Count would come secretly and unofficially to Paris, he would greet him most heartily and would make a public visit to Berlin in return.[23] Although very much interested, Count Bülow refused to run the risk. The time was inopportune, he said; the French government and people must first be more solicitous of closer relations with Germany.[24] That reply postponed the matter to the Greek calends.

In 1902 M. Delcassé made a concentrated effort to establish the French claim to ascendancy in Morocco. His negotiations with Italy, which led to the agreement of November of that year, and those with Spain, which in December proved abortive, have already been considered. Simultaneously therewith, M. Delcassé again endeavored to negotiate with Great Britain and, perhaps, with Germany on the same question.

On several occasions in January and February, M. Cambon, the French ambassador at London, discussed Anglo-French differences, including the Moroccan one, with Mr. Chamberlain, British colonial minister, and with Lord Lansdowne, British foreign secretary since November, 1900. While the British officials showed some interest, no progress was made.[25] For after the

[23] The identical project was also proposed to Radolin by Pallain, governor of the Banque de France. Hansen also remarked that an important Russian personage had told him positively that Lamsdorff had spoken to Delcassé of the trip to Berlin. The idea seems to have been suggested to the Russian Minister by the German Emperor (Radolin to Bülow, Oct. 27, 1901, ibid., 782 ff., No. 5873).

[24] Bülow to Radolin, Nov. 6, 1901, ibid., 785, No. 5874.

[25] Metternich to F. O., Jan. 30, 1902, ibid., XVII, 342 f., No. 5186; Hermann Freiherr von Eckardstein, Lebenserinnerungen und politische Denkwürdigkeiten (Leipzig, 1919, 1921), II, 379; Lansdowne to Monson, Jan. 22, 1902, B.D., II, 262 f., No. 320; interview with Cambon published in the London Times, Dec. 22, 1920; Monson to Lansdowne, Feb. 6, 1902, B.D., I, 274, No. 339. Lansdowne was

publication of the Anglo-Japanese treaty of alliance in February, France was forced to declare with her ally that the Dual Alliance extended to the Far East.[26] Under pressure from Russia[27] and with the hope of obtaining support while negotiating a treaty with Siam,[28] the French government drew closer to Germany. Late in June the French Ambassador, in asking the German views on the Siamese question, remarked to Count Bülow that "the present good relations between Germany and France justified the hope that France would receive the support [*coup d'épaule*] of Germany in the Siamese affair."[29] As the German government ignored the suggestion, however, and as the French government was alarmed at the growing influence of certain Englishmen, particularly Kaid Maclean, over the Sultan of Morocco, M. Delcassé determined, in spite of probable Russian objection,[30] to open the Moroccan question with the British government.

On July 23, when M. Cambon asked Lord Lansdowne about

so much interested in the French Ambassador's ideas that the latter wrote him a letter enumerating the differences which might be treated. King Edward read the letter and declared to Cambon, "It is excellent. You must go on" (interview with Cambon published in the *London Times*, Dec. 22, 1920).

[26] A few days later, however, Delcassé spoke in the Chamber so vaguely of this declaration and emphasized so strongly France's pacific intentions that he cast great doubt upon its value. See Mévil, pp. 81 f. n.; Tardieu, *La France et les alliances*, pp. 21 f.; see also Newton, pp. 226 f.

[27] Memo. by Bülow of a conversation with the French Ambassador, March 20, 1902, *G.P.*, XVII, 179 f., No. 5064. In February the Russian government urged the German government to enter into an agreement against the new alliance, but the offer was refused (*ibid.*, chap. cx, Part B).

[28] On Siamese affairs, an old cause of trouble between Great Britain and France, see *ibid.*, XVIII, 795 ff., Nos. 5881–83; Schefer, *D'une guerre à l'autre, etc.*, p. 242; *Quest. dipl. et col.*, Nov. 15, 1902, pp. 577 ff.; and others.

[29] Richthofen to Metternich, June 30, 1902, *G.P.*, XVIII, 795 f., No. 5881.

[30] Memo. by Bülow of a conversation with the Russian Ambassador, Feb. 25, 1902, *ibid.*, XVII, 160 ff., No. 5051; Alvensleben to F. O., Feb. 25, 1903, *ibid.*, 349, No. 5195.

discussing fully the Moroccan problem, the British Minister replied that he would be ready to consider it "in the frankest possible manner."[31] On August 6, therefore, the Ambassador officially proposed an accord over the future of Siam and Morocco. After a consideration of the former question, the two men took up the latter one. While asserting that the French government preferred that the Moroccan problem should not become acute, the Ambassador desired that the two governments "frankly discuss the action which they might be constrained to adopt in the event of Morocco passing 'into liquidation.' " Spain, he explained, could be satisfied by a sufficient allowance of hinterland behind her coastal possessions; Tangier could be converted into an international and open port—for France could not allow it to pass into the hands of any European Power; and beyond the Spanish line, France would expect "exclusive influence."

Lord Lansdowne replied that although he listened to the French proposal with great interest, yet since Italy, Spain, and Germany had also at various times manifested a concern in the Moroccan question, he regarded with the "greatest apprehension" any attempt to deal prematurely with a liquidation of that land, which "would be sure to lead to serious complications." The Ambassador answered that at any rate there could be no harm "in discussing these eventualities in good time." He pointed out that Spain and Germany had both failed egregiously in their attempts to establish themselves in Morocco, and that at present Germany was "not to the front there or elsewhere in the Mediterranean." But the British Foreign Secretary, denying that his government had made any difficulties in Morocco for France, postponed further consideration of the proposal until after the government holiday.[32] When in October M. Cambon returned to the subject, Lord Lansdowne not only replied that the French

---

[31] Lansdowne to Monson, July 23, 1902, *B.D.*, II, 263 f., No. 321.

[32] Lansdowne to Monson, Aug. 6, 1902, *ibid.*, 264 ff., No. 322.

terms were unsatisfactory, but he also refused to discuss the possibility of a liquidation of Morocco.[33]

In the meantime, M. Delcassé had been again seeking the cooperation of Germany. In September the German government assured France of its disinterestedness in Siam, provided German economic interests remained uninjured. Although this reply contained no mention of the larger request for support made by the French Ambassador in June, yet the latter, in expressing the satisfaction of his government with the German answer, added that this opportunity had been used to emphasize the community of French and German interests, and not only in Siam. To this broad hint the German government made no response.[34]

In the next month the Spanish Ambassador in Paris reported to Prince Radolin that the French Foreign Minister had recently said to him:

I do not believe that Germany wishes to come to an understanding with France. . . . . Four years ago it was said to M. de Noailles at Berlin that there were points upon which the two countries might place themselves in accord. I found the matter so important that I immediately took it to the president of the Republic and to the premier. I was authorized by them to telegraph to M. de Noailles that I was disposed to treat with Germany on all points on which the two countries would be able to agree. M. de Noailles reported that they had informed him in the *Wilhelmstrasse* that in view of its importance the question deserved to be studied. That was four years ago. Since then not a word more has been said on that subject. Our ambassador still awaits a response.[35]

The German government replied to this overture with recriminations against the French Minister. It complained that his proposals had lacked in concreteness, that France had rejected sev-

[33] Lansdowne to Monson, Oct. 15, 1902, *ibid.*, 268 ff., No. 325; Newton, pp. 268 f.

[34] Mühlberg to Radolin, Aug. 18, 1902, *G.P.*, XVIII, 795 f., No. 5882; Schlözer to F. O., Sept. 22, 1902, *ibid.*, 797, No. 5883.

[35] Radolin to Bülow, Oct. 15, 1902, *ibid.*, 797 ff., No. 5884.

eral German offers of co-operation, and it accused M. Delcassé of consistent bias in favor of Great Britain.[36] When this reply was passed on to M. Delcassé by the Spanish Ambassador late in November, he remarked, "Then M. de Noailles is a fool"; thereafter he had no business to transact with the German representative.[37]

The refusal by both the British and the German governments of the French overtures was followed in December by that of the Spanish government to sign the agreement over Morocco. So M. Delcassé's campaign of 1902 terminated in failure. At the end of the year he reverted to the policy of the *status quo,* and, anxious about the situation in Morocco, proposed to Lord Lansdowne that if disorders there should necessitate action "the Powers interested should take counsel together as to its nature and scope, and should agree that there should be no single-handed intervention . . . . on the part of any one Power." In approving this policy the British Minister asked M. Cambon for a further explanation of the phrase "interested Powers." The latter replied that Great Britain, France, and Spain were the ones referred to, that Italy had no interest in Morocco, and that the French government was solicitous of excluding the United States, and, above all, Germany from that group. He thought that "it

---

[36] Richthofen to Radolin, Oct. 23, 1902, *ibid.,* 799 f., No. 5885. These accusations were unfair. In the previous June in a dispatch to Metternich, ambassador at London, two instances had been mentioned in which the French government had tried to secure the co-operation of Germany. The editors of *G.P.* admit that one of these proposals was definite; and in August, 1901, Holstein of the German foreign office had written that the French government was "not in itself irreconcilable." That admission speaks volumes. Moreover, the German reply admitted that the French Ambassador had usually taken the initiative in these attempts at co-operation. See Richthofen to Metternich, June 30, 1902, *ibid.,* 795 f., No. 5881; Holstein to Bülow, Aug. 8, 1901, *ibid.,* XVII, 341, No. 5184.

[37] Radolin to Bülow, Dec. 4, 1902, *ibid.,* XVIII, 801, No. 5886. As an explanation for this very marked attitude, Delcassé said to a third party that he had tried to co-operate with Germany but had been refused (Memo. by Klehmet, April 19, 1903, *ibid.,* 801 f., No. 5887). None the less, up to Oct., 1903, the French government continued to approve the investment of French capital in the Bagdad Railway (memo. by Rosen, Oct. 29, 1903, *ibid.,* 456 ff., No. 5274).

would be most desirable that if Germany were at any moment to come forward and attempt to assume a conspicuous rôle, it should be intimated to her that she had no *locus standi.*" Upon that point Lord Lansdowne refused to commit himself.[38]

M. Delcassé had shown a pro-British inclination from the start, and it may be that his approaches to Germany had been intended primarily to press Great Britain to an agreement. Certainly they had been sufficiently vague to be in harmony with the traditional French attitude of irreconcilability with the victor of 1870–71. But they had also been concrete enough to show the difficulty, if not the impossibility, of negotiating with Germany on acceptable terms. Whether M. Delcassé was sincere in those overtures cannot be said, although he seems to have been. At any rate, despairing of Germany, he devoted his full energies in 1903 toward achieving an accord with Great Britain, from whom no irredentist problem separated France.

[38] This conversation occurred on Dec. 31, 1902. Lansdowne to Monson, Dec. 31, 1902, *B.D.*, II, 274 ff., No. 330; Lansdowne to Monson, Dec. 28, 1902, Monson to Lansdowne, Dec. 31, 1902, Newton, pp. 269 f.

CHAPTER V

THE ANGLO-GERMAN ALLIANCE NEGOTIATIONS, 1898–1901

The international position of Great Britain at the end of the nineteenth century was uncomfortable. The major Powers were all busy in the colonial world more or less in opposition to her interests; *Weltpolitik* was the order of the day; the navies of all states were growing rapidly and by combining might be able to threaten her maritime supremacy. On the Continent, the German Emperor's courtship of an apparently complaisant France, cordial relations between Russia and Germany, an agreement in 1897 between Russia and Austria-Hungary over Balkan affairs, and a growing amity between France and Italy and between France and Spain gave evidence of a developing *rapprochement* between the two systems of alliance. Trouble in West Africa with France in 1897 and early in 1898 made Anglo-French relations acute. Fashoda was on the way; so was the Boer War. British markets in China were being menaced by Russia, and the British feared that the Russian, French, and German governments might co-operate on Chinese affairs to their injury. Public opinion demanded that the government defend British interests more actively.[1] These were the more important of the difficulties confronting the island empire.

[1] Memo. by Bertie, March 14, 1898, *B.D.*, I, 17 f., No. 24; memo. by Tilley, on relations between Russia and Great Britain, 1892–1904, Jan. 14, 1905, *ibid.*, 1 ff., No. 1; O'Conor to Salisbury, March 15, 1898, *ibid.*, 20, No. 29; Salisbury to O'Conor, March 24, 1898, *ibid.*, 24 f., No. 38; Monson to Salisbury, Feb. 26, 1898, *ibid.*, 146, No. 172; Monson to Salisbury, March 6, 1898, *ibid.*, 147, No. 173; Monson to Salisbury, May 19, 1898, *ibid.*, 154, No. 179; memo. by Bertie, June 30, 1898, *ibid.*, 54, No. 72; Erich Brandenburg, *Von Bismarck zum Weltkriege* (Berlin, 1924), chaps. iv, v; Sir A. W. Ward and G. P. Gooch (eds.), *The Cambridge History of British Foreign Policy, 1783–1919* (Cambridge, 1923), Vol. III, chaps. iii, iv, *passim; G.P.*, Vol. XIV, chap. xci. The British were especially concerned over maintaining the open door in China. See Alfred L. P. Dennis, *Adventures in American Diplomacy, 1896–1906* (New York, 1928), pp. 179, 182 f.

To dispel these dangers, two policies were advocated by members of the Unionist cabinet. Lord Salisbury, prime minister and foreign secretary, did not believe that a Continental alliance against Great Britain would be made.[2] He clung to the traditional position of "splendid isolation," of making special agreements with the various Powers over specific issues. As he realized the inadequacy of this policy if Great Britain attempted to expand her influence too largely in China, South Africa, and elsewhere, he only half-heartedly supported a vigorous program of aggression.[3] In January, 1898, he proposed to the Russian government a general agreement over China and Turkey.[4] On March 8 he asked the United States government to co-operate in maintaining the open door in China.[5] However, he was old, in poor health, and inclined to permit Mr. Chamberlain, the colonial secretary, to force his hand. In fact, the last five years of his administration have been called the "Chamberlain period," so great was the latter's influence.[6]

This "stormy petrel" from Birmingham favored an entirely new policy.[7] Determined to maintain and extend British interests in the whole world, he sought to form a corporation for directing world-affairs by close co-operation with the United States and Germany. He was supported more or less fully by the Prince

[2] For expressions of this fear see Gwynn, *The Letters and Friendships of Sir Cecil Spring Rice,* I, 182 f., 225 f., 331 f.

[3] Hatzfeldt to Hohenlohe, April 26, 1898, *G.P.,* XIV, 221 ff., No. 3793; dispatches from Hatzfeldt recounting conversations with Salisbury, May 12, 15, 1898, *ibid.,* 230 ff., and notes; Hatzfeldt to F. O., May 15, 1898, *ibid.,* 233 ff., No. 3797. The best exposition of Salisbury's views is given in a memorandum by him, May 29, 1901, *B.D.,* II, 68 f., No. 86. See also J. A. Spender, *The Public Life* (New York, 1925), I, 79; Salisbury to Lansdowne, April 21, 1897, Newton, *Lord Lansdowne, A Biography,* pp. 145 f. On Aug. 30, 1899, Salisbury wrote to Lansdowne that the British army would not be needed for a Continental war "in a blue moon" (*ibid.,* p. 157).

[4] Salisbury to O'Conor, Jan. 17, 25, 1898, *B.D.,* I, 5, No. 5; 8, No. 9; and others in *ibid.,* chap. i.

[5] Dennis, pp. 170 f.   [6] Salisbury was prime minister from 1895 to 1902.

[7] On Chamberlain see Spender, I, 79.

of Wales (who in 1901 became King Edward VII), in the cabinet by Mr. Balfour (who in 1902 succeeded Lord Salisbury as prime minister), and by the Duke of Devonshire;[8] while his influence with the masses and with the business elements seemed to assure him of popular approval.

Various difficulties had in recent years arisen between Great Britain and Germany. But Mr. Chamberlain thought that in view of the German Emperor's offers of alliance to the British government at various times during the 1890's, one as late as January, 1898,[9] the German government would eagerly accept a proposal to that effect. When Lord Salisbury's policy toward Russia failed and trouble with Russia[10] and with France[11] threatened, in March and April, 1898, the British Colonial Minister declared to Count Hatzfeldt, the German ambassador, that Great Britain would have to relinquish her isolation. Under threat of coming to terms with Russia or France if his overture were refused, he made an unofficial offer of defensive alliance to Germany.[12]

---

[8] Hatzfeldt, German ambassador to London, also thought that the Liberal leaders, Lord Rosebery and Sir William Harcourt, approved of Chamberlain's plan. Hatzfeldt to Hohenlohe, April 7, 1898, *G.P.*, XIV, 209 ff., No. 3788. See also Gwynn, I, 188, 191.

[9] Lieut. Col. Grierson, British military attaché at Berlin, reported to the British Ambassador a conversation with the Emperor on Jan. 15, 1898, as follows: "He [the Emperor] said that for eight years he had striven to be friendly with Great Britain to gain her alliance, and to work hand in hand with her, but had failed" (Grierson to Lascelles, Jan. 19, 1898, *B.D.*, I, 42, No. 62). The Emperor said the same to Lascelles on Feb. 1. See Lascelles to Salisbury, Feb. 1, 1898, *ibid.*, 43 f., No. 63; memo. by Tilley on the relations between Germany and Great Britain (1892–1904), Jan. 5, 1905, *ibid.*, Appendix, 322 ff.; Brandenburg, chaps. i–iv.

[10] Russia had just occupied Port Arthur. In speaking to the Russian Ambassador about that act on March 24, Balfour declared that the British government regarded it with "grave objection," as a "menace" to the friendship of the two countries. See Salisbury to O'Conor, March 24, 1898, *B.D.*, I, 24 f., No. 38.

[11] Monson to Salisbury, March 6, 1898, *ibid.*, 147, No. 173. Salisbury tried to obtain the support of the United States on Chinese affairs (Dennis, p. 170).

[12] It was on March 24 that Hatzfeldt reported that Alfred Rothschild had arranged a meeting between him and Chamberlain and Balfour. See Hatzfeldt to F. O., March 24, 1898, *G.P.*, XIV, 193 f., No. 3779. For reports of the conversations between Hatzfeldt and Balfour and Chamberlain see the following dis-

Mr. Chamberlain's proposal was coolly received. Count Bü-low, the German secretary of state for foreign affairs, and his inspirer and guide, Herr von Holstein, privy councilor (*vortra-gender Rat*) in the foreign office, who with occasional interference from the Emperor were the directors of the German foreign policy, not only were mistrustful of British intentions, but also saw no reason for dissatisfaction with the current international position and prospects of their state.[13] Besides, this overture so increased the power of their situation that they were able to lay down a policy of the "free hand" to be followed during the next few years. A telegram from Emperor William II to Count Bülow on April 10, 1898, together with the latter's marginal notes, best expressed this policy. After stating that Germany had less need of a British alliance since Great Britain had turned her attention from the Continent to the colonial world, the Emperor wrote:

If the English need of support direct itself in the future toward European affairs also, we could consider it more closely than now. Nevertheless, it is

---

patches: Hatzfeldt to F. O., March 25, 29, April 1, 1898, *ibid.*, 195 ff., Nos. 3781, 3782, 3784; Hatzfeldt to Hohenlohe, April 26, 1898, *ibid.*, 221 ff., No. 3793. The editors of the *British Documents* could find "practically no evidence" concerning this proposal in the archives of the British foreign office, and have stated that Chamberlain apparently treated the affair as private (*B.D.*, Vol. I, Foreword). See also the dispatch from Lascelles to Balfour, Aug. 23, 1898, *ibid.*, 101, No. 122. That Chamberlain was uncertain about the sort of agreement he wished was evident from the different formulations of the proposal which he made. As to the American aspect of his plan, Chamberlain was influenced by Ambassador John Hay, who supported the idea of an Anglo-American alliance. On May 13, 1898, at Birmingham the British Minister spoke publicly in favor of that alliance (Dennis, pp. 117 f., 122). Nothing of course came of the matter. The great affinity for the United States on the part of the British government was shown in July, 1898, by its indirect warning to Germany not to interfere in the Spanish-American War (Gwynn, I, 251, 253). On the Anglo-German negotiations for an alliance see Friedrich Meinecke, *Geschichte des deutsch-englischen Bündnisproblems, 1890–1901* (München and Berlin, 1927); Eugen Fischer, *Holsteins Grosses Nein* (Berlin, 1925).

[13] Holstein thought that the possibility for this alliance would first enter "when (1) Russia threatens us; (2) England acts less haughty than today." See Holstein's minute to a dispatch from Hatzfeldt to Hohenlohe, April 26, 1898, *G.P.*, XIV, 223, No. 3793. On the German reaction see also the dispatch from Bülow to Hatzfeldt, April 3, 1898, *ibid.*, 204 ff., No. 3785, and the following documents.

also of great significance for the present to keep the official attitude in England favorable and hopeful toward us [Bülow's comment, "Yes"]. . . . . Through an England friendly to us we hold another card in our hand toward Russia. [Bülow's comment, "Very true, we must remain independent between them, be the tongue to the wagon, not the pendulum restlessly swinging about."] And we thereby have prospects of gaining colonial and commercial advantages from England. [Bülow's comment, "Also the reverse. The calmer relations we have with Russia, the more will England treat us with respect, not to say take great care with respect to us."]

The Emperor proposed that Count Hatzfeldt be instructed not to refuse the overture abruptly, but rather to express pleasure at the prospect of a profitable co-operation leading toward an alliance. To the Emperor's remark that the pro-German sentiment of the British cabinet would not long remain concealed from Russia, Count Bülow wrote, "It does not matter, if only the English cannot prove to the Russians and *vice versa* with the evidence in hand that we have played falsely."[14] In accordance with the Emperor's suggestion, Mr. Chamberlain's offer was for the time refused.[15]

The German leaders had found the policy by which they hoped to carry out their program of *Weltpolitik*, already so resoundingly proclaimed in their speeches and acts.[16] "I am the balance of power," declared the Emperor in 1901;[17] and by utilizing the advantages of that position, he and his advisers hoped to gain colonial concessions from the Powers, to construct the Bagdad

[14] William II to F. O., April 10, 1898, *ibid.*, 217 f., No. 3790.

[15] Bülow to Hatzfeldt, April 3, 24, 1898, *ibid.*, 207, No. 3785; 218 ff., No. 3792.

[16] In January, 1896, the Emperor had sent the famous telegram to President Krueger of the Transvaal which was regarded by the British as showing a desire to take the Boers under Germany's wing. On Dec. 6, 1897, Bülow in his first speech before the Reichstag as secretary of state for foreign affairs declared: "The days are past when the German left to one neighbor the earth, to another the sea, and reserved for himself the air. . . . . We do not wish to place anyone in the shadow, but we demand also our place in the sun" (Bülow, *Reden*, I, 7 f.). In 1898 the first important navy bill was passed by the Reichstag. On September 23, 1898, the Emperor declared, "Our future lies on the sea" (G. P. Gooch, *History of Modern Europe, 1878–1919* [New York, 1923], pp. 225 ff.). These were merely a few examples of Germany's changed interests.

[17] William II to Bülow, Jan. 29, 1901, *G.P.*, XVII, 28, No. 4987.

Railway, and to build the German battle fleet. It was a policy of finesse and at times of intrigue, one nicely suited to Count Bülow's ingratiating nature, but one full of pitfalls. Success depended upon whether Anglo-Russian and Anglo-French hostility was temporary or relatively permanent, upon whether Mr. Chamberlain was in earnest in declaring that Great Britain must abandon her policy of isolation,[18] upon whether German diplomacy would be competent to force concessions from those Powers without driving them together. Guided by Emperor William II, Count Bülow, and Herr von Holstein, the policy of the "free hand" seemed almost foredoomed to failure.

In 1898 the Emperor was thirty-nine years of age, but experience had taught him very little caution, moderation, or political understanding. He remained the spoiled sovereign of a spoiled country; each had risen to power so rapidly as to be unable to take this position for granted and not to demand explicit recognition of it, and as to be inclined consequently to abuse its power. The Emperor's belief in and practice of his divine right to rule were not tempered by any consistent application to his task. While not devoid of political intuition, he lacked most of the qualities of a statesman. He was brilliant, but erratic and impulsive. In spite of his seeming wide knowledge, he was mentally lazy and devoid of profundity. Of a highly nervous temperament, he was guided chiefly by his emotions. He appeared rigid, severe, and forbidding on state occasions, but he loved to relax, to be jocose and sociable. He could be cordial and wonderfully amiable and charming, like his mother, and again, when his temper was aroused, he could be ruthless and crushing. He spoke often and dramatically, and traveled as much and as widely as he could. He frequently antagonized and angered people unintentionally by his imperious obtuseness. Then he would feel aggrieved and abused, for he expected all the understanding to come from the other side. One could not take him at his word; one had to interpret his meaning from his acts and intentions as well. At

[18] Hatzfeldt to Hohenlohe, April 26, 1898, *ibid.*, 224, No. 3793.

times his words would leave exactly the opposite meaning from that which he intended. He once remarked to Sir Frank Lascelles, the British ambassador, that "the noodles seem to have had a lucid interval," when upon further conversation it developed he had intended thereby to express his great satisfaction with the communication from the British government.[19] He loved to set countries at odds by his intrigues and gossip. His jealousy of Great Britain, her empire, and her fleet was a cardinal reason both for his being constantly attracted to England and for his desiring to become her colonial and naval rival. Nevertheless, after twelve years of personal contact with the Emperor, Sir Frank Lascelles came to the following sane conclusion about him:

> In spite of his habit of twirling his moustache and rattling his sabre (I trust that this sentence may be taken in its metaphorical and not in its literal sense, for, as a matter of fact, I have never either seen him twirl his moustache or heard him rattle his sword), which he may think a befitting attitude for the ruler of a mighty Empire, he is really animated by the most pacific sentiments, and . . . . his great ambition now is that his name should be handed down to posterity as that of the German Emperor who kept the peace. It would seem that this is the estimate which the Emperor has formed of his own character, as in a recent conversation with Prince Radolin[20] he said he was at a loss to understand how, with his well-known peaceful intentions, he had come to be looked upon as a disturbing element—an instance, perhaps, of that "inconscience" which M. Herbette[21] considered a characteristic of the German nation, and concluded with the almost pathetic sentence, "Ich bin doch kein böser Mensch" [I am really not a bad person].[22]

The Emperor's deficiences were in part made up by Count Bülow, who had been chosen secretary of state for foreign affairs in 1897 to execute the program of *Weltpolitik*. Born in 1849 of an old North German family, he had had diplomatic service

[19] The occasion for this remark was the conclusion of the Anglo-Japanese Alliance early in 1902 (Lascelles to Lansdowne, Feb. 8, 1902, Newton, p. 247).

[20] German ambassador at Paris at the time.

[21] Formerly French ambassador at Berlin.

[22] Extract from "General Report on Germany for 1906, May 24, 1907," *B.D.*, III, 437 f.

at St. Petersburg, Vienna, Athens, Paris, Bucharest, and Rome where he had been ambassador since 1894. He came to his task at a crucial time in the history of Germany's foreign relations, but he lacked the farsightedness, decision, and firmness of character necessary to deal with the problems adequately. Although he learned with time, recognized his mistakes, and tried to readjust the German foreign policy, he was then unable to do so. While his cosmopolitan culture and knowledge enabled him to understand other nations better than most Germans did, he seemed incapable of using this understanding practically. Under him the German policy appeared to demand something for nothing, anywhere or everywhere, merely because Germany was so strong a Power. In 1907 Lord Sanderson, British permanent undersecretary of state for foreign affairs, 1894–1906, a sane, sympathetic witness, stigmatized the German method of handling foreign affairs as follows:

The Germans are very tight bargainers, they have earned the nickname of *"les Juifs de la diplomatie."* The German Foreign Office hold to a traditional view of negotiation that one of the most effective methods of gaining your point is to show how intensely disagreeable you can make yourself if you do not. They are surprised that the recollection of these methods should rankle, and speaking generally the North Germans combine intense susceptibility as regards themselves with a singular inability to appreciate the susceptibilities of others.[23]

Under Count Bülow, German foreign policy lacked direction and stability. It aroused the mistrust of the other Powers, who could not comprehend what Germany wanted. The Count was abler at extricating himself from difficulties than at avoiding them. A confirmed optimist at all times, he was suave and reassuring; the French Ambassador complained that he "was a fluent speaker but when one came to recall and note down what he had said very little came out of it." Sir Frank Lascelles called him a perfect master at expressing vague generalities.[24] Count Bülow no

---

[23] Memo. by Sanderson, Feb. 21, 1907, *ibid.*, p. 429.

[24] Whitehead to Lansdowne, June 28, 1905, *ibid.*, 108 f., No. 135; extract from "General Report on Germany for 1906," *ibid.*, p. 435.

doubt had a difficult time keeping the Emperor within bounds and undoing the latter's mischief, but he was by no means an able statesman himself, and he relied for advice upon a person whom many considered a psychopath.

Since Prince Bismarck's dismissal in 1890, Herr von Holstein had been a dominant influence in the German foreign office as the preserver of the Bismarckian tradition. Strangely secretive, he avoided all publicity and all responsible offices, yet he lusted after power behind the scenes. He was irascible, morbidly suspicious, both timorous and bold, by nature unfit to handle foreign affairs. He could not make up his mind to act. He could not understand the other government's viewpoint. He knew few of the foreign representatives in Berlin personally, and rarely consulted with any of them. He relied for information chiefly upon the dispatches and upon newspapers, thus lacking the intimate contact with reality which might have balanced his recluse judgment. His mobile mind could make two plus two equal three, five, or seven and a half, but seldom four. His training under Prince Bismarck had taught him that master's use of threats and force but not his caution and comprehensive sagacity. His adroit and intricate analysis of diplomatic situations and policies made him a power in the foreign office. The Emperor urged his dismissal, but Count Bülow clung to him, consulted him on all matters, and generally followed his advice.[25]

During the next year the German plan worked. On the one hand, with troubles coming to a head in China, the Sudan, and South Africa, the British government was grudgingly compelled to play the German game by agreeing to a division of the Samoan Islands and a prospective partition of the Portuguese colonies and

[25] Emil Ludwig, *Wilhelm der Zweite* (Berlin, 1926); G. P. Gooch, "Baron von Holstein," *Cambridge Historical Journal*, Vol. I; Johannes Haller, *Die Ära Bülow; eine historisch-politische Studie* (Stuttgart and Berlin, 1922); Otto Hammann, *Bilder aus der letzten Kaiserzeit* (Berlin, 1922); extract from "General Report on Germany for 1906," *op. cit.*, III, 434 ff.; Wilhelm Spickernagel, *Fürst Bülow* (Hamburg, 1921); André Tardieu, *Le Prince de Bülow* (Paris, 1909).

by acknowledging the utility of similar accords.[26] On the other hand, an indirect bid for a *rapprochement* by M. Delcassé in December, 1898,[27] and a proposal from the Russian government in 1899 for an agreement over Asia Minor[28] signified equal success, although the German government refused both offers. Then when the Boer War began late in 1899, Great Britain, surprised by the universal outburst of hatred against her on the Continent and apprehensive of German, French, and Russian intervention in favor of the Boers, had urgent need of Germany's friendship. Hence the pressing invitation to the Emperor William II and his foreign secretary in the autumn of 1899 to visit England.[29]

As Count Bülow cared nothing about the fate of the Boers, the visit took place (November 21–24). He and the Emperor were received enthusiastically by government, court, and people. The British ministers showed anger at France and Russia and a desire for co-operation with Germany.[30] Mr. Chamberlain, who boldly asserted that the two countries "must sooner or later come to a general understanding because we need each other," repeated his wish for a grouping of Germany, the United States, and Great Britain.

The German leaders responded as in the previous year that

[26] *G.P.*, Vol. XIV, chaps. xcii, xcvi; *B.D.*, Vol. I, chaps. ii, iii.

[27] Memo. by Huhn, Dec. 5, 1898, *G.P.*, XIII, 247 ff., No. 3558. See above.

[28] Memo. by Bülow, April 18, 1899, *ibid.*, XIV, 540 f., No. 4017, and the following documents. According to a memorandum by Bülow on May 5, 1899, Count Osten-Sacken, the Russian ambassador, attempted "in every way" to convince him that Germany "should hold in all questions to Russia and France and take position against England." "England is strong only because Germany and France do not co-operate," said the Ambassador (*ibid.*, 546 ff., No. 4020).

[29] Hatzfeldt to F.O., Sept. 30, 1899, *ibid.*, XV, 397, No. 4386; Bülow to F. O., Sept. 25, 1899, *ibid.*, 396 f., No. 4385; Monson to Salisbury, Aug. 14, 1899, *B.D.*, I, 213, No. 259; Monson to Salisbury, Oct. 1, 1899, *ibid.*, 233, No. 285; and other documents in *ibid.*, chap. vii.; Dennis, pp. 125 ff.

[30] Salisbury was absent on account of the death of his wife, but the officials in the British foreign office assured Hatzfeldt that the premier was not at all prejudiced against Germany, as the latter supposed. See Hatzfeldt to Hohenlohe, Dec. 2, 1899, *G.P.*, XV, 423, No. 4401; cf. Gwynn, I, 351.

more intimate relations between the two countries should be prepared for by special agreements. The British Colonial Minister,
readily accepting this program, suggested two subjects for negotiation, the Bagdad Railway and Morocco; whereupon it was
agreed that he should take up the latter question with the German Ambassador in the very near future.[31]

The visit to Windsor was apparently a complete success. Both
governments were highly pleased with the results. The only discord in the harmony was the expression of mutual antagonism on
the part of the English and German press. To counteract this
opposition, Mr. Chamberlain, at Count Bülow's suggestion,[32]
openly advocated his project in a speech at Leicester on November 30 as follows:

The same sentiments which bring us into closer sympathy with the United
States of America may also be evoked to bring us into closer sympathy and
alliance with the Empire of Germany. . . . . If the union between England
and America is a powerful factor in the cause of peace, a new triple alliance
between the Teutonic race and the two great branches of the Anglo-Saxon
race will be a still more potent influence in the future of the world.[33]

The Colonial Secretary's act had the very reverse effect of that
intended, for the German people rejected with vituperation the
idea of allying with the oppressors of the Boers. The German
Foreign Minister, ambitious for the chancellorship when the
aged Prince Hohenlohe should retire, and inclined to follow the
dictates of public opinion, felt compelled to take cognizance of
this feeling. Speaking before the Reichstag on December 11, he
made a cool rejoinder to Mr. Chamberlain's proposal. In a chauvinistic declaration of Germany's need for colonies and a navy,

---

[31] On this visit see Lee, *King Edward VII*, I, 747; Eckardstein, *Lebenserinnerungen und politische Denkwürdigkeiten*, Vol. II, chaps. iv, v; memo. by Bülow,
Nov. 24, 1899, *G.P.*, XV, 413 f., No. 4398; Eckardstein to Hatzfeldt, Nov. 30, 1899,
ibid., 421 f., No. 4400; Hatzfeldt to Hohenlohe, Dec. 2, 1899, *ibid.*, 422 ff., No.
4401.

[32] Eckardstein, II, 107.

[33] *Annual Register* (1899), p. 227. Salisbury agreed to this act, but warned
Chamberlain that Germany would very probably disappoint him (Spring Rice to
Miss Lascelles, April 17, 1902, Gwynn, I, 351).

he proclaimed: "As for England we are gladly willing to live with her in peace and harmony on a basis of complete reciprocity. But since our international position is at present a favorable one, we must utilize it in order to safeguard ourselves for the future."[34] Mr. Chamberlain was indignant at this reply, even though the German government made special efforts to explain it away.[35] Hence, as the two presses were at each other's throats and the governments were wrangling over minor troubles arising out of the Boer War, he dropped the idea of an alliance, presumably also that of a Moroccan accord, at least until the close of the war.[36]

In 1900, with the French advance on Touat, the Moroccan question became acute. In April the German government for the first time weighed carefully its ambitions with reference to Morocco and the means for realizing them.[37] Count Bülow held that

---

[34] Bülow, I, 88 ff.   [35] Eckardstein, II, 126 ff., 133 ff.

[36] *Ibid.,* p. 125.

[37] On several previous occasions Morocco had been the topic of conversation between British and German officials. In January, 1897, not to go back any farther, Lord Salisbury had sounded the German government on that question, but the latter had not been interested (*G.P.,* XVII, No. 4979 n.). But when the subject was brought up in a conversation between the Premier and Hatzfeldt in February and again in June, 1899, the German policy, now launched on its career of *Weltpolitik,* was different. Salisbury stated that in case of the break-up of the Sherifian Empire, "Great Britain could not with indifference see the Atlantic seaboard pass under any other dominion." Hatzfeldt replied that in his personal opinion his government would approve a British acquisition of territory in that land only in case Germany received her share; and he added that it would be very desirable to exchange views and ideas on the subject whenever action should become pressing. Salisbury, however, expressed the wish for the *status quo* to be indefinitely maintained, and refused to enter into details. See Hatzfeldt to Bülow, Feb. 8, 1899, *ibid.,* 295 f., No. 5152; Salisbury to Lascelles, June 7, 1899, *B.D.,* II, 256 f., No. 307.

A short time before the visit to Windsor in Nov., 1899, Chamberlain suggested to Eckardstein that the two governments make a secret agreement over Morocco by which the Mediterranean coast should be left free for Great Britain while Germany should receive far-reaching concessions on the Atlantic seaboard. See Hatzfeldt to F. O., *G.P.,* XVII, 297, No. 5153. Eckardstein also states that in Jan., 1901, Chamberlain and Devonshire both told him that in 1899 Salisbury had approved the idea of a solution of the Moroccan problem with Germany (Eckardstein, II, 359).

Germany had maritime interests of her own in that land, and was
no longer concerned merely for the sake of Italy, as she had been
ten years before. He coveted particularly the southern area on
the Atlantic Coast. A British seizure of Moroccan territory without consideration for German interests, he stated, "would within
Germany greatly weaken and discredit the Government and in
its foreign relations make any future co-operation with England
impossible and force us to seek connection with Russia and
France at almost any price"; while an Anglo-French settlement
of the question to the exclusion or detriment of Germany "would
have incalculable results for the further course of German internal and external policy." In either case German foreign policy
would be forced to take another direction whether the government wished it or not; and relations with Great Britain would
become more strained than ever before. In fact, the German government "could not possibly accept either eventuality."[38]
(In these words lies the key to the understanding of Germany's
precipitation of the Moroccan crisis in 1905.)

To obviate those dangers, the German government preferred
an agreement with Great Britain. In May, 1900, it proposed to
Mr. Chamberlain that they negotiate a Moroccan accord. But
the Colonial Minister, while acknowledging that the only peaceful way to solve the Moroccan problem was by an agreement between Great Britain and Germany, had become more wary and
requested the German government to make an official proposal
which he could submit to the cabinet. He felt sure, he said, that
it would be favorably received, and promised to support it, provided his well-known desires were given due consideration.[39]

---

[38] These remarks by Bülow were chiefly contained in his minutes to the dispatches from Hatzfeldt. See Bülow to Münster, April 27, 1900, *G.P.*, XVII, 299 ff.,
No. 5156; Hatzfeldt to Hohenlohe, May 1, 1900, *ibid.*, 303 ff., No. 5159; Hatzfeldt
to F. O., May 27, 1900, *ibid.*, 309 ff., No. 5162; Bülow to Hatzfeldt, May 29, 1900,
ibid., 313 f., No. 5165; Hatzfeldt to Hohenlohe, June 1, 1900, *ibid.*, 314 ff., No. 5166.

[39] Bülow's plan was also to associate Italy later in the Moroccan settlement.
See Bülow to Hatzfeldt, May 14, 1900, *ibid.*, 302 f., No. 5158; Hatzfeldt to Hohenlohe, May 21, 1900, *ibid.*, 303 ff., No. 5159; Bülow to Hatzfeldt, May 23, 1900,
ibid., 308 f., Nos. 5160 f.; Hatzfeldt to F. O., May 27, 1900, *ibid.*, 309 ff., No. 5162.

Fearing a rejection, the German government deemed it inadvisable to follow Mr. Chamberlain's suggestion. Nor did Count Bülow warn the British government that Germany must participate in any Moroccan settlement, since he believed it possible to prevent the Moroccan affair from becoming serious until the opportunity for an Anglo-German agreement arose.[40] He held that an Anglo-French understanding about Morocco was impossible because of the conflict of French and British interests over the possession of the south shore of the straits. To avert a crisis, he issued a discreet warning to M. Delcassé in May, 1900, not to go beyond treaty limits in the action against Touat;[41] he incited the Russian Foreign Minister, who, he thought, would be opposed to any Anglo-French agreement or to a European disturbance over Morocco, to restrain the French Minister;[42] and he instructed the German representative at Tangier to retard the collapse of the Sherifian Empire.[43] Thereafter the Moroccan question remained in abeyance for a time.[44]

In November, 1900, Lord Salisbury resigned the secretaryship of foreign affairs to Lord Lansdowne. Lord Lansdowne had had a varied life. Of high aristocratic and wealthy family, he had entered politics as a matter of course and had served as governor-general of Canada, viceroy of India, and secretary of state for war. He fitted admirably into his new position as foreign secretary, for he possessed patience, tact, and the ability to inspire confidence, and he assumed responsibility with decision and courage. While he entered office with very few preconceptions,

[40] Hatzfeldt to Hohenlohe, May 21, 1900, *ibid.*, 303 ff., No. 5159; Bülow to Hatzfeldt, May 23, 1900, *ibid.*, 308, No. 5160; Hatzfeldt to F. O., May 27, 1900, *ibid.*, 309 ff., No. 5162; Bülow to Hatzfeldt, May 28, 1900, *ibid.*, 311 f., No. 5163; Hatzfeldt to F. O., May 29, 1900, *ibid.*, 312 f., No. 5164; Hatzfeldt to Hohenlohe, June 1, 1900, *ibid.*, 314 ff., No. 5166.

[41] Bülow to Münster, April 27, 1900, *ibid.*, 299 f., No. 5156; Münster to Hohenlohe, May 9, 1900, *ibid.*, 301 f., No. 5157.

[42] Bülow to Tschirschky, June 5, 1900, *ibid.*, 318 ff., No. 5167; Bülow to Hatzfeldt, June 13, 1900, *ibid.*, 321 ff., No. 5168.

[43] Derenthall to Mentzingen, Aug. 2, 1900, *ibid.*, 324, No. 5170.

[44] Bülow to Hatzfeldt, June 30, 1900, *ibid.*, 323 ff., No. 5169 and note.

he wrote to Sir Frank Lascelles, he did believe that "we should use every effort to maintain and, if we can, to strengthen the good relations which at present exist between the Queen's Government and that of the Emperor" of Germany.[45] In his foreign policy he sided with the new school, already represented by Mr. Balfour and Mr. Chamberlain. When King Edward VII gave royal support to this group after his accession to the throne in January, 1901, the Victorian policy of "splendid isolation" definitely terminated. However, the old Marquess of Salisbury remained premier until 1902; and the foreign policy eventually adopted was a compromise between the old and the new.

The international position of Great Britain remained bad. If anything, it had grown worse since 1899; for the Boer War lingered on, and France and Russia were endangering important British interests, the one by her active policy with reference to Morocco, the other by her use of the Boxer Rebellion to extend her power in China and by her activity in Persia and Afghanistan.

In the autumn of 1900, the British government had negotiated an accord with Germany over China to hold Russia in check.[46] In January of the next year Mr. Chamberlain, after repeating his assertion that Great Britain must ally either with Germany and the Triple Alliance or with France and Russia, proposed to Baron Eckardstein, first secretary of the German embassy in London, that as an introduction to the project for an alliance the two governments agree over Morocco. The subject could be taken up with Lord Lansdowne, he said, as soon as Lord Salisbury, still in feeble health, left for the south.[47] Before any negotiations were

---

[45] Newton, pp. 196 f.

[46] *G.P.*, Vol. XVI, chap. cv; *B.D.*, Vol. II, chap. ix, Part I.

[47] Eckardstein, II, 235 ff.; Hatzfeldt to F. O., Jan. 18, 1901, *G.P.*, XVII, 14 ff., No. 4979. In the same month Lansdowne expressed to the German government the desire to remain in "complete harmony" with it on Chinese affairs. See Lascelles to Lansdowne, Jan. 4, 1901, *B.D.*, II, 20 f., No. 25; Lascelles to Lansdowne, Jan. 18, 1901, *ibid.*, 21 f., No. 26.

begun, however, far eastern affairs, as more pressing and vital, brought to the fore the question of alliance.[48]

Early in 1901, reports were spread of a Russo-Chinese agreement which would give Russia practically a protectorate in Southern Manchuria. The problem which thereupon confronted the British government was illuminatingly summed up by Mr. Bertie, undersecretary of state for foreign affairs, as follows (March 11, 1901):

Germany has assured Japan that there is no secret understanding between Germany and Russia respecting the Far East; and that, in the event of a crisis, Germany will observe a benevolent neutrality, the effect of which would be to keep the French fleet in check.

The Japanese Government ask whether His Majesty's Government have been consulted by Germany, and whether they believe the assurances given to Japan; and they further ask: "How far may Japan rely upon the support of Great Britain in case Japan finds it necessary to approach Russia?"

It is assumed by the Japanese Minister that "approach" in the context means "resist," which is war.

Unless Japan can make sure of neither Germany nor France taking an active part on the side of Russia, she will not fight Russia over the Manchurian Agreement. If the possession of Corea by Russia were at issue, Japan would fight, with or without support, and independently of whether France or Germany would remain neutral.

If Germany and England, in answer to the Japanese Government's inquiries, deprecated war, and said that if unfortunately war broke out between Japan and Russia, it would be the object of England and Germany to restrict as much as possible the theatre of it, and they would consequently remain neutral, so long as no third Power attempted to take a part in it, then I think that such an assurance. might be sufficient to satisfy Japan that France would not be allowed to join with Russia, and that Japan might fight Russia single-handed. . . . .

If France were allowed to side with Russia, and they crushed Japan, the result might be a renewal of the triple understanding—viz., Russia, France, and Germany. Those three Powers would become supreme in China, and we should go to the wall.

If Russia alone, or in combination with France, defeated Japan, and we came to the rescue to prevent the obliteration of Japan, we should incur the lasting enmity of Russia and France, and a defeated, and probably ungrate-

[48] On those far eastern troubles see *G.P.*, Vol. XVI; *B.D.*, Vol. II, chap. ix.

ful, Japan would not be of much use to us as against Russian encroachments.

It has been suggested that if Japan defeated Russia there would be grave danger to European interests in the Far East.

A great military and naval Power, with unbounded natural resources and an immense population such as Russia, is not likely to accept defeat permanently. She would reorganize for a further trial of strength, but such a trial might be a long way off, and it would be greatly retarded by Japan being allowed to take as the spoils of war the Liaotung Peninsula. Its possession by Japan would be a guarantee that there would be no reconciliation between Russia and Japan. This would be an advantage to England and Europe. The yellow danger would be kept in check by Russia and the Russian danger by Japan.

If we do nothing to encourage Japan to look upon us as a friend and possible ally against Russia and France, we may drive her to a policy of despair, in which she may come to some sort of terms with Russia. I do not say that it is probable, but it is possible, and our interests would greatly suffer if she did.[49]

Therein lies the deciding reason why the British government tried to secure the support of Germany; why it made the alliance with Japan when this attempt came to naught; and why it subsequently established the entente with France. An agreement with Germany, supplemented by one with Japan, would have solved Great Britain's difficulty of defending her colonial interests by assuring the maintenance of the balance of power in Europe. Failing this, an alliance with Japan and a policy of reconciliation and entente with the other Powers furnished the best solution. But in any case either alliance or close friendship with a European Power was essential.

At the time the prospect of obtaining German aid looked favorable. The German Emperor had rushed impetuously to the bedside of the dying Queen Victoria late in January, 1901, and had remained for her funeral. In his talk with the British officials he had denounced Russia for her aggressions in China, had informed them that Great Britain needed an alliance, and, in a dinner speech at Marlborough House on February 5, had de-

---

[49] B.D., II, 43, No. 54. On Anglo-Russian relations see also Newton, pp. 215 f.

clared: "We ought to form an Anglo-German alliance, you to keep the seas while we would be responsible for the land."[50]

Late in January the British government tried to obtain German aid against the Russian aggressions in Manchuria by calling into action the Anglo-German agreement of the previous year; but the German government refused to permit an interpretation of that accord which would embroil it with its eastern neighbor.[51] Instead, it tried to persuade the British government to connive at embroiling Russia and Japan in war without binding themselves.[52] It assured Japan of the localization of that conflict by remarking that Germany would remain neutral and would thereby hold France neutral. In March, Lord Lansdowne, following up this assertion, asked Baron Eckardstein if Germany would undertake to hold France neutral in case of war (March 16). In violation of strict orders from Herr von Holstein "not to breathe à word of alliance" to the British government,[53] Baron Eckardstein replied that "if there were a defensive alliance between Germany and Great Britain covering all eventualities," Germany would be able to do so.[54] Two days later Lord Lansdowne declared to the Baron that "England now stands at a turning point and must decide upon her future policy"; and in accordance with the Baron's strong hint, a defensive alliance was tentatively set forth for consideration. By its terms each Power should preserve neutrality in case of an attack upon the other by either France or

---

[50] Quoted in Lee, II, 11. This was against Bülow's advice (Bülow to William II, Jan. 21, 1901, G.P., XVII, 20 f., No. 4983). On the Emperor's visit see Eckardstein to F. O., Jan. 29, 1901, ibid., 23 f., No. 4986; William II to Bülow, Jan. 29, 1901, ibid., 24 ff., No. 4987; Lansdowne's memo., Jan., 1901, Newton, p. 199. The Emperor had been given an enthusiastic welcome in England. The Harmsworth press had called him "A Friend in Need" (Newton, p. 198).

[51] Memo. by Mühlberg, Jan. 28, 1901, G.P., XVI, 286, No. 4785, and following documents.

[52] Lansdowne to Lascelles, March 18, 1901, Newton, pp. 199 f.

[53] Eckardstein, II, 279.

[54] He naturally did not report this statement to Berlin (ibid., pp. 280 f.).

Russia but should come to its aid in case of an attack by those two Powers combined.[55]

Baron Eckardstein reported the proposal as coming from the British Minister, and his government looked upon it as a British offer. Lord Lansdowne made the Baron responsible for the initiative. With the existing evidence, the contradiction cannot be cleared up; yet as each government was under the impression that the other had taken the first step and was therefore more eager for the alliance than was really the case, the negotiations endured longer than they might otherwise have done.[56]

In the next two and a half months the course of the negotiations was checkered. On March 22, Baron Eckardstein unofficially brought up the subject with Lord Lansdowne. During their discussion they agreed that it would be best for the *casus foederis* to arise when one of the Powers was attacked by two or more Powers, and that the accord should be ratified by the two parliaments. The British Secretary declared that the Premier approved "in principle of a strictly defined defensive alliance."[57] On March 29 they again touched on the matter; but owing to Lord Lans-

[55] *Ibid.,* pp. 277 ff.; Eckardstein to F. O., March 19, 1901, *G.P.,* XVII, 41 f., No. 4994; Lansdowne to Lascelles, March 18, 1901, *B.D.,* II, 61, No. 77; Newton, pp. 199 f. As the Ambassador was ill during most of this time, Eckardstein carried on the negotiations.

[56] Eckardstein has written in his memoirs that in his private correspondence with Holstein he took the latter's peculiarities into account and used expressions that were adapted to his "complex mentality." "For instance, I very often avoided using the word *alliance* and spoke of a *defensive arrangement;* then I emphasized that the whole affair was yet in embryo, although in fact the negotiations progressed very smoothly and were on the point of conclusion, etc. As soon as the negotiations began to run smoothly and lightly, Holstein became suspicious, and if the other party were willing to accede to our wishes, smelled a rat." The truth seems to be that for this very reason Eckardstein sent home not less but more favorable reports of the British desire for an alliance than was really the case, and by stretching his instructions to the utmost in his ardent desire to ally the two Powers, may have been responsible for the contradiction mentioned above (Eckardstein, II, 273).

[57] Hatzfeldt to F. O., March 23, 1901, *G.P.,* XVII, 46 ff., No. 4997; Eckardstein, II, 321 ff.

downe's inability to consult his chief, who was ill, and owing to a flare-up between the two governments over a minor matter connected with the Chinese customs, Baron Eckardstein postponed the negotiations.[58] On April 9 he was ready to resume the discussion; and for the first time he mentioned to the British Minister the indispensable stipulation of his government, that Austria-Hungary and Italy must also be included in the alliance.[59]

From the start the attitude of the German government toward these proposals was mistrustful. Since the British government had been disinclined to execute the Anglo-German accord of 1898 for a future division of the Portuguese colonies, the German government was reluctant to consider even Mr. Chamberlain's suggestion for an accord over Morocco, at least until events permitted its immediate execution.[60] Count Bülow and Herr von Holstein refused to believe that the British government would make an alliance so long as Lord Salisbury remained in authority. Moreover, they feared that if the negotiations failed and became known to France and Russia, owing to British perfidy or to Parliament's rejecting the treaty—and either outcome seemed likely to them—Germany would be the one to suffer from the wrath of those two Powers while Great Britain, protected by the sea, would enjoy greater international security than before.

I am especially mistrustful of this present storm of friendship by Chamberlain and comrades [wrote Herr von Holstein to Count Metternich] because the threatened understanding with Russia and France is such complete fraud. A retreat by England would postpone her struggle for existence for a few years, but would then make it all the more certain, because the opponents [France and Russia] will have been strengthened, while the English will have been weakened in power and prestige. A reasonable agreement with England, that is, one in which a proper consideration is given to the almost certain danger of war to which we should thereby expose ourselves, can in

[58] Lansdowne to Lascelles, March 29, 1901, *B.D.*, II, 62, No. 79; Eckardstein, II, 326 ff.

[59] Lansdowne to Lascelles, April 9, 1901, *B.D.*, 62 f., No. 80; Eckardstein, II, 335.

[60] Bülow to Hatzfeldt, Jan. 20, 1901, *G.P.*, XVII, 17 f., No. 4981.

my opinion first be achieved when the appreciation of her constrained position has become more general in England than it is at present.[61]

Count Bülow, chancellor since the previous October, held the same view. In fact, he was even more inclined to preserve the policy of the "free hand." "Facts, sir, facts," he wrote in connection with this question of alliance, and above all he wanted facts in the form of colonial acquisitions in Africa.[62] So while sensible of the power of such an alliance, these two would have it only on German terms, an alliance between the British Empire, on the one hand, and the Triple Alliance, on the other; or, as an alternative formulation, an alliance by which Great Britain joined the Triple Alliance.[63] To obviate all possibility of betrayal, they instructed Baron Eckardstein to demand of Lord Lansdowne the acceptance of this basic condition before continuing the negotiations. Not until then, they declared, should the terms of the Triple Alliance be imparted to the British government.[64]

Conversations were resumed in the second half of May. When, on May 23, Count Hatzfeldt made clear to Lord Lansdowne the provision of his government, an *impasse* was soon reached. The British Foreign Secretary approved the project of alliance in principle, but he had never expected much to come of it. Upon ascertaining the German condition he foresaw a breakdown when the time came to formulate the terms.[65]

[61] Holstein to Metternich, Jan. 21, 1901, *ibid.*, 22, No. 4984. Metternich accompanied the Emperor to England at that time.

[62] See his minutes to the dispatch from Holstein to Hatzfeldt, Feb. 11, 1901, *ibid.*, 37, No. 4989; Bülow to Hatzfeldt, Jan. 20, 1901, *ibid.*, 17 f., No. 4981; Bülow to William II, Jan. 21, 1901, 20 f., No. 4983.

[63] The two formulations were in no way identical, but the negotiations never proceeded far enough to permit their being discussed.

[64] Bülow to Hatzfeldt, March 24, 1901, *ibid.*, 49, No. 4998; Bülow to Hatzfeldt, May 11, 1901, *ibid.*, 54 ff., No. 5003; Richthofen to Hatzfeldt, May 18, 1901, *ibid.*, 60 ff., No. 5007; Richthofen to Hatzfeldt, May 20, 1901, *ibid.*, 64 f., No. 5009; and the following documents.

[65] Lansdowne to Lascelles, April 13, 1901, *B.D.*, II, 63, No. 81; Lansdowne to Lascelles, March 18, 1901, Newton, pp. 199 f.

Moreover, Lord Salisbury persistently refused to admit that Great Britain needed an alliance. He asserted that it would be a bad bargain to join the Triple Alliance, for the "liability of having to defend the German and the Austrian frontiers against Russia is heavier than that of having to defend the British Isles against France." He opposed any secret agreement on the grounds that Parliament had the right to decide questions of war and peace; and he continued to favor isolation and dependence on public opinion to determine governmental policy in a crisis. Nor did he believe that German public opinion, so hostile to Great Britain, would accept an Anglo-German defensive alliance.[66] Thus while some of the members of the cabinet discussed the possible terms of an alliance, and Sir Thomas Sanderson, permanent undersecretary of state for foreign affairs, even drew up two trial drafts of a treaty, the opposition of Lord Salisbury together with the German refusal to communicate the terms of the Triple Alliance forced the negotiations to a halt in June.[67]

The German Chancellor readily accepted this turn of affairs. After expressing a desire for a future alliance, he assured the British government that Germany would continue the policy of the "free hand."[68]

The visit of the Moroccan embassy to London and Berlin in June and July afforded an opportunity to revive the Moroccan question. Lord Lansdowne's uneasiness about the French actions with reference to Morocco was not allayed by the French Am-

[66] Memo. by Salisbury, May 29, 1901, *B.D.*, II, 68 f., No. 86.

[67] Memo. by Sanderson, May 27, 1901, *ibid.*, 66 ff., No. 85; Lansdowne to Eckardstein, May 24, 1901, *ibid.*, 66, No. 84; Lansdowne to Lascelles, May 30, 1901, *ibid.*, 69 ff., No. 87 and inclosures; Hatzfeldt to Lansdowne, May 30, 1901, *ibid.*, 71, No. 88; Hatzfeldt to F. O., May 27, 1901, *G.P.*, XVII, 68 f., No. 5012; and the following documents.

[68] Lascelles to Lansdowne, Aug. 25, 1901, *B.D.*, II, 73, No. 90; memo. by Holstein, June 14, 1901, *G.P.*, XVII, 83 ff., No. 5019. Late in October, 1901, Holstein and Bülow had long talks with Valentine Chirol of the *London Times* to a like effect. See memo. by Holstein, Oct. 31, Nov. 1, 1901, *G.P.*, XVII, 101 ff., Nos. 5026 f.; Sir Valentine Chirol, *Fifty Years in a Changing World* (London, 1927), pp. 288 ff.

bassador's assertion to him on July 3 that France had no intention of raising that problem.[69] But nothing was done.[70]
When el-Menebhi, the leader of that embassy, was dismissed in disgrace on his return home, the British Foreign Secretary expressed the wish to remain in constant touch with the German government on the Moroccan question.[71] Each Power, however, acted separately in defending the Moroccan Minister; and the German government looked on this as another occasion in which Great Britain was trying to employ Germany to defend British interests. The German leaders likewise thought that by refusing to make any separate agreements with Great Britain they would eventually force the latter to accept their terms for an alliance.[72]

[69] On April 13, 1901, Lansdowne had written to Lascelles: "Things in Morocco look ugly. Do you hear anything?" See B.D., II, 64, No. 81; Lansdowne to Monson, July 3, 1901, ibid., 261, No. 318.

[70] Eckardstein gives the following story:
Early in July, soon after the arrival of the Moroccan embassy in London, Sir Arthur Nicolson, British minister in Morocco, told him that France was intriguing in that land for the establishment of a protectorate. At Lansdowne's request he suggested the co-operation of Great Britain and Germany for the maintenance of the status quo in Morocco. Then he touched upon the subject of a common Anglo-German peaceful penetration of that country, which should be inaugurated by a commercial treaty with the Sultan. Between the two European states an agreement should be made to determine which concessions each should receive. He proposed that Germany be given, among others, the right of supplying all railway and electrical materials and of installing them, and that all further political, financial, or economic measures should be carried through by the two Powers together. Eckardstein states that he sent a long telegram to Berlin in regard to this conversation, but received no reply (Eckardstein, II, 357 f.). The editors of G.P., however, found no such telegram (G.P., XVII, 333 n.), nor is there any mention of the proposal in any of the documents published by them or by the British. Still the offer may have been made, as will be evident later. Hammann, director of the press department in the German foreign office at that time, has also written that on the dismissal of el-Menebhi, the British government proposed common action to the German government, but that it was refused (Otto Hammann, Zur Vorgeschichte des Weltkrieges. Erinnerungen aus den Jahren 1897–1906 [Berlin, 1918], pp. 139 f.).

[71] Eckardstein to F. O., July 29, 1901, G.P., XVII, 338 f., No. 5182.

[72] Memo. by Mühlberg, Aug. 8, 1901, ibid., 339 f., No. 5183; Holstein to Bülow, Aug. 8, 1901, ibid., 341, No. 5184; Bülow to F. O., Aug. 9, 1901, ibid., 341 f., No. 5185.

As soon as the negotiations with Germany showed no prospect of success, the British government followed up Japan's offer of an alliance and in August began official conversations on that subject.[73] None the less it continued its efforts to make some kind of agreement with Germany. But on August 23, at Wilhelms-höhe, a meeting between Emperor William II and King Edward VII, which the British leaders hoped would pave the way for an understanding, had no result.[74] In November, Lord Lansdowne regarded the difficulties in the way of an alliance as "at the present moment virtually insuperable," enumerating some of them as follows:

1. The impossibility of arriving at a definition of the *casus foederis* which would not be either so rigid as to greatly hamper our freedom of action or so vague as to deprive the alliance of all practical value.

2. The certainty of alienating France and Russia.

3. Complications with the Colonies, which might not at all approve of the idea of hanging on to the skirts of the Triple Alliance.

4. The risk of entangling ourselves in a policy which might be hostile to America. Without knowledge of the German Emperor's views in regard to the United States, this is to my mind a formidable obstacle.

5. The difficulty of carrying Parliament with us at a moment when the Parliamentary situation is as little satisfactory as it is at present.[75]

[73] *B.D.*, Vol. II, chap. x; Newton, pp. 221 ff.

[74] On that meeting see Lee, II, 130 f.; Lascelles to Lansdowne, Aug. 25, 1901, *B.D.*, I, 259, No. 323; Lascelles to Lansdowne, Aug. 23, 1901, *ibid.*, II, 73, No. 90; memo. by William II, Aug. 23, 1901, *G.P.*, XVII, 94 ff., No. 5023. For the meeting Lansdowne gave to King Edward a memorandum on the questions which might be brought up. "With regard to Morocco," he wrote, "the policy of the German and British Governments would appear to be identical. Both desire the maintenance of the *status quo*, and both would probably resent any indignity offered to the Moorish Envoy who lately visited, and was received with honours at the German and British Courts" (*ibid.*, 124, No. 5033). By mistake King Edward gave a copy of this memorandum to the Emperor, whose government responded with a similar communication to the British government. The statement about Morocco was as follows: "In Morocco we follow a policy of reserve. The Morocco question by itself is not sufficiently important for us to justify a policy by which Germany might incur the risk of serious international complications" (*ibid.*, 129, No. 5025, Anlage).

[75] Memo. by Lansdowne (very secret), Nov. 11, 1901, *B.D.*, II, 78, No. 92. Late in July, Lascelles had expressed to Eckardstein his personal opinion that an alli-

But, he wrote, "the argument that, because we have in the past survived in spite of our isolation, we need have no misgivings as to the effect of that isolation in the future," could be pushed too far. Besides, since negotiations then in progress for an alliance with Japan virtually signified that Great Britain did not wish to remain alone, he proposed that the government seek "a much more limited understanding with Germany as to our policy in regard to certain matters of interest to both Powers"—for instance, they might agree to co-operate for the preservation of the territorial *status quo* on the shores of the Mediterranean, the Adriatic, the Aegean, and the Black Seas, for the maintenance of the "freedom for the commerce and navigation . . . . in the Persian Gulf, and the prevention of any territorial acquisitions on its shores by other Powers which might interfere with that object." But only "whenever the occasion for it might arise" should the nature of their co-operation be determined.[76]

The Premier remained vigorously opposed to the project; but Lord Lansdowne urged that the German government probably expected him to reopen the negotiations, and that if he made this offer, that government would be deprived of any grounds for complaining that Great Britain "had treated it inconsiderately or brusquely rejected its overture." As he also suspected that "the German Gov't. (or the German Emperor) desire something much more precise and far-reaching . . . . and that they would refuse an overture on the above lines," he maintained that the proposal could cause no damage.[77]

On December 19 the British Foreign Minister recalled to Count Metternich, the new German ambassador at London, the negotiations for an alliance and stated that "while . . . . we

---

ance between Great Britain and the Triple Alliance was hardly possible, that at most one between Great Britain and Germany was all that could be expected (Eckardstein to F. O., July 29, 1901, *G.P.*, XVII, 91, No. 5021).

[76] Memo. by Lansdowne, Nov. 11 and Dec. 4, 1901, *B.D.*, II, 76 ff., Nos. 92 f.

[77] Memo. by Lansdowne, Dec. 4, 1901, *ibid.*, 79 f., No. 93, and Salisbury's minutes.

certainly did not regard the German proposal with an unfriendly or indifferent eye, I did not think that for the moment we could afford to take it up." Instead he suggested that the two governments arrive at "an understanding with regard to the policy which they might pursue in reference to particular questions or in particular parts of the world in which they are alike interested." Count Metternich expressed surprise that the British government had not "jumped at" this "magnificent opportunity" to end its isolation, and replied that he did not expect his government to favor this restricted proposal. "It was a case of the whole or none."[78]

There the matter rested. Lord Lansdowne and King Edward were both dissatisfied with Count Metternich's critical tone;[79] but they continued to voice their solicitude, which the German Emperor and Count Bülow reciprocated, that the two governments keep in close touch.[80] However, public opinion in both countries remained bitterly hostile, and when in October, 1901, Mr. Chamberlain spoke disparagingly of the actions of the German army in the war of 1870–71, the protest of the German press was so vehement that the Chancellor, on January 8, 1902, declared in the Reichstag, "let the man go and do not become excited. He bites on granite."[81] The pleasant visit of the Prince of Wales to Germany a short time later did not offset the discord re-

[78] Lansdowne to Lascelles, Dec. 19, 1901, *ibid.*, 80 ff., No. 94; memo. by Metternich, Dec. 28, 1901, *G.P.*, XVII, 111 ff., No. 5030.

[79] Lee, II, 133 ff.

[80] Lascelles to Lansdowne, Jan. 16, 1902, *B.D.*, I, 268, No. 331; Plunkett to Lansdowne, April 11, 1902, *ibid.*, 274 f., No. 340; Lascelles to Lansdowne, Jan. 3, 1902, *ibid.*, II, 84, No. 95; memo. by Mühlberg, Dec. 27, 1901, *G.P.*, XVII, 109 f., No. 5028; William II to Edward VII, Dec. 30, 1901, *ibid.*, 110 f., No. 5029.

[81] He was quoting Frederick the Great (Bülow, I, 242). See Metternich to Bülow, Nov. 19, 1901, *G.P.*, XVII, 194 f., No. 5073; Bülow to Metternich, Nov. 26, 1901, *ibid.*, 195 ff., No. 5074; Metternich to F. O., Nov. 26, 1901, *ibid.*, 197 ff., No. 5075; Buchanan to Lansdowne, Nov. 20, 1901, *B.D.*, I, 263, No. 325; Lansdowne to Buchanan, Nov. 26 and Dec. 3, 1901, *ibid.*, 263, No. 328; Lansdowne to Lascelles, Jan. 14, 1902, *ibid.*, 266 f., Nos. 329 f.; Lascelles to Lansdowne, Jan. 16, 1902, *ibid.*, 268 f., No. 332. Cf. Chirol, p. 297; Gwynn, I, 350.

sulting from this war of words.[82] By March, Count Metternich wrote that he "wouldn't give two pence for Anglo-German relations"; while the Chancellor admitted that so far as Great Britain was concerned the Emperor was Germany's "best card."[83] It was a dismal fiasco for so momentous a negotiation. The British government thought that by considering an alliance the German leaders had manifested friendly feeling. Lord Lansdowne did not believe that the animosity of Germany toward Great Britain would last forever or that Germany would "let us 'go under' before a great European coalition." "Is it not more likely," he wrote, April 22, 1902, to Sir Frank Lascelles, "that she will stick to her rôle of the honest broker, taking advantage, if you like, of our difficulties in order to pursue a *politique de pourboire* at our expense, but without pooling her ironclads with those of France and Russia?" The Ambassador agreed with him; but after talking to the British naval attaché in Berlin he pointed out for the first time that the German navy was definitely aimed at Great Britain.[84] The future for Anglo-German relations was therefore none too bright for the British government, and British public opinion cordially approved when on January 30, 1902, the Anglo-Japanese Alliance was concluded.

The German government was not at all alarmed by this failure. Its relations with France and Russia were of the best. As a result of the Anglo-German intimacy in 1901, M. Delcassé had twice endeavored to approach Germany, while in September, during a meeting at Danzig of the Russian and German rulers together with their foreign ministers, the Russian Minister had asserted that "an alliance between Germany and Russia would be the greatest blessing and is a goal to be striven for." The overtures were disregarded.[85] When the Anglo-Japanese Alliance was

[82] Lee, II, 138 ff.; *B.D.*, I, Nos. 334 ff.

[83] Bülow to Metternich, March 13, 1902, *G.P.*, XVII, 149 ff., No. 5046.

[84] Newton, pp. 247 f.

[85] Bülow to F. O., Sept. 12 and 14, 1901, *G.P.*, XVIII, 28 f., Nos. 5393 f.; memo. by Bülow, Sept. 14, 1901, *ibid.*, 29 ff., No. 5395.

concluded in February, 1902, the Russian government urged Germany to enter a Continental combination against those Powers; but Count Bülow, pleased to see obviated the possibility of an Anglo-Russian understanding, bluntly rejected the proposal.[86] Nor did he believe that, since Russia and Great Britain were so decisively at odds, France would dare make an accord with the latter.[87] And Herr von Holstein wrote on December 31, 1901, that "at the present day Germany with her enormous strength on land and sea is a factor which no Power that wishes to perform an important act dare leave in its rear without having previously come to an understanding with her."[88]

Thus, the German apostles of *Weltpolitik* guiding the destinies of an acquisitive and chauvinistic nation, refused to co-operate with Great Britain, France, or Russia. Apparently they did not know what they wanted or how they might utilize their favorable situation; for they derived no benefits whatever from any of the opportunities offered. An Anglo-German agreement would have prevented the formation of the Entente Cordiale and would very likely have brought about a settlement of the Moroccan question to Germany's advantage. By cultivating France and encouraging her to draw closer, Germany might have come to some agreement with that Power through which she could have prevented the later Entente Cordiale from becoming so cordial, and through which she might have shared in the general improvement of relations between the Powers and in the settlement of the Moroccan question. The whole Moroccan crisis and many others to follow might thereby have been avoided. In a world of shifting friendships, of swiftly changing policies, a world demanding resolute and judicious statesmanship, the German Chancellor and Herr von Holstein refused to take risks.

[86] Alvensleben to F. O., Feb. 19, 1902, *ibid.*, XVII, 156 f., No. 5049; Bülow to Alvensleben, Feb. 22, 1902, *ibid.*, 157 ff., No. 5050; memo. by Bülow, Feb. 25, 1902, *ibid.*, 160 ff., No. 5051; and the following documents.

[87] See below.

[88] Memo. by Holstein, Dec. 31, 1901, *ibid.*, XVIII, 737, No. 5844.

Toward the British government they had showed themselves too sensitive, suspicious, and peremptory in their demands.[89] The French and Russian governments they had rebuffed even more brusquely. Deluded by wrong preconceptions of international politics and overprudent in their negotiations, they believed themselves entirely safe in playing their favorite rôle of sphinx and of aligning with no one.[90] Their naval program alarmed Great Britain; their construction of the Bagdad Railway antagonized Russia; their Moroccan policy exasperated France. They played against all three Powers, and still did not expect them to draw together against a common opponent. Instead of alliances or ententes, they reaped animosities. By their refusals and their clumsy diplomacy, they paved the road for the Anglo-French and the Anglo-Russian ententes. And when, a few years later, those Powers came to agreement, the German leaders feared that their country was being encircled and isolated.

[89] Eckardstein, III, 93.

[90] Hammann, *Zur Vorgeschichte des Weltkrieges*, pp. 144 f.

CHAPTER VI

THE MAKING OF THE ENTENTE CORDIALE

I

The Boer War had revealed to Great Britain the depth of antagonism toward her among the European nations and the haphazard inadequacy of her defensive preparations. The British government had therefore sought the support of Germany and of Japan. But the alliance with the second had not compensated for the rebuff from the first; and in 1902 the future direction of the British foreign policy, particularly with reference to Europe, remained undecided.

In February, 1903, Mr. Balfour, who succeeded Lord Salisbury as premier in 1902, appointed as a permanent body a Committee of Imperial Defence, whose duty, he said, was

to survey as a whole the strategical military needs of the Empire, to deal with the complicated questions which are all essential elements in that general problem, and to revise from time to time their own previous decisions, so that the Cabinet shall always have at its disposal information upon these important points.[1]

Great Britain also wanted to maintain peace, to settle her outstanding international difficulties, and to form ententes. In the first part of 1903 the government tried to co-operate with the various Powers. In January and February it asked the aid of Austria-Hungary and Italy in preventing Russia from sending ships of war through the Dardanelles and the Bosphorus. The two states refused although both were cordial friends of Great Britain.[2] Moreover, the British government associated itself with

[1] 4 Hansard, Vol. CXVIII, col. 1579.

[2] See Rodd to Lansdowne, Jan. 9, 1903, *B.D.*, IV, 41 f., No. 32, and following documents. However, an extract from *Defence Committee Paper 1b* (Feb. 11, 1903), read as follows: "What difference would it make to the balance of power

Germany in the Venezuela affair and expressed its willingness to participate in the Bagdad Railway. British public opinion protested strenuously, however, for it mistrusted Germany, regarding her as so chauvinistic, so hungry for colonies, so bold in her naval ambitions as to be not a friend but a rival. Hence the government had to settle the one affair as quickly as possible and, in March, to recede entirely from its stand on the other.[3]

Anglo-Russian relations were most troublesome. Early in 1903 the antagonism of these two Powers became acute all along the line from the Bosphorus and the Dardanelles to Persia to Afghanistan to Tibet to China. The British government offered in March to negotiate over Afghanistan, but Russia refused.[4] Still more pressing for Great Britain was the problem which resulted from the Anglo-Japanese Alliance. In April, 1903, the renewal of Russian activity in Manchuria and its extension into the Yalu Valley caused a grave increase of tension between Rus-

in the Mediterranean if Russia were to obtain, through possession of Constantinople, free egress from the Black Sea through the Dardanelles, these remaining closed, as at present, against other Powers?

"The answer to this question unanimously accepted by the Committee was that, while Russia would no doubt obtain certain naval advantages from the change, it would not fundamentally alter the present strategic position in the Mediterranean."

An extract from *Defence Committee Paper 2b* of the same month read as follows: "It may be stated generally that a Russian occupation of the Dardanelles, or an arrangement for enabling Russia to freely use the waterway between the Black Sea and the Mediterranean, such as her dominating influence can extract from Turkey at her pleasure, would not make any marked difference in our strategic dispositions as compared with present conditions" (*B.D.*, IV, 59 f.). This opinion was approved on April 22, 1904, by King Edward and by Sir Charles Hardinge, who had just been appointed ambassador at St. Petersburg (Lee, *King Edward VII*, II, 289 f.). It apparently led to a change of policy in the autumn of 1903 (see below).

[3] Chirol, *Fifty Years in a Changing World*, pp. 276 ff.; *G.P.*, Vol. XVII, chaps. cxii, cxiv, Part A; *B.D.*, Vol. II, chap. xii. See also Lansdowne to Curzon, April 24, 1903, Newton, *Lord Lansdowne*, p. 254.

[4] See *B.D.*, IV, 41 ff., Nos. 32 ff.; memo. on British policy in Persia, Oct. 31, 1905, *ibid.*, 365 ff., No. 321; memo. respecting Russia and Afghanistan, Oct. 14, 1903, *ibid.*, 512 ff., No. 465; Newton, pp. 271 ff.

sia and Japan.[5] The revived danger of war between those two states brought home to the British government the urgent need of assurance that it would not become involved if hostilities did ensue. By the terms of the Anglo-Japanese Alliance, the *casus foederis* would arise only in case of an attack upon one of the allies by two or more Powers. Manifestly it would depend upon France and upon the nature of her obligations as ally to Russia whether Great Britain could preserve neutrality in case of a conflict.[6] Hence the British government, which in the previous year had refused to touch the dangerous Moroccan question, now concluded to accept the French proposal for a Moroccan accord and to liquidate the various differences with France. It would thereby win a friend who could act as mediator between Great Britain

[5] The Japanese Foreign Minister, in communicating to the British Minister on April 27 the Russian demands to China, spoke "with unwonted seriousness" and asserted "that he considered the situation exceedingly grave" (MacDonald to Lansdowne, April 27, 1903, *B.D.*, II, 198 ff., No. 226. The dispatch was received first on June 2, but there is no reason to doubt that the view expressed therein was immediately known to the British government since the two governments were in constant communication. See Lansdowne to MacDonald, April 29, 1903, *ibid.*, 200 f., No. 228; memo. communicated by Hayashi, Japanese minister to London, to Lansdowne, April 27, 1903, *ibid.*, 201 f., No. 228, inclosure; William L. Langer, "Der Russisch-Japanische Krieg," *Europäische Gespräche*, June, 1926, pp. 310 ff.; Tyler Dennett, *Roosevelt and the Russo-Japanese War* (New York, 1925), pp. 139 f., 355 ff.

[6] When Russo-Japanese relations became strained early in 1901, Lansdowne asked Monson whether he thought "that France is under any engagement to take part on the side of Russia in the event of war, or that without such obligation she would attempt to do so" (Lansdowne to Monson, March 8, 1901, *B.D.*, II, 40, No. 49). Monson replied that he did not know whether the Dual Alliance laid down the obligation of military aid outside of Europe, and that while the French people showed little zeal for far eastern affairs, yet nationalistic hatred against Great Britain might be aroused at any time and might make the French stand uncertain (Monson to Lansdowne, March 13, 1901, *ibid.*, 44 f., No. 56). The Franco-Russian declaration of 1902 in reply to the Anglo-Japanese Alliance stated that the Dual Alliance was extended to the Far East, although a few days later Delcassé cast doubt upon the significance of this engagement. While French public opinion was opposed to becoming involved in the Far East for the sake of Russia, yet this ambiguity left the French position in case of a war in doubt (see above).

and Russia and would make certain that a Russo-Japanese war would not involve the allies of those Powers.

The way toward France instead of Germany was indicated clearly by the drift of British public opinion; for while the animosity between the British and German peoples had increased in 1902 and 1903, the flow of vituperation between the British and French press over the Boer War and the Dreyfus case[7] had practically ceased, and concerted movements were on foot to create a popular basis for an "entente cordiale."

Political and business groups took the lead in this work. By 1903 King Edward, who two years previously had desired an alliance with Germany, advocated strongly a *rapprochement* with France. His personal dislike and mistrust of his nephew, William II, and of Germany, his wide knowledge of men and of international affairs, his sensitiveness to currents of public opinion, caused him to incline toward France.[8] His willingness to take the initiative in clarifying public opinion and in defending British interests enabled him to play an important rôle in transforming British foreign relations.[9] One of his advisers was Lord Esher, a man who held no official position but who exerted quiet influence upon court, government, and press. Particularly interested in naval and military problems, he was instrumental in creating the Committee of Imperial Defence, of which he became a perma-

---

[7] See Pinon, *France et Allemagne*, pp. 79 f.; Jean Darcy, *France et Angleterre. Cent années de rivalité coloniale: L'Afrique* (Paris, 1904); Barclay, *Thirty Years: Anglo-French Reminiscences, 1876–1906*, chaps. xiii–xvi.

[8] Philippe Crozier, who in 1903 was French minister at Copenhagen, states that to his intimate friends King Edward "even foresaw the hypothesis of a positive alliance" with France ("L'Autriche et l'avant guerre," *Revue de France*, April 15, 1921, p. 271).

[9] Lee, II; Newton, pp. 292 f. Early in 1915 Balfour wrote to Lansdowne denying that King Edward was the author of the Entente Cordiale. "Now, so far as I remember, during the years which you and I were his Ministers, he [King Edward] never made an important suggestion of any sort on large questions of policy" (Newton, p. 293). This estimate may be true, but it does not give the King credit for what he actually did.

nent member. Through him the press leaders were kept informed about the needs of defense and were guided toward friendship with France.[10] The influence of the business world in the same direction was represented by Mr. Thomas Barclay, former president of the British Chamber of Commerce in Paris and an active worker for the improvement of international relations. In 1901 he began a campaign in both France and England for a *rapprochement*, to which during the next two years he devoted his entire time and fortune.[11] In England these efforts had complete success.[12] In France they encountered more difficulty, for France had usually been the loser in Anglo-French diplomatic battles. However, the *revanche* anti-German group, the socialists and internationalists, and the commercial and business elements approved. Then, after the French people at large became convinced that Great Britain was not so thoroughly egoistic and chauvinistic as they had supposed, and that she really felt amicable toward France, they heartily welcomed a *rapprochement* as flattering and beneficial to their country.[13] Nevertheless, they remained skeptical about the durability of any entente with their old rival. The French press laid down as conditions for one that the Dual Alliance should not be weakened thereby and that Great Britain should convince France of her serious intentions by treating her equitably in the settlement of their colonial differences, particu-

[10] Spender, *Life, Journalism and Politics,* I, 185 ff. Esher had been furnishing information to Spender, who was editor of the *Westminster Gazette,* a Liberal paper, since 1900. Spender denies that the British foreign office inspired the newspapers (*op. cit.,* I, 185).

[11] J. L. de Lanessan, *Histoire de l'entente cordiale franco-anglaise* (Paris, 1916), pp. 218 ff., 229, 234; Barclay, chaps. xvii–xx.

[12] The *Times,* the Northcliffe Press, the Chamberlain Press, the *National Review, Fortnightly Review, Contemporary Review,* the Liberals as well as the Conservatives, supported the movement. See *G.P.,* XVII, Nos. 5081–83, 5087–88, 5094, 5026–27; Hammann, *Zur Vorgeschichte des Weltkrieges,* pp. 175 f.; Wolff, *Das Vorspiel,* p. 135; Barclay, pp. 177 f.

[13] See Barclay, chaps. xvii, xx.

larly the Moroccan question.[14] This mistrust was not entirely dispelled for several years.

Informal conversations for an agreement were resumed in April, 1903, between representatives of the two governments.[15] Then King Edward visited Paris (May 1–5); and, although at first he was met with cold silence, his felicity of speech and act soon won the French people. As a French Anglophobe said to a friend: "I can't think what has come over the population of Paris. The first day they behaved well; the second day, they merely displayed interest; but the third day, *c'était attristant— ils ont acclamé le Roi!*"[16] This visit, so unexpectedly successful,

[14] Reports from the Belgian ministers in Paris and London, May 4, 1902, *Zur europ. Politik,* I, 105 f. Impressed with the unanimity of friendliness toward France among the British, M. Delcassé expressed to Monson his regret that the French did not fully reciprocate this feeling. See Monson to Lansdowne, July 24, 1903, *B.D.,* II, 302 f., No. 361; *Bulletin,* July, 1903, pp. 211 ff.; *Quest. dipl. et col.,* XV, 656 f., XVI, 147; articles from *Figaro* and the *Temps* quoted in the *London Times,* May 5, 1903; article by Etienne in the *National Review,* July 1, 1903, esp. p. 748a.

[15] So Eckardstein asserts, *Lebenserinnerungen, etc.,* II, 337; cf. Schefer, *D'une guerre à l'autre, etc.,* p. 249.

[16] King Edward's trip was a bold move, for Paris was the center of anti-British feeling, and some members of the British government were doubtful about its success. But the King initiated the visit and took the entire responsibility for it, feeling certain that he would be well received. In his first public speech, more optimistically than truthfully, he declared: "There may have been misunderstandings and causes of dissension in the past [between the two countries], but all such differences are, I believe, happily removed and forgotten, and I trust that the friendship and admiration which we all feel for the French nation and their glorious traditions may in the near future develop into a sentiment of the warmest affection and attachment between the peoples of the two countries. The achievement of this aim is my constant desire." Quoted in the *London Times,* May 2, 1903, M. Paul Cambon's estimate of the significance of the King's visit is as follows: "Of course, King Edward helped immensely. His visit to Paris in the spring of 1903 really made it [the Anglo-French entente] possible. . . . ." See interview with Cambon in *ibid.,* Dec. 22, 1920. On the visit see Captain the Hon. Sir Seymour Fortescue, *Looking Back* (London, 1920), pp. 279 ff.; *Quest. dipl. et col.,* XV, 656 f.; Lee, II, 221 ff., 236 ff.; Barclay, p. 218; Viscount Esher, *The Influence of King Edward and Essays on Other Subjects* (London, 1915), pp. 57 ff.; Pinon, p. 114; Herbert H. Asquith, *The Genesis of the War* (New York, 1923), p. 30; Metternich to Bülow, June 2, 1903, *G.P.,* XVII, 590 ff., No. 5376; Crozier, pp. 272 ff.; Newton, pp. 275 f., 278 f.

created a favorable atmosphere for further negotiations.[17] Later in the month, at M. Cambon's initiative, the project of a treaty of arbitration was taken up.[18] In July, when President Loubet, accompanied by M. Delcassé, returned the King's visit, the newspapers reported a statement by King Edward to the effect that M. Loubet would be more heartily welcomed in England than any chief of state had ever been. The President was able to speak of the Entente Cordiale as established.[19]

During the visit the foreign ministers agreed that the time was "in every way propitious for a frank exchange of opinions." They began that long negotiation from which the Entente Cordiale was to result. They discussed the question of the fishing rights off the coast of Newfoundland, the question of Siam, of the New Hebrides, of Sokoto, of the treatment of British firms in French Congo, and of Morocco. The French Minister frankly stated that if they could come to terms over Morocco, "all other difficulties would disappear, or become comparatively easy to deal with." While denying any desire "to get rid of the Sultan or to annex his country" or to "force the pace," he declared that in view of the rapidly waning authority of the Sultan, France could not regard with indifference the prevalence of chronic disorder in Morocco or permit any other Power to undertake the task of regenerating the land. What France wished, said M. Del-

[17] Shortly before this visit Chamberlain remarked to Eckardstein: "Here in England the King's visit to Paris is very popular, and if France gives him a good reception then everything will go well between us in the future." See Eckardstein to Bülow, May 10, 1903, *G.P.*, XVII, 568, No. 5369; Metternich to Bülow, June 2, 1903, *ibid.*, 590 ff., No. 5376.

[18] Monson to Lansdowne, Jan. 20, 1902, *B.D.*, II, 261 f., No. 319; Lansdowne to Monson, May 19, 1903, *ibid.*, 289, No. 352; Monson to Lansdowne, May 22, 1903, *ibid.*, 290, No. 353; Monson to Lansdowne, May 29, 1903, *ibid.*, 290 f., No. 354; Lansdowne to Monson, July 21, 1903, *ibid.*, 301 f., No. 360, and inclosures; *Annual Register* (1903), pp. 216 f.; Barclay, pp. 235, 242; expressions of public opinion on this project contained in *Quest. dipl. et col.*, July 1 and 15, Aug. 1, Sept. 1 and 15, 1903.

[19] King Edward's assertion had direct reference to the German Emperor, with whom he had never agreed (*Zur europ. Politik*, I, 110; Lee, II, 244 ff.; *Quest. dipl. et col.*, XVI, 147 ff.).

cassé, was a "reasonable assurance that their policy would not be obstructed by Great Britain."

In reply, Lord Lansdowne made three conditions for an accord over Morocco. First, British interests in the Mediterranean seaboard of Morocco, particularly in Tangier and the neighboring coast, must be protected. Second, Spanish ambitions must be fairly dealt with. Third, complete equality of economic opportunity in Morocco must be assured. M. Delcassé unhesitatingly accepted all three stipulations. Then the British Minister proposed that they make the settlement a comprehensive one by including the Egyptian question. Again the French Minister agreed, provided they reached accord "as to the position of France and Morocco."[20]

A few days later M. Cambon made to the British Minister a more detailed statement of the French proposal. Concerning Morocco, he said, the two governments could agree that the existing constitution *au point de vue politique* as well as *au point de vue territorial* should be maintained. But the British should acknowledge that France "has a peculiar interest in maintaining peace within that country, and in assisting the Moorish Government to bring about the administrative, economical, and financial improvements of which Morocco stands so much in need." The French, in turn, should expressly attest that these improvements would not infringe in any way upon the principle

[20] On this interview see the dispatch from Lansdowne to Monson, July 7, 1903, *B.D.*, II, 294 ff., No. 357; also Delcassé's interview in *Petit Parisien*, April 10, 1904, reprinted in *Quest. dipl. et col.*, April 16, 1904, pp. 616 f. Delcassé's conversation with Lansdowne had been prefaced by the talks between Cambon and Lansdowne during the previous year and also by a long talk on July 2, 1903, between Lansdowne and Etienne. Etienne had stated one of the reasons for an Anglo-French entente as follows (the account is from the hand of the British minister): "M. Etienne expressed his belief that the most serious menace to the peace of Europe lay in Germany, that a good understanding between France and England was the only means of holding German designs in check, and that if such an understanding could be arrived at, England would find that France would be able to exercise a salutary influence over Russia and thereby relieve us from many of our troubles with that country" (Lansdowne to Monson, July 2, 1903, *B.D.*, II, 293, No. 356).

of commercial liberty. The two governments, continued M. Cambon, might co-operate in securing a free passage through the Straits of Gibraltar by preventing the erection of any fortifications on the southern shore. When Lord Lansdowne raised the objection that Great Britain was interested in other parts of the Moorish littoral besides that abutting on the straits, the Ambassador readily acknowledged this point, and remarked that France wished to prevent any Power from establishing itself at any strategic position on the Moroccan coast.

As M. Cambon did not mention the Egyptian problem, the British Minister immediately stated that its inclusion was an absolute condition to any consideration of the Moorish question. The Ambassador proposed that they leave Egypt alone for the present; but, when this suggestion was refused, he declared that if the French government, by acknowledging the permanency of the British hold upon that land, extracted this "big thorn from the foot of Great Britain," it would expect *une grosse compensation*. This, he said, "might take the shape of greater liberty of action in Morocco—something less remote and conjectural . . . . than she [France] had yet asked for."[21]

After this agreement upon the questions to be included in the negotiation there remained the other preliminary matter of how to deal with Spain. Lord Lansdowne thought that "it would not be difficult for us to come to terms with France if Spain were out of the way."[22] But, bound by the promise of the previous March to that Power and more desirous of having weak and decadent Spain than powerful France control the south shore of the straits, he upheld Spain's interest in Morocco. M. Cambon declared that his government acknowledged this position, mentioning the Franco-Spanish negotiations of 1902 as proof. At his suggestion they decided on August 5 that a subsequent settlement between France and Spain in harmony with the proposed

---

[21] Lansdowne to de Bunsen, July 15, 1903, *ibid.*, 298, No. 358; Lansdowne to Monson, July 29, Aug. 5, 1903, *ibid.*, 304 ff., Nos. 363 f.

[22] Lansdowne to Durand, July 14, 1903, Newton, p. 280.

Anglo-French accord be made and be communicated to the British government.[23]

The negotiations over these complex problems lasted almost ten months. Two months passed before the British answer was ready; for the members of the cabinet were on their vacation, a ministerial crisis occurred in September as a result of which several resigned,[24] and Lord Cromer, British consul-general and agent in Egypt, had to be consulted. This influential official had previously received permission to send Sir Eldon Gorst, financial adviser to the Egyptian government, to Paris in the autumn in order to sound the French government about converting the Egyptian debt and abolishing the *caisse de la dette*. Foreseeing the failure of that effort unless the British government made concessions in Morocco, Lord Cromer urged it to do so. He realized that thereby Morocco would "to all intents and purposes become before long a French province"; none the less he supported the proposed accord fully to strengthen British control in Egypt, and played a major rôle during the negotiations in determining the British policy.[25]

On October 1 Lord Lansdowne stated to M. Cambon the British conditions for an arrangement.[26] He accepted the French proposal about Morocco with slight modifications. He suggested that France should agree not to erect any military or naval works along the Moroccan coast from Algeria to Mazaghan, and that the two Powers should engage not to permit any others to do so;

[23] Then Lansdowne notified the Spanish government of the steps which he had taken and asked for a statement of its views on the Moroccan question. Whether Spain replied is not evident. See Lansdowne to Monson, Aug. 5, 1903, *B.D.*, II, 306 f., No. 364; Lansdowne to Durand, Aug. 11, 1903, *ibid.*, 309 f., No. 366; Newton, p. 280.

[24] J. A. Spender, *The Life of the Right Hon. Sir Henry Campbell-Bannerman* (London), Vol. II, chaps. xxiii–xxiv.

[25] Cromer to Lansdowne, July 17, 1903, *B.D.*, II, 298 ff., No. 359; memo. by Cromer, Aug. 7, 1903, *ibid.*, 307 ff., No. 365; Newton, pp. 280 ff.

[26] Lee, II, 245 f.; Lansdowne to Cambon, Oct. 1, 1903, *B.D.*, II, 311 ff., No. 369; 400 n.

that a certain amount of territory in Northern Morocco "should be recognized as destined to fall under Spanish influence" and that "in the event of a complete collapse of the Sultan's authority," Spain should be intrusted with the administration of the Moroccan seaboard as far south as Mazaghan. However, Spain was to "be precluded from fortifying this portion of the coast, and also from alienating it or her existing possessions in Morocco to another Power." As the *quid pro quo* for these concessions to France, the British Minister required in Egypt the lifting of the time limit to the British occupation and the French sanction of the abolishment of the *caisse de la dette,* the reorganization of the railway administration, and the conversion of the Egyptian debt. He also requested the consent of the French government to examine at some future time proposals abolishing the capitulations in Egypt and "tending to assimilate the Egyptian legislative and judicial systems to those in force in other civilized countries." "His Majesty's Government would, on their side," he continued, "be ready to examine, in consultation with the Government of the French Republic, similar proposals with regard to Morocco, if at any future period France should acquire so predominant a position in Morocco as to become outwardly responsible for the good government of the country." The other questions considered in the Minister's reply, those of Newfoundland, Siam, New Hebrides, Nigeria, Zanzibar, and Madagascar, were less significant.[27]

With the offers of each party known, the bargaining began. On October 27 M. Cambon replied. He was still averse to dealing with the Egyptian affair so fully, and declared that the terms offered were unequal; for, whereas France received "hopes" alone in Morocco, Great Britain would enjoy immediate and concrete benefits in Egypt. Moreover, France would have to settle with Spain, and might even have to reckon with the pretensions of Germany. So he suggested that the proposed changes

[27] Lansdowne to Cambon, Oct. 1, 1903, *ibid.,* 311 ff., No. 369.

in Egypt be introduced *pari passu* with correlative ones in Morocco. He also objected to giving Spain control over any seacoast farther south than the Sebou River. He further suggested that Great Britain and France undertake "to maintain, save for the consequences of the present accord, the territorial *status quo* within a radius of 500 miles around the straits."[28]

When these terms were submitted to Lord Cromer, he was pleased with the progress that had been made. "Who would have imagined, only a short time ago," he wrote Lord Lansdowne, November 1, "that we should ever have got so far? . . . . We *must* manage to come to terms. . . . . I regard this as by far the most important diplomatic affair that we have had in hand for a long time past. . . . . *We must not fail.*" He added that Great Britain was asking for much more in Egypt than she offered France in return in Morocco. Lord Lansdowne agreed with him; but, he said, the French "are extremely anxious to have their position in Morocco recognized, and we must turn this feeling to account." His suggestion to Lord Cromer that consideration of the conversion of the Egyptian debt be postponed so as to diminish the difficulties was not carried into execution.[29]

On November 19 Lord Lansdowne replied to M. Cambon that he was willing to limit the Spanish and the neutralized portions of the Moroccan coast to those between Melilla and Rabat; but he refused the French proposal concerning the simultaneous introduction of changes in Egypt and Morocco, particularly the change by which the "abandonment of financial control by France in Egypt would proceed *pari passu* with the acquisition of financial control by France in Morocco." He likewise wished the French government to join Great Britain "in addressing the other Powers for the purpose of securing their assent" to the

[28] Lansdowne to Monson, Oct. 7, 1903, *ibid.*, 317 f., No. 370; Cambon to Lansdowne, Oct. 26, 1903, *ibid.*, 320 ff., No. 373.

[29] Cromer to Lansdowne, Nov. 1, 1903, Lansdowne to Cromer, Nov. 17, 1903, Newton, pp. 283 ff.

suggested British changes in Egypt. And he held out for absolute guaranties of full economic liberty in Morocco.[30]

In the French response of December 9 M. Cambon reported
that his government agreed to assist the British government
in obtaining the assent of the other Powers to the Egyptian
changes; but he objected strongly to the exclusion of Rabat
from the French sphere. Moreover, he desired that the period
of commercial liberty in Morocco be limited to fifteen or twenty
years, and that the construction and administration of railways
and ports there be kept under governmental control. In explaining the five-hundred-mile proposal, M. Cambon pointed out
Germany's designs upon Morocco which had recently been renewed, in all probability under the encouragement of Spain. He
recalled the Spanish proposal in 1887 for the assembly of a
European conference to discuss the Moroccan question, and
added:

> It was quite likely that some such proposal might now be revived. It was
> in view of these circumstances that the French Government had proposed
> the maintenance of the *status quo* within a radius of 500 miles from the
> Straits—a radius which would include the Balearic Islands, in which Ger-
> many might perhaps desire to obtain a footing.[31]

Both Lord Lansdowne and Lord Cromer knew that Germany
was interested in the fate of Morocco, and they fully anticipated
a request from her for some territory there, for example, Rabat
or some other port. They also realized that the French expected
Great Britain to help in keeping Germany out of Morocco, and
Lord Cromer gathered from conversations with French officials
in Egypt that the French would like to embroil Great Britain
and Germany, bring about an Anglo-Russian agreement, and isolate Germany. As both statesmen felt that a demand on the part

---

[30] Cromer to Lansdowne, Oct. 30, 1903, *B.D.*, II, 323, No. 374; Lansdowne to
Cambon, Nov. 19, 1903, *ibid.*, 324 ff., No. 376.

[31] The French government, Cambon said, knew that "the Queen of Spain during
her recent visit to the Continent had been in communication with the German
Emperor upon the subject of Morocco" (Lansdowne to Monson, Dec. 9, 1903,
ibid., 329 ff., No. 378).

of Germany for a coaling station would be very awkward to meet, Lord Lansdowne did nothing to clarify the situation beyond refusing M. Cambon's anti-German project.[32] He thereby left to the French the possibility of forcing Great Britain to aid them in case Germany did try to intervene in the Moroccan question.

In reply to M. Cambon on December 11 Lord Lansdowne signified his apprehension that if Rabat were not neutralized France might later transform it into a torpedo-boat station. The other points concerning Morocco he agreed to, except that he extended the limit for commercial equality to fifty years.[33]

Thus far the negotiations had proceeded smoothly. The Anglo-French arbitration treaty had been signed on October 14. Agreement over the two main questions, those of Egypt and of Morocco, had practically been reached.[34] And on November 23 M. Delcassé had been able to declare in the French Chamber, with evident reference to Great Britain, that "when one speaks today of a Moroccan problem, the idea that in the solution the decisive word pertains to France has become almost familiar and appears almost natural, even to those who in the past would have believed themselves obliged to oppose it with the greatest vigor."[35]

II

These discussions had been closely connected with another diplomatic movement. The Anglo-French *rapprochement* was logically followed by attempts at an Anglo-Russian settlement

---

[32] Lansdowne to Cromer, Nov. 17, 1903, Cromer to Lansdowne, Nov. 27, 1903, Newton, pp. 285 f.

[33] Lansdowne to Monson, Dec. 11, 1903, *B.D.*, II, 333 f., No. 380. It was evident that in view of the monopolistic tendencies of the French, British trade in Morocco would practically cease at the end of the time limit (Cromer to Lansdowne, Dec. 11, 1903, *ibid.*, 332 f., No. 379).

[34] Lansdowne to Monson, Jan. 13, 1904, *ibid.*, 338, No. 384; Cromer to Lansdowne, Dec. 11, 1903, *ibid.*, 332, No. 379.

[35] Quoted in *Quest. dipl. et col.*, Dec. 1, 1903, p. 821.

which in turn would have an alleviating effect upon Russo-Japanese relations. The British and French governments immediately recognized this fact, as did also Count Lamsdorff, Russian foreign minister. In July, just after M. Delcassé's visit to England, conversations began, at the instigation of the French Foreign Minister,[36] between Lord Lansdowne and the Russian Ambassador. The British Foreign Secretary remarked to Count Benckendorff, July 29, as follows: "If Russia would put us in full possession of her ideas, and if she would bear in mind that for any concessions which she obtained from us we should expect corresponding concessions from her, I believe that we might put an end to the unfortunate rivalry which had so long prevailed between us in China and in the other parts of Asia." But he declared a few days later that until he was "thoroughly satisfied" by Russia, especially as to Manchuria, he "must remain observant and critical." The Ambassador, who seemed favorable toward a general agreement, left in August for a visit to St. Petersburg, and did not see Lord Lansdowne again until November 7.[37]

An understanding along the lines mentioned by Lord Lansdowne would have settled both the Anglo-Russian and the Russo-Japanese problems. As an inducement to a *rapprochement* the British Foreign Secretary was showing compliance with Russia's policy in the Balkans,

even to the extent [wrote on October 26 Sir Louis Mallet, précis writer to Lord Lansdowne] of suggesting reforms which will give them [Russia] a foothold in the Balkans. H. M. G. are therefore committed to a certain extent to a policy of not opposing Russia's advance to Constantinople. At least,

---

[36] Delcassé had received the hint from Chamberlain (see next reference).

[37] Lansdowne to Scott, July 29, Aug. 12, 1903, *B.D.*, II, 212 f., Nos. 242 f. In September, Lansdowne wrote in a memorandum for the cabinet as follows: "A good understanding with France would not improbably be the precursor of a better understanding with Russia" (Lee, II, 246). In July, Lansdowne also sought the co-operation of the United States in checking Russia in the Far East (Dennis, *Adventures in American Diplomacy*, p. 359).

I read it in that light. . . . . It's a chance Russia will never get again of buying off our opposition to their advance to Constantinople.[38]

Russia, however, continued her Asiatic activity, so objectionable to Great Britain and Japan. She dallied with the Japanese offer of agreement over their Chinese differences while she made new demands on China, extended her interests in the Yalu Valley and in Seoul itself, and seemed on the way to take Korea.[39] She asserted her right to send agents into Afghanistan at will, contrary to the old understanding with Great Britain; and on October 5 made a communication to the British government on that subject which Sir Charles Hardinge, assistant undersecretary of state for foreign affairs, regarded as "peremptory in tone, and almost discourteous in its terms."[40]

In this grave situation Lord Lansdowne besought the help of the French government in restraining Russia. On October 26 he expressed regret to M. Cambon over the absence of frankness in Anglo-Russian intercourse. "Their conduct [the Russian government's]," he complained, "placed us in a very embarrassing position." The pledges which they gave—for example, with respect to the evacuation of Manchuria—remained unfulfilled. "We were . . . . told that the obstructiveness of the Chinese was to blame. There might be some truth in this, but it was impossible to test the truth of the assertion unless the Russian Government would really tell us what they wanted." Lord Lansdowne expressed the hope that during Count Lamsdorff's forthcoming visit to Paris (October 29–31) his conversations with M.

[38] Mallet to Spring Rice, Oct. 26, 1903, Gwynn, *Letters and Friendships of Sir Cecil Spring Rice*, I, 366 f.

[39] Lansdowne to MacDonald, July 3, 13, 1903, *B.D.*, II, 206 ff., Nos. 237 f., and the following documents. See MacDonald to Lansdowne, Sept. 4, Oct. 1, 1903, *ibid.*, 214 ff., Nos. 246, 248; Alfred von Hedenström, *Geschichte Russlands von 1878 bis 1918* (Stuttgart and Berlin, 1922), p. 170; *Cambridge History of British Foreign Policy*, III, 324 f.; Langer, pp. 312 ff.

[40] *B.D.*, IV, 621; memo. respecting Russia and Afghanistan, Oct. 14, 1903, *ibid.*, 518 f., No. 465; memo. on Russo-Afghan relations, Oct. 11, 1905, *ibid.*, 519 f., No. 466; Hardinge to Lansdowne, Nov. 22, 1903, *ibid.*, 194, No. 181(*b*). There was also trouble over Tibet and the Persian Gulf (see Newton, p. 287).

Delcassé "might indirectly have an effect upon the attitude of the Russian Government towards that of this country."[41]

M. Delcassé took the hint. Count Lamsdorff agreed with him on the value of an arrangement with both Great Britain and with Japan.[42] He also expressed publicly Russia's satisfaction with the Anglo-French and the Franco-Italian *rapprochements*.[43]

This intercession had an immediate result. When Count Benckendorff returned to London, Lord Lansdowne summed up his assertions, November 7, as follows:

> Count Lamsdorff felt strongly that it was of importance that an endeavour should be made to remove all sources of misunderstanding between the two Governments, and that there should be "a change for the better" in our relations. Count Benckendorff was therefore instructed to discuss frankly with me the various questions outstanding between Great Britain and Russia, with the object of arriving at an agreement as to the manner in which they should be dealt with. In the meantime, the Russian Government would be careful to avoid any action bearing the appearance of hostility to this country.

Lord Lansdowne was pleased at this response, for, as he said, he "had been seriously concerned at the position into which the two Powers were apparently drifting." The two men then discussed in general terms the questions dividing their countries.[44] On November 17 and 25 they returned to the subject, and on November 22 King Edward and Sir Charles Hardinge each had an interview with Count Benckendorff. The Count stated that "the moment was riper now for a friendly understanding than at any time during the past twenty years." He said that the matters for consideration "seemed naturally to group themselves into (1) questions concerning China in which Russia had a special interest (2) questions concerning India, in which Great Britain had a special interest and (3) questions concerning Per-

[41] Lansdowne to Monson, Oct. 26, 1903, *B.D.*, II, 217 f., No. 250.

[42] Lansdowne to Monson, Nov. 4, 1903, *ibid.*, 221 f., No. 257.

[43] Spring Rice to Grey, Feb. 12, 1906, *ibid.*, IV, 224, No. 209; Bülow to F. O., Oct. 31, 1903, *G.P.*, XVIII, 853, No. 5918.

[44] Lansdowne to Spring Rice, Nov. 7, 1903, *B.D.*, II, 222 ff., No. 258.

sia in which both Powers were interested." But it became clear from these conversations that the Ambassador was instructed merely to discuss the problems, that he had no definite proposals to make. Nor were the discussions satisfactory. The Ambassador could make no statement about Russian aims in China. He objected to the division of Persia into spheres of influence. He protested strongly against the British expedition to Tibet announced in that month. He refused to put anything on paper about Afghanistan.

In order to make some headway, Lord Lansdowne made a frank exposition of the British desires. On December 11 Count Lamsdorff voiced "much satisfaction" with this "ready response." The British Ambassador urged him to make "an early and equally frank expression of the views of the Russian Government," which might "lead to a satisfactory understanding." Count Lamsdorff promised to try to reply before February 2, when Parliament was to reassemble. And Count Benckendorff planned to go to St. Petersburg early in 1904 for consultation.[45]

Just as Lord Lansdowne had expected, the negotiations did not proceed beyond that point; Russia would not limit her Asiatic ambitions. She would not accept the British terms, which of course included stipulations concerning China satisfactory to Japan, nor would she settle with Japan alone. Count Lamsdorff was willing to do so; but, as was well known by the other governments, he had no control over Russia's far eastern policy. Since August this policy had been directed by the viceroy in the Far East, back of whom stood the Czar and the coterie around him interested in Russian expansion into Manchuria and Korea. Count Lamsdorff's hands were tied; Russian activity made war with Japan a certainty. Toward the end of 1903 this menace grew so ominous that on December 11 Lord Lansdowne warned M. Cambon as follows:

[45] Lansdowne to Spring Rice, Nov. 7, 17, 25, 1903, *ibid.*, 222 ff., No. 258; IV, 183 ff., Nos. 181 f.; 306 f., No. 289; Scott to Lansdowne, Dec. 22, 1903, *ibid.*, II, 226, No. 262; Lee, II, 280 f.; Lansdowne to Cromer, Dec. 7, 1903, Newton, p. 287.

H. E. [His Excellency] was no doubt aware that, under the Agreement with Japan, our intervention could only be demanded in case that Power were assailed by two others. On the other hand, public opinion here might render it extremely difficult for us to remain inactive if Russia were to find some pretext for attacking Japan and were to endeavour to crush her out of existence.

It seemed to me in these circumstances that it was the duty of our two Governments, which were, I rejoiced to think, at this moment in such friendly relations, to do all in their power to keep the peace.[46]

The French government reciprocated this wish, and let the British government perceive that it would not enter a Russo-Japanese war. Early in January the other Powers also asserted their intention of remaining neutral.[47]

Having been fully informed about Russo-Japanese relations, the British government had recognized the danger of war since July and had in consequence not let the negotiations with France lag or fail.[48] But since it now felt reasonably certain of not being drawn into the impending struggle, it allowed the transactions with France, on January 13, 1904, to come to a deadlock over a question hitherto cursorily considered. M. Delcassé requested territorial indemnity for the relinquishment of certain fishing rights off the coast of Newfoundland; and the British government refused to give the amount desired. The difficulty imperiled the entire settlement since both sides were so fearful of public opinion that they refused to make concessions.[49] But on Feb-

[46] Lansdowne to Monson, Dec. 11, 1903, *B.D.*, II, 224, No. 259.

[47] In Dec., 1903, Delcassé informed the Japanese Minister in Paris that he did not approve of all of Russia's designs in the Far East (Dennis, p. 385). Hayashi, Japanese minister in London, believed as early as Dec. 23 that France would remain neutral. See Eckardstein, III, 62, 188; see also Metternich to F. O., Jan. 8, 1904, *G.P.*, XIX, 20 f., No. 5931; memo. by Eckardstein, Jan. 17, 1904, *ibid.*, 38 ff., No. 5945; Langer, p. 317; Bülow to William II, Jan. 12, 1904, *G.P.*, XIX, 26, No. 5936.

[48] Lee, II, 282; Langer, pp. 316 f.; Dennis, chap. xiii. However, as late as Nov. 4, 1903, Lansdowne did not expect war, nor did Sir Charles Hardinge as late as Dec. 25. By Jan. 5, the latter did (Gwynn, I, 391 f.).

[49] Cambon to Lansdowne, Dec. 27, 1903, *B.D.*, II, 336, No. 382; and the following documents, particularly the dispatch from Lansdowne to Monson, Jan. 18,

ruary 10 the Russo-Japanese War began. Admiral Fisher was certain that Japan would be defeated.[50] Rumors were abroad concerning Russo-German negotiations for closing the Baltic Straits,[51] and some British officials had misgivings that a coalition of Russia, France, and Germany might be formed against their country.[52] Moreover, the British government feared that a Balkan war might break out in the spring.[53] Under these circumstances the British government could not afford to risk alienating France.[54]

M. Delcassé was surprised by the outbreak of the war.[55] His

1904, *ibid.*, 339, No. 386. The British were also surprised to learn early in January that Delcassé had kept his colleagues in the dark concerning the details of the arrangement, and feared some trouble on that account. It seems that as late as March 2 Delcassé had not consulted the French Colonial Minister (Lansdowne to Cromer, Jan. 5, 1904, Monson to Lansdowne, Jan. 8, 1904, Newton, pp. 287 ff.).

[50] *Ibid.*, p. 307.

[51] *G.P.*, XIX, 89 f., editor's note, and the documents in *G.P.*, Vol. XIX, chap. cxxix; Gwynn, I, 391.

[52] Spring Rice to Ferguson, Feb. 4, 1904, Spring Rice to Roosevelt (no date given, though written in Feb. or March, 1904), Gwynn, I, 392 ff.; Sternburg to F. O., March 21, 1904, *G.P.*, XIX, 112, No. 5992. See also the dispatch from Alvensleben to Bülow, Dec. 20, 1903, *ibid.*, 18, No. 5929. Sir Charles Dilke summed up the danger of the situation as follows: "If Germany were to declare war on Japan, Great Britain would be forced by her treaty engagement to declare war on Russia and Germany; and France, it is understood, to declare war upon Great Britain and Japan" (Dilke, "The War in the Far East," *North American Review*, April, 1904, quoted in Dennett, p. 94).

[53] Lansdowne to Monson, Feb. 17, 1904, *B.D.*, V, 67 f., and following documents.

[54] Lansdowne to Monson, Feb. 25, 1904, *ibid.*, II, 346, No. 391, and following documents; on March 1, King Edward wrote to Balfour strongly advising in favor of the territorial sacrifice asked by the French on the Newfoundland question, for, he wrote, *"more than ever now"* [in italics in the original] we must leave no bone of contention between ourselves and the French Government" (Lee, II, 248). See also Holstein's keen analysis of the situation on Jan. 23, 1904, *G.P.*, XIX, 48 ff., No. 5951. Cromer also urged his government to make concessions (Newton, p. 289).

[55] Tardieu, *La France et les alliances*, p. 23; E. J. Dillon, *The Eclipse of Russia* (New York, 1918), pp. 330 ff.; Eckardstein, III, 57 ff., 187 ff.; Crozier, pp. 282 f.; Mévil, *De la paix de Francfort, etc.*, pp. 83 ff.; Radolin to F. O., Feb. 11, 1904, *G.P.*, XIX, 60 f., No. 5960.

ambition had been for the Anglo-French *rapprochement* to be supplemented by an Anglo-Russian one. Then as Italy was also trying to approach Russia, a more or less loose grouping of France, Russia, Great Britain, Italy, Spain, and Japan would be created.[56] Busy with the Anglo-French negotiations, he had been misled by the optimism of the Russian government into thinking that war would not occur.[57] He had not appreciated fully the weakness of Count Lamsdorff's position. Not until January, 1904, did he perceive the danger and make belated efforts to maintain peace. But Great Britain refused to aid him.[58] Immediately after the war began he tried again to secure British co-operation in stopping it. When the British government again refused, M. Delcassé became incensed, for he saw the defeat of his larger program.[59] His better judgment soon calmed him, however, for with France's ally eliminated from European affairs, he needed British co-operation more than ever in order to keep the war from spreading[60] and to offset the increased power of Germany. Late in February both parties were therefore ready to compromise.[61] And, after a threat by Lord Lans-

[56] Mévil, p. 82.

[57] For an illustration of that optimism see Nicholas II to William II, Jan. 24, 1904, *G.P.*, XIX, 53, No. 5952.

[58] Lansdowne to Scott, Jan. 19, 1904, *B.D.*, II, 237, No. 280; Lansdowne to Monson, Jan. 27, 1904, *ibid.*, 240, No. 283.

[59] In July, 1905, Spring Rice reported to his friend Roosevelt a conversation which he had recently had with Lansdowne, as follows: "In speaking in general terms of our relations with Japan, he [Lansdowne] pointed out that from the very first our political interest had been to prevent the war [between Russia and Japan] which would not only expose us to great dangers of loss in Asia itself, but would seriously imperil our good understanding with France. . . . ." Then after explaining why Great Britain refused to press Japan to maintain peace, he continued: "As a result we all but lost our agreement with France" . . . . (Dennett, pp. 213 f.). Cf. Eckardstein to Schwabach, Feb. 10, 1904, *G.P.*, XIX, 60, No. 5959. Spring Rice's assertion was no doubt exaggerated in order to prove to Roosevelt that Great Britain really desired peace between Russia and Japan.

[60] See Radolin to Bülow, March 15, 1904, *ibid.*, XX, 3 f., No. 6366.

[61] See Lansdowne to Monson, March 1, 1904, *B.D.*, II, 347, No. 393, and following documents.

downe on March 31 to break off negotiations when the French Foreign Minister, alarmed by French public opinion, attempted to reopen the Newfoundland question,[62] the accord was finally completed on April 8, 1904.

This agreement consisted of three documents: first, a convention which settled the Newfoundland question, modified certain boundaries between French and British colonies in Africa, and gave the Iles de Los to France; second, a declaration concerning Siam, Madagascar, and the New Hebrides; and third, a declaration concerning Egypt and Morocco. Only the convention had to be submitted to the two parliaments, since it alone provided for territorial changes in the existing possessions of the two states. While the solution of all these difficulties established the Entente Cordiale, the last-named declaration gave to the entente its great significance in international affairs; for through it two of the old sore spots in Anglo-French diplomacy were healed, and the basis for the future co-operation of the two Powers was laid.

By the terms of this declaration France relinquished her rights and interests in Egypt in favor of Great Britain; Great Britain, in favor of France in Morocco. Only the clauses concerning Morocco are of interest here. Article II read as follows:

The Government of the French Republic declare that they have no intention of altering the political status of Morocco.

His Britannic Majesty's Government . . . . recognize that it appertains to France . . . . to preserve order in that country, and to provide assistance for the purpose of all administrative, economic, financial, and military reforms which it may require.

They declare that they will not obstruct the action taken by France for this purpose, provided that such action shall leave intact the rights which Great Britain, in virtue of Treaties, Conventions, and usage, enjoys in Morocco. . . . .

[62] See Monson to Lansdowne, March 30, 1904, *ibid.*, 357, No. 405; Lansdowne to Monson, March 30, 31, 1904, *ibid.*, 358, No. 406; 359 f., No. 408; Newton, pp. 289 f.

Article IV provided for full commercial liberty, which, however, should obtain for only thirty years. Each government reserved the right "to see that the concessions for roads, railways, ports, etc. [in Morocco and Egypt], are only granted on such conditions as will maintain intact the authority of the State over these great undertakings of public interest." By Article VII the free passage and non-fortification of the south shore of the Straits of Gibraltar were assured. According to Article VIII the interests of Spain in Morocco were to be respected, and the compact over them to be worked out between the Spanish and French governments was to be communicated to the British government. Article IX was included at the insistence of the British government, which planned thereby to enjoy French support in obtaining the acquiescence of the other Powers to the proposed changes in Egypt. Although the French reluctantly agreed to it, it eventually proved to be of the greatest value to them. It read as follows: "The two Governments agree to afford to one another their diplomatic support, in order to obtain the execution of the clauses of the present Declaration regarding Egypt and Morocco."

Five secret articles supplemented the public agreement. Article I was as follows:

In the event of either Government finding themselves constrained, by the force of circumstances, to modify their policy in respect to Egypt and Morocco, the engagements which they have undertaken towards each other by Articles IV, VI and VII of the Declaration of to-day's date would remain intact.

Article II was included at the wish of the British:

His Britannic Majesty's Government have no present intention of proposing to the Powers any changes in the system of the Capitulations, or in the judicial organization of Egypt.

In the event of their considering it desirable to introduce into Egypt reforms tending to assimilate the Egyptian legislative system to that in force in other civilized countries, the Government of the French Republic will not refuse to entertain any such proposals, on the understanding that His Britannic Majesty's Government will agree to entertain the suggestions that the Government of the French Republic may have to make to them with a view of introducing similar reforms in Morocco.

Articles III and IV marked out the portion of Morocco which should come within the "sphere of influence" of Spain "whenever the Sultan ceases to exercise authority over it," and provided for the validity of the Anglo-French declaration in case Spain refused to make an agreement.[63] Article V concerned the Egyptian debt.

The contradictions in the accord are apparent. The "political status" in Morocco was to be preserved, but it would take a statesman trained in diplomatic casuistry to explain how this was possible with France alone making all the proposed internal reforms. Of course, what was meant was that the "international status" of the land should be respected. However, the terms of the secret articles foresaw a future change even in that; and it can hardly be called showing a nice regard for Morocco's international and sovereign independence for two alien Powers to set a time limit to the right of commercial liberty in that land. The doctors were agreeing upon a division of the patient's property before they began to operate. That Morocco, an independent state, would eventually be partitioned into French and Spanish protectorates was evident to anyone with an understanding of contemporary political practices. To preserve peace and amity between themselves, Great Britain and France had simply made a division of spoils at Morocco's expense.[64]

The new accord was most cordially welcomed by all parties in

[63] The first two articles were kept secret at Delcassé's desire; the next two for obvious reasons.

[64] Ministère des Affaires Etrangères, *Documents diplomatiques. Accords conclus, le 8 avril, 1904, entre la France et l'Angleterre au sujet du Maroc, de l'Egypte, de Terre-Neuve, etc.* (Paris, 1904); *Parliamentary Papers. Declaration between the United Kingdom and France Respecting Egypt and Morocco, together with the Secret Articles Signed at the Same Time. Signed at London, April 8, 1904* (Cd. 5969), Vol. CIII (1911); *B.D.*, II, 373 ff., No. 417. The secret articles were first revealed in 1911.

Great Britain. In the House of Commons on June 1, Earl Percy, speaking for the government, and Sir Edward Grey, speaking for the opposition, both emphasized the need for Great Britain henceforth to follow a policy of "administrative concentration and consolidation" of her empire, and declared that similar agreements should be made with other Powers. Not all troubles with France had been disposed of, said Earl Percy, but the chief ones had been, and the others could now be more easily settled. As to the terms dealing with Morocco, while he admitted that the Sultan had not been consulted beforehand, he declared that Morocco needed setting to rights and that France had a better claim to execute that work than anyone else. He also emphasized the unique quality of the Entente Cordiale.

The parties pledge themselves not merely to abstain from poaching on each other's preserves but to do all in their power to further one another's interests. We promise to give to one another, as friends, advantages which are ordinarily given only to allies, and it is as a pledge of friendship rather than as the terms of a compromise between jealous and exacting litigants that we ask the House to consent to these concessions.

Sir Edward Grey approved of the relinquishment of Morocco to France. Together with other speakers, he praised the spirit of the agreement, and he expressed the hope that Article IX would enable the two nations to draw closer together by increasing the "opportunities for the interchange of international courtesies between them."

During the debates Mr. Gibson Bowles declared that the agreement amounted to a "partition of three new Polands" (Egypt, Morocco, and Siam), "a compact of plunder." But from a European point of view he considered it of "the highest import," for it signified a "return to the . . . . system of the balance of power." "There are stalking through Europe," he stated, "ambitions which must be curtailed and which may be developed to a greater extent than seems at present. Against such it is well to raise a visible barrier in England and France." Mr. Balfour, the premier, however, denied that there had been "any reversal of the traditional policy of our party," or that anything had been done "prejudicial to the interests of Germany or any other Power."

The *Times* did not agree with him. Its Paris correspondent wrote on April 14 as follows:

> The Triple Alliance has long since ceased to be the European bogey which it once was. . . . . There is the Dual Alliance, the Anglo-French Agreement, and the Franco-Italian *rapprochement*, with benevolent diplomatic neutrality on the part of Russia. Now, in the midst of this happy family, the Triple Alliance only appears as the ghost of its former self.

The editorial comment of that paper was in a similar tone.

> The days have gone by when the Germans could assume with some shadow of plausibility that in the larger questions of international politics Great Britain must follow in the wake of the Triple Alliance, and that the attitude of France might be ignored. There is no alliance between them, but there is a cordial understanding which will induce both to discuss all subjects affecting them fairly and without jealousy or suspicion, and which, combined with the relations in which they stand to Italy, must exercise a great influence upon all States, and, it may be, a great attraction upon some of them.

Events soon proved that the *Times's* estimate of that entente was more accurate than that of Mr. Balfour.[65]

Although happily surprised by the conclusion of the Anglo-French agreement, French public opinion did not accept the accord as whole-heartedly as did the British. Opposition to various parts of the settlement was expressed by extremists who regretted the final renunciation of French ambitions in Egypt and who thought that French interests in Siam and elsewhere had not been adequately upheld; by those in the maritime districts of Northern and Northwestern France who criticized the terms

[65] On the reaction of the British people to the accord see Spender, *Life, Journalism and Politics,* I, 188 ff.; *London Times,* April 12 and 14, 1904; *Spectator,* quoted in Schulthess, *Europäischer Geschichtskalendar 1904,* p. 223. For the debates in the British Parliament see 4 Hansard, Vol. CXXXV, cols. 502 ff. Adverse opinion was expressed by Lord Rosebery, the *Daily Chronicle,* the *Morning Post,* and Mr. Aflalo who had lived in Morocco and was particularly interested in the fate of the land; but their voices were lost in the general applause (Metternich to Bülow, April 9, 1904, *G.P.,* XX, 13 f., No. 6375).

concerning Newfoundland as disastrous to French fishing interests in that region; and more or less openly by the enemies of M. Combes, the premier, whose stringent anticlerical policy had aroused bitter antagonism among the French. These critical forces, however, were more than offset by the elements who praised the agreement. "It is equitable, the equilibrium of the accord is irreproachable," wrote M. de Caix. The recognition of France's special interests in Morocco was especially commended by almost all parties. The strengthening of France's international position was also acknowledged with satisfaction. In reporting the agreement to the Chamber of Deputies on November 3 M. Deloncle declared: "We do not wish a . . . . passing entente between our two countries. We think . . . . of the formation of accords always more intimate and durable, which, loyally executed by both parties, ... on the basis of reciprocal confidence, will cement the community and solidarity of the two countries." Alliance with Russia, friendship with Great Britain, was the popular formula.

Nevertheless, the convention over Newfoundland was accepted by the Chamber only on condition that M. Delcassé attempt to reopen the question with the British government. Many warned M. Delcassé not to trust Great Britain too far, not to permit the entente to assume in any way the character of an alliance, and not to involve France in the Anglo-German rivalry. In the Chamber on November 8 M. Delafosse declared that the accord signified a "detente," not an "entente." M. René Millet, former governor of Tunis, wrote that the arrangement was "a retreat in good order" which "does not justify the enthusiasm with which it has been received." M. Millet found insufficient the diplomatic preparation for the French action in Morocco.

It is not possible [he wrote] for France to undertake anything without knowing the thoughts of Germany. . . . . Our bad will toward the Germans will only render them more imperious, and, without declaring war, they will have more than one means of being disagreeable to us, especially at the time when Russia . . . . is unable to help us. . . . . Of all pretensions, the most foolish would be to wish to isolate the German Empire, as certain musketeers of the press advise.[66]

Alarmed by the criticism of the Newfoundland convention, M. Delcassé tried in June and July to obtain some further concessions from the British government.[67] Although he had no success, he felt compelled during the debates in the French Chamber, November 3–10, to promise to reopen negotiations on the Newfoundland question. Otherwise, he feared a rejection. This meaningless concession, together with the fact that the entente had already proved its value by enabling M. Delcassé to mediate between Great Britain and Russia in October for a peaceful settlement of the Dogger Bank episode,[68] smoothed the path for parliamentary approbation. Hence M. Delcassé, in his speech of defense, was able to confine himself to generalities. He reviewed his achievement of the ententes with Italy, Spain, and Great Britain, by which the Moroccan question had been settled in favor of France and by which the French position in the world had been elevated. He advocated a policy of peace and conciliation, but he also declared that France must maintain her defenses.

And this is what procures for France [he concluded], augmented in her credit and prestige, the trust and sympathy of the world. The world is convinced to-day that French policy does not seek the advantage for France other than in the harmony of French interests with the interests of others. And she is happy to affirm that that harmony, which no one believes or pretends to believe unrealisable, is being realised each day to the benefit of all.

It will be the honor of our democracy to have practiced that policy.

[66] *Bulletin*, April, 1904, p. 107: Millet, *Notre politique extérieure 1898–1905*, pp. 168, 173. Millet was a follower of Hanotaux, Delcassé's predecessor at the foreign office, and a consistent critic of the latter.

[67] Count de Montferrand, who in company with M. Cambon talked with Sanderson about the Newfoundland question, remarked that "if M. Delcassé was not able to inform the French Chambers that they had secured this right, the Convention would be rejected" (memo. by Sanderson, June 30, 1904, *B.D.*, III, 6, No. 5; see *ibid.*, chap. xvi, Part I).

[68] See below.

He was roundly applauded, and his achievements were approved by both Parliament and people. The accord was ratified in the Chamber by a vote of 443 to 105, and in the Senate by one of 215 to 37.[69]

[69] For a summary see the article by Louis-Jaray, "L'Accord entre la France et l'Angleterre. L'Opinion publique et le rapprochement franco-anglais," *Quest. dipl. et col.*, XVIII (Nov. 16, 1904), 593 ff. The debates in the Chamber, Nov. 3–10, 1904, and in the Senate, Dec. 5–7, 1904, are to be found in the *Journal officiel, Debats. parlem.* (Chambre), pp. 2255 ff.; *ibid.* (Sénat), pp. 1013 ff. See also Monson's reports to Lansdowne, Nov. 9, Dec. 8, 1904, *B.D.*, III, 11 ff., Nos. 8 ff.

CHAPTER VII

ANGLO-RUSSIAN RELATIONS AFTER THE MAKING OF THE ENTENTE CORDIALE

After the Russo-Japanese War began, the British and Russian governments decided that for the present nothing further could be done toward an understanding.[1] Russian anger was directed as much against Great Britain as against Japan for having caused the conflict;[2] while Great Britain could hardly jeopardize her alliance with Japan by coming to a settlement with the latter's enemy. A few days after the signing of the Anglo-French agreement, King Edward tried to revive the negotiations in a talk at Copenhagen with M. Iswolski, Russian minister at the capital. When Count Benckendòrff mentioned the King's conversation to Lord Lansdowne, the latter reiterated his former opinion, adding that in the meantime the two governments should so handle any differences which might arise as to permit the renewal of the discussions for an agreement after the conclusion of the war.[3]

This suggestion was acted upon, for, even apart from other reasons, Count Lamsdorff wished to hold Great Britain to the strictest neutrality during the war with the lure of an understanding. The British government assured him of its neutral inten-

[1] Lansdowne to Spring Rice, April 22, 1904, *B.D.*, IV, 188 f., No. 183. The breakdown of the negotiations as a result of the war had been anticipated early in January by Sir Charles Hardinge (Gwynn, *The Letters and Friendships of Sir Cecil Spring Rice*, I, 392).

[2] Hardinge to Lansdowne, June 8, 1904, *B.D.*, IV, 194 f., No. 188; Radolin to Bülow, Feb. 28, 1904, *G.P.*, XIX, 165 ff., No. 6028, and following documents; Lansdowne to Scott, March 4, 1904, *B.D.*, V, 73; Spring Rice to Ferguson, March 2, 1904, Gwynn, I, 403 ff.

[3] Lee, *King Edward VII*, II, 283 ff.; Lansdowne to Spring Rice, May 4, 1904, *B.D.*, IV, 189 f., No. 184, and following documents; Savinsky, *Recollections of a Russian Diplomat*, pp. 90 f.; Crozier, *Revue de France*, April 1, 1921, pp. 275 ff.; Newton, *Lord Lansdowne*, pp. 307 ff.; cf. *ibid.*, pp. 243 f.

tions.[4] King Edward cultivated assiduously the friendship of the Czar during the next months.[5] Early in June the British government gave reassurances about its policy toward Tibet, in return for which the Russian government approved the Khedivial decree putting into execution the reforms in Egypt foreseen in the Anglo-French declaration.[6] Fraught with more danger was the possibility that Russia might send her Black Sea fleet through the straits. Lord Lansdowne warned her that that act "could not be tolerated by this country," that it "might render conflict inevitable."[7] So the fleet was never sent. In spite of British protests, however, Russia dispatched several vessels belonging to the volunteer fleet through the Dardanelles and the Bosphorus. When, in July and August, two of these ships seized some British merchant vessels suspected of carrying contraband, British public opinion demanded that the government defend British commerce. When Lord Lansdowne expressed indignation at the depredations, the Russian government immediately agreed to a conciliatory settlement.[8] In September the Russian government objected strongly to the terms of the recent Anglo-Tibetan Treaty, but without avail. Being in no position to follow up that protest, it had to acquiesce in the British action.[9]

[4] Hardinge to Lansdowne, June 8, 1904, *B.D.*, IV, 194 f., No. 188; Newton, pp. 310 ff.

[5] Lee, II, 287 ff.

[6] Lansdowne to Spring Rice, May 4, 10, 1904, *B.D.*, IV, 189 f., No. 184; 307 ff., No. 291; Hardinge to Lansdowne, May 18, 1904, *ibid.*, 190, No. 185; Monson to Lansdowne May 27, 1904, *ibid.*, 193, No. 186.

[7] Lansdowne to Monson, April 29, 1904, *ibid.*, II, 401; Lansdowne to O'Conor, June 7, 1904, *ibid.*, IV, 51, No. 46; Metternich to F. O., Aug. 18, 1904, *G.P.*, XIX, 240, No. 6070.

[8] *B.D.*, Vol. IV, chap. xxiii, Part III; *G.P.*, Vol. XIX, chap. cxxxii; Newton, pp. 313 ff.; Gwynn, I, 424 f. King Edward was in favor of showing to Germany, whose commerce was also being molested by those ships, a mark of friendship by co-operating with her in handling the matter with Russia. Lansdowne disapproved the idea (Lee, II, 297 f.).

[9] Hardinge to Lansdowne, Sept. 23, 1904, *B.D.*, IV, 317, No. 299; Lansdowne to Hardinge, Sept. 27, 1904, *ibid.*, 319 f., No. 301.

In October the two countries came dangerously close to war over the Dogger Bank affair. The Russian Baltic fleet, a make-shift, heterogeneous collection of vessels, was on its way to the war zone. While passing through the North Sea, it shot into a British fishing fleet off the Dogger Bank in the night of October 21, sinking one vessel and damaging others, killing two men and wounding members of the crews. The Russian fleet thought that it had fired at two Japanese torpedo boats, and continued its voyage without stopping to see what damage it had inflicted. The previous mishandling of British merchant ships by the Russians had already so irritated the British nation that it became incensed at this latest act. Public opinion was bellicose. Sir Charles Hardinge, British ambassador at St. Petersburg, described the fleet's conduct to Count Lamsdorff as "an unqualified and brutal outrage." The British government demanded a full investigation, punishment of those culpable, "ample apology and complete and prompt reparation as well as security against the recurrence of such intolerable incidents." "The matter is one which admits of no delay," asserted Lord Lansdowne to the Russian Ambassador; "if an attempt were made to fence with the question, public feeling here would become uncontrollable." Unless prompt action were taken by the Russian government, he continued, "we should certainly be obliged to take our own measures for guarding against a repetition of these acts."[10] The British admiralty mobilized the fleets at Portland and at Malta, rushed reinforcements to the fleet at Gibraltar, and advised the commander there that "it may become necessary for you to stop the Baltic Fleet, by persuasion if possible, but by force if necessary."[11]

This energetic procedure brought immediate results. The Russian government agreed quickly to the British demands. With the help of French mediation, the crisis passed within a week, and

[10] Lansdowne to Hardinge, Oct. 24 and 25, 1904, *ibid.*, 6, No. 6; 7 f., No. 8; 10 f., No. 12; Hardinge to Lansdowne, Oct. 24, 1904, *ibid.*, 7, No. 7.

[11] Admiralty to F. O., Oct. 28, 1904, *ibid.*, 18 f., No. 19 and inclosures.

the final settlement was left to international arbitration. But on October 29 Lord Lansdowne warned the Russian Ambassador as follows:

I owned . . . . that I lived in dread of new troubles arising. . . . . It had not been without the greatest difficulty that we had avoided a conflict. . . . . I would not, in these circumstances, dwell upon the results of a repetition of the North Sea incident.

There was however another peril against which it was our duty to guard. . . . . If, during its [the Russian fleet's] long voyage, the Russian captains considered themselves justified in the wholesale seizure of vessels suspected of carrying contraband, public feeling in this country would become uncontrollable.[12]

A few days later the British Foreign Secretary again warned the Ambassador, somewhat more mildly to be sure, against permitting two particularly predatory ships of the volunteer fleet which had just been added to the Russian fleet itself to prey on neutral commerce.[13] No more trouble arose.

After events of this kind, an Anglo-Russian *rapprochement* seemed far off. The British and Russian presses were at each other's throats. On December 2 Sir Charles Hardinge reported his French colleague's views as follows:

He [M. Bompard] impressed upon me that the attitude of His Majesty's Government during the next year when the conditions of peace would be under discussion would be decisive of the relations between England and Russia for the next twenty five years. Thanks to the Japanese war the German Government were only now recovering the position which they had lost at the congress of Berlin. If His Majesty's Government continued to maintain the same strained relations during the forthcoming year as in the past twelve months there would be no prospect of a rapprochement between the two countries for another generation. He begged me to remember that the many incidents which had occurred had redounded solely to the advantage of the German Emperor who now had a position at the Russian Court which a year ago would have been regarded as impossible.[14]

[12] Lansdowne to Hardinge, Oct. 29, 1904, *ibid.*, 23 f., No. 23.

[13] Lansdowne to Hardinge, Nov. 3, 1904, *ibid.*, 55, No. 52. On the Dogger Bank affair see *ibid.*, chap. xxiii, Part ii; *G.P.*, Vol. XIX, chap. cxxxiv; Lee, II, 301 ff.; Newton, pp. 315 ff.; Gwynn, I, 432 f.

[14] Hardinge to Lansdowne, Dec. 2, 1904, *B.D.*, IV, 66 f., No. 58.

In the next month M. Delcassé urged upon the British Ambassador the desirability of an Anglo-Russian *rapprochement* and asked about the possibility of bringing Italy also into new quadruple grouping. Lord Lansdowne saw no reason why a permanent understanding with Russia should be impossible, but he pointed out the difficulty. "The Russian diplomatic currency has become debased and discredited," he wrote to the Ambassador at Paris, "and it will not be easy to restore it to its face value."[15] None the less he hardly needed the French warning and advice, for he had already been acting in accordance with them. The British government had shown as much consideration for Russian feeling in the Dogger Bank affair as circumstances permitted. In February of the next year it tried to reach accord on the Afghan question, but Count Lamsdorff was too much occupied with other matters.[16] Great Britain could well afford to be friendly since the Japanese victories were so eminently satisfactory to her. Moreover, she wanted no war, for, apart from her aversion to war as such, she feared what Germany might do in case of one.[17] Rumors of a Russo-German treaty were already abroad and spread rapidly toward the end of 1904.[18] British public opinion was becoming more mistrustful of Germany than of Russia. Having regarded the growing German navy, so near at hand in the North Sea, as a distinct menace for over a year, it now feared

[15] Newton, pp. 339 f.

[16] Lansdowne to Benckendorff, Feb. 17, 1905, *B.D.*, IV, 520 f., No. 466a; Lansdowne to Hardinge, March 8, 1905, *ibid.*, 521, No. 466b.

[17] On Nov. 5, 1904, Spring Rice wrote to Roosevelt as follows: "Emperor William has got the ear of the Emperor here. . . . . It is plain that Germany naturally enough wants to see Russia have a free hand in Asia and hopes in exchange to have one in Europe; that if England could be engaged in a war with Russia which would require her fleet to be absent in the East, the German fleet, especially if France would come in, would have a good chance for a sudden descent on England" (quoted in Dennett, *Roosevelt and the Russo-Japanese War*, pp. 73 f.; see also Gwynn, I, 414 ff., 436, 438 ff.).

[18] Lascelles to Lansdowne, Sept. 23, 1904, *B.D.*, IV, 4 f., No. 4; Gwynn, I, 427 f.; see also below.

that Germany might try a sudden descent upon the English coast.[19] The British government viewed the situation more sanely, but it appreciated the danger of the German navy. As Mr. Spring Rice, first secretary of the British embassy in St. Petersburg, had written to his friend, President Roosevelt, in the summer of 1904:

> We are trying our best to come to some sort of understanding with Russia (when the war is over), so as to put an end to the continual régime of panic in India, Persia, etc. The reason we are doing so is that with the establishment of a strong German navy on our flanks we cannot afford to have a life-and-death struggle in Asia and the Far East. Germany is rapidly acquiring a very strong position in Russia. . . . . In any case, if we were at war with Russia, Germany would either take Russia's side, or exact very hard terms from us for her neutrality. The German fleet has really revolutionized politics.[20]

In August, 1904, Sir John Fisher, first sea lord of the British admiralty, had warned the government that " 'instant readiness for war' was imperative, ... unless naval reforms were 'ruthless and remorseless, ... we may as well pack up and hand over to Germany.' "[21] In accordance with his recommendation, the British government reorganized and redistributed its fleet late in 1904 in such a way as to concentrate the main strength in home waters. And at the close of the year, when the German statesmen expressed fears of a British attack on their country, Lord Lansdowne wrote to Sir Frank Lascelles:

> They cannot seriously believe that we are meditating a coup against them. Are they perchance meditating one against us and are they seeking to justify it in advance? All this talk about one driving them to lean towards Russia looks a little like it.

[19] Bernadotte Everly Schmitt, *England and Germany, 1740–1914* (Princeton, 1916), p. 180; *G.P.*, Vol. XIX, chap. cxxxvi. Balfour denied in the House of Commons that an attack was likely or would succeed if it were made. But the British fear continued. See 4 Hansard, Vol. CXLII (March 7, 1907), col. 595; Vol. CXLVI (May 11, 1905), cols. 72 f.

[20] Dennett, pp. 152 f.; Gwynn, I, 422 f. The letter was a reply to one from Roosevelt dated June 13, 1904. The approximate date given by Dennett is incorrect.

[21] Fisher to Knollys, Aug. 19, 1904, Lee, II, 328.

The knowledge gained early in 1905, that Germany was making approaches not only to Russia and the United States but to Japan as well, augmented British mistrust of her policy.[22]

The pressure of events and the insistence of such men as King Edward, Admiral Fisher, and others were completing the change of policy which Great Britain had been making since 1901. Great Britain had abandoned her policy of splendid isolation; she was more and more taking an active share in European international relations and assuming a definite position in the Continental system of alliances.

[22] Newton, p. 332.

CHAPTER VIII

FRENCH POLICY AFTER THE MAKING OF THE ENTENTE CORDIALE

As friend of Great Britain and ally of Russia, France was in an uneasy situation after the outbreak of the Russo-Japanese War. Hostility between those two Powers was increasing. Thereby the influence of Germany in St. Petersburg was greatly augmented, and Germany was assiduously courting Russia. M. Delcassé had to show enough sympathy and give enough help to Russia to prevent Germany from usurping France's position at St. Petersburg and at the same time hold to the Anglo-French entente.

The task did not prove to be unduly arduous, for Russia did not require much of her ally. M. Delcassé sought to maintain harmony between Great Britain and Russia by helping them settle their disputes.[1] He also did what favors he could for Russia, such as permitting the Russian Baltic fleet to use French ports on the way to the Far East. But otherwise he left Russia to her own resources and devoted himself to other tasks.

The Anglo-French accord did not complete M. Delcassé's work of establishing France's right to preponderance in Morocco and of elevating her position in Europe, but it made the completion possible. The Foreign Minister still had to negotiate an agreement with Spain, to exclude Germany from the Moroccan settlement, and to execute the policy of pacific penetration in the

---

[1] On Oct. 28, 1904, at the height of the Dogger Bank crisis, Lansdowne reported the following assertion by Cambon: "His Excellency [M. Cambon] said that he did not himself know precisely what obligations France had undertaken in virtue of that understanding [the Dual Alliance]. He did not however believe that if there was a collision, France would join Russia against us, but if a collision occurred, and particularly if it were brought on by unreasonable demands on our part, there would be a *revirement* of public feeling, and the Anglo-French *entente* could not fail to suffer" (Lansdowne to Monson, Oct. 28, 1904, *B.D.*, IV, 22, No. 21.

Sherifian Empire. During the succeeding months he was occupied with these problems.

I. THE FRANCO-SPANISH AGREEMENT, 1904

When M. Delcassé, in accordance with Article VIII of the Anglo-French declaration, proposed to the Spanish government in April, 1904, that they negotiate over the Moroccan question, he immediately met with difficulty. Relying upon promises by Lord Lansdowne and M. Delcassé, the Spanish government had expected to be consulted before the conclusion of the bargain. It therefore complained because the negotiations had not been conducted à trois.[2] The Spanish Queen Mother branded the act as an "unfriendliness" to Spain, and the Marquis del Muni (M. Leon y Castillo), Spanish ambassador at Paris, "clinched his fist in his pocket" at the two Powers.[3] When the Cortes met, the Liberals took occasion on June 6, 7, and 9, to expose the main terms of the Franco-Spanish accord of 1902 which the Conservatives had refused to sign, and to accuse that party of having inadequately upheld Spain's interests. As the nation remained apathetic, M. Maura, the prime minister, had no difficulty in

[2] According to a speech in the Spanish Senate on March 21, 1904, by M. Abarzuza, who had been a member of Silvela's cabinet from Dec. 6, 1902, to July 20, 1903, both the British and the French governments promised Spain in the first half of 1903 not to touch the Moroccan question or to make any alterations in North Africa without Spain's previous knowledge and acquiescence. The speech is quoted by Becker, *Historia de Marruecos* (Madrid, 1915), pp. 440 f. See above for Lansdowne's promise. The Spanish government did try to participate in the Anglo-French negotiations by way of both London and Paris; but it was put off with general assurances of friendship by both Lansdowne and Delcassé. See Lansdowne to Durand, Aug. 11, 1903, *B.D.*, II, 309 f., No. 366; Lansdowne to Monson, Jan. 23, 1904, *ibid.*, 341, No. 388; Lansdowne to Egerton, April 11, 1904, III, 25 f., No. 24; Bülow to F. O., Sept. 18, 1904, *G.P.*, XVII, 354, No. 5199, and the following documents. For expression of Spanish public opinion over the Anglo-French accord see the *London Times*, April 11-16, 1904; Gay, *España ante el problema del mediterráneo*, pp. 31 ff.; Maura, *La Question du Maroc, etc.* (Paris, 1911), pp. 32 f.; Mousset, *La política exterior de España, 1873-1918* (Madrid, 1918), pp. 149 ff.

[3] *G.P.*, XX, 169 f.

defending his government.[4] Urged by the British government,[5] he accepted M. Delcassé's overture.

The course of the negotiations, which began in April, was a rocky one. The Spanish accused the French of being too-hard bargainers; the French thought that the other party was too prone to alarm.[6] The Spanish government, ignorant of the secret articles in the Anglo-French agreement by which the Spanish sphere was already limited,[7] demanded the territorial terms which had been informally agreed upon in 1902. But M. Delcassé refused to give them, for, he asserted, Spain ought to bear her part of the sacrifice which France had had to make to Great Britain. Aroused by this reply, the Spanish government appealed late in April to the German government for an "active expression" of "sympathy . . . . at the opportune moment." Although the German Chancellor was eager to give it,[8] Spain aimed to use this intimacy merely as a threat. While continuing the conversations more or less dilatorily with Germany, she asked for and relied chiefly upon the support of Great Britain to obtain satisfactory terms with France.

Through Lord Lansdowne's mediation, M. Delcassé agreed in May to extend the Spanish sphere of influence in the north from Melilla to the mouth of the Moulouya—a particularly sore spot with the Spanish since they owned islands just off this coast—and to expand the limits of the Spanish sphere in Southern Morocco. The French Minister made these concessions dependent upon

[4] The debates in the Cortes are to be found in the *Diario de las sesiones de Cortes*. Congreso de los Diputados *(Legislatura de 1903)*, pp. 4883 ff., 4917 ff., 4944 ff., 4959 ff. Also see Maura, pp. 85 ff.

[5] Lansdowne to Egerton, April 11, 1904, *B.D.*, III, 25 f., No. 24; Egerton to Lansdowne, April 11, 1904, *ibid.*, 26 f., No. 25.

[6] Egerton to Lansdowne, May 6, 1904, *ibid.*, 34, No. 35.

[7] The British government kept these articles secret (Lansdowne to Egerton, April 11, 1904, *ibid.*, 25 f., No. 24).

[8] Bülow to Radowitz, April 27, 1904, *G.P.*, XX, 169 f., No. 6481, and following documents.

Spain's accepting his other conditions, and asserted to the Spanish Ambassador that "he was not prepared to prolong the discussion of these details, and his offer was *à prendre ou à laisser*."[9] This bold speech did not impress the Spanish government, which, knowing France's need for an agreement with it, followed Count Bülow's advice of drawing out the negotiations.[10] Its views differed from those of M. Delcassé in that it desired Spanish control in Tangier, full commercial liberty throughout Morocco without any time limit, and the publication of the agreement—all of which the French Minister refused.[11] However, by the last of June accord was virtually reached, when M. Delcassé brought forth a new condition to the effect that Spain should be precluded from taking any action in her prospective sphere until the *status quo* in Morocco came to an end.[12]

M. Delcassé was confronted with the problem of how to maintain a unified Franco-Spanish policy in the peaceful penetration of Morocco, how to retain the initiative in that work in French hands, how to minimize Spain's rights in Morocco in favor of France. Mistrusting Spain's competence to handle subject peoples, he wished to prevent her from taking any action in her sphere that would arouse the Moroccans to a war not only against Spain but also against France and thus ruin the work of pacific penetration. He feared that Spain might precipitate the liquidation of Morocco so as to obtain full control of her area. The

[9] Lansdowne to Monson, April 20, 1904, *B.D.*, III, 29, No. 28, and following documents.

[10] Bülow to Radowitz, May 22, 1904, *G.P.*, XX, 173 f., No. 6484. Bülow repeated his offer of aid on May 31. Bülow to Radowitz, May 31, 1904, *ibid.*, 175 f., No. 6487. The Spanish Ambassador at Paris remarked to Monson that if Great Britain did not help Spain the latter "would be done out of half her rights in that country [Morocco]" (Monson to Lansdowne, May 20, 1904, *B.D.*, III, 37, No. 41).

[11] Romanones, *Las responsabilidades políticas, etc.*, pp. 49 ff.; reports from Madrid, June 15 and 21, 1904, *Zur europ. Politik*, I, 121; see also *G.P.*, Vol. XX, chap. cxliv.

[12] Egerton to Lansdowne, July 1, 1904, *B.D.*, III, 38, No. 43; Lansdowne to Egerton, July 2, 1904, *ibid.*, 38 f., No. 44.

French policy was to postpone that event until a suitable occasion, in the meantime undermining Morocco's integrity and independence while pretending to maintain them. He was legally within his rights in taking this line toward Spain, and was fortified against British intervention in the latter's favor, because secret Article III of the Anglo-French agreement provided that the specified area should come within the sphere of influence of Spain and be administered by her "whenever the Sultan ceases to exercise authority over it."[13]

The Spanish government, protesting that this proposal would reduce its position to that of a subprotectorate, demanded the same rights in its sphere of influence as France would enjoy in hers. It desired particularly that Tangier be policed by Spanish altogether. The Spanish Foreign Minister asserted that Spain was averse to disturbing the *status quo* in Morocco, but he and his colleagues suspected that France would never acknowledge a change in the political status in Morocco and would thus exclude Spain from any share in the land. The Spanish Minister declared that he "would not sign an agreement which abandoned Spanish rights," and in complaining to the British government he threatened to "appeal to the Powers."

Lord Lansdowne knew that by "Powers" was meant Germany, who was just then showing marked interest in helping Spain in the Moroccan affair. Wishing to obviate German intervention, he advised the Spanish to make concrete proposals to France concerning ways of exercising an influence in the proposed Spanish sphere—for instance, as to "the construction of railways and other useful works." He also cautioned Spain against undertaking to police Tangier. At the same time he urged M. Delcassé to be more conciliatory toward Spain so as to avoid the possibility of "international difficulties."[14]

[13] *Ibid.*, II, 393 f.

[14] Egerton to Lansdowne, July 1, 1904, *ibid.*, III, 38, No. 43; Lansdowne to Egerton, July 2, 6, 1904, *ibid.*, 38, No. 44; 40, No. 46; Lansdowne to Monson, July 4, 1904, *ibid.*, 40, No. 45; Leon y Castillo, *Mis tiempos*, II, 182 ff.

M. Delcassé was willing to permit Spanish participation in the economic development of Morocco and also to associate Spanish officials with French ones in two of the three ports whose customs revenues were to be collected as security for the recent French loan. He refused to recede on the other points.[15] This reply so excited the Spanish that when M. Delcassé proposed a clause whereby Spain would be prohibited from alienating the Moroccan territory over which she should have control, the Spanish government rejected it as beneath its dignity. It offered instead to give France a right of preference in case Spain wished to alienate any or all of that area. Lord Lansdowne, who did not want France to gain this preferential right, persuaded the Spanish to accept the French proposal.[16]

The main issue, however, that of Spain's independence of action in her sphere, remained unsolved. In the middle of July, while leaving the impression that the cause of difference was the question of full commercial freedom, the Spanish government informally asked the German government to give Spain a *coup d'épaule* in Paris. As the German government desired a more definite proposal, it did not carry out the request.[17] Nor was much support to be obtained from Great Britain. But as both French and British governments knew of Germany's interest in the negotiations, M. Delcassé, in August, agreed to restrict Spain's action for fifteen years only.[18] The Spanish government rejected that concession, but offered to take no action for that period without previous accord with France, provided France recognized that she "ought to proceed in accord with the Spanish Government in that which touches the zone of influence reserved

[15] Lansdowne to Monson July 8, 1904, *B.D.*, III, 41, No. 47.

[16] Lansdowne to Monson, July 29, 1904, *ibid.*, 42, No. 49; Lansdowne to Egerton, July 29, 1904, *ibid.*, 43, No. 50; Egerton to Lansdowne, July 31, 1904, *ibid.*, 44, No. 52.

[17] Memo. by Richthofen, July 16, 1904, *G.P.*, XX, 186 f., No. 6503; and other documents in *ibid.*, Vol. XX, chap. cxliv.

[18] At first Delcassé said thirty years.

to Spain." Lord Lansdowne supported this proposal. So while M. Delcassé held to his previous stand, he agreed that "France would take no steps within the Spanish Sphere without giving previous notice to Spain." Thus, although the Marquis del Muni thought that the two parties had reached a deadlock, there was in reality no great difference between the two demands. On October 3 the agreement was signed.[19]

The accord consisted of a published declaration and of sixteen secret articles. The former merely expressed the fact that Spain adhered to the Anglo-French declaration of April 8 concerning Morocco and Egypt and that Spain and France were in agreement "to fix the extension of their rights and guaranty of their interests" in Morocco.[20] The secret articles were of a far different caliber. Spain received as her sphere of influence not only the area from the Moulouya to Larache in Northern Morocco but also the coastal territory and hinterland extending from her possession Rio de Oro northward to the Wad Sus, just south of Agadir. The rest of Morocco constituted the French sphere (Arts. II, IV, V). Provision for a future change was included.

In case the political state of Morocco and of the Sherifian Government are unable to subsist, or if by the feebleness of the Government and by its continued impotence to introduce security and public order, or for any other cause to be stated in a common accord, the maintenance of the *status quo* becomes impossible, Spain will be permitted freely to exercise her action in . . . . her sphere of influence [Art. III].

Although the same rights of action were permitted to Spain in her sphere as to France in hers, yet for a period of not over fifteen years from the date of signing the convention Spain was prohibited from taking action in her sphere without previous understanding with France. The latter, however, could take action unrestricted by Spain in the French zone, and could also act in the Spanish zone after having notified Spain of her intention.

[19] Egerton to Lansdowne, July 31, 1904, *B.D.*, III, 44, No. 52, and following documents; also Leon y Castillo, II, 183 f.

[20] *L.j., 1901–5*, 164, No. 187.

After that first period expired and as long as the *status quo* obtained, France could not act in the Spanish zone without previous agreement with Spain (Art. II). By Articles VII and VIII Spain agreed not to cede or to alienate in any form any of the territory assigned to her or to seek the aid of a foreign Power other than France in taking any military action in her sphere of influence. Article IX preserved "the special character" of Tangier "which the presence of the diplomatic corps and the municipal and sanitary institutions give it." Article X ran as follows:

So long as the actual political status continues, the enterprises for public works, railroads, roads, canals . . . . shall be executed by such companies as may be formed by French and Spanish. In the same manner it will be permissible for French and Spanish in Morocco to co-operate for the exploitation of mines, quarries, and, in general, of enterprises of an economic order.[21]

The two Powers immediately communicated the agreement to the British government, which accepted it.[22] The Spanish government thanked both British and German governments for their aid during the negotiations, and briefly informed the latter that by the treaty Tangier had been neutralized and complete equality and freedom of commerce and trade had been guaranteed.[23]

In Spain the agreement, grudgingly approved by the government as the best that it could obtain, was shown by the Premier to the various party leaders, and received their indorsement.[24] M. Delcassé informed none of the French politicians of the content of the treaty. During the debates in the French Parliament on the Anglo-French accord in November and December, how-

---

[21] The text of the agreement, which became public in 1909, is to be found in *British and Foreign State Papers*, CII (London, 1913), 432 ff.; and in *B.D.*, III, 49 ff., No. 59.

[22] Lansdowne to Adam, Oct. 5, 1904, *B.D.*, III, 52, No. 60.

[23] Radowitz to F. O., Oct. 7, 1904, *G.P.*, XX, 191 f., No. 6509.

[24] Maura, p. 54; Radowitz to F. O., Oct. 7, 1904, *G.P.*, XX, 191 f., No. 6509.

ever, the Franco-Spanish agreement was also accepted on faith.[25] The convention was a logical extension of the accord of April 8. Both agreements anticipated a change in the political status of Morocco and made provisions for a future division of the land. The one permitted commercial restriction at the end of thirty years; the other arranged for a Franco-Spanish monopoly of all economic enterprises. Both accords violated the principle of the open door. In fact, had the secret articles of the two agreements been known, they would have proved that the clauses concerning the independence and integrity of Morocco and the sovereignty of the sultan were complete shams. In declaring to the other Powers that commercial freedom would be absolutely respected, M. Delcassé was equivocating and attempting to disarm suspicions concerning his real intention of destroying economic freedom in Morocco.[26]

II. DELCASSÉ AND GERMANY, 1904

It was manifest during the Anglo-French negotiations that the French government planned to prevent Germany from gaining any foothold in Morocco or the Western Mediterranean.[27] Fearing that that Power might try to share in the Moroccan settlement when the Anglo-French accord became known, M. Delcassé endeavored to avoid a discussion of the agreement with it.[28]

When, therefore, on March 23, Prince Radolin asked the French Minister an "indiscreet question" about the reported

[25] Maura, p. 78; Tardieu, *Questions diplomatiques*, 1904, pp. 75 ff.; Millet, *Notre politique extérieure 1898–1905*, pp. 179 ff.; and the French debates cited above.

[26] For an estimate of this accord see Tardieu, *Revue des deux mondes*, Dec. 1, 1912, pp. 637 ff.; Stuart, *French Foreign Policy from Fashoda to Serajevo (1898–1914)* (New York, 1921), pp. 154 ff.

[27] See, among others, the dispatch from Lansdowne to Monson, Dec. 9, 1903, *B.D.*, III, 332, No. 378.

[28] Lansdowne to Monson, March 11, 1904, *ibid.*, II, 353, No. 398. One day long after signing the accord Radolin remarked to Delcassé that he "had heard of an apparent treaty with England but had never read the text of it in any authentic form." The Minister replied that he could find it in the *Livre jaune* (letter from Radolin, apparently to Holstein, March 25, 1905, *G.P.*, XX, 266 n.).

Anglo-French negotiations, the latter replied that they had been going on for some time and would probably be successfully concluded. He said that they treated of Newfoundland, Egypt, and Morocco (the other questions he did not mention); and he explained the terms of the proposed agreement concerning the last-named land. "You know already our point of view on this subject. . . . . We wish to maintain in Morocco the existing political and territorial status; but that status, to endure, must manifestly be sustained and improved." After citing the many occasions for intervention of which France had taken no advantage, he stated that the Sultan had already requested French aid. "It is now a matter of continuing it to him," he said, and he assured the Prince that commercial liberty would be "rigorously and entirely respected. . . . . France wishes no special rights in Morocco, but it should be her task in the interest of all nations trading there to put an end, according to her power, to the anarchy in that land." Moreover, the free passage through the straits should be secured by neutralizing their southern shore. As for Spain, her "positive interests and legitimate ambitions" in Morocco would be amicably treated. He did not mention either the clause limiting commercial freedom to thirty years or Article IX assuring mutual diplomatic support in the fulfilment of the accord. And of course he gave no hint of the existence of the secret articles.[29]

This informal and incomplete notification misrepresented the true aims of the agreement with respect to Morocco. M. Delcassé expected that by avoiding an official notification of the accord to the German government and by omitting to request an expression of opinion from it he would cause the German government either to permit him a diplomatic victory or to take the

[29] In repeating these assertions to the German government on April 26 the French Ambassador added that "the Anglo-French entente was directed against no other Power and in no way menaced the German commercial interests." See Delcassé to Bihourd, March 27, 1904, *L.j., 1901–5*, 122, No. 142; Radolin to Bülow, March 23, 1904, *G.P.*, XX, 5 ff., No. 6368; Bihourd to Delcassé, April 27, 1904, *L.j., 1901–5*, 131, No. 155.

initiative for a Franco-German understanding.[30] He felt safe in his policy,[31] because France, in addition to her alliance with Russia, whose victory over Japan M. Delcassé and the French people confidently expected,[32] now enjoyed with her ally's public approval[33] the friendship of Great Britain, Italy, and Spain, whereas the Triple Alliance was weakened by internal strife. Moreover, the French Minister learned on March 30[34] that at Vigo a few days before the Emperor William had denied having any territorial interests in Morocco. Hence by shunning the word "protectorate" he hoped to avoid the responsibility for endeavoring to establish one.[35] In October his notification of the Franco-Spanish agreement to the German government was even more perfunctory.[36]

[30] See Bertie to Lansdowne, March 22, 1905, B.D., III, 60, No. 67.

[31] Bihourd, the French ambassador at Berlin, warned Delcassé in April that Germany had not said her last word on the Moroccan question and that more complete guaranties of commercial liberty should be given to her; but Delcassé disregarded the warning. See Bihourd to Delcassé, April 18, 1904, L.j., 1901–5, 128, No. 151; Delcassé to Bihourd, April 18, 1904, ibid., 129, No. 152; Bihourd to Delcassé, April 21, 1904, ibid., 129 f., No. 153; cf. Lee, King Edward VII, II, 338.

[32] Michon, L'alliance franco-russe, 1891–1917, pp. 101 f.

[33] Statement made by Nelidow, Russian ambassador to Paris, to a reporter of the Temps, reprinted in Quest. dipl. et. col., XVII, 607 f.

[34] Radolin to Bülow, March 30, 1904, G.P., XVII, 365, No. 5210.

[35] There is some evidence, however, that Delcassé did make some vague attempts to approach the German government on the Moroccan affair in 1904. Bülow, in a dispatch of March 22, 1905, stated that if Delcassé should declare that he had discussed Moroccan affairs "thoroughly with German diplomats passing through" Paris, Radolin was to reply that those conversations were only private ones and showed plainly the inclination to avoid the official and proper authorities. See Bülow to Radolin, March 22, 1905, ibid., XX, 267, No. 6568. Theodor Wolff, at that time Paris correspondent of the Berliner Tageblatt, also has written that in the spring of 1904 Delcassé said to Lichnowsky, an official in the German foreign office, that they should come to an understanding over Morocco. According to Wolff, Holstein became furious at the dispatch from Lichnowsky (Wolff, Das Vorspiel, pp. 154 f.; cf. Ludwig, Wilhelm der Zweite, p. 342). Lichnowsky may have been the person to whom Bülow referred, although, if any such conversation occurred, it was not mentioned later by either the French or the Germans.

[36] The French Ambassador merely left a copy of the published declaration and added verbally that the accord in no way infringed upon commercial liberty

III. "PACIFIC PENETRATION," 1904

After the signing of the Anglo-French agreement, the French Parliament voted 600,000 francs with which to carry on the work of pacific penetration in Morocco.[37] The French government immediately dispatched a preliminary mission to Fez under Count de Saint-Aulaire, first secretary of the legation in Tangier. The Count gave the Sultan an exact Arabic translation of the published declaration of April 8; and, after setting forth the need for progressive reforms in Morocco and the special interest of France in executing them, he offered the friendly co-operation of his government to that end.[38] Thus, in spite of the persistent Moroccan raids across the Algerian border, the Sultan was asked to believe that France was once more manifesting her patience and good will.[39]

The Sultan scarcely knew what line of policy to take toward the Anglo-French agreement.[40] His subjects, from the religious groups to the merchants of Fez, were all hostile to any form of foreign control. Alarmed at the news of the agreement, they feared an immediate invasion by the Christians. Suspecting their ruler of conniving with the French, they became even more rebellious; many denied that he possessed the *baraka*, the divine

---

in Morocco. See Richthofen to Radowitz, Oct. 7, 1904, *G.P.*, XX, 191, No. 6508; memo. by Richthofen for Bülow, Oct. 7, 1904, *ibid.*, 230, No. 6534; Delcassé to Bihourd, Oct. 6, 1904, *L.j., 1901–5,* 164, No. 187; Bihourd to Delcassé, Oct. 7, 1904, *ibid.*, 166, No. 190; Delcassé to Bihourd, Oct. 8, 1904, *ibid.*, 167 f., No. 193.

[37] This was done on a motion by Jaurès, made on Nov., 1903, and passed on April 25, 1904 (Tardieu, *La Conf. d'Algés.*, p. 35).

[38] Saint-René Taillandier to Delcassé, April 14 and 24, 1904, *L.j., 1901–5,* 124, No. 146; 130, No. 154; Delcassé to Saint-René Taillandier, April 27, 1904, *ibid.*, 131, No. 156; Saint-René Taillandier to Delcassé, May 19, 1904, *ibid.*, 133, No. 159 and annexe; Lansdowne to Nicolson, April 19, 1904, *B.D.*, III, 28, No. 27.

[39] *L.j., 1901–5,* Nos. 148, 157, 158, 183, 186, 189, 194–98, 202–7.

[40] On the Moroccan reaction see report by A. Bernard, who was in Morocco at the time, in *Bulletin*, June, 1904, pp. 203 f.; Saint-René Taillandier to Delcassé, Jan. 1 and 24, Feb. 22, April 24, May 19, 1904, *L.j., 1901–5,* 119 ff., Nos. 135, 137, 140, 154, 159.

benediction. At court the Conservative party, led by Si Feddoul Gharnet, grew stronger in its opposition to all French actions and policies. The Sultan realized the precariousness of his position, and was very anxious about the effects of his acts upon his people. He was uneasy and angry at having been ignored in the negotiations over his land. Nevertheless, as he did not comprehend the full significance of the accord, particularly since the French had explained it to him in soothing terms, he soon became calmer. Some of his officials were not opposed to the French, as they realized that the present conditions could not last and that the French had the power to change them. Furthermore, certain practical considerations prevented him from closing his ear to the French altogether. His ambition was, with the help of Europeans selected by himself, so to strengthen his land as to enable it to maintain its independence.[41] The Sultan had no funds; the small French, English, and Spanish loans of the previous year were exhausted, and he could not collect taxes or maintain an army. Forced to seek foreign aid, he had begun negotiations with the Banque de Paris et des Pays-Bas for a large loan late in January, and had besought the help of the French government in obtaining it. M. Delcassé had readily promised his support.[42]

In this situation the Sultan neither accepted nor rejected the Anglo-French agreement and Count de Saint-Aulaire's explanation of it although he showed favor toward them.[43] On June 12

[41] Kühlmann to Bülow, Jan. 31, 1905, G.P., XX, 250, No. 6553.

[42] Saint-René Taillandier to Delcassé, Jan. 29, 1904, L.j. 1901–5, 119, No. 138.

[43] Ben Sliman, Moroccan minister of foreign affairs, wrote to Saint-René Taillandier on June 17 as follows: "The Sultan . . . . has instructed me to reply to you that he does not doubt your favorable sentiments nor those of your Government, either the humanity of your actions or the sincerity of your counsels. . . . . Your letter is an argument the more in favor of the reaffirmation of that conviction and a testimony of your good intentions, conforming to the desire of the two countries. This is confirmed also by the conversations which we have had with your secretary to clarify the difficult points of the accord. . . . . I express to you in his [the Sultan's] name the fullest thanks for your happy efforts past and present which, we hope, will characterize the conduct of our future relations" (ibid., 156 ff., No. 177, annex; Mévil, De la Paix de Francfort, etc. [Paris, 1909], pp. 172 f. n.).

with the aid of the French government he concluded the transaction for the loan.

The loan, made by a consortium of eleven French banks headed by the Banque de Paris et des Pays-Bas, fulfilled political as well as economic purposes, for it was backed by the French government and was admirably adapted to the work of pacific penetration. The amount was 62,500,000 francs (Art. I), of which 80 per cent was actually to be credited to the Sultan (Art. XXIV). The interest was set at 5 per cent (Art. III). The loan was to be redeemed within thirty-six years, but the schedule of amortization was fixed and could not be hastened during the first fifteen years (Arts. IV, VII). The loan, guaranteed by the customs duties in all the ports of Morocco, was to have preference and priority over all other loans which might be similarly guaranteed (Art. XI). Sixty per cent of the customs revenues were reserved for the repayment of the obligation. If the necessary amount was not obtained thereby, the Moroccan government was to make up the deficit (Art. XVII). Two million francs were left in the bank at Paris to cover short payments; if withdrawn, this amount was to be re-established immediately by the Sultan's government (Art. XXI). The remainder, after the Sultan's outstanding loans were liquidated, was placed at the ruler's disposal to be drawn upon at will (Arts. XXV, XXXV). By Article XIV the existing customs treaties and arrangements of Morocco with the Powers were guaranteed. Article XXXII prohibited the Sultan from using the customs receipts at his disposal to guarantee any other loan without a previous agreement with the French banks. By Article XXXIII those banks were given the right of preference in contracting new loans, coining money, or buying and selling gold and silver for Morocco, provided the conditions they offered were equal to those offered by others. The collection of the customs was to be supervised by a special group of French officials under the protection of the French legation. Their director should communicate with the Moroccan government through the French Minister at Tangier. Furthermore, if the stipulated funds were not turned over to the supervisors, the agents could appeal to the French Minister; and, with his consent and with due notification to the Sultan, they could collect the sums themselves. Thus, when by the last of July those officials were installed, the control of the customs was practically lost to the Sultan.[44]

In May an act of banditry occurred in Morocco which convinced public opinion everywhere that reform in that land was immediately necessary and which enabled France to take another step in her work of penetration. On May 18, Raisouli, a sherif, ex-cattle thief, robber and rebel, avenger of wrongs, opponent to Europeans—in short, a Moroccan Robin Hood—took prisoner an American citizen, Ion Perdicaris, and his English son-in-law, Varley, in their home near Tangier. As the price of their release he demanded a large ransom, the dismissal and punishment of certain of the Sultan's loyal officials who were his enemies, and his own appointment as pasha for the district around Tangier. The Sultan had to accept his terms. On June 24, through the good offices of the French government, working through some of its Algerian religious leaders with followers in Morocco, the release was effected.[45] But the panic-stricken foreigners in Tan-

---

[44] The prominent part played by the French government in making this loan is attested as follows: As already stated, in January, at the Sultan's request, Delcassé promised his help in making the loan. Furthermore, Saint-Aulaire and his interpreter, in Fez at the time, took an active part in bringing the negotiation to a satisfactory conclusion, being consulted on various points and helping in the formulation of the terms (Saint-René Taillandier to Delcassé, July 30, 1904, *L.j.*, *1901–5*, 162 f., No. 184.). The contract was signed and sealed by the French Consul at Fez (*ibid.*, 142 f., No. 170, Annex I). And the terms of the loan were such as could never have been obtained without the approval of the French government. The contract is printed in *ibid.*, 143 ff., No. 170, Annex II. On the instalment of customs officials see the dispatches from Saint-René Taillandier to Delcassé, July 24, and 30, 1904, *ibid.*, 159 ff., Nos. 181, 184; also Tardieu, *Questions diplomatiques, 1904*, pp. 60 ff.

[45] On this episode see the various dispatches in *L.j.*, *1901–5*, 135 ff., Nos. 160 ff. On Raisouli see Rosita Forbes, *El Raisuni, the Sultan of the Mountains* (London, 1924). On June 22, 1904, Secretary of State Hay cabled to the American Consul at Tangier, "We want Perdicaris alive or Raizuli dead." See William Roscoe Thayer, *The Life and Letters of John Hay* (Boston and New York, 1915), II, 383; Dennis, *Adventures in American Diplomacy*, pp. 443 ff. Both the British and the American governments requested the good offices of the French government in

gier, fearing that Raisouli would continue such lucrative business and that he would have imitators, demanded protection.[46] Thereupon the French government stationed two warships in Moroccan waters and secured the appointment of French and Algerian officers over the Tangier police.[47] The work of "pacific penetration" was most auspiciously under way.

Private French enterprise did not lag behind that of the government. Moroccan towns swarmed with hungry fortune-seekers eager to enjoy the opportunities for quick wealth which the opening of Morocco was expected to bring. The Comité du Maroc, formed in the preceding December from the ranks of the larger Comité de l'Afrique française, engaged energetically in directing and expanding the work of scientific exploration in the Sherifian Empire and of disseminating propaganda in France.[48] It received the financial support of the chief banks, maritime companies, steel works, railway companies, and some of the leading newspapers of France.[49] The list of guests present at a banquet held by it on June 15 to enlist public support reads like a French *Who's Who.*[50]

---

effecting the release. Mr. Hay, the American secretary of state, gave assurance that if more serious action were subsequently necessary in Morocco, it would not take place "without a previous exchange of views" with France. Thus he acknowledged France's special position with reference to that country. See Saint-René Taillandier to Delcassé, May 30, 1904, *ibid.*, 137, No. 163; Delcassé to Saint-René Taillander, May 31, 1904, *ibid.*, 137, No. 164; Jusserand to Delcassé, June 20, 1904, *ibid.*, 152, No. 171; Porter to Delcassé, June 27, 1904, *ibid.*, 155, No. 176; Mévil, pp. 172 f.

[46] Saint-René Taillandier to Delcassé, June 2 and 27, July 2, 1904, *L.j., 1901–5*, 137 ff., Nos. 165, 175, 178.

[47] Saint-René Taillandier to Delcassé, June 11 and 27, July 2, 1904, *ibid.*, 140 ff., Nos. 168, 175, 178; Delcassé to Saint-René Taillandier, July 26, 1904, *ibid.*, 160, No. 182; Saint-René Taillandier to Delcassé, July 29, 1904, *ibid.*, 160 f., No. 183, and annex.

[48] *Bulletin*, Dec., 1903, p. 377; Jan., 1904, pp. 3 ff.; March, 1904, pp. 76 f.; and others.

[49] See the list of the large subscribers in *ibid.*, July, 1904, p. 224.

[50] The names of those present, 355 in all, are given in *Quest. dipl. et col.*, XVIII, 62 ff. See also *Bulletin*, June, 1904, p. 185.

In the autumn and early winter the French government made preparations to send a larger mission to Fez under the resident minister, M. Saint-René Taillandier, to obtain the Sultan's approval of the French program of reforms. According to M. Delcassé's instructions on December 15,[51] the Minister's foremost task should be to institute police reforms similar to those inaugurated in Tangier, first in the towns already in contact with Europeans and then gradually in the other areas. In the border region order should be preserved by extending the co-operation of the two governments. The establishment of a state bank, the construction of means of transportation and of communication, the improvement of harbors, the support of philanthropic works, the spread of the French language, and the settlement of claims for damages inflicted on Algeria by Moroccan raiders were the other matters to be taken up. It was a comprehensive program, the achievement of which would end Moroccan isolation and independence.

The departure of the mission was delayed by the long negotiations for an accord with Spain and by the fact that the French Chamber did not approve the Moroccan accords until November. When the mission was prepared to start in December, the situation in Morocco, apparently favorable for France in the spring, had become adverse. The natives had grown bolder in their attacks upon foreigners, venting their hatred upon them even in Fez. The Sultan had begun to show signs of resisting. In September he had disgraced the pro-foreign minister el Menebhi and confiscated his property. Later in the year he had supplanted his pro-French ministers by anti-foreign ones, such as Si Feddoul Gharnet. In December he had dismissed all foreign

[51] Delcassé to Saint-René Taillandier, Dec. 15, 1904, L.j., 1901–5, 179 ff., No. 209. In October a conference had been held in Paris with Jonnart, governor-general of Algeria; Gen. Lyauty, commander of the French troops at Ain-Sefra in Southern Oran; and Saint-René Taillandier, on the Moroccan question (Monson to Lansdowne, Oct. 7, 1904, B.D., III, 54 f., No. 63.

employees at Fez and Rabat.[52] These signs augured trouble for the French. While assuming an optimistic manner publicly, M. Saint-René Taillandier acknowledged to his chief on December 12 that he might "be powerless to make the Sultan accept the minimum of reforms that the present state of Morocco demands."[53] But as firmness was the best means to "recall the Moroccan government to a sense of reality,"[54] he immediately countered the dismissal of the French officers by a sharply worded letter to the Moroccan Foreign Minister. After reminding the latter of the *acte international* by which France had "assumed the task of aiding" the Makhzen[55] to reform the land, he stated that the Sultan's co-operation was expected and desired, but that

if that co-operation were not forthcoming, France would know how to accomplish the work alone. Dangerous counselors [he wrote] have led the Sultan astray as to the true state of affairs. And in consequence the French Government has decided to postpone the departure of the mission, and to recall to Tangier from Fez within ten days the French military mission, vice-consul, and all French subjects resident there.[56]

The Sultan's opposition wilted immediately. The French vice-consul at Fez reported that the Makhzen was "ready to welcome all French counsels and to accept all the reforms," that it "withdrew all the actions which have offended us."[57] But the Sultan's submission was not so complete as it seemed. Although France was the victor in this encounter, the conflict had only begun.

[52] *L.j., 1901–5*, Nos. 199, 210–12, 215, 218–20, 222–24; *B.D.*, III, 55, No. 64; *Bulletin*, Sept. and Oct., 1904, pp. 279, 320.

[53] Saint-René Taillandier to Delcassé, Dec. 12, 1904, *ibid.*, 179, No. 208; Tardieu, *Questions diplomatiques, 1904*, pp. 78 ff.

[54] The words are Delcassé's (Delcassé to Saint-René Taillandier, Dec. 20, 1904, *L.j., 1901–5*, 186, No. 213.

[55] The term is used to designate the Moroccan court and government.

[56] Saint-René Taillandier to Delcassé, Dec. 19 and 24, 1904, *L.j., 1901–5*, 185 f., No. 212; 186 f., No. 214.

[57] Saint-René Taillandier to Delcassé, Dec. 30, 1904, Jan. 2, 1905, *ibid.*, 188 ff., No. 216 f.

CHAPTER IX

GERMANY AND THE ENTENTE CORDIALE, 1903-4

I

In the early part of 1903, although one of Germany's allies was rent by nationalistic conflicts[1] and the other was no longer reliable, and although British and German public opinion remained so hostile that the former prevented Anglo-German co-operation,[2] Count Bülow and Herr von Holstein were untroubled about the international situation. Upon the announcement of King Edward's forthcoming visit to Paris, the latter wrote to his chief, on April 2, that an Anglo-French alliance was "music of the future," and that the Franco-Russian alliance was slowly breaking under the strain of conflicting interests in the Balkans. "We have blocked M. Delcassé's policy in Turkey as well as in Morocco," he stated. The Chancellor agreed with him.

> Delcassé's coquetting with England [he wrote] would become serious for us only in case he should also succeed in bringing about a *rapprochement* between England and Russia. . . . . Otherwise his wooing of England will . . . . strengthen Count Lamsdorff in the thought that the former League of the Three Emperors is, all things considered, the best combination for Russian autocracy. But the present groupings will not change soon, and in my opinion, we cannot take things too coolly.[3]

Soon after King Edward's visit to Paris the equanimity of the German government was somewhat disturbed by a dispatch of

[1] See among others Richard Charmatz, *Österreichs äussere und innere Politik von 1895 bis 1914* (Leipzig and Berlin, 1918).

[2] On the state of British public opinion see Eckardstein, *Lebenserinnerungen und politische Denkwürdigkeiten*, II, 397 f.; and the various dispatches from Metternich and Eckardstein, *G.P.*, XVII, Nos. 5046, 5071, 5094, 5104, 5371, 5375, and others.

[3] Holstein to Bülow, March 30, 1903, *G.P.*, XVII, 573 n.; memo. by Holstein, April, 1903, *ibid.*, XVIII, 802 ff., No. 5888; Holstein to Bülow, April 2, 1903, *ibid.*, 838 f., No. 5910; Bülow to F. O., April 3, 1903, *ibid.*, 839 f., No. 5911.

May 10 from Baron Eckardstein, formerly first secretary of the German embassy in London. The Baron expressed his belief that a general Anglo-French settlement of colonial differences including that of Morocco was under way; and that since the two nations were reconciled, it would very likely be concluded. He denied that this agreement would cause a breach in the Dual Alliance, as was supposed in Germany; rather, he wrote, "a new Triple Alliance is being formed, which, although it may assume no written form and perhaps may endure only for a number of years, will for a time cause us everywhere at least economic and political difficulties."[4]

This dispatch was referred by Count Bülow to the German ambassadors at St. Petersburg, Paris, and London, and to the first secretary of the embassy in London for consideration. Not one of these men believed possible an Anglo-Russian settlement or the formation of a new Triple Alliance. The Chancellor and Prince Radolin, the ambassador at Paris, were both very skeptical about the prospects for an Anglo-French agreement; but the German representatives in London thought that one might be achieved. Count Metternich's opinion was that Great Britain and France were merely negotiating another colonial accord, which he admitted might lead to closer co-operation between them, but which need not cause alarm so long as Great Britain, already pacifically inclined, enjoyed only the fickle friendship of France and was confronted by the antagonism of Russia.[5]

[4] An ardent advocate of the proposed Anglo-German alliance and a sufferer from the "nightmare of coalitions," Eckardstein had resigned his position in October, 1902, because he disapproved of the diplomatic method and the policy of his foreign office and "saw black ahead" for his country; also perhaps because of personal pique at not having been appointed ambassador in London upon the death of the aged Count Hatzfeldt (Eckardstein, II, 412 f.). For his dispatch to Bülow see *G.P.*, XVII, 567 f., No. 5369; also published with minor changes in Eckardstein, II, 425 f. The few changes from the original which occur in some of the documents in Eckardstein's memoirs are not of any great importance. On the whole his judgments were sound.

[5] The dispatches are to be found in *G.P.*, Vol. XVII, chap. cxv. In July, however, the German Emperor could not conceal from the French Ambassador his

In September the German government believed that the Anglo-French settlement was already far advanced;[6] and, learning from the Spanish Queen Mother, who was visiting in Austria, that France and Spain were also negotiating over Morocco,[7] it resolved to intervene. To that end on September 24 it instructed Herr von Radowitz, German ambassador at Madrid, as follows:

> By virtue of our political international position and especially by virtue of the great significance of our economic interests in Morocco, we must seek to be considered also in a division of the land by obtaining territorial compensation, for example in the region of the Sus, or elsewhere in the colonial world, perhaps by the cession of Fernando Po. Your Excellency should weigh thoroughly the means by which we should best reach that goal, whether through direct negotiations with Spain, through breaking the way for participation in the negotiations of the most interested states, or through proposing a conference.[8]

Thus the German government, realizing the improvement in the diplomatic position of France and the decline in its own, was apparently willing to make a division of Morocco with Great Britain, France, and Spain.

When Herr von Radowitz immediately unfolded the German desire to the Spanish Foreign Minister, the latter, admitting the German right to a share, agreed to study the proposal.[9] After this the conversations appear to have ceased.

---

irritation at Delcassé's success in the Anglo-French *rapprochement*. After expressing the wish that French vessels might repeat the visit of 1895 to Kiel, he remarked to M. Bihourd, July 16: " 'I know well that nothing is to be accomplished with M. Delcassé. The advances to England are the work of M. Delcassé and M. Cambon. . . . . But the Russians are not content with that and some day they will make you. . . . .' Here a gesture of disappointment, concluded M. Bihourd, made clear the prediction" (quoted from a dispatch from Bihourd in Bourgeois et Pagès, *Les origines et les responsabilités de la grande guerre*, p. 293).

[6] Groeben to F. O., Sept. 17, 1903, *G.P.*, XVII, 353 f., No. 5198; Richthofen to Radowitz, Sept. 28, 1903, *ibid.*, 357 ff., No. 5202.

[7] Bülow to F. O., Sept. 18, 1903, *ibid.*, 354, No. 5199; Richthofen to Radowitz, Sept. 24, 1903, *ibid.*, 354 ff., No. 5200.

[8] Richthofen to Radowitz, Sept. 24, 1903, *ibid.*, 355, No. 5200.

[9] Radowitz to F. O., Sept. 29, Oct. 4, 1903, *ibid.*, 359 ff., Nos. 5203, 5205.

Simultaneously with these efforts, in the autumn of 1903 the German government planned by maintaining strict reserve to allow the Franco-Russian antagonism about the Balkans and the Russo-Japanese hostility in the Far East to grow. It thought that any German leanings toward Russia would pull France back into line and cause Japan to recede before the danger of a new Continental triple entente.[10] On the Chancellor's advice, William II, during his meeting with the Czar at Wiesbaden and Wolfsgarten on November 4-5, 1903, kept Germany's hands entirely free. Nevertheless, after the Czar's approval of the Anglo-French and the Franco-Italian *rapprochements* was made public late in October, the Emperor began to suffer from the "nightmare of the coalitions." During the visit he sought to incite Nicholas II against France and Great Britain and to urge him further into far eastern enterprises. In his correspondence with the Czar in December and January he continued these tactics.[11] Count Bülow remonstrated, but the Emperor, haughtily replying that these were private letters, advised the Chancellor to mind his own business.[12]

[10] Radolin to F. O., Oct. 17, 1903, *ibid.*, XVIII, 845 ff., No. 5915; Bülow to William II, Oct. 19, 1903, *ibid.*, 847 ff., No. 5916.

[11] William II wrote to Nicholas II, Dec. 1, 1903, as follows: "The visit of the hundred British Parliamentary—gentlemen and ladies—to Paris shows how 'the Crimean combination' is warming to its work. Your ally is making rather free with his flirt [with Great Britain]. You should pull him up a little." Again on Jan. 3, 1904, he wrote to the same: "Therefore it is evident to every unbiassed mind that Korea must and will be Russian. When and how that is nobody's affair and concerns only you and your country." See Bülow to F. O., Oct. 31, 1903, *ibid.*, 853 f., No. 5918; memo. by Bülow, Nov. 7, 1903, *ibid.*, 70 ff., No. 5422; Walter Goetz (ed.), *Briefe Wilhelms II an den Zaren, 1894-1914* (Berlin, 1920), pp. 330 ff.; Savinsky, *Recollections of a Russian Diplomat*, pp. 63 ff. William II addressed Nicholas in various letters as "Admiral of the Pacific" and signed himself "Admiral of the Atlantic." In spite of these words, to hold the Emperor responsible for the Russo-Japanese War is to underestimate the force of Russian foreign policy.

[12] See *G.P.*, Vol. XIX, chaps. cxxviii, cxxix, especially Bülow to William II, Jan. 4, 1904, *ibid.*, 87 ff., No. 5972, and the Emperor's minutes; memo. by Bülow, Feb. 14, 1904, *ibid.*, 62 f., No. 5961.

To the satisfaction of the German government,[13] the Russo-Japanese War broke out in February, 1904. In anger at Great Britain, Russia immediately drew nearer to her neighbor;[14] and, with a war in progress, the German statesmen planned by a wise manipulation of their power to improve their international position and to gain concrete advantages.[15] For the time, however, they endeavored by assuring the British government that Germany would preserve strict neutrality to obviate the need for Great Britain to come to terms with France, arguing that a neutral Germany would entail a neutral France.[16] Moreover, carrying out a suggestion of the Prince of Monaco, the *Wilhelmstrasse* sought to effect, through the mediation of the Italian government, a meeting between the Emperor William and President Loubet of France during their visits to Italy in March and April.[17] But on March 23 Prince Radolin surprised his government[18] by reporting a conversation with M. Delcassé which showed that the

[13] Bülow to Holstein, Jan. 15, 1904, *ibid.*, 33 f., No. 5942; memo. by Eckardstein, Jan. 17, 1904, *ibid.*, 38 ff., No. 5945, and the Emperor's minutes thereto.

[14] Count Benckendorff, Russian ambassador at London, spoke of the Dual Alliance as going to pieces, and there was talk among other Russian diplomats of renewing the former League of the Three Emperors. See Radolin to Bülow, Feb. 28, 1904, *ibid.*, 165 ff., No. 6028; Metternich to Bülow, March 14, 1904, *ibid.*, 167 ff., No. 6029; Alvensleben to Bülow, March 18, 1904, *ibid.*, 172 ff., No. 6030; memo. by Holstein, Jan. 16, 1904, *ibid.*, 35 ff., No. 5944.

[15] "Because of the importance of German neutrality we shall perhaps find opportunity to utilize our central position in case of further sharpening of the hostility in the same way that M. Delcassé intends doing with reference to Morocco," wrote Holstein in a memo. on Jan. 23, 1904 (*ibid.*, 48 ff., No. 5951). Also see memo. by Holstein, Jan. 16, 1904, *ibid.*, 48 ff., No. 5951.

[16] Bülow to Metternich, Jan. 9, 1904, *ibid.*, 22, No. 5932; Lascelles to Lansdowne, Jan. 8, 1904, *B.D.*, II, 232, No. 273. Bülow later complained that the British had offered very weak resistance to the French demands (Bülow to Metternich, June 4, 1904, *G.P.*, XX, 28, No. 6383).

[17] Radolin to Bülow, Feb. 4, 1904, *ibid.*, 105 f., No. 6431; Bülow to Radolin, Feb. 18, 1904, *ibid.*, 106 f., No. 6432, and following documents.

[18] For proof that the German government had not expected the signing of the accord then see Eckardstein, II, 426 f.; Otto Hammann, *Der misverstandene Bismarck. Zwanzig Jahre deutscher Weltpolitik* (Berlin, 1921), p. 110.

Anglo-French agreement was near completion. By March 26 it became evident that the French had refused to permit the proposed meeting.[19] So Count Bülow recommended to the Emperor on March 30 the dispatch of three small warships to Tangier as a direct intervention in the Moroccan affair. By thus arousing French animosity, Germany would show Great Britain that the formation of a Continental *bloc* was impossible, that there was no cause for her to sacrifice her interests in Morocco.[20] The Emperor regarded the move as "entirely inopportune"; for, he argued, since France, Great Britain, and Spain were about to settle the Moroccan question, "a one-sided bellicose action by Germany . . . . would undoubtedly arouse the suspicion of those Powers, would undermine belief in our repeatedly expressed assurance, reiterated to the King of Spain at Vigo, that we claim no exclusive rights in Morocco, and would put the stamp of duplicity upon our policy." He suggested that if the government wished to take action in Morocco, it should first consult those three Powers and secure their co-operation.[21]

Without relinquishing the idea, Count Bülow had to content himself for the time with a renewed declaration to the British Ambassador on April 6 of neutrality during the Russo-Japanese War.[22] On April 8 the Anglo-French accord was signed.

II

German public opinion was disquieted by the Anglo-French agreement and by the Franco-Italian intimacy. Apart from the "lunatic fringe" as represented by the Pan-German League,

[19] Monts to F. O., March 26, 1904, *G.P.*, XX, 116, No. 6439.

[20] Although Bülow did not say so, it is manifest that this was one of his intentions (Bülow to William II, March 30, 1904, *ibid.*, 197 ff., No. 6512).

[21] Tschirschky to Bülow, April 3, 1904, *ibid.*, 199 ff., No. 6513. On the interview at Vigo see below.

[22] Bülow to Tschirschky, April 3, 1904, *ibid.*, 8 f. No. 6370; memo. by Bülow, April 6, 1904, *ibid.*, 10 f., No. 6372; Bülow to Tschirschky, April 6, 1904, *ibid.*, 201 and note, No. 6514. The last dispatch was not sent, for on April 8 the accord was signed.

which demanded an immediate seizure of a portion of Morocco,[23] no one expressed particular concern over the loss of that country.[24] The scandals in the colonial administration and the costly war with the natives of German Southwest and German East Africa had momentarily turned the nation against further colonial ventures.[25] The new international alignments, however, were viewed by the nation with some alarm. In the Reichstag on April 12 Herr Sattler, a National Liberal and a supporter of the government, expressed satisfaction that the Triple Alliance remained firm; but, he continued, "one has the feeling that otherwise a transformation has occurred in the relations of the great Powers which can be of the gravest influence also on German relations." On the next day the Nationalist Count Reventlow sarcastically remarked that he could not understand why Germany should rejoice since France and Great Britain had settled their differences. "If the world is divided, we must assume a somewhat different attitude thereto," he declared; "even in prudent circles of our people the course of our foreign policy is being followed with national sorrow," for the government was trying to be overcordial to all without gaining anything. Herr Bebel, the Social Democratic leader, greeted the Anglo-French settlement on April 14; but he also regarded it as weakening the Triple Alliance and strengthening the Dual Alliance. Like Count Reventlow, he said that Germany's international position in the last few years had in no way improved, acknowledging with regret the increasing antipathy to Germany in foreign lands.[26]

Count Bülow endeavored to calm the public opinion by declaring in the Reichstag, April 12 and 14, that "we have no rea-

[23] *Zwanzig Jahre alldeutscher Arbeit und Kämpfe*, pp. 219, 233, 235, 238 f.

[24] See, for instance, *Berliner Tageblatt*, April 17, 1904; Dr. Th. Schiemann, *Deutschland und die grosse Politik, 1904* (Berlin, 1905), p. 118, and others; *Grenzboten*, June 23, 1904, p. 668.

[25] Alfred Zimmerman, *Deutsche Kolonialpolitik* (Berlin, 1914), pp. 241 ff.

[26] *Stenographische Berichte von den Behandlungen des Reichstages*, CXCIX, 2019, 2053 f., 2058 f.; Hammann, *Bilder aus der letzten Kaiserzeit*, p. 42; reports from the Berlin correspondent to the *London Times*, April 11 and 16, 1904.

son to suppose that the Anglo-French colonial accord is directed at any other Power." To this apparently "amicable understanding . . . . from the standpoint of German interests we have nothing to object." As to Morocco, "in the main" Germany had economic interests which "we must and shall protect. . . . . We have no cause to fear that these . . . . could be disregarded or injured by any Power." While scoffing at the allegation that Germany was isolated, he added: "If we keep our sword sharp, we need not fear isolation very much. Germany is too strong not to be able to make alliances. Many combinations are possible for us." Denying any thought of waging a war over Morocco, he upheld a policy of "prudent quiet and even of reserve"; but he concluded with the significant statement that "if one wishes to arouse friction in the world, one does not shout it from the house-tops. Frederick the Great may now and then have made a Machiavellian move in politics, but he previously wrote the Anti-Machiavelli."[27]

The Chancellor's speech expressed only a temporary acquiescence in the Anglo-French agreement, an intimation to France and Great Britain to consult Germany over Morocco.[28] The German government liked that accord less than the German people did, even though it knew nothing of the content of the secret articles. The Emperor feared that now Great Britain "would put every consideration for us more and more into the background."[29] And Count Bülow, who knew that the new alignment placed Germany in no actual danger,[30] admitted that "doubtlessly both

[27] Bülow, *Reden*, II, 74, 84, 90 f.; see also Hammann, *Bilder aus der letzten Kaiserzeit*, pp. 42 f.

[28] This was Sanderson's opinion. He was at the time British permanent undersecretary of state for foreign affairs. See memo. by Sanderson, Feb. 25, 1907, *B.D.*, III, 421.

[29] William II to Bülow, April 19, 1904, *G.P.*, XX, 22 ff., No. 6378.

[30] From London, Bernstorff, first secretary of the embassy, reported that the British were entirely pacific in their intentions and inclinations (Bernstorff to Bü-

Powers [France and Great Britain] win in international influence and in freedom of movement by this accord and by their
rapprochement, and that the drawing force of the Anglo-French
Entente on Italy will also be strengthened."[31] The prospective
loss of Morocco to Germany and the general dissatisfaction within Germany over the conduct of her foreign affairs accentuated
Count Bülow's ill will toward the new agreement.

III

The Chancellor's prophecy about Italy came true almost immediately.

Italy's policy was, of course, to play between the Triple Alliance and France for her own advantage. Italian opinion interpreted the Anglo-French *rapprochement,* following upon the
Franco-Italian entente, as a setback to Germany, and became
more independent toward its allies. After Italy's special interest
in the future of Tripoli was recognized, the Italian people raised
the irredentist question in the summer and autumn of 1903. In
the winter relations with Austria became so tense that war clouds
loomed up.[32] Count Goluchowski, the Austrian foreign minister,
desired to replace the Triple Alliance by the old League of the
Three Emperors, and declared that if the present relations with
Italy continued, Austria could not renew the alliance.[33]

Count Bülow succeeded in patching up the raveling fabric of

---

low, April 16, 1904, *ibid.,* 14 ff., No. 6376). The Emperor considered this report
"excellent." Alvensleben also wrote from St. Petersburg that Russia was not so
well satisfied with the Anglo-French accord as French newspapers would have one
believe (Alvensleben to Bülow, April 15, 1904, *ibid.,* 21 f., No. 6377).

[31] Bülow to William II, April 20, 1904, *ibid.,* 24, No. 6379.

[32] On Austro-Italian relations see Wedel to Bülow, Sept. 14, 1903, *ibid.,* XVIII,
621 ff., No. 5779; memo. by Bülow, Sept. 20, 1903, *ibid.,* 624 ff., No. 5780; Monts
to F. O., *ibid.,* XX, 47 f., No. 6399; Monts to Bülow, April 25, 1904, *ibid.,* 54 ff.,
No. 6404; Monts to Bülow, April 30, 1904, *ibid.,* 64 ff., No. 6412.

[33] Memo. by Bülow of conversation with Goluchowski at Vienna, Sept. 20,
1903, *ibid.,* XVIII, 625 f., No. 5780; Wedel to Bülow, Oct. 20, 1903, *ibid.,* 627 f.,
No. 5783.

the Triple Alliance.[34] He suspected that Italy had made a rein-surance treaty with France after the renewal of the Triple Alliance in 1902, by which the alliance was nullified in case of a Franco-German war.[35] Neither he nor General Schlieffen, German chief of staff, expected Italy to support Germany in that instance or even to hold inactive the French troops on the Italian frontier. None the less, at the request of the Italian chief of staff, the Chancellor permitted the German-Italian military conversations to continue as before.[36] He endeavored to preserve at least the outward appearance of harmony.[37]

But in the spring of 1904 the Triple Alliance almost went on the rocks over an intrinsically insignificant affair—whether or not the entertainment of the French and of the German chiefs of state, who were both to visit Italy at about the same time in March and April, should be on a similar scale.

After the Emperor's visit on March 26–27 had passed off quietly enough[38] the French government sought to expand the program of reception for President Loubet in order to demonstrate the great popularity of France in Italy,[39] while the German

[34] An interview between the Italian and the Austrian foreign ministers at Abazzia on April 9, 1904, attested to this fact. See Wedel to Bülow, April 14, 1904, *ibid.*, XX, 50 ff., No. 6401; memo. by Bülow, May 9, 1903, *ibid.*, XVIII, 613 ff., No. 5775; Bülow to Monts, June 9, 1903, *ibid.*, 616 ff., No. 5776; and following documents in *ibid.*, chap. cxxii, Anhang.

[35] Monts to Bülow, April 30, 1904, *ibid.*, XX, 64, No. 6412; memo. by Holstein, March 3, 1904, *ibid.*, 37 ff., No. 6388.

[36] Chelius to Schlieffen, Dec. 1, 1903, *ibid.*, XVIII, 705 ff., No. 5827; Richthofen to Schlieffen, Dec. 11, 1903, *ibid.*, 707 f., No. 5826; Schlieffen to Richthofen, Dec. 14, 1903, *ibid.*, 708, No. 5829.

[37] Memo. by Holstein, March 3, 1904, *ibid.*, XX, 37 ff., No. 6388; Monts to F. O., March 7, 1904, *ibid.*, 41, No. 6390.

[38] Bülow to William II, March 11, 1904, *ibid.*, 46, No. 6397; Monts to F. O., March 26, 1904, *ibid.*, 47 f., No. 6399; *Quest. dipl. et col.*, April 1, 1904, XVII, 524 f.

[39] Monts to Bülow, April 16, 1904, *G.P.*, XX, 53 f., No. 6403. Giovanni Giolitti, who was then Italian premier, has written as follows about this visit: "In Delcassé I noticed particularly his finesse and ability, as well as the insistence with which he attempted to loosen or weaken our bonds with Germany, without however putting forward anything at all in the nature of a definite proposal" (*Memoirs*

government endeavored to restrict it. Under threat of breaking the alliance, the latter forced M. Tittoni, the Italian foreign minister, to promise that Italy's loyalty to the Triple Alliance would be warmly mentioned in the toasts.[40] But when the visit occurred, April 24–28, the Italian King, playing his own hand, helped the French to enjoy an unbroken triumph.[41] On April 25 and 26 affection for them was extravagantly displayed by the Italians while no mention of the Triple Alliance was made.[42] In an endeavor to stop further exchange of toasts, the German ambassador, Count Monts, complained bitterly to M. Luzzati, Italian secretary of the treasury, of the pro-French attitude of the King, government, and press; of the non-fulfilment of promises; of the King's ignoring him at the festivals; of the failure to mention the alliance in the speeches. "My training and instructions prohibit me from using that tone toward the *Consulta* which would correspond with its behavior," he declared. He demanded that no more toasts be made.[43]

Doubtless this peremptoriness would have produced the desired result if at the crucial moment the German Emperor had not sent a telegram of warm thanks for his reception to the Italian government and nullified the entire effect of the Ambassa-

---

of My Life [London, 1923], p. 183). On March 5, 1904, Sir Francis Bertie, British ambassador in Rome, wrote to Lansdowne as follows: "M. Ba[rrère] does all he can to create friction between Italy and Austria to alienate Italy from her partner in the Triplice" (*B.D.*, V, 74). In contrast the British Ambassador in Vienna was in April, 1904, reassuring his Italian colleague about Austrian intentions in the Balkans now that Russia was in a far eastern war (Plunkett to Lansdowne, April 7, 1904, *ibid.*, V, 80, No. 41).

[40] Memo. by Holstein, March 3, 1904, *G.P.*, XX, 37 ff., No. 6388; Bülow to Monts, March 6, 1904, *ibid.*, 39 ff., No. 6389, and following documents.

[41] Monts to F. O., March 17, 1904, *ibid.*, 45, No. 6396; Bülow to Monts, March 26, 1904, *ibid.*, 46 f., No. 6398; Monts to Bülow, April 2, 1904, *ibid.*, 48 f., No. 6400; Monts to Bülow, April 16, 1904, *ibid.*, 52 f., No. 6402; Monts to Bülow, April 16, 1904, *ibid.*, 53 f., No. 6403.

[42] Monts to Bülow, April 25, 1904, *ibid.*, 54 ff., No. 6404; Monts to F. O., April 26, 1904, *ibid.*, 57 f., No. 6405; *Quest. dipl. et col.*, XVII, 688 ff.

[43] Monts to Bülow, April 28, 1904, *G.P.*, XX, 60 ff., No. 6410.

dor's indignation.[44] At Naples the King again exchanged toasts with M. Loubet without mentioning the alliance.

Although the demands of the German government had been flouted, it could not execute its threat; for a dissolution of the Triple Alliance, occurring so soon after the conclusion of the Entente Cordiale, would have been too great a victory for France. "One would say," wrote Count Bülow, "that our policy since the retirement of Bismarck has lost us first the alliance with Russia, then good relations with England, and finally the Triple Alliance itself."[45] So, feigning cool indifference toward the renegade ally, he remarked to the Italian Ambassador that as the conditions out of which the Triple Alliance had developed no longer obtained, Germany had no need of Italy's aid, nor, he supposed, had Italy of Germany's.[46] Then came apologies. On May 18 M. Tittoni declared in the Italian Chamber that "the policy of Italy is not one of balancing, which would be unworthy of a great state, but one of loyal honesty. The alliance with Germany is not incompatible with friendly relations with France."[47] Although the German government did not believe him, it accepted his excuses. The Triple Alliance resumed its precarious course.[48]

[44] Monts to Bülow, April 29, 1904, *ibid.*, 63 f., No. 6411.

[45] Bülow's minutes to a dispatch from Monts, May 21, 1904, *ibid.*, 78, No. 6419.

[46] Holstein advised informing the Italian government that the Triple Alliance "practically speaking has had its day," while Monts confined his relations with Tittoni to written communications. See Richthofen to Monts, April 28, 1904, *ibid.*, 59 f., No. 6409; Bülow to Monts, May 7, 1904, *ibid.*, 67 ff., No. 6414; memo. by Holstein, May 12, 1904, *ibid.*, 71 f., No. 6416; memo. by Bülow, May 12, 1904, *ibid.*, 73 f., No. 6417.

[47] Quoted in *ibid.*, p. 75 nn.; Tommaso Tittoni, *Italy's Foreign and Colonial Policy. A Selection from the Speeches Delivered in the Italian Parliament by Tommaso Tittoni* (New York, 1915), pp. 12 f., quoting a speech by Tittoni on May 14, 1904.

[48] Memo. by Bülow, May 12, 1904, *G.P.*, XX, 73 f., No. 6417 and Anlage; Monts to Bülow, May 12, 1904, *ibid.*, 74 ff., No. 6418; and the following documents. At a personal meeting on Sept. 27, 1904, Premier Giolitti affirmed to Bülow Italy's loyalty to her alliance and promised to show more reserve toward France (memo. by Bülow, Sept. 28, 1904, *ibid.*, 81 ff., No. 6422).

As a result of this episode, the anger of the German government at France, already aroused over the diminution of German influence through the Entente Cordiale, was increased. The Emperor, who had tarried near the Italian coast in the persistent hope of a chance meeting with M. Loubet,[49] returned home feeling like the poor kinsman uninvited to the feast. On May 1, at the opening of the new Rhine bridge at Mainz, he gave vent to his chagrin in the following warning: "I desire sincerely that peace . . . . be kept. But I am convinced that if this bridge should have to be used for more serious transports, it would stand the test completely."[50]

IV

"We need a success in our foreign policy," wrote Prince Lichnowsky, councilor in the German foreign office, on April 14, "because the Anglo-French understanding as well as the Franco-Italian *rapprochement* is generally considered a defeat for us."[51] The German government immediately took steps toward obtaining that success.

To manifest its dissatisfaction at being excluded from the Moroccan settlement and to force M. Delcassé to agree with Germany on that question, the German government first considered in April the project of dispatching a warship to Tangier, ostensibly to settle certain grievances against Morocco.[52] As a pre-

[40] The Emperor tarried so long that Bülow finally advised him to come home; otherwise he would make himself ridiculous. See Monts to F. O., April 17, 1904, *ibid.*, 117, No. 6440; Bülow to William II, April 17, 1904, *ibid.*, 117 f., No. 6441.

[50] The Emperor made similar speeches at Karlsruhe, April 28, and at St. Johann-Saar-brücken, May 14 (Schulthess, *Europäischer Geschichtskalender 1904*, pp. 76, 92). At Karlsruhe he declared: "I hope that peace will not be disturbed and that the events which we see occurring will have the effect of . . . . making our eyes clear, of steeling our courage, and of uniting us if it should become necessary to interfere in the *Weltpolitik*."

[51] Memo. by Lichnowsky, April 13, 1904, *G.P.*, XX, 203, No. 6516.

[52] Dr. Genthe of the *Kölnische Zeitung* had recently been murdered by some of the Moroccans; a native employee of a German firm had been illegally impris-

caution, General Schlieffen, chief of staff, was consulted, April 19, about the possibility of success in case of a Franco-German war. Herr von Holstein summed up the General's reply as follows: "In case of the outbreak of a Franco-German war at the present, Russia's participation would be improbable, but England's attitude would be uncertain."[53]

The proposal was not executed at the time,[54] for Count Bülow had other plans. The first one was to test the strength of the Entente Cordiale, to weaken its force, and to include Germany among the Powers making ententes by endeavoring to negotiate an arbitration treaty and a general settlement with Great Britain similar to the Anglo-French ones. If accord, even in principle, were reached on Anglo-German difficulties, the Chancellor was willing to propose a naval agreement. He felt certain that by careful handling he could win the Emperor's approval of the whole transaction.[55]

The opportunity to make the proposal was afforded when about the first of May the British government asked the other Powers interested in Egypt to approve the changes which France had accepted in the declaration of April 8. The German foreign office replied that Germany must receive the same guaranty of her rights in Egypt that France had received, and proposed to include in the negotiations the Anglo-German troubles concern-

---

oned; and certain indemnities from the Moroccan government had to be collected. See Mentzingen to Bülow, April 5 (received April 11), 1904, *ibid.*, 202, No. 6515; memo. by Lichnowsky, April 13, 1904, *ibid.*, 202 f., No. 6516; memo. by Bruning, April 23, 1904, *ibid.*, 203 ff., No. 6517, and Richthofen's minutes thereto.

[53] Memo. by Lichnowsky, April 19, 1904, *ibid.*, XIX, 174 f., No. 6031; Schlieffen to Bülow, April 20, 1904, *ibid.*, XX, 175 ff., No. 6032.

[54] On May 21, Mühlberg, of the German foreign office, telegraphed to Mentzingen, German minister at Tangier, that since "a forceful action could be easily misunderstood and lead to erroneous conclusions about the German policy," the ship would not be sent (*ibid.*, 206, No. 6502).

[55] Memo. by Holstein, April 19, 1904, *ibid.*, 123 f., No. 6443; Bülow to Richthofen, April 19, 1904, *ibid.*, 124, No. 6444. All three men approved of the idea.

ing Samoa, Transvaal indemnities, and the Canadian preferential tariff.

The British government refused to broaden the basis of negotiations, declaring that the Egyptian affair must be settled on its own merits. How Lord Lansdowne regarded the German proposal was shown in his letter of May 6 to Sir Frank Lascelles.

The proposal of the German Government to make their concurrence in regard to the Khedivial Decree dependent upon an all-round settlement [he wrote] . . . . looks to an ordinary observer like a great piece of effrontery. . . . . The suggestion that the consent of the German Government to a perfectly innocuous arrangement in Egypt can only be bought at the price of concessions elsewhere does not become more palatable when we find it connected with an intimation that Germany is hesitating whether "she shall turn to the East or to the West." This is a veiled threat of which I remember Hatzfeldt used to be fond.[56]

Pointing out the fact that Germany held only a very small per cent of the Egyptian bonds (he said only $\frac{1}{4}$ per cent), that the other Powers had agreed to the Egyptian changes unconditionally, and that France had made reciprocal concessions to Great Britain in return for the guaranty of her rights in Egypt, Lord Lansdowne refused to give Germany the special guaranty which she requested.[57]

Count Bülow agreed (May 28) to confine the negotiations to Egypt alone; but he would not recede from the other demands. For, he argued, France had been given large compensation in return for her renunciations in Egypt while Germany merely asked an equal assurance of her rights and interests in that land, particularly of her commercial interests. Thus the two governments reached a deadlock. Each felt that it had a just griev-

---

[56] Newton, *Lord Lansdowne*, pp. 329 f.

[57] Richthofen to Lascelles, May 4, 1904, *G.P.*, XX, 127 f., No. 6446. Whether or not the communication was sent in this form is not known. See Rücker-Jenisch to F. O., May 18, 1904, *ibid.*, 128 f., No. 6447; Villiers to Lascelles, May 24, 1904, *ibid.*, 129 ff., No. 6448; Lascelles to Lansdowne, May 18, 1904, *B.D.*, III, 1, No. 1; Lansdowne to Lascelles, May 4, 1904, *ibid.*, 18, No. 16, and following documents.

ance.[58] Herr von Holstein, considering the occasion a "test of strength," thought that if Germany receded, the world would perceive that sharp handling was sufficient to vanquish her.[59] Count Metternich reported, however, that the British refusal was caused not by any malign designs against Germany, but rather by the fact that the government was opposed to weakening or endangering the Entente Cordiale by treating Germany in the same way as France, and by the fact that it saw no reason for making an exception of Germany after the other Powers had unconditionally accepted the modifications. Above all, he wrote, the British government feared another outburst of vituperation against Germany from British public opinion and of indignation against the British government itself for permitting Germany again to browbeat it.[60] So about the middle of June at the Count's suggestion, a compromise was effected. The British government gave Germany a guaranty of its Egyptian interests in return for an acceptance of the French obligations in that land. The other Powers were to be asked to approve this new agreement.[61]

Late in June King Edward enjoyed a pleasant visit as the Emperor's guest at a naval review at Kiel; on July 10, at the King's suggestion, some German warships touched at Plymouth; and on July 12 an arbitration treaty was signed between the two Powers. Their relations seemed to be improving. At Kiel, Count Bülow once more assured the King that Germany intended to guard strict neutrality during the Russo-Japanese War; and

[58] Memoir handed to Richthofen to Lascelles, May 28, 1904, *G.P.*, XX, 132 f., No. 6449; Metternich to F. O., June 1, 1904, *ibid.*, 147 f., No. 6454.

[59] Memo. by Holstein, June 5, 1904, *ibid.*, 144 f., No. 6461; William II to Bülow, June 6, 1904, *ibid.*, 147 f., No. 6463.

[60] Dispatches from Metternich to F. O., June 2, 3, 4, 8, 9, 1904 (*ibid.*, 138 ff., Nos. 6455, 6458, 6460, 6464, 6466). Cf. Mallet to Spring Rice, early summer, 1904 (Gwynn, *The Letters and Friendships of Sir Cecil Spring Rice*, I, 414). Mallet stated that the British government did not want to weaken the advance toward France by a settlement with Germany, especially since the Anglo-French accord had not been definitely ratified.

[61] *G.P.*, XX, 148 ff., Nos. 6464–80; *B.D.*, III, 21 ff., Nos. 19–23.

Edward VII declared that "no special agreements were needed between England and Germany since no conflict of political interests divided them." He also stated that he wished a settlement with Russia, in fact, that he desired to diminish animosities among all Powers; but he added that he had no thought thereby of isolating Germany.[62]

In spite of the King's cordial words, the fact remained that Germany was still regarded with marked mistrust and antipathy by the British people, while the British government had shown a preference, not yet appreciated by Germany, for the friendship of France. Germany's bid to participate in the formation of ententes had failed.

V

Count Bülow's second plan was to share in the settlement of the Moroccan problem. He had made preparations to that end in the previous autumn, but his policy had been repudiated by the German Emperor (who personally had no interest in Morocco)[63] during an interview with the King of Spain at Vigo on March 16, 1904. In one of his expansive and oracular moods William II advised the youthful King to keep on good terms with France and to make his first foreign visit to Paris, to be on his guard against Great Britain and her satellite, Portugal, but to maintain friendly personal relations with King Edward, and to come to an agreement over the future of Morocco with the other nations, especially France, interested in North Africa. Germany, he said, aimed at no territorial acquisitions in North Africa, but only the maintenance of the open door for, among others, "rail-

---

[62] Memo. by Bülow, June 26, 29, 1904, *G.P.*, XIX, 186 ff., Nos. 6038, 6040; memo. by Richthofen (undated though probably written about July 4, 1904), *ibid.*, 194 ff., No. 6042; Richthofen to Metternich, June 20, 1904, *ibid.*, XX, 163, No. 6478; Lee, *King Edward VII*, II, 292 ff. See also MacDonald to Lansdowne, June 23, 1904, *B.D.*, IV, 1, No. 1; Lansdowne to MacDonald, June 24, 1904; *ibid.*, 2, No. 2.

[63] In 1896 the Emperor had shown a decided interest in Morocco (*G.P.*, XI, No. 2820). In the next years, however, his attitude had changed. The motive force behind the German policy toward Morocco was Bülow.

way concessions, open ports, and importation of manufactured articles."[64]

In spite of the Emperor's renunciation, Count Bülow did not relinquish his ambitions although the difficulty of realizing them was enormously increased. The indefiniteness and apparent duplicity of the German policy on the Moroccan question were caused by Count Bülow's dilemma of gaining a share in Morocco without violating the Emperor's assertions.

Late in April, 1904, the Chancellor was afforded an opportunity to intervene through Spain, whose government asked for Germany's sympathy and "practical proof of it at the opportune moment" during the Franco-Spanish negotiations then under way. Count Bülow was eager to fish in troubled waters by lending aid, and in his optimism went so far as to instruct Herr von Radowitz on April 29 as follows:

> Port Mahon we leave entirely out of consideration. Primarily Fernando Po interests us, for which under circumstances we would also pay well. If, moreover, a harbor in West Morocco is obtainable, that would be very useful. Perhaps Your Excellency can use the prevailing opinion in Spain against the Anglo-French accord in this direction.[65]

The Chancellor advised the Spanish government to draw out the negotiations; for, he argued, if Great Britain were given time in which to recover from her fear that the far eastern entente of 1895 might be renewed, she would begin to rue her bargain, and would at least passively support Spain or acquiesce

[64] The Emperor thought of buying Fernando Po, but said nothing of this to the King. On this incident and the Emperor's attitude toward Morocco see his minutes to Radolin to Bülow, Oct. 20, 1903, *ibid.*, XVII, 362, No. 5206; William II to Bülow, March 16, 1904; *ibid.*, 363, No. 5208; Radowitz to Richthofen, March 23, 1904, *ibid.*, 364, No. 5209; Radolin to Bülow, March 30, 1904, *ibid.*, 365, No. 5210. On Oct. 20, 1903, Radolin had reported from Paris a conversation with the Spanish Ambassador in which the latter, after admitting that France and Spain were well on the way toward an accord over Morocco, remarked to him, "I suppose that you have nothing to object to our entente." Radolin replied, "We have only commercial interests in those parts, which, however, are of very great importance and which we must safeguard" (Radolin to Bülow, Oct. 20, 1903, *ibid.*, 361 f., No. 5206).

[65] Bülow to Radowitz, April 29, 1904, *ibid.*, XX, 169 f., No. 6481.

in the latter's receiving better terms from the more powerful France.[66] When the Chancellor heard of difficulty between the two negotiating Powers over the control of Tangier, he decided to give diplomatic support to Spain in obtaining that port and its hinterland provided Great Britain was not obliged to aid France diplomatically in acquiring them. In other words, he was making it very easy for Great Britain to sin against her obligations to France. When the German Ambassador sounded Lord Lansdowne early in June, the latter, while not objecting, made it evident that he preferred and expected a satisfactory settlement directly between the two Powers themselves.[67] By June 10 the German government learned that this matter had been arranged, but that trouble had arisen over the question of publishing the agreement. Count Bülow immediately urged Spain in favor of it.[68] On June 17 Herr von Radowitz reported that Spain was insisting upon complete commercial freedom in Morocco without the thirty years' limitation. As this was also a sensitive point for Germany Count Bülow on the next day instructed the Ambassador to advise Spain strongly to insist upon the assurance of the fullest economic freedom even for obtaining government contracts and concessions. He left it to Herr von Radowitz to determine "whether it would be advantageous for the achievement of the German goal to let the Spanish percieve that Germany would assume and maintain the same standpoint at the proper moment." "Naturally," he added for the Ambassador's personal information, "it would be . . . . a great help to us for Spain to take the lead."[69]

[66] Bülow to Radowitz, May 22, 1904, *ibid.*, 173 f., No. 6484; Bülow to Radowitz, May 25, 1904, *ibid.*, 174 f., No. 6486.

[67] Bülow to Metternich, May 31, 1904, *ibid.*, 176 f., No. 6488; Metternich to F. O., June 1, 1904, *ibid.*, 177 f., No. 6489, and following documents; also Lansdowne to Lascelles, June 1, 1904, *B.D.*, III, 53, No. 61.

[68] Radowitz to F. O., June 10, 1904, *G.P.*, XX, 180 f., No. 6494; Bülow to Radowitz, June 16, 1904, *ibid.*, 181, No. 6496.

[69] Radowitz to F. O., June 17, 1904, *ibid.*, 182, No. 6497; Bülow to Radowitz, June 18, 1904, *ibid.*, 182 f., No. 6498 and following documents.

By July, however, there seemed little prospect of Germany's profiting from the Franco-Spanish negotiations.[70] German grievances against Morocco remained unsettled. German firms trading there demanded protection against the French monopolistic actions. In June, France practically gained control over the Sultan's finances, and she was preparing an important mission to Fez in the autumn. Nor did M. Delcassé show any inclination to open negotiations with Germany. Already disgruntled at the French Foreign Minister, the German government came to feel itself slighted and humiliated by his disregard. Its resentment toward him became concentrated upon the one grievance which could be best supported in public, that he was infringing upon Germany's economic interests in Morocco. It therefore decided to assume a more active policy, and late in July held a discussion of ways and means. The government did not follow up a hint from the Sultan for co-operation because of its unsettled claims against Morocco. Nor could it tender him financial support or begin an economic penetration of the land similar to that of France because, as Baron Richthofen wrote late in July, "the German banks all strike immediately when one mentions Morocco." The German Foreign Secretary advised against keeping pace with every act of the French in Morocco as too venturesome; while to take the initiative directly with the French government by requesting guaranties for economic freedom he regarded as both doubtful of success and beneath German dignity. So at the Baron's suggestion a "gradual, purely matter-of-fact advance, ignoring as long as possible a special position of France," was decided upon. German warships should appear from time to time in Moroccan waters, and during one of these visits the grievances against Morocco should be settled.[71]

[70] Radolin to Bülow, July 27, 1904, *ibid.*, 216, No. 6524; memo. by Richthofen, July 16, 1904, *ibid.*, 186, No. 6503; Radowitz to F. O., July 21, 1904, *ibid.*, 188, No. 6504.

[71] Bülow to Radolin, July 21, 1904, *ibid.*, 210 ff., No. 6523; Radolin to Bülow, July 27, 1904, *ibid.*, 215 ff., No. 6524; memo. by Richthofen, July 29, 1904, *ibid.*,

The uncertain international situation also caused the German government to proceed warily. On June 3 the Belgian Minister at Berlin had stated to the German foreign office that he suspected the presence of a secret article in the Anglo-French accord concerning the Rheinish frontier. Although believing that the agreement did contain secret clauses regarding Egypt, Count Metternich refused to credit this suspicion. Upon mentioning the rumor to Lord Lansdowne on June 19, he received a full denial that the accord contained any articles which concerned European complications.[72] Nevertheless, the Chancellor realized that "any attempt on the part of Germany to interfere in the Moroccan question in its present phase can lead to an action with far-reaching consequences and therefore deserves special precaution."[73] For that reason he first sought to learn how the British government regarded its obligations to France with respect to Morocco.[74]

217, No. 6525, and Bülow's minutes. In the negotiations with Germany over the acceptance of the Khedivial decree, Lansdowne informed Metternich that France had agreed to support Great Britain fully if at some future time the latter should propose "a revision of the international agreements affecting the position of the Powers in Egypt" (Lansdowne to Whitehead, June 19, 1904, B.D., III, 22 f., No. 21). This was, of course, the content of one of the secret articles in the Anglo-French agreement of April 8, although naturally Lansdowne did not say so. Whether the German government inferred therefrom that a reciprocal concession had been made by Great Britain to France with respect to Morocco is not evident, but it probably did. Lansdowne also stated to Metternich on June 1 what the area was which should be supervised by Spain, although he spoke only of having emphasized this point verbally to the French government and said nothing of a secret article to that effect. So far as the documents show, the German government does not seem to have recognized the import of this statement, although this negative proof is not conclusive (Metternich to F. O., June 1, 1904, G.P., XX, 177 f., No. 6489).

[72] Bülow to Metternich, June 4, 1904, ibid., 27 f., No. 6383; Metternich to F. O., June 4, 1904, ibid., 29 f., Nos. 6384 f.

[73] Bülow to Radolin, July 21, 1904, ibid., 210 f., No. 6523. Radolin also warned that if "English diplomatic support of France does not signify much, we have a free hand, while an Anglo-French resistance could easily force us to retreat" (Radolin to Bülow, July 27, 1904, ibid., 216 f., No. 6524).

[74] Mühlberg to Metternich, Aug. 7, 1904, ibid., 217 ff., No. 6526.

On August 15 Count Metternich declared to Lord Lansdowne that "the French effort aimed at a monopolization in Morocco. We could not permit this." Asserting that Germany was in no way bound by the Anglo-French agreement, he said that Germany's economic interests in regard to governmental concessions and industrial enterprises in Morocco were endangered by France. "We could very soon be put in a situation in which we should have to protect our commercial interests [in the widest sense] against France." He asked Lord Lansdowne how the British government interpreted the last part of Article IV of the Anglo-French declaration stating that concessions for roads, etc., in Morocco were to be granted "only on such conditions as will maintain intact the authority of the State over these great undertakings of public interest," and Article IX obliging Great Britain to lend diplomatic aid to France.

Lord Lansdowne denied that Great Britain had renounced her right to share in the concessions in Morocco, but he refused to interpret Article IX until a concrete instance arose. He declared that in the French agreement

we [Great Britain] made no attempt to dispose of the rights of other Powers, although we made certain concessions in respect of the rights and opportunities to which we were ourselves entitled. I could at any rate say that it was not at all probable that, if any third Power were to have occasion to uphold its Treaty rights, we should use our influence in derogation of them.

Count Metternich inferred from that interview that Lord Lansdowne would limit the scope of Article IX, and that in case Germany's actions did not infringe upon the Sultan's authority Germany would be safe in opposing France in Morocco. However, he wrote, if Germany sought, for instance, to acquire control of a harbor there, Great Britain would support France. He warned his government that Great Britain would not connive at blocking the French advance in Morocco or endanger her friendship for the sake of that land. If a third Power disputed politically the French position there, both government and people would support France. Within those limits Germany could execute her Moroccan policy. But, he continued, "in the present international situation, it will be difficult for us to arrest the process of France's establishing herself in Morocco."[75]

Even before receiving Count Metternich's reply, the Chancellor proposed to dispatch an ultimatum to the Sultan demanding under threat of a naval demonstration that he satisfy the German claims within three months.[76] But the Emperor, who remained strongly opposed to active interference in the Moroccan affair, refused his consent for the third time, and upset the Chancellor's policy.[77] In September the foreign office discussed the plan to seize the Moroccan transport ship and even Agadir, but nothing was done.[78] Early in October Baron Richthofen suggested that since the Emperor was so averse to intervention the government should take up the Moroccan question directly with the French government. This project also came to naught.[79]

While no action was taken German feeling continued to smolder. The noncommittal communication from the French government about the agreement with Spain early in October[80] and the repeated petitions of German firms for the defense of their interests in Morocco[81] augmented the bitterness against France. So while the German government itself played the

[75] Metternich to Bülow, Aug. 15, 1904, *ibid.*, 219 ff., No. 6527; Lansdowne to Lascelles, Aug. 15, 1904, *B.D.*, III, 53 f., No. 62.

[76] Metternich's dispatch was sent on Aug. 18, although dated Aug. 15. Bülow approved of the new measures on Aug. 17. See Mentzingen to Bülow, Aug. 6, 1904, *G.P.*, XX, 222 f., No. 6528; Mühlberg to Bülow, Aug. 16, 1904, *ibid.*, 223 f., No. 6529; Bülow to Tschirschky, Aug. 17, 1904, *ibid.*, 224 f., No. 6530.

[77] Mentzingen to F. O., Sept. 13, 18, 1904, *ibid.*, 226 ff., Nos. 6532 f.

[78] See editor's note, *ibid.*, p. 225; also memo. by Richthofen, Oct. 7, 1904, *ibid.*, 228, No. 6534.

[79] Memo. by Richthofen, *ibid.*, 228 ff., No. 6534.

[80] Richthofen to Radowitz, Oct. 7, 1904, *ibid.*, 191, No. 6508; memo. by Richthofen for Bülow, Oct. 7, 1904, *ibid.*, 228 ff., No. 6534.

[81] Memo. by Kries, Oct. 22, 1904, *ibid.*, 231 f., No. 6535.

sphinx, it showed its resentment through the semiofficial press and through conversations between German and French officials in Morocco and elsewhere. By the end of the year the Moroccan question was still very much alive. As an influential Moor remarked, "Germany has not yet spoken, and so long as that has not occurred, we cannot believe that anything definite has been decided."[82] Before Germany did speak, she endeavored to solve her difficulties by an effort to ally with Russia.

[82] Kühlmann to Bülow, Nov. 9, 1904, *ibid.*, 232 ff., No. 6536.

CHAPTER X

THE NEGOTIATIONS FOR A RUSSO-GERMAN ALLIANCE, 1904

Early in July, 1904, Herr von Holstein offered his resignation because of personal differences with Baron Richthofen. In doing so, he stated that the prestige of Germany had diminished during the past years "while our opponents and rivals are on the point of encircling us"; and as "difficult situations" were to be anticipated, he was happy to be relieved of responsibility. Count Bülow patched up the quarrel, but his comment to Herr von Holstein's remarks is illuminating:

Now he [Herr von Holstein] speaks of our shrunken prestige just as the Bismarckian press does. But I cannot believe that Holstein, like that press, attributes the decline of our authority to the dismissal of the great Chancellor. Since that dismissal, from the non-renewal of the Russian Reinsurance Treaty and the East Asiatic Triple Alliance to the handling of the Moroccan and Egyptian questions, from the so-called Urias letter to Vienna to the publication of the Swinemünde dispatch, from the turn in 1896 against England to the Shanghai and Pauncefote difference with that Power, nothing of significance has happened in our foreign policy without Holstein's advice.[1]

The results of those errors, so frankly confessed, were apparent: the conclusion of the Entente Cordiale, the exclusion of Germany from the entente movement and from the Moroccan settlement, the British efforts to approach Russia,[2] animosity between Great Britain and Germany. They all caused that attempt at a new orientation of policy which in 1900 Count Bülow had threatened in this eventuality.

One of the most favorable aspects of the German foreign rela-

[1] Both letters, the one by Holstein, the other by Bülow, dated July 11 and July 13, respectively, are given in Hammann, *Bilder aus der letzten Kaiserzeit,* pp. 33 ff.

[2] It is of course apparent that the German government anticipated no immediate success from these British efforts. Signs of Anglo-Russian antagonism were too numerous (see *G.P.,* Vol. XIX, chap. cxxxi).

tions was the *rapprochement* with the United States in 1903 and
1904. There was cordial friendship between President Roosevelt
and Baron Sternburg, the German ambassador,[3] and the two
governments both desired to maintain the integrity of China during the current war.[4] The President mistrusted Russia, about
whom he could say nothing good, and France in their policy toward China, and he met difficulty in trying to co-operate with
Great Britain.[5] As he was ambitious to mediate peace between
Russia and Japan when the time came, he turned to Germany
for aid, in August expressing the wish "to go hand in hand with
Germany in East Asia."[6] The German government perceived in
this co-operation a means of protecting its interests in China, of
issuing from its relative international isolation, and of preventing France and Great Britain from mediating peace—an event
which might enable them to form a triple grouping with Russia
or even a quadruple combination with Russia and Japan.[7] Count
Bülow therefore cordially responded to the President's invitation,[8] seeking at the same time to increase the latter's suspicion
of France and Great Britain.[9]

As the German government realized the limitations to this intimacy with the United States, it sought a more effective associa-

[3] Dennett, *Roosevelt and the Russo-Japanese War*, p. 36.

[4] *G.P.*, Vol. XIX, chap. cxxx, A; Gwynn, *The Letters and Friendships of Sir
Cecil Spring Rice*, I, 397 f.

[5] Dennett, pp. 36 ff., 42; Sternburg to F. O., Sept. 27, 1904, *G.P.*, XIX, 542,
No. 6266.

[6] Bülow to William II, Aug. 31, 1904, *ibid.*, 536, No. 6264.

[7] Bülow to William II, Aug. 31, 1904, *ibid.*, 535 ff., No. 6264; Bülow to Bernstorff, Sept. 1, 1904, *ibid.*, 217 f., No. 6051; Bernstorff to Bülow, Sept. 6, 1904,
ibid., 218 ff., No. 6052. Eckardstein informed Bülow in August, 1904, of attempts
being made by Witte to introduce negotiations for peace with Hayashi. Bülow
was not in favor of an early peace. See Eckardstein, *Lebenserinnerungen und
politische Denkwürdigkeiten*, III, 76 ff.; Goetz, *Briefe Wilhelms II an den Zaren
1894–1914*, p. 341; Dillon, *The Eclipse of Russia*, p. 297; memo. by Bülow, Nov. 2,
1904, *G.P.*, XIX, 387 f., No. 6167.

[8] Bülow to Sternburg, Sept. 5, 1904, *G.P.*, XIX, 541, No. 6265.

[9] See *ibid.*, Nos. 5977, 6259 ff.

tion in an alliance with Russia. In January, 1904, the Chancellor had been unconcerned about such an alliance;[10] but by July he was waiting for the "psychological moment" in which to propose a renewal of the former "League of the Three Emperors."[11] The advent of that moment seemed highly probable. Since the beginning of the Russo-Japanese War, the Russian people, government, and sovereign had drawn closer to Germany.[12] On June 1, "dearest Nicky" wrote to his cousin "Willy" (so they addressed each other), "I know that you feel for us in this serious time and it is a comfort to realize that one's *real friends* think and sympathize with one."[13] And "Willy," in his replies, overflowed with affection and advice—advice that varied from directing "Nicky" upon how to conduct war to lecturing him on the "piratical" practices of his ships, from urging him to send his Black Sea fleet through the Dardanelles in spite of British opposition to reporting gossip which would antagonize him against Great Britain and France.[14]

In October the opportunity arose for the German move toward an alliance. A Russian company had given a contract to the Hamburg-American Line to furnish coal for the Russian Baltic

[10] Memo. by Bülow, Jan. 16, 1904, *ibid.*, 34, No. 5943; memo. by Holstein, Dec. 23, 1903, *ibid.*, 73 ff., No. 5967.

[11] Bülow to William II, July 15, 1904, *ibid.*, 202, No. 6043. Richthofen opposed the project (memo. by Richthofen, undated although probably written early in July, 1904, *ibid.*, 194 ff., No. 6042. This intention did not prevent Bülow from negotiating a commercial treaty with Russia in July, 1904, which Witte, Russian minister, declared exacted a tribute from Russia "much greater than any war indemnity on record" (Bülow to William II, July 15, 1904, *ibid.*, 196 ff., No. 6043; Dillon, pp. 323 ff.; Witte, *Memoirs,* pp. 413 f.).

[12] Radolin to Bülow, Feb. 28, 1904, *G.P.*, XIX, 165 ff., No. 6028; Metternich to Bülow, March 14, 1904, *ibid.*, 167 ff., No. 6029; Alvensleben to Bülow, May 11, 1904, *ibid.*, 177 ff., No. 6033, and following documents.

[13] Nicholas II to William II, June 1, 1904, *ibid.*, 181, No. 6034.

[14] See their correspondence in Goetz, pp. 337 ff.; also in *G.P.*, XIX, Nos. 6028 n., 6034, 6035, 6037, 6039, 6056, 6057, 6062 and n., 6064 and n., 6073 and n. The Emperor's letters were dated Feb. 11, March 29, June 6, June 12, June 28, July 17, July 23, Aug. 19, Oct. 8, Oct. 10; the Czar's replies were dated June 1, July 20, July 31, Sept. 28, 1904.

fleet which was to sail for the war zone about the middle of that month.[15] As the German firm intended to use mainly English coal, it had chartered a number of British ships and had given a subcontract to a British firm to aid it in the transportation. None the less, on learning of the transaction, the British press bitterly attacked Germany for thus violating neutrality. In view of this attack Count Bülow on October 4 instructed Baron Romberg, first secretary of the German embassy in St. Petersburg, to make a communication to the Russian government as follows: Baron Romberg should state to Count Lamsdorff that this press campaign might provoke a war but that the German government would not prevent the execution of the coaling contract, that it "would run the risk of having the English kindle fire-rockets in Japan." If war did occur with Japan and Great Britain, Germany would hold France also responsible; for not only would a large element among the French advocate grasping the opportunity for revenge against Germany, but also the arousing of the British zeal for war would be a direct result of the Entente Cordiale. "So if we lose our colonies, trade, merchant marine, and perhaps also a part of our war fleet in an unequal battle on the sea . . . . a reckoning with France on land would become unavoidable for us."[16]

Count Lamsdorff showed no inclination to respond to this feeler. On October 19, while thanking the German government for its friendship, he refused to credit either Great Britain or Japan with bellicose intentions against Germany. He interrupted Baron Romberg to assure him that nothing was to be feared from France; not a word did he utter about an alliance.[17]

Meantime, the Russian Baltic squadron sailed, and in the night of October 21 occurred the Dogger Bank disaster which brought war between Great Britain and Russia dangerously

---

[15] Bernhard Huldermann, *Albert Ballin* (Berlin, 1922), pp. 146 ff.; *G.P.*, XIX, Nos. 6077 ff.

[16] Bülow to Romberg, Oct. 4, 1904, *G.P.*, XIX, 257 ff., No. 6084.

[17] Romberg to F. O., Oct. 19, 1904, *ibid.*, 259, No. 6085.

close.[18] The "psychological moment" had come, reasoned Count Bülow and Herr von Holstein. Defeated in the Far East, menaced by revolution, and excited by this new danger, Russia should welcome the project of an alliance with the strongest military power in Europe. So on October 24 Herr von Holstein, who usually held aloof from all ambassadors, explained the German proposition to Count Osten-Sacken,[19] the Russian representative. Three days later the Emperor's influence with the Czar, who was thought to be more pliable and more favorably inclined than his Foreign Minister, was brought into play. In a letter to Nicholas II the Emperor wrote:

For some time English press has been threatening Germany, on no account to allow coals to be sent to your Baltic Fleet now on its way out. It is not impossible, that the Japanese and British Governments may lodge a joint protest against our coaling your ships coupled with a *sommation* to stop further work. The result aimed at by such a threat of war would be absolute immobility of your fleet and inability to proceed to its destination from want of fuel. This new danger would have to be faced in community by Russia and Germany together, who would both have to remind your ally France of the obligations she has taken over in the treaty of Dual Alliance with you, the *casus foederis*. It is out of the question, that France on such an invitation, would try to shirk her implicit duty towards her ally. Though Delcassé is an Anglophile *énragé*, he will be wise enough to understand that the British fleet is utterly unable to save Paris! In this way a powerful combination of 3 of the strongest continental Powers would be formed to attack, whom the Anglo-Japanese group would think twice before acting. . . . . My news from London say, that the Press and mob make a noise, the Admiralty some fuss, but that Government, Court and Society look with greatest calm at the event as an unhappy accident, arising from to great nervousness.[20]

[18] See above.

[19] Osten-Sacken to Lamsdorff, Oct. 27, 1904, *Kriegsschuldfrage*, Nov., 1924, pp. 456 ff.; Savinsky, *Recollections of a Russian Diplomat*, p. 97.

[20] William II to Nicholas II, Oct. 27, 1904, *G.P.*, XIX, 303 f., No. 6118. Their correspondence was entirely in English, in the use of which they made frequent mistakes. Osten-Sacken reported on Nov. 4 a conversation with Bülow in which the latter, repeating the remarks of Holstein, declared that in case the British government objected to the coaling of the Russian ships by the German firm, "we should apparently be forced to ask the St. Petersburg cabinet whether we should refuse this objection and thus assume the risk of a war with England and become

This broad hint, amounting almost to a proposal of alliance itself, was immediately effective. The Czar replied two days later:

> As you say . . . . Germany, Russia, and France should at once unite upon an arrangement to abolish Anglo-Japanese arrogance and insolence. Would you like to lay down and frame the outlines of such a treaty and let me know it? As soon as accepted by us France is bound to join her ally. This combination has often come to my mind. It will mean peace and rest for the world.[21]

On the next day a draft of a treaty and a long explanatory letter, both composed by the Chancellor and Herr von Holstein,[22] were sent by the Emperor to the Czar. This draft, which was intended to test how far the Russian government would go, provided for a "defensive alliance . . . . to localize as far as possible the Russo-Japanese War." The first article was the most important:

> In case one of the two Empires shall be attacked by a European Power, its ally will aid it with all its force on land and sea. The two allies, in that case, would make common cause for the purpose of recalling to France the obligations which she has assumed by the terms of the Franco-Russian treaty of Alliance.

By the second article neither Power was to conclude a separate peace with a common adversary. The third article was designed to safeguard Germany in the coaling affair and to continue the alliance after the current war was over. It read:

> The engagement of mutual aid is equally valid in case acts performed by one of the high contracting parties during the war such as the delivery of coal to a belligerent should give place after the war to reclamations of a third Power, as pretended violations of the right of neutrality.

---

your [Russia's] ally; or would Russia prefer to dispense with . . . . the coaling . . . . which in this case we should have to prohibit as incompatible with Germany's neutrality" (*Kriegsschuldfrage*, Nov., 1924, p. 463).

[21] Nicholas II to William II, Oct. 29, 1904, *G.P.*, XIX, 305, No. 6119.

[22] Bülow and Holstein were the proponents of the alliance. Richthofen and Tirpitz, secretary of the Navy Department, opposed it (Alfred von Tirpitz, *Erinnerungen* [Leipzig, 1920], pp. 143 ff.).

In the letter the Emperor emphasized the defensive and the purely European character of the alliance. "It is very essential that America should not feel threatened by our agreement," he wrote. He denounced France, "this republic of miserable civilians," "the French radicals, Clemenceau and all the rest of the tag-rag and bobtail" for not fulfilling France's obligations to her ally.

I positively know that as far back as last December the French Finance Minister Rouvier told the Finance Minister of another power, France would on no account join in a Russo-Japanese war, even though England sided with Japan. To make doubly sure, the English have handed Morocco over to France. The certainty, that France intends to remain neutral and even to lend her diplomatic support to England, is the motive, which gives English policy its present unwonted brutal assurance. This unheard of state of things will change as soon as France finds herself face to face with the necessity of eventually choosing sides. . . . . The radical party . . . . abhors war and militarism, while the nationalist party while not objecting to war in itself, hates fighting for England and against Russia. Thus it will be in the interests of both parties to bring pressure to bear on and warn England to keep the peace. The main result will be, if you and I stand shoulder to shoulder, that France must formally and openly join us, thereby fulfilling her treaty-obligations toward Russia. . . . . This consummation once reached, I expect to maintain peace and you will be left an undisturbed and free hand to deal with Japan. . . . . Of course, before we can take any steps in this question and approach France that tiresome North Sea incident must first have been brought to a close.

For, he continued, the French foreign office had already accepted the British view of the incident, and in case of difficulty over this matter, France would choose the British side. At the close of his letter the Emperor wrote that only he and Count Bülow knew of the project, and that when they had finished the draft the Chancellor had said: "May God's blessings rest upon the work of the two monarchs and may the mighty three-Power group, Russia, Germany, France, preserve forever the peace of Europe. God grant it!"[23]

[23] William II to Nicholas II, Oct. 30, 1904, Goetz, pp. 346 ff.; Bülow to William II, Oct. 30, 1904, G.P., XIX, 305, No. 6120, and Anlage I and II.

The real object of this extravagant show of devotion to Russia was of course to inveigle her into an alliance. It did not signify a desire for a general conflict; the German government appreciated the British naval power too keenly for that.[24] Moreover, since it knew how averse the Russian government and especially the Czar were to an extension of the war, it emphasized the pacifying influence which the proposed alliance would exercise. The German leaders doubtlessly realized, however, that they were running a big risk, since Count Bernstorff, first secretary of the embassy in London, had warned them that Great Britain would regard an alliance between Germany and Russia, no matter how defensive in character, as an aggression directed against the security of the British Empire.[25]

The Chancellor and Herr von Holstein considered the risk worth while, because, if the alliance could be concluded, they expected France, under the combined pressure of Russia and Germany, to enter the new grouping. If she did so, they no doubt reasoned, the Entente Cordiale would be destroyed, the work of M. Delcassé would be blocked, and, instead of Great Britain, Germany would be the center of the new combination. France, as the weakest member of the firm, would have to take orders from both her partners. In fact, the German government openly expressed to the Czar the expectation that in case of a war the control over the French army and navy would be put into German hands. If France, refusing to enter the alliance, elected to range herself with Great Britain and if the Russo-German alliance alone were made, the German statesmen apparently thought that the Dual Alliance would be broken, France would again be at the mercy of the German military power, and the possibility of an Anglo-Russian accord would be destroyed. The gains, both positive and negative, to be derived by Germany from such an

[24] Mühlberg to Tschirschky, Aug. 10, 1904, *G.P.*, XIX, 238 f., No. 6069; Bülow to William II, July 15, 1904, *ibid.*, 204, No. 6043.

[25] Bernstorff to Bülow, Sept. 6, 1904, *ibid.*, 220, No. 6052.

alliance would be enormous. Its completion would constitute a far-reaching diplomatic revolution.[26] In Russian governmental circles opinion was divided. The Czar, who had proposed the alliance without consulting his Foreign Minister,[27] was its staunchest supporter. Weak and dependent, he usually agreed with his most recent adviser. His imagination, which could be vivid at times, was given freer rein because of his indolence. In 1903 he had succumbed to the arguments and ambitions of the adventurer, M. Bezobrazov, about Manchuria and Korea and had brought on the war with Japan. As the necessary European part of that program, M. Bezobrazov had advocated an understanding between the Dual and the Triple alliances. This aspect had not been achieved, probably owing to Count Lamsdorff's opposition.[28] But the war was taking a disastrous course for Russia, revolution was threatening, and the German Emperor's telegram arrived while the crisis with Great Britain was still acute and when Russia, according to the British Ambassador, would have welcomed a war with that Power.[29] The forlorn and troubled Czar returned readily to the idea of an alliance when William II suggested it.

Count Lamsdorff was wary of this move from the start. Not a very strong personality, he was unable at times to maintain control of the foreign policy, yet he was a capable and loyal official who, when necessary, spoke frankly to his master. The Czar was actuated chiefly by sentiment and emotion; his Minister by shrewd diplomatic calculations. Although the one did not grasp

[26] "It is a matter here of a really great and, for the onlooking world, wholly unexpected transformation [*Weichenstellung*]," wrote Bülow to the Emperor, Nov. 16, 1904 (*ibid.*, 312, No. 6125).

[27] See the report from Lamsdorff to the Czar of Holstein's conversation with Osten-Sacken on Oct. 24, and the Czar's minute to it (*Kriegsschuldfrage*, Nov., 1924, pp. 455 f. and n.; cf. Savinsky, p. 97).

[28] Langer, *Europ. Gespr.*, June, 1926, pp. 397 f.; Dennis, *Adventures in American Diplomacy.* pp. 354 f.

[29] Hardinge to Lansdowne, Nov. 7, 1904, *B.D.*, IV, 35, No. 26.

the German motives, the other did; and the prospect of feeling
"the heavy weight . . . . of the iron bands" of a German alliance was not to his liking. Count Lamsdorff did not believe that
Russia needed this alliance as he felt certain that Great Britain
would not attack her.[30] Furthermore, the conclusion of an agreement of neutrality about Balkan affairs with Austria-Hungary
late in October relieved his country from danger in that quar-
ter.[31]

On the other hand [he wrote to Count Osten-Sacken], we manifestly need
the friendship of our powerful neighbor for the security of our extensive
frontier, for our provisioning with coal and other contrabands, etc. All this
must be seriously considered and we must endeavor not to permit our relations with Berlin to deteriorate, although Paris must also not be disregarded.
Only through the preservation of this balance will Russia succeed in obtaining all possible advantages from both sides.[32]

When the German draft of the treaty arrived, the Dogger
Bank crisis was over, but the Russian government remained embittered because Great Britain had made special naval preparations and a detachment of British cruisers, cleared for action,
had followed the Russian fleet from Vigo to Tangier.[33] Still, that
was no reason to assume the "iron bands" of a German alliance.
The Czar and his Foreign Minister immediately set to work to
make the terms more favorable for Russia.[34] They modified the

[30] A. Savinsky, "Guillaume II et la Russie. Ses Dépêches à Nicholas II, 1903–
1905," *Revue des deux mondes*, XII (1922), 790 f.; *G.P.*, XIX, Nos. 6044 ff.; Savinsky, p. 97. Savinsky was an official in the Russian foreign office in the confidence of Lamsdorff, *G.P.*, XIX, 505, editor's note).

[31] *Ibid.*, Vol. XXII, chap. clviii.

[33] Lamsdorff to Osten-Sacken, Nov. 10, 1904, *Kreigsschuldfrage*, Nov., 1924, pp.
464 f.; cf. Savinsky, p. 99.

[33] Hardinge to Lansdowne, Oct. 31, Nov. 7, 1904, *B.D.*, IV, 25, No. 24; 34 f.,
No. 26.

[34] On receipt of that draft the Czar wrote to Lamsdorff: "To-day I received
the Emperor's letter with the treaty draft. As I read it, I laughed aloud. The content of the three articles touches France mostly. The last point concerns the particular object of dissatisfaction of the German Government with the British action
in the coaling operation. This, however, is a private affair of both states. . . . .
The matter must be considered from all sides, and a more desirable counter-
proposal for us must be composed" (*Kriegsschuldfrage*, Nov., 1924, p. 461).

first and third articles.[35] In the latter, to be kept secret, they incorporated a *quid pro quo* by which Russia should receive German support in the Russo-Japanese negotiations for peace. The revised first article was the more important. The first sentence remained as before; but, instead of stipulating that Russia and Germany both advise France to enter the alliance, the second sentence was changed to read: "His Majesty the Emperor of all the Russias will take the steps necessary to initiate France into this accord and to invite her to associate herself in it as ally." The Czar told the Emperor that the revised Article I must stand without change.[36]

When the Russian government had been brought to this point, the German leaders revealed their real aim. They were, of course, obliged to accept the new first article; but the Emperor, in his reply to Nicholas II, November 17, made it plain that France would have to choose sides, even though, as he frankly wrote, "doubtless the French would much prefer any other grouping of Powers to that of the Alliance *a trois* as in 1895." The chief revisions asked by the German government were in the introduction and in Article III. The former was changed to read: The Emperor and the Czar "for the purpose of assuring the maintenance of peace in Europe have agreed on the following articles of a treaty of defensive alliance." According to an entirely new Article III the treaty should remain in force until denounced one year in advance; however, it was left to the Czar to set any time limit he wished.

These revisions transformed the basis of the negotiation. They made the alliance a general one to continue after the war. The changes were explained on the ground that, in the previous version, the treaty had been aimed too openly at Great Britain, and that, while this was the case, it was not politic to make the fact too evident.

[33] Lamsdorff to Nicholas II, Nov. 4, 1904, *ibid.*, pp. 462 f.

[36] Nicholas II to William II, Nov. 7, 1904, *G.P.*, XIX, 310 ff., No. 6124 and Anlage.

The Russian *quid pro quo* in Article III was also rejected. Germany preferred not to help Russia in the negotiations for peace for fear of antagonizing the United States and of driving her into British arms, although the Emperor excused this refusal by explaining that if this secret clause became known, public opinion might consider the treaty an aggressive one binding Germany to defend the Russian conquests. Instead, he proposed that the previous Article III be made into an extra secret article in which the second sentence should read: "It follows from the the terms of the first sentence of Article I that Germany will associate herself with no action whatever that might imply hostile tendencies to Russia." That clause, wrote the Emperor, would safeguard Russia against the repetition of any such congress as that of 1878, whereby she had been deprived of her Turkish conquests.

In his accompanying letter to the Czar, for which Count Bülow and Herr von Holstein furnished the rough draft, the Emperor urged a quick signing of the agreement, adding the extraordinary proposal that Russia make some military demonstration on the Persian-Afghan frontier. "Even should the forces at your disposal not suffice for a real attack on India itself," he wrote, "they would do for Persia—which has no army—and a pressure on the Indian frontier from Persia will do wonders in England and have remarkably quieting influence on the hot headed Jingoes in London." He also warned the Czar against Anglo-French ambitions to mediate at the desire of Japan.[37]

In St. Petersburg, Count Lamsdorff persuaded the Czar to proceed slowly with the negotiations, and, more important still, to consult France before concluding any agreement. So on November 23 Nicholas II telegraphed the German Emperor to that effect, adding:

[37] William II to Nicholas II, Nov. 17, 1904, Goetz, pp. 349 ff.; Savinsky, p. 102; Bülow to William II, Nov. 16, 1904, *G.P.*, XIX, 312 ff., No. 6125 and Anlage. The treaty draft is given in Goetz, pp. 146 f. See also Alexander Iswolsky, *Recollections of a Foreign Minister* (New York, 1921), pp. 34 f.

As long as it is not signed one can make small modifications on the text; whereas if allready approved by us both, it will seem as if we tried to enforce the treaty on France. In this case a failure might easily happen, which I think is neither your wish.[38]

The Germans realized that this answer spelled defeat for them; because if the treaty became known to the French government that government would of course strenuously resist its completion. In fact, the Emperor was sure that M. Delcassé would at once publish the news of the proposed alliance, that a war cry in England would then burst forth, and that the timid Czar would back out. As he aptly expressed it, Count Lamsdorff and M. Witte had "spat in the German soup."[39] On November 26 he replied with a refusal to let France know a word of the affair; it would be better to drop the whole matter until a more suitable moment, he declared. Although disgusted at this display of "cold feet," as he put it, William II showed no especial anger or uneasiness in his answer and asked Nicholas II to continue their intimacy as before.[40]

On the receipt of that reply Count Lamsdorff had to persuade his master all over again, because the latter was more anxious to make the alliance than he was to be considerate of his ally.[41] Certainly his letter of October 29 to William II was such as to warrant confidence that he would be willing to force the alliance upon France whether she wished it or not. Count Lamsdorff argued that the relations of Russia and Germany were sufficiently close to hold them together without an alliance. He declared that France's intimacy with Great Britain had not caused her to be disloyal to her ally. While he doubted whether she could be

[38] Nicholas II to William II, Nov. 23, 1904, G.P., XIX, 317, No. 6126, Anlage; Savinsky, pp. 102 f.

[39] William II to Bülow, Nov. 23, 1904, G.P., XIX, 316 f., No. 6126.

[40] Bülow to William II, Nov. 24, 1904, ibid., 318 f., No. 6127 and Anlage; William II to Nicholas II, Nov. 26, 1904, Kriegsschuldfrage, Nov., 1924, pp. 471 f.; Savinsky, pp. 103 f.

[41] Iswolsky makes an attempt to exonerate the Czar of the charge of disloyalty to France, but his argument is not convincing (Iswolsky, pp. 27, 36 f.).

won to the proposed combination, he urged her right to be consulted beforehand and denied that she would disclose the secret. She must be won gradually, he said, and not confronted with a *fait accompli* which might force her back upon Great Britain.[42] It is obvious that Count Lamsdorff sought by this method to quash the project or render it harmless. He succeeded only partly in winning over his master. In the reply to the Emperor on December 7 Nicholas II once more asked permission to obtain the French reaction to the main lines of the alliance, even though the original document itself be kept secret from her. "In case of a negative answer," he wrote in conclusion, "the second phase of Art. I of the draft of the treaty ought to be left out I think."[43] Thus, even in case Germany refused his request, the Czar was still apparently willing to make an alliance with her to the entire exclusion of France.

While the Russian government was preparing this answer, the Germans lost patience. Prospects for success seemed doubtful if not entirely hopeless. The declarations of the French press that the Dual Alliance remained as firm as ever and that Germany's attempts to win Russia had failed caused the Chancellor to suspect that news of the negotiations had leaked out. Threats to seize the German vessels coaling the Russian fleet appeared in the Japanese press; the British government laid restrictions upon the shipping of coal to that fleet. In November and December Germany began to fear a British attack.[44]

Since October the British press had returned to its campaign of calumniation against Germany, seeing a German plot behind every British difficulty. In the autumn a redistribution of the British naval forces had weakened the Mediterranean fleet and

[42] Report of Lamsdorff for Nicholas II, Nov. 23, 1904, *Kriegsschuldfrage*, Nov., 1924, pp. 473 ff.; Savinsky, *Revue des deux mondes*, XII (1922), 789 ff.; Savinsky, pp. 104 ff.

[43] He inclosed a draft of the proposed communication to France. See Nicholas II to William II, Dec. 7, 1904, *G.P.*, XIX, 322 ff., No. 6131.

[44] Bülow to William II, Dec. 6, 1904, *ibid.*, 263 ff., No. 6088; *ibid.*, chap. cxxxvi.

concentrated the main strength in home waters. Germany perceived in this rearrangement a tangible proof of the new alignment of Great Britain with France and of the growing British animosity toward her.[45] Hence when in November several articles appeared in *Vanity Fair* and in the *Army and Navy Gazette* proposing that the German fleet be "Copenhagened"[46] as useless for any other purpose than to attack Great Britain,[47] German public opinion took these threats seriously. The Emperor wrote to Count Bülow on November 23 that "the situation assumes more and more the aspect of that immediately preceding the Seven Years' War."[48] The German navy department began hurried measures to recall the vessels in foreign waters.[49] Taking a saner view, the Chancellor, by means of an interview published in the *Nineteenth Century* for December and a speech in the Reichstag on December 5, sought to calm both his own and the British people by an absolute disclaimer of the thought of war between the two countries and by a denial that in the construction of her fleet Germany intended any hostility toward Great Britain.[50] But by December 5 Herr von Holstein himself came to credit the possibility of a British attack.[51]

[45] Metternich to F. O., Oct. 20, 1904, *ibid.*, 652, No. 6349, and following documents; Flotow to Bülow, Oct. 26, 1904, *ibid.*, 286 f., No. 6105 and following documents.

[46] This was the expression used.

[47] Memo. by Metternich for Bülow, Dec. 25, 1904, *ibid.*, 367 ff., No. 6156; report of Marine Attaché Coerper, Jan. 15, 1905, *ibid.*, 379 f., No. 6161; Lee, *King Edward VII*, II, 329; Admiral Sir Edward E. Bradford, *Life of Admiral of the Fleet Sir Arthur Knyvet Wilson* (London, 1923), p. 197.

[48] William II to Bülow, Nov. 23, 1904, *G.P.*, XIX, 316 f., No. 6126; Graf Robert Zedlitz-Trützschler, *Zwölf Jahre am deutschen Kaiserhof* (Stuttgart, 1925), pp. 86 f.

[49] On this war scare see *G.P.*, Vol. XIX, chap. cxxxvi.

[50] J. L. Bashford, "Great Britain and Germany: A Conversation with Count von Bülow, German Chancellor," *Nineteenth Century*, Dec., 1904, pp. 873 ff.; Bülow, *Reden*, II, 123 ff.

[51] Memo. by Holstein, Dec. 5, 1904, *G.P.*, XIX, 358 f., No. 6153.

While this situation seemed serious, the Chancellor was more concerned by the fact that the completion of the coaling of the Russian fleet would soon deprive Germany of her hold over Russia.[52] On December 6 he instructed the German Ambassador at St. Petersburg to inquire peremptorily of the Russian government whether Germany could rely upon its full support in case the coaling led to war. The Ambassador was to state that if no satisfactory answer were received by the time the Russian fleet reached Madagascar the Hamburg-American Line would be forbidden to continue its task. This telegram, which was followed on the next day by a similar one from the Emperor to Nicholas II,[53] forced the negotiations back to the very point from which they had started.

Upon receipt of this message the Czar, highly agitated, immediately telegraphed that his letter of the same date (December 7) had evidently crossed the other on the way and would explain everything.[54] But when that letter arrived, William II demanded that they settle the coaling affair by signing a convention concerning it at once.[55] Thus, Germany herself destroyed the possibility of continuing the previous negotiations and of concluding, perhaps, a defensive alliance with Russia alone. The Czar could only acquiesce.[56] On December 12 Count Lamsdorff gave written assurance to the German government that Russia would make common cause with it in case the coaling led to war.[57]

[52] Bülow to William II, Dec. 6, 1904, *ibid.*, 263 ff., No. 6088.

[53] Bülow to Alvensleben, Dec. 6, 1904, *ibid.*, 320 f., No. 6129; William II to Nicholas II, Dec. 7, 1904, *ibid.*, 322, No. 6130.

[54] Savinsky, *Revue des deux mondes*, XII (1922), 794 f.; Savinsky, p. 107.

[55] William II to Nicholas II, undated, *G.P.*, XIX, 325, No. 6132.

[56] Nicholas II to William II, Dec. 11, 1904, *ibid.*, 325 f., No. 6134.

[57] On December 11 Lamsdorff stated to Alvensleben that as soon as the Czar had made a decision he would be ready to agree with Germany on the "modality of co-operation" in case of a conflict. On the next day in his note to that government he did not mention this matter, and as Germany seemed satisfied, he never returned to it. See Alvensleben to F. O., Dec. 11 and 12, 1904, *ibid.*, 325 ff., Nos. 6134 ff.; Lamsdorff to Alvensleben, Dec. 13, 1904, *ibid.*, 329, No. 6137; Savinsky, p. 108.

The promptness with which the Russian government agreed to the German demand showed how essential to Russia was the continued coaling of her fleet, which within about a week would reach Madagascar. Count Lamsdorff felt entirely safe in making the assurance of support, for, as he frankly said to the German Ambassador, he did not believe that either Great Britain or Japan would let things come to war.[58] Also he particularly wished to avoid antagonizing Germany while she was permitting a Russian loan of 231,000,000 rubles to be made in Berlin.[59] The Minister was elated over the turn which the Russo-German negotiations had taken. By changing the basis of discussion from that of a defensive alliance to that of a specific agreement limited to a definite eventuality, the German government had adopted his own policy of close friendship and co-operation without an alliance. His battle with both Germany and the Czar was won by the German government itself.

On riper thought the German foreign office perceived that this Russian promise did not cover all cases in which war might arise as a result of German friendliness. It had no doubt had time since the arrival of the Czar's letter of December 7 in which to appreciate its mistake in hastily changing the basis of negotiation. Hence on December 12 it instructed Count Alvensleben to propose to the Russian government a general defensive agreement. By its terms Russia would be bound to aid Germany in case of a conflict arising: first, because of any German act of "benevolent neutrality" in favor of Russia during the current war; or, second, because of the coaling affair during and after the war. The Ambassador was to declare that if Russia did not accept this agreement the coaling would be discontinued.[60] What

---

[58] Alvensleben, to F. O., Dec. 11, 1904, *G.P.*, XIX, 325 f., No. 6134.

[59] M. A. de Wolfe Howe, *George von Lengerke Meyer: His Life and Public Services* (New York, 1920), pp. 121 f.; Schulthess *(Europäischer Geschichtskalender 1905)*, p. 255.

[60] Bülow to Alvensleben, Dec. 12, 1904, *G.P.*, XIX, 326 f., No. 6135; Bülow to Alvensleben, Dec. 21, 1904, *ibid.*, 342 f. Nos. 6142 f.

was here proposed amounted practically to Articles I and III of the first German treaty draft with the parts pertaining to France omitted, and was in keeping with the Czar's letter of December 7.

Since the instructions arrived after Count Lamsdorff had accepted the earlier German demand, the exasperated Ambassador consulted his government before executing them.[61] Count Bülow then realized that the Russian Minister would not receive the proposal favorably and that the German government would seem not to know its own desires if it persisted in this new demand. Furthermore, on December 18, he was assured by Count Metternich that, although a Dogger Bank affair between Great Britain and Germany or the passage by Germany of a stronger naval law might precipitate a crisis, the British did not seek a war and had no intention of starting one.[62] Hence the Chancellor can-

---

[61] Editor's note giving a summary of a dispatch from Alvensleben on Dec. 13, 1904, *ibid.*, p. 342.

[62] On Dec. 13 Metternich was called to Berlin for consultation as to the effect which a Russo-German agreement of any sort would have on Anglo-German relations. Schulenburg and Eulenburg, of the German embassy in London, also were asked about the attitude of the British toward Germany. They all believed that the British would not tolerate as much from Germany as they would from Russia. See memo. by Bülow, Dec. 16, 1904, *ibid.*, 331 f., No. 6139, and editor's note; memo. by Metternich, Dec. 18, 1904, *ibid.*, 332 ff., No. 6140; Schulenburg to Bülow, Dec. 14, 1904, *ibid.*, 359 ff., No. 6154; memo. by Eulenburg, Dec. 15, 1904, *ibid.*, 366 f., No. 6155; Alfred von Tirpitz, *Politische Dokumente*, Band I; *Der Aufbau der deutschen Weltmacht* (Stuttgart and Berlin, 1924), pp. 13 f. A few days later Lascelles tried to argue with both Bülow and Holstein that the British fear of the German navy was more reasonable than the German fear of the British navy. And on Dec. 26 Holstein declared to Lascelles as follows: "In the present instance a situation had been created by the action of the Press which was fraught with the gravest of all dangers, viz.: that of two great nations being involved in war, for if any untoward incident had arisen which gave rise to an acrimonious discussion between the two Governments it would have been almost impossible to have settled it owing to the atmosphere which the Press campaign had created." Nevertheless both parties agreed that Anglo-German relations had become easier. See Lascelles to Lansdowne, Dec. 28, 1904, *B.D.*, III, 56 ff., No. 65. At about the same time King Edward, Lansdowne, and Balfour all branded the German fears of a British attack as foolish; and the British condemned them as hypocritical. But the press war continued into January

celed the instructions. Instead, he notified the Russian Minister, December 26, that "within the limits which care for our own safety prescribes, we shall be glad to aid Russia as previously."[63] The coaling was continued without mishap.[64]

On December 21 William II repeated to the Czar his refusal to permit the consultation of France about the project of alliance, hoping thereby to reopen the discussion.[65] But Nicholas II, in his reply of December 25, did not mention the matter.[66]

Just at this moment of profound disappointment to the German government another outlet seemed to open up. On December 26 it learned that the Japanese government was thinking of sending Viscount Aoki to Berlin in the next year in order to establish closer contact with it on the questions to be considered in the Russo-Japanese negotiations for peace.[67] The German government reacted cordially to this project. The Emperor William, still unable to comprehend the failure of the Russian negotiations, had visions of Germany's so mediating peace between Russia and Japan as to form an agreement *à trois* with them.[68] Apparently without consulting the foreign office he appealed to the Czar on January 2 "as your faithful friend" for a statement of his plans for the future, "so that if possible, I make myself

as bitterly as before. See Bülow to William II, Dec. 26, 1904, *G.P.*, XIX, 372 f., No. 6157; and following documents. See also Schulthess (1905), p. 3; Newton, *Lord Lansdowne*, pp. 331 f.; Friedrich Thimme, "Auswärtige Politik und Hochfinanz: Aus den Papieren Paul H. von Schwabach's," *Europäische Gespräche*, June, 1929, p. 307.

[63] Bülow to Alvensleben, Dec. 21, 1904, *G.P.*, XIX, 342 f., Nos. 6142 f.; Alvensleben to Bülow, Dec. 26, 1904, *ibid.*, 343 ff., No. 6144.

[64] Mühlberg to Tirpitz, Jan. 27, 1905, *ibid.*, 265 ff., No. 6089, and following documents.

[65] William II to Nicholas II, Dec. 21, 1904, *ibid.*, 340 f., No. 6141; also Goetz, p. 354. The letter was written by the foreign office.

[66] Nicholas II to William II, Dec. 25, 1904, *G.P.*, XIX, 346, No. 6145.

[67] Memo. by Eckert, Nov. 18, 1904, Received Dec. 26, 1904, *ibid.*, 395 ff., No. 6176.

[68] Bülow to William II, Dec. 26, 1904, *ibid.*, 400 ff., No. 6178.

useful to you and be enabled to shape the course of my policy."[69] As Nicholas II ignored this request—the third rebuff from Russia within two months—the Emperor wanted to cultivate Japan so zealously that Count Bülow had to hold him back for fear of antagonizing Russia.[70] The German government, particularly Herr von Holstein, continued to apprehend that France and Great Britain would endeavor to mediate peace and form a new quadruple grouping with Russia and Japan by partitioning China.[71] To obviate that possibility it had attempted during the past months to draw closer to President Roosevelt[72] and to keep check upon the Russian views about peace. But since Russia had rebuffed this endeavor[73] as well as an alliance, Count Bülow turned late in December, 1904, to Japan and the United States in order to escape from "the sulking-corner in which not only England but also Russia is seeking to hold us."[74] In January, 1905, the German government intensified its campaign to arouse President Roosevelt's mistrust of Great Britain and France. Articles in the semiofficial press in Paris, assertions by M. Doumer, president of the French Chamber and intimate friend of M. Delcassé, and discreet soundings by French, British, and Russian diplomats gave

[69] William II to Nicholas II, Jan. 2, 1905, *ibid.*, 404 f., No. 6180.

[70] William II to Bülow, March 11, 1905, *ibid.*, 411, No. 6187; Bülow to William II, March 11, 1905, *ibid.*, 412, No. 6188. On Jan. 16, 1905, the Emperor wrote: "The action of Delcassé and Lamsdorff is unspeakably treacherous and common. This trio [France, Great Britain, and Russia, who he thought desired to divide China] must be opposed by a German-American-Japanese league. That must be done quickly and energetically. Above all America's mistrust of France and Russia be nourished" (Emperor's minute to the dispatch from Bülow to William II, Jan. 15, 1905, *ibid.*, 562, No. 6280).

[71] Memo. by Holstein, Dec. 29, 1904, *ibid.*, 551 ff., No. 6275. The Emperor also suffered from the "nightmare of the coalitions," but his suffering assumed more varied forms. At one moment he feared a Franco-Anglo-American-Japanese grouping; at another, an Anglo-Franco-Russian grouping; at another, an Anglo-Franco-Russo-Japanese grouping (see *ibid.*, Nos. 5925, 5945, 6187, 6280).

[72] See *ibid.*, chap. cxxxix.

[73] Romberg to Bülow, Dec. 1, 1904, *ibid.*, 394 f., No. 6175.

[74] Bülow to William II, Dec. 26, 1904, *ibid.*, 402 f., No. 6178.

body to the German fears. Count Bülow emphasized to the President the menace of this new quadruple alliance to both the United States and Germany. At the Count's suggestion in January Mr. Roosevelt obtained from the Powers an assurance of the territorial integrity of China during the negotiations for peace.[75] This move brought the German government and Mr. Roosevelt into greater intimacy. The latter suspected France and Russia, but not Great Britain.[76] He refused to believe rumors of a Russo-German agreement, and credited the German denials of those reports.[77] With Japan, however, the German government was not so successful; hearing those same rumors, the Japanese government decided in February not to send Viscount Aoki to Berlin.[78]

In the same month the German government tried once more to make an agreement with Russia, this time over Austria-Hungary. Torn by national conflicts, that empire was not expected to survive the death of the aged Emperor Francis Joseph. Count Bülow therefore proposed to the Russian Foreign Minister that they sign a public treaty of territorial disinterestedness in case of the disruption of the Hapsburg Empire. While Count Lamsdorff agreed to make the accord, he stipulated that it be kept secret, and left its formulation to the proposer. Thereupon the German foreign office, fearing that the existence of a secret Russo-German treaty might become known and might make Japan and the United States mistrustful of Germany and doubting whether the Russian Minister would really conclude the accord, decided to drop the project.[79]

Thus the negotiations between Germany and Russia worked

[75] See Dennett, pp. 77 ff., 162, 171 f.; Dennis, pp. 392 f., 397; Bülow to William II, Dec. 24, 1904, *G.P.*, XIX, 547 ff., No. 6274, and following documents.

[76] See, among others, Sternburg to F. O., Feb. 3 and 9, 1905, *G.P.*, XIX, 567 f., No. 6285; 570, No. 6287.

[77] Dennett, pp. 73 ff., 50; Dennis, pp. 367 f., 385 ff. The anonymous document which Dennis quotes must have been written some time early in 1905, for it refers to events which occurred in January, 1905.

[78] Arco to F. O., Feb. 10, 1905, *G.P.*, XIX, 407, No. 6183; Arco to Bülow, March 16, 1905, *ibid.*, 413 ff. No. 6190.

[79] *Ibid.*, Vol. XXII, chap. clix.

only to the detriment of Germany's international relations. They were in large part responsible for the acuteness of British anger at Germany and for the collapse of the proposed Aoki mission. And had it not been for President Roosevelt's ignorance of Continental affairs, they would no doubt have turned him against Germany. Although protestations of friendship were exchanged between the German and Russian rulers and governments, the German Emperor and his government were greatly chagrined at their failure.[80] They had found the bonds of the Dual Alliance tighter than they had expected, and had suffered a rebuff by a Power in the very worst straits. Believing that another opportunity to solve Germany's international problems in this way would likely not be offered, the German foreign office next attempted the employment of force.

[80] Alvensleben to Bülow, Dec. 26, 1904, *ibid.*, XIX, 343 f., No. 6144; William II to Bülow, Dec. 28, 1904, *ibid.*, 346 f. No. 6146; Bülow to Alvensleben, Jan. 1, 1905, *ibid.*, 347 f., No. 6147; Bülow to William II, Dec. 26, 1904, *ibid.*, 400 ff., No. 6178.

CHAPTER XI

THE VISIT TO TANGIER

Upon the refusal of an alliance by Russia, the German government, in the early part of 1905, regarded its international situation and loss of prestige with concern. The continued defeats of Russia by Japan in the Far East, culminating in that at Mukden, February 23 to March 10, and the outbreak of revolution in Russia had for the time neutralized the effectiveness of the Dual Alliance. But the Anglo-German animosity persisted. On February 2 at Eastleigh, Mr. Arthur Lee, first civil lord of the British admiralty, frankly explained the redistribution of the fleet as follows:[1]

> The balance and center of naval power in Europe had been shifted during the last few years. They [Great Britain] had not so much to keep their eyes upon France and the Mediterranean as they had to look with more anxiety, though not fear, towards the North Sea. It was for that reason that the Fleets had been distributed to enable them to deal with any danger in that direction. . . . . If war should unhappily be declared, under existing conditions the British Navy would get its blow in first, before the other side had time even to read the papers that war had been declared.

The German Emperor regarded those assertions as an "open threat of war" by that "vengeance-breathing corsair."[2] An Anglo-German press war ensued. Count Bülow declared to Admiral Tirpitz that he would agree to any sum for the German naval law for 1906.[3]

The state of the Triple Alliance also worried the German foreign office; Austria-Hungary was in internal turmoil, Italy more unreliable than ever. Irredentist troubles, which had flamed up

---

[1] Reported in the *London Times*, Feb. 4, 1905. When Lee saw how the German press took offense at his words, he published a "correct version" of these passages in a somewhat milder form (*ibid.*, Feb. 7, 1905; *Annual Register, 1905*, pp. 21 f.).

[2] Von Tirpitz, *Politische Dokumente*, I, 14.   [3] *Ibid.*, pp. 17 ff.

again in the previous November,[4] and Balkan rivalries had so antagonized those two allies that during 1904 the main military force of Italy had been transferred from the French to the Austrian frontier. During the winter, reports of a Franco-Italian agreement nullifying the Triple Alliance and of the activity of Ambassador Barrère in attempting to foment difficulty between Austria and Italy came to the German government.[5] But when, toward the end of February, 1905, Count Bülow mentioned these rumors to the Italian Ambassador, King Victor Emmanuel and his government both formally denied that Italy had made any agreement "that is in contradiction with the Triple Alliance or that may diminish the value of our obligations toward our allies," and asserted that M. Prinetti's declarations to France did not "vary, modify, or attenuate the bearing or obligations that result from it [the Triple Alliance] for us."[6]

Although the Chancellor did not believe these asseverations, he continued to hold to Italy. As he wrote to the Emperor on March 5 and 9:

For times of peace and for all international combinations it is to our interest to maintain the façade of the Triple Alliance as intact as possible, if only because the Italians, so long as they remain in it, will meet with mistrust from hostile sides. In case of complications, however, we need have no illusions concerning active Italian co-operation. Still, it is an advantage if Italy remains neutral instead of siding with France. . . . . The general international situation is so tense that we must endeavor to sacrifice as few tricks as possible.

[4] Monts to Bülow, Nov. 19, 1904, *G.P.*, XX, 85 ff., No. 6423.

[5] Monts to Bülow, Dec. 18, 1904, *ibid.*, 88 f. No. 6424; report of Military Attaché Chelius to Schlieffen, Dec. 18, 1904, *ibid.*, 89 ff., No. 6424 Anlage; Metternich to Bülow, Jan. 12, 1905, *ibid.*, 93, No. 6425. The relation of Italy to France and Germany was well shown in the following incident. Shortly after Loubet's visit to Rome, an Italian officer was caught delivering to the French important documents dealing with the Italian plan of mobilization. At about the same time the Italian chief of staff gave to the German government photographs of the French border fortifications (*ibid.*, Nos. 6423–24, 6426).

[6] Bülow to Monts, Feb. 21, 1905, *ibid.*, 93 f., No. 6426; Monts to F. O., Feb. 25, 1905, *ibid.*, 94 f., No. 6427; Bülow to William II, March 5, 1905, *ibid.*, 95, No. 6428 and Anlage.

Therein was expressed the German policy toward Italy until the latter's final entry into the World War. Upon reading this confession, the Emperor, who already feared that King Edward VII was trying to establish a Franco-Russo-British alliance, summed up the international position of his country as follows: "The Triple Alliance loosened by the antagonism of Austria and Italy, Russia unchanged or indifferent toward us, England hostile, France revengeful." As to Italy, he wrote severely to the Chancellor: "Your Excellency is easily satisfied. My grandfather and I looked upon the co-operation of the Italian army as a matter of course. In case of a French attack on us that must be adhered to."[7]

The diminution in Germany's prestige was felt most acutely in her relationship to France, whose Foreign Minister showed by the dispatch of the French mission to Fez in January that he intended to establish French control over Morocco without consulting Germany. Hence, after the failure of the move toward Russia, the German government began, in December, to turn its attention to the Moroccan question. Conveniently disregarding its unsettled grievances against the Sultan, it responded to certain overtures for a *rapprochement* from that monarch by quietly and unofficially encouraging him to resist the French demands.[8]

This action could the more easily be taken since the Sultan had already begun to oppose the French by convoking an assembly of Moroccan notables to consider the French proposals for reform. The Sultan selected two men from each town, who were moderate conservatives, more or less amenable to his influence,

[7] Bülow to William II, March 5 and 9, 1905, *ibid.*, 95 ff., Nos. 6428 f., and the Emperor's minutes.

[8] The German representatives in Morocco unofficially assured the Sultan early in February that Germany had a political interest in the Moroccan question, that Germany as well as several other Powers had not yet taken the question in its existing form into consideration, that Germany would not actively support Morocco, but that, with a silent Germany on her frontier, France would not attack the latter (see *ibid.*, Nos. 6538–40, 6544–47, 6550, 6553).

hostile to French control but not in principle opposed to foreigners or to reforms.[9] Count Bülow, much pleased, advised the Sultan about the middle of February to unite with the rebel, Bou-Amama [sic], and to threaten a holy war in case France tried to prevent the meeting of the assembly.[10] Early in February a German warship appeared casually in Moroccan waters. A few days later Herr von Holstein instructed Herr von Kühlmann, first secretary of the German legation in Tangier, to avoid official utterances toward France "until we are more certain about the attitude of the Sultan"; for "according as the Sultan shows himself firm or yielding, German policy will endeavor as much as possible to strengthen his back or will confine itself to defending German economic interests."[11]

The Moroccan government lived up to the German hopes by convening the assembly of notables on February 22 and by requiring M. Saint-René Taillandier to explain the French program to it. To stiffen the Moroccan resistance against France, Herr von Kühlmann suggested that the German government send a note to the Sultan manifesting its disapproval of the French policy.[12] Before following that suggestion, however, the German government endeavored to interest President Roosevelt in the Moroccan question.

As Mr. Roosevelt and the German government were co-operating so cordially for the preservation of the open door in China, Count Bülow sought to extend this effort to Morocco and to involve the United States against France and Great Britain, or at least to prepare the President for isolated German action on the Moroccan question. On February 25, after calling Mr. Roosevelt's attention to the Franco-Spanish monopolistic plans, the Chancellor invited him to unite with Germany in advising the

---

[9] Kühlmann to Bülow, Jan. 29, 1905, *ibid.*, 248, No. 6552.

[10] Bülow to Kühlmann, Feb. 11, 1905, *ibid.*, 251 ff., No. 6554.

[11] Bülow to Kühlmann, Feb. 16, 1905, *ibid.*, 255, No. 6556. The dispatch was written by Holstein.

[12] Kühlmann to Bülow, Feb. 21, 1905, *ibid.*, 255 f., No. 6557.

Sultan that the calling of the assembly was a correct move toward fortifying his government and inaugurating reforms. This action, argued the Chancellor, would stop the French advance and make possible a peaceful solution of the Moroccan question. Even if the United States did not participate, he continued, France would scarcely risk a Moroccan war with a silent Germany on her frontier.[13]

Although not interested in Morocco, the President agreed to instruct the American representative in Tangier to keep in close touch with his German colleague.[14] The answer satisfied the German government, which now felt assured of Mr. Roosevelt's moral support in case Germany took action alone. On March 10 the note was sent.

Through this note and the supplementary statements of the German representatives in Morocco the German government informed the Sultan that, although he must reorganize his country, Germany

hopes that the rumors of a prospective change in the existing conditions in Morocco—equal rights and freedom for all nations—are unfounded. Germany would disapprove of such a change. Germany and the United States are favorably inclined toward the maintenance of the present conditions; . . . . the attitude of the other Powers is not definitely known. In England the Government has bound itself to a certain extent in favor of France, even though in the English commercial world a current in favor of the maintenance of the independence of Morocco and in favor of equal rights of the Powers is present.[15]

Germany here showed her strong disapproval of the whole French action and sought to augment Moroccan resistance without committing herself to any definite policy.

Immediately after the dispatch of the note the German govern-

---

[13] Bülow to Kühlmann, Jan. 16, 1905, *ibid.*, 245, No. 6547; Bülow to Sternburg, Feb. 25, 1905, *ibid.*, 256 ff., No. 6558.

[14] Sternburg to F. O., March 9, 1905, *ibid.*, 258 f., No. 6559; Dennett, *Roosevelt and the Russo-Japanese War*, pp. 83 f.

[15] Only a summary of the note is given in *G.P.*, XX, 260 n. The quotations are taken from this summary and from a telegram from Bülow to Kühlmann, March 10, 1905, *ibid.*, 260 f., No. 6561.

ment heard that at the opening session of the assembly of notables on February 22 M. Saint-René Taillandier had claimed to
have "the assent of other foreign representatives at Tangier" to
the French program of reform.[16] Considering this a deliberate
misrepresentation for the purpose of overawing the Moroccans,
the German government sought further means for blocking
French efforts. The Chancellor intimated in the Reichstag on
March 15 that Germany intended taking steps to defend her economic interests in Morocco.[17] Five days later the newspapers
announced the forthcoming visit of the German Emperor to Tangier.[18]

When Count Bülow saw the strong opposition which this proposed visit aroused in the French and English press, he immedi-

[16] Report from Vassel, German vice-consul at Fez, Feb. 23, 1905. According
to a second report from him, March 7, the French Minister had claimed to have
"the approval of his proposals by the foreigners" (ibid., pp. 255 f. n.; Auswärtiger
Amt, Aktenstücke über Marokko, 1905 [Berlin, 1905], No. 3). The latest communication received by the German government from Vassel, before the dispatch
of the note of March 10, was of Feb. 17. See Kühlmann to Bülow, Feb. 21, 1905,
G.P., XX, 255, No. 6557; Bülow to Kühlmann, March 10, 1905, ibid., 260, No.
6561.

[17] The Chancellor declared as follows: "I understand entirely the attention
which is given here to the events in and about Morocco. I regard it as a duty of
the German Government to see that . . . . our economic interests in Morocco
are not injured. But the present moment is unsuitable for further explanations"
(Bülow, Reden, II, 186 f.). As a matter of fact, German economic interests ran
a very poor third behind those of France and Great Britain (Zeitschrift für Kolonialpolitik, Dec., 1904, pp. 885 ff.).

[18] The information was given out to the London Standard, London Times, and
the Kölnische Zeitung, at Tangier on March 19. The origin of the visit is obscure.
Theodor Wolff relates that Kühlmann and Hornung, correspondent in Tangier of
the Kölnische Zeitung, were responsible for proposing in February that the Emperor include Tangier in his itinerary (Wolff, Das Vorspiel, p. 156). The plan for
the Emperor's voyage in the Mediterranean submitted to the Chancellor on March
13 included a stay of four hours in Tangier (editor's note, G.P., XX, 263). Probably Bülow aimed to use this visit politically from the start, just as he had intended using the dispatch of a warship to Tangier in the previous year. But only
after he saw the effect of the announcement upon public opinion did he realize
the full political significance of the visit (cf. ibid., pp. 262 ff.). Crozier's story of
the origin of this voyage is unsubstantiated by any evidence (Revue de France,
April 1, 1921, pp. 279 f.).

ately determined to put it to a political use.[19] He wrote to the Emperor: "Your Majesty's visit to Tangier will embarrass M. Delcassé, thwart his plans, and be of benefit to our economic interests in Morocco." For, he wrote a few days later,

apart from the fact that the systematic exclusion of all non-French merchants and promoters from Morocco according to the example in Tunis would signify an important economic loss for Germany, it is also a want of appreciation of our power when M. Delcassé has not considered it worth the effort to negotiate with Germany over his Moroccan plans. M. Delcassé has completely ignored us in this affair.[20]

[19] Editor's note, *G.P.*, XX, 263 f.; Bülow to William II, March 20, 1905, *ibid.*, 262, No. 6563; 264 f., No. 6565.

[20] Bülow to William II, March 20, 1905, *ibid.*, 263, No. 6563; Bülow to William II, March 26, 1905, *ibid.*, 274 f., No. 6576. It was reported in the German foreign office soon after the Anglo-French accord was made that Delcassé had said to some intimate friends: "Je viens de rouler Radolin; il ne me reste plus qu'à rouler l'empereur d'Allemagne" (Guibert et Ferrette, *Le conflit franco-allemand en 1905* [Paris, 1905], p. 83, quoted in Stuart, *French Foreign Policy from Fashoda to Serajevo*, p. 136 n.). On Feb. 21, 1907, Lord Sanderson, permanent undersecretary of state for foreign affairs, 1894–1906, wrote as follows: "M. Delcassé . . . . ignored Germany entirely when he commenced operations in Morocco. The action of France and her demands on the Sultan were undoubtedly much exaggerated and misrepresented. But in addition there is no doubt that M. Delcassé was steadily pursuing a series of manœuvres for the purpose of isolating Germany and weakening her alliances. The German Gov[ernmen]t and the German nation are extremely sensitive about being ignored or neglected in the discussion of important questions, and it is not surprising that on this occasion they should have been much exasperated, and determined on inflicting on France a severe humiliation. That they also wished to separate us from France, to prevent the Agreement from developing into an alliance, and to obtain any share they could in the eventual development of Morocco is no doubt also true. The methods adopted were characteristic of German policy, and as on some other occasions they failed" (memo. by Lord Sanderson, Feb. 21, 1907, *B.D.*, IV, 421). Whether the German government knew the exact terms of the Franco-Spanish agreement is a question. Tardieu says that it did know them (*La conf. d'Algés*, p. 156). Hammann has written, "One may assume that it learned the main content" (*Zur Vorgeschichte des Weltkrieges*, p. 200). It also suspected that the Moroccan accords contained stipulations for the exclusion of Germany from any participation in the territorial division of Morocco (*ibid.*, p. 201). See also the dispatch from Stumm to Bülow, Feb. 20, 1906, *G.P.*, XXI, 191, No. 7024, and the Emperor's minute thereto: "And the rascals [the Spanish government] will not even admit what sort of a pact they have made with the devil [France]." See also Veit Valentin, *Deutschlands Aussenpolitik von Bismarcks Abgang bis zum Ende des Welkkrieges* (Berlin, 1921), p. 54; report

William II was lukewarm about the project. He had persistently opposed interfering in the Moroccan question both for reasons of general policy and for lack of interest in Morocco itself. At the insistence of the Chancellor he agreed to execute the *coup;* but Count Bülow had to employ every means to hold him steady. When the Emperor learned from the papers that the natives and the German and British colonies in Morocco intended to exploit his visit against the French, he wrote to the Chancellor on March 20 as follows: "Telegraph immediately to Tangier that it is *highly* doubtful whether I shall land and that I shall only travel incog[nito] as a tourist, that is, no audiences, no receptions."[21] Count Bülow overcame his objections by arguing that otherwise M. Delcassé would spread the rumor that the program of reception for the Emperor had been curtailed after remonstrances had been made in Berlin.[22]

Aside from the communication with President Roosevelt, the German government made no diplomatic preparation for this action.[23] Direct contact with the French government was cut off as

---

from Madrid, Dec. 10, 1904, *Zur europ. Politik,* I, 126 f. However, the German government did know the terms of the Franco-Spanish agreement of Sept. 1, 1905, so Ojeda of the Spanish foreign office admitted to Cartwright of the British embassy (Cartwright to Grey, Jan. 22, 1906, *B.D.,* III, 233, No. 252. The probability is therefore that it also learned in good time the terms of the other secret accords. Failure to mention that knowledge or even denials of being informed in the documents is not conclusive proof that the secret articles were not known to the German foreign office.

[21] William II to Bülow, undated, *G.P.,* XX, 263, No. 6564. The editors of *G.P.* presume the date of this communication to have been March 21; but Bülow's reply to it was dated March 20. See Bülow to William II, March 20, 1905, *ibid.,* 264, No. 6565. The Emperor had dined at the French embassy on March 17 and had said nothing about his proposed visit. Furthermore, just before leaving on his trip he made at Bremen one of his half-militaristic, half-pacific speeches which did not indicate what was to follow (Schulthess, *Europäischer Geschichtskalender 1905,* pp. 67 f.; Ludwig, *Wilhelm der Zweite,* p. 275; Mévil, *De la Paix de Francfort, etc.,* pp. 193 ff.).

[22] Bülow to William II, March 20, 1905, *G.P.,* XX, 264 f., No. 6565.

[23] The unexpectedness of this action was shown by the remarks made on March 21 by Bernstorff, first secretary of the embassy in London, to a reporter of the

early as March 22.[24] Two days later the Chancellor issued general orders to play the sphinx on the subject of Morocco.[25] A Franco-German press war alone revealed the tension of the situation.[26]

With the performance ready to start, the chief actor began to suffer from stage fright. Learning of an attempt at Tangier a day or so before to assassinate Mr. Harris of the *London Times*, the Emperor telegraphed Count Bülow from Lisbon on March 28 as follows: "In Tangier the devil is already loose. Yesterday an Englishman almost murdered. I consider the affair there as very doubtful."[27] Furthermore, he learned that at Tangier he would have to disembark in an open boat, and that after he was in the town he would have to walk through the narrow streets or be carried in a sedan or ride some unknown Berber horse. The first two ways were decidedly beneath imperial dignity, while the last one, on account of the Emperor's crippled left arm, might be too dangerous. Not only the anxious sovereign, but members of his company as well, were inclined to advise against the attempt. But Count Tattenbach, former minister at Tangier and at the time minister at Lisbon, whom the Emperor had brought along from Portugal, and Prince Eulenburg clung to the plan and kept up their master's courage,[28] while from Berlin the Chancellor sent

---

Daily Chronicle. He asserted that Germany had only economic interests in Morocco over which it ought not to be difficult for France and Germany to agree (Bülow to Metternich, March 22, 1905, *G.P.*, XX, 268 f., and note, No. 6569).

[24] Bülow to Radolin, March 22, 1905, *ibid.*, 267 f., No. 6568; Flotow to F. O., March 23, 1905, *ibid.*, 269, No. 6570; Flotow to F. O., March 28, 1905, *ibid.*, 278, No. 6578; Bülow to Flotow, March 28, 1905, *ibid.*, 278, No. 6579; Mévil, pp. 197 f.

[25] Memo. by Bülow, March 24, 1905, *G.P.*, 271, No. 6573.

[26] Mévil, p. 205; *G.P.*, XX, 262 f., n. 266 n., Nos. 6570, 6584, 6590; *Quest. dipl. et. col.*, XIX, 442 ff.; Schulthess, *1905*, pp. 78 f.

[27] William II to Bülow, March 28, 1905, *G.P.*, XX, 279, No. 6580.

[28] Tattenbach to F. O., March 29, 1905, *ibid.*, 283, No. 6585; Freiherr von Schoen, *Erlebtes. Beiträge zur politischen Geschichte der neuesten Zeit* (Stuttgart and Berlin, 1921), pp. 19 ff.

one telegram after the other to effect the visit. To the Emperor he telegraphed that it would be a "historic act," that the attention of the world was focused on him, that "if the visit . . . . turns out as desired, Delcassé with his anti-German policy will stand there as a disgraced European," and that the French Foreign Minister would probably then be overthrown by his enemies in France. He agreed with Count Tattenbach that since press and people were discussing the matter so fully the Emperor could not recede without exposing himself to the accusation of cowardice. He likewise sent a telegram of four pages to the Emperor on March 26 with instructions about his speeches at Tangier. It read in part as follows:

Naturally it is not to German interest for the Sultan to be discouraged now at the beginning of the French negotiations and to place himself under a French protectorate. To oppose this . . . . Your Majesty should receive the Sultan's representative expressly as a representative of a sovereign, and should . . . . express the hope that he [the Sultan] would soon suppress the rebellion of Bou-Amama. . . . . Your Majesty might ask where the rebel Bou-Amama obtains the means for his long resistance. If the representative should reply, "Probably from France," Your Majesty might answer, "It is difficult to believe the French capable of such baseness."

. . . . Without saying an unfriendly word about France, Your Majesty should ignore her in Morocco, should not mention at all the French advance against Morocco, and should honor the French chargé d'affaires with . . . . only a silent greeting.

It is improbable that any diplomat will mention France's Moroccan policy to Your Majesty. If that subject should be brought up, Your Majesty might reply that the French policy is entirely unknown to you. The case is different, however, if the Sultan's representative at his master's command . . . . asks Your Majesty's advice. On the reply will depend whether the Sultan will continue to defend the independence of Morocco or will submit to France. The question whether Your Majesty can risk a war with France for the sake of Morocco cannot be considered at all. But on the other hand it is more than doubtful whether the present civil Government of France . . . . would risk a war with Morocco so long as the least possibility exists that Germany might sooner or later interfere. Therefore we must for the present leave our goal uncertain. We cannot conveniently make an alliance with the Sultan. But if we withdraw our moral support entirely from him and destroy all hope, we shall relinquish important German interests. Therefore I conceive Your Majesty's reply to the Sultan's minister somewhat as follows: "It is known that I desire no Morocco territory, but that I value equality of treatment with other nations in trade and commerce with Morocco. Other commercial nations have the same interest. As my view is known, the English colony greeted me joyfully today. It is to the interest of the Sultan as well as of almost all seafaring and commercial peoples that he preserve his independence and therewith freedom to permit them all equal rights in his empire. The main strength of every ruler lies in having his people back of him at decisive moments. In that case no foreign Power will attack him lightly. Therefore the Sultan should make certain that the notables whom he has summoned to Fez for advice are of one mind with him and should direct his policy in accordance therewith."

Since it is well known that the Moorish delegates at present assembled at Fez are entirely hostile to the Sultan's conciliation toward France, definite advice would herewith be imparted to the Sultan. If the representative should ask whether Your Majesty would support the Sultan in a war against France, Your Majesty might reply: "In case I promised today to support you, you would attack the French at once. But I desire, if possible, to maintain peace, although I have a very strong army. Therefore I must reserve decision until it really comes to war between France and Morocco. I do not expect this event. France will try to see how far she can advance with threats. But France knows that her situation would be dangerous if she attacked Morocco without having assured herself of Germany's neutrality."

Next in importance to the conversation with the Sultan's representative is Your Majesty's reply to a probable short English greeting. . . . . There Your Majesty might well stress the common interest in equality for all nations. By emphasizing this principle at that place Your Majesty will make it half impossible for the English Government in later Franco-German discussions about Morocco to place itself on the French side.

Finally, in case Your Majesty has to reply to a question from a non-Moroccan source about what attitude Germany would take in case of a Franco-Moroccan war, Your Majesty might reply somewhat as follows: "Germany has no obligations which would prevent her from being guided in that case by her own interests." This reply sounds disquieting for our opponents but binds us to nothing.

Thus, Count Bülow instructed the Emperor to encourage the Moroccans in their resistance to France, to make France uneasy by his actions and words, but not to bind Germany to anything definite.

At the same time, to assure his master's safety, the Chancellor telegraphed to Herr von Kühlmann that German and Spanish secret police should be present in abundance, that the visit should perhaps be shortened, and that "a horse, guaranteed gentle, which should be exercised early in the morning for several hours by some trustworthy rider in order to quiet it, would be best and could obviate all difficulties as well as any curtailment of the program."[29] Then, to cut off any possibility of retreat, the Chancellor declared on March 29 to the Reichstag that Germany had no aggressive intentions toward Morocco, but that she did aim to defend her economic interests and the open door.

The speech and attitude of a diplomat . . . . must vary according to circumstances [he stated]. The moment suitable . . . . for the preservation of our interests I shall choose as I think best. But in this case the tendency of the German policy has not changed. Whoever seeks a *fait nouveau* will not find it in the German policy. In the same degree as it is attempted to change the international position of Morocco or to control the open door in the economic development of the land, we must also to a greater degree than before be heedful that our economic interests in Morocco remain safe. For this reason we are entering into relations with the Sultan of Morocco.[30]

When the Emperor's boat arrived at Tangier early in the morning of March 31, a stiff east wind made landing impossible.[31] Herr von Kühlmann and the captain of one of the French warships stationed in the harbor succeeded only with the greatest difficulty in coming aboard. The Emperor immediately drew the latter into conversation about the weather prospects. It looked as if the "historic act" would not occur. A few hours later, however, the wind died down, and General Scholl, a member of the Emperor's party, went ashore to make a tour of inspection. He returned with an enthusiastic report of the reception in view from

[29] See his telegrams from March 26 to March 30, 1905, *G.P.*, XX, 272 ff., Nos. 6574 ff.

[30] Bülow, II, 209 f.

[31] For a description of the visit see Schoen, pp. 19 ff.; Schoen to F. O., March 31, 1905, *G.P.*, XX, 285 ff., Nos. 6588 ff.; Tardieu, pp. 69 f.

the natives, declared the horse to be trustworthy, and said that if one did not mind getting wet, one could make the landing. So the Emperor intrusted himself to the wind and the waves, the Moroccans, and a Berber horse. The landing was made; the horse, which at first shied at the splendor of the imperial costume, was quieted; and

followed by about twenty attendants all on horseback [according to Herr von Schoen's account], the Emperor entered the town, the narrow streets of which, filled with the joyous, noisy masses, permitted only a slow advance. The flat roofs of the houses were thickly packed with Moorish, Christian, and Jewish women who hailed the Emperor in the most varied tones and scattered flowers. Finally the procession arrived at the Soko, the open place before the garden of the legation, filled with a turbulent sea of human beings who expressed their enthusiasm in deafening cries and wild shooting. The confused din was increased still more by a military band sent by the Sultan which endeavored in vain to drown out the uproar of the people. The restlessness of the horses caused me to ask the French officer, apparently leading a command, whether he could not stop the wild shooting. He replied dejectedly that he had some influence only over the handful of regular troops entrusted to his instruction but not the least over the sportively shooting, half-wild Kabyle.

However, the company reached the legation in safety where the German colony, the diplomatic corps, and the representative of the Sultan were received.

In the speeches which the excited Emperor delivered, he permitted his tongue to become looser than usual. Whereas he had previously been opposed to intervention in the Moroccan affair, he now fixed the German policy with respect to Morocco more tightly than the Chancellor had wished and exposed himself to the criticism of having taken another backward monarch under his wing. In reply to the greeting of the Sultan's representative, Abd-el-Melik, the Emperor declared that

he . . . . had great interest in the welfare and prosperity of the Moroccan Empire, that he visited the Sultan as an independent ruler, and that he hoped that under the authority of the Sultan a free Morocco would be opened to the peaceful competition of all nations without monopoly or exclusion.

The Sultan's representative read to the Emperor a message from his master in which the latter stated that

he remembered the friendship which had always existed between his predecessors and Germany and that he was filled with the wish to strengthen and extend those friendly relations in every way. In reply the Emperor William expressed his thanks for this cordial message. He shared the feelings of the Sultan [he said] and agreed with Abd-el-Melik's assertations concerning the divine power and wisdom which directs the fate of peoples. He wished sincerely for the development and welfare of the Moroccan Empire for the sake of his subjects and for that of the other European nations who traded there, as he hoped, on the basis of full equality.

The Emperor then decorated Abd-el-Melik and his three companions. Later, he said to Abd-el-Melik that

his visit to Tangier aimed to assert that German interests in Morocco would be protected and preserved. Concerning the best means to achieve this, he would enter into direct relations with the Sultan, whom he regarded as an independent ruler. The Emperor closed with the remark that prudence was necessary in the reforms which the Sultan planned and that regard should be paid to the religious feelings of the Moroccan people in order to avoid disturbing public order.[32]

[32] The foregoing is the official version of the speeches published in the German press (see *Allgemeine Zeitung* [Munich], April 4, 1905). There were various versions of the speeches since the Emperor spoke extemporaneously. Schoen on March 31 sent to the foreign office a report of William II's assertions as follows: When Count de Chérisey attempted to greet the Emperor in the name of Delcassé in such a way as to imply a French predominance in Morocco, William II replied sharply that his visit "signified that Germany demanded free trade there and full equality with other nations." When the Count admitted this, the Emperor remarked that "he would treat directly with the Sultan as a peer, as a free ruler of an independent land, that he would know how to assert his just claims and expected that these also be respected by France." Those words crushed the Count. To the Sultan's representative the Emperor spoke as follows: "He regarded the Sultan as the ruler of a free and independent Empire, subject to no foreign suzerainty. He expected for German trade and commerce the same advantages as for all other commercial nations. He would always negotiate with the Sultan directly. Reforms which the Sultan planned to introduce ought always to be executed within the limits of the customs and views of his people and without violation of the precepts of the Koran, in honest administration and strengthening of peace and order that would make the best impression outside. European customs and usages would not be taken over without further consideration. Let the Sultan therein listen carefully to the counsel of the great ones of his land" (Schoen to F. O., March 31,

After the speeches were over, the imperial party hurried back on shipboard before some accident should occur or a contrary wind arise. Count Bülow was so relieved upon learning that his master was safe on board that, as he later confided to the Emperor, he had a "nervous fit of tears."[33] The Emperor himself did not at first realize the great political significance of his act. When he met Prince Louis of Battenberg at Gibraltar on April 1, he expressed the time-honored shibboleth, that "Germany, Great Britain and the United States must make common cause and march shoulder to shoulder."[34] When he received the reports from the press several days later, he awoke from his illusions.[35] For, although the whole event smacked of a comic opera, it none the less threw down the gauntlet to M. Delcassé and French policy in Morocco[36] and ushered in a long period of crisis in international relations. The echoes which the Emperor's speeches aroused in Europe reverberated like the distant rumblings of cannon.

1905, *G.P.*, XX, 286 f., No. 6589. It was also stated in the press, although not in the official version of the speeches, that the Emperor replied to the greetings from the German colony at Tangier that that colony "could rely on the support of the German Government to prevent any obstacle in that free country [Morocco] from hindering the success of its efforts in favor of the national commerce" (Quoted in *Quest. dipl. et col.*, XIX, 504). Schoen made no mention of this assertion. Cf. Schoen, pp. 20 f.; Mévil, pp. 210 ff.; *B.D.*, III, 62 f., Nos. 71 f.; 64, No. 74; Prince Louis of Battenberg's report of a conversation with the Emperor, April 1, 1905, Newton, *Lord Lansdowne*, pp. 333 f.

[33] William II to Bülow, Aug. 11, 1905, *G.P.*, XIX, 497, No. 6237.

[34] Memo. by Prince Louis of Battenberg, April 1, 1905, Newton, p. 333.

[35] Schoen, p. 22.   [36] Mévil, p. 210.

CHAPTER XII

THE MOROCCAN CRISIS FROM THE VISIT TO TANGIER TO THE FALL OF DELCASSÉ

I

The visit to Tangier, because of its very unexpectedness, did not at first alarm the French, who refused to credit the German Emperor with hostile intentions.[1] Better-informed personages in Paris, however, interpreted the event more accurately. They were asking seriously whether war would ensue and were declaring that "no such critical moment has occurred since the Schnäbele affair." The Austrian Ambassador was reminded by the Franco-German press war of the days immediately preceding the conflict of 1870.[2]

The French government had been warned by both German and British representatives of Germany's interest in Morocco. As early as November, 1904, Herr von Kühlmann had declared to the French chargé d'affaires at Tangier that Germany had expected France to acquaint her with the new situation in Morocco created by the Anglo-French and Franco-Spanish accords, but that she had since realized that she was being "systematically excluded." "The Imperial Government is ignorant of all the accords made over Morocco and does not consider itself bound in any way on that question," he said. The French chargé d'affaires had not regarded these remarks as sufficiently significant to re-

[1] *Quest. dipl. et col.*, XIX, 516.

[2] Radolin to F. O., April 9, 1905, *G.P.*, XX, 317, No. 6612; Radolin to Bülow, April 14, 1905, *ibid.*, 330 ff., No. 6622. After having talked with President Loubet early in April, Edward VII wrote to Lansdowne as follows: "President Loubet was most amiable . . . . but I could see from his manner that he considers the German conduct at Tangier, if not a direct menace to France, at any rate a covert insult" (Lee, *King Edward VII*, II, 341). The Schnäbele affair brought France and Germany almost to war in 1887.

port until the following February. Upon direct inquiry in Berlin the French government had had them corroborated by the German foreign office.[3] On February 12, 1905, Sir Arthur Nicolson, British ambassador at Madrid, had remarked to his French colleague that "the attitude assumed by the German Government in response to the petition of their subjects in Morocco was an invitation to the French Government to initiate some discussion with a view to obtain their concurrence with the provisions of the Convention."[4] M. Delcassé had not heeded this advice. By March 22 he had become uneasy over the German policy, about which he was so uncertain.[5] He was determined, however, to maintain intact France's accords with the other Powers and her position in Morocco.[6] Ascertaining on the eve of the voyage to Tangier that Great Britain, Spain, and Italy would hold loyally to their agreements,[7] he declared in the Senate on March 31, the same day on which William II spoke at Tangier, that

nothing in our Moroccan policy, nothing in our execution of the accords of April 8 and October 3, 1904, can explain the movements of the German

[3] Kühlmann to Bülow, Nov. 9, 1904, *G.P.*, XX, 232 ff., No. 6536; Chérisey to Delcassé, Feb. 11, 1905, *L.j., 1901–5*, 196, No. 225; Delcassé to Bihourd, Feb. 14, 1905, *ibid.*, 196 f., No. 226; Bihourd to Delcassé, Feb. 15, 1905, *ibid.*, 197 f., No. 227; Lowther to Lansdowne, April 26, 1905, *B.D.*, III, 67, No. 81.

[4] Nicolson to Lansdowne, D. Feb. 12, 1905, R. March 4, 1905, *B.D.*, III, 59, No. 66.

[5] Bertie to Lansdowne, March 22, 1905, *ibid.*, 60, No. 67. For the uncertainty about the Emperor's proposed action see Lascelles to Lansdowne, March 23, 1905, *ibid.*, 61, No. 69; Nicolson to Lansdowne, March 23, 1905, *ibid.*, 62, No. 70.

[6] Delcassé stated to Bertie, June 10, that "his policy had been to be ready to make commercial concessions to Germany if she were willing to discuss with the French Government the question of Morocco, but not to yield anything politically or territorially" (Bertie to Lansdowne, June 10, 1905, *ibid.*, 78, No. 96).

[7] Mévil, *De la Paix de Francfort, etc.*, pp. 206 f., 231; Imperial Foreign Office, *Reports of the Belgian Representatives in Berlin, London, and Paris to the Minister of Foreign Affairs in Brussels, 1905–1914. European Politics during the Decade before the War as Described by the Belgian Diplomatists* (. . . ., 1915), No. 3 (hereafter cited as *Belg. Docs., 1905–1914*); *Quest. dipl. et col.*, XIX, 517; Henry Wickham Steed, *Through Thirty Years, 1892–1922: A Personal Narrative* (London, 1924), I, 229. Delcassé also made strenuous efforts during the succeeding

press. . . . . You may legitimately hope that in the western basin of the Mediterranean . . . . France will succeed, without ignoring any right, without injuring any interest, in assuring her future.[8]

The semiofficial French press threatened the formation of a new Dual Alliance between France and Great Britain supported by Italy and Spain in case Germany attempted to gain any special advantages in Morocco.[9] At the same time, M. Delcassé instructed M. Saint-René Taillandier, who since March 24 had been making substantial progress in the negotiations with the Sultan,[10] to warn that monarch against following the proposal of the German press for an international conference over the Moroccan question.[11] He also informed the Italian government, April 12, that France could not entertain such a proposal.[12]

The Emperor's move nevertheless forced M. Delcassé to open negotiations with Germany for an understanding regarding Mo-

---

weeks to mediate peace between Japan and Russia so that the latter Power could resume its obligations as France's ally. See Radolin to F. O., April 27, 1905, *G.P.*, XX, 345, No. 6635; Lansdowne to MacDonald, April 19, 1905, *B.D.*, IV, 76 f., No. 68; Dennett, *Roosevelt and the Russo-Japanese War*, pp. 176 f.

[8] *Journal officiel, Debats parlem.* (Sénat, March 31, 1905), pp. 540 f.

[9] Articles in *Temps* of April 3, and in the *Dépêche de Toulouse* of April 10. Mévil, the official apologist for Delcassé, asserts that the latter article was based on the "best" information (pp. 218 ff.).

[10] By April 13 the Sultan had expressed his general approval of the French proposals, and the details for military reorganization in six of the Moroccan towns were ready for final formulation and signature (Mévil, p. 200 n.; Vassel to Tattenbach, April 21, 1905, *G.P.*, XX, 339 ff., No. 6631; and the various dispatches from Saint-René Taillandier to Delcassé during Feb., March, April, 1905, in *L.j.*, *1901–5*, Nos. 228–31, 233, 240, 243, 248, 266.

[11] Delcassé instructed the Minister to make the following statement to the Sultan: "We cannot conceive that, changing from the way of accords which he [the Sultan] has followed for several years, he will decide to assume an attitude which will oblige us to consider strict right alone as the basis of our relation with him" (Delcassé to Saint-René Taillandier, April 9, 1905, *ibid.*, 208, No. 239).

[12] Egerton to Lansdowne, April 12, 1905, *B.D.*, III., 66, No. 78. The French government was afraid that Spain would not loyally uphold their agreement if some other Power intervened in Morocco (Nicolson to Lansdowne, Feb. 12, 1905, *ibid.*, 59, No. 66). But with M. Villa-Urrutia at the foreign office, Spain remained entirely on the French side (Nicolson to Lansdowne, April 14, 1905, *ibid.*, 66, No. 79).

rocco. From March 28 he endeavored indirectly to approach the German government.[13] On April 7 a threatened interpellation in the Chamber forced him to state publicly that France was "ready to dissipate any misunderstanding which . . . . may still exist."[14] Under pressure from the French cabinet[15] as well as from public opinion M. Delcassé, while dining at the German embassy on April 13, repeated that statement directly to Prince Radolin. He denied that M. Saint-René Taillandier had ever claimed before the Sultan to have a mandate of Europe. He excused his failure to transmit the Anglo-French agreement to the German government; and, while admitting that the conversation of March 23, 1904, had been unofficial, he declared that his intention had been to show special favor to Germany by communicating the contents of the accord to her beforehand. He had also believed, he said, that freedom of commerce for all nations had been completely safeguarded in that agreement and in the one with Spain.[16] Immediately thereafter the French government

[13] On March 22 Bihourd advised Delcassé to "establish by an exchange of notes the bearing of the Anglo-French and Franco-Spanish accords on the commercial and industrial interests of Germany," adding that "until then we shall remain under the menace, very clearly formulated by the German press, of some inopportune surprise" (Bihourd to Delcassé, March 22, 1905, *L.j., 1901–5*, 202 f., No. 232). On March 28 an article by André Tardieu, a journalist with close governmental connections, stated that the French Foreign Minister would give satisfaction to Germany if she wished it on the subject of Morocco, "provided it is a question solely of commercial interests" (Flotow to F. O., March 28, 1905, *G.P.*, XX, 282 f., No. 6584). On April 4 Billy, a press writer in the French foreign office, sounded Theodor Wolff, Paris correspondent for the *Berliner Tageblatt*, upon how the German government would receive a French overture (*ibid.*, p. 305 n.). On April 7 Hedeman, London correspondent of *Matin*, talked with Hammann to the same effect (memo. by Hammann, April 7, 1905, *ibid.*, 310 ff., Nos. 6608 f.).

[14] Quoted in *Quest. dipl et col.*, XIX, 511 f.

[15] Radolin to Bülow, April 14, 1905, *G.P.*, XX, 331, No. 6622.

[16] Radolin to F. O., April 14, 1905, *ibid.*, 328 ff., No. 6621; Radolin to Bülow, April 14, 1905, *ibid.*, 330 ff., No. 6622; Mévil, pp. 238 ff.; Delcassé to Bihourd, April 14, 1905, *L.j., 1901–5*, pp. 211 f., No. 244; Bihourd to Delcassé, April 18 and 25, 1905, *ibid.*, 214, Nos. 246 f.; memo. by Mühlberg, April 19, 1905, *G.P.*, XX, 332 f., No. 6623. Saint-René Taillandier's denial that he had ever claimed to have a mandate of Europe must be balanced against the Sultan's personal assertion that

informally asked the British government to "help to convince the Emperor that German interests were in no way threatened" in Morocco.[17]

To carry out his policy, M. Delcassé needed the loyal support of all France. That he did not have. Political jealousy because of his long tenure in office, dislike of his secretiveness, enmity between him and M. Rouvier (the premier), hostility because of his defending the Russian government in the massacre of January 22, 1905[18]—all these forces of opposition were now strengthened by the fact that the Foreign Minister had blundered and that, aroused by the fear of complications, France sought a victim whose sacrifice might dispel the danger. Quickly deserting M. Delcassé, the nation pressed him on too rapidly to take the initiative with Germany. As time passed with nothing settled, nothing known, the French grew more and more alarmed, until on April 19 the Chamber denounced the Foreign Minister for having neglected to consult Germany, and demanded information. M. Deschanel declared that the Foreign Minister should have heeded Germany's well-known imperialistic ambitions by negotiating with that Power about Morocco. "There are not lacking in England people who desire to utilize the French power against Germany," he said. "And there are not lacking in Germany people who will try to utilize the French power against England. We should not offer ourselves to that play." M. Tournade accused M. Delcassé of having hoped that if he "juggled the question with Germany" and confronted her with a *fait accompli,* she would venture no opposition. M. de Pressensé, charging him with deliberately having avoided an official notification

---

he had claimed it. The truth would seem to be that the French Minister had sought to make more out of France's international accords over Morocco than the facts justified by speaking vaguely and by not clearing up misunderstandings in the Sultan's mind (*L.j., 1901–5,* Nos. 214, 231, 238, 263; *G.P.,* XX, Nos. 6621, 6631, 6658, 6662, 6551 n.; *Aktenstücke über Marokko, 1905,* Nos. 1, 3). Cf. the report from the Belgian Minister at Paris, Dec. 19, 1905, *Zur europ. Politik,* II, 96.

[17] Lansdowne to Lascelles, April 23, 1905, *B.D.,* III, 67, No. 80.

[18] Michon, *L'alliance franco-russe 1891–1917,* pp. 117 ff.

to Germany of the Moroccan accords, asserted: "You have not followed an exact conception of the interests of France. Your policy is unworthy of a great country." M. Delafosse, sensing the reason for the German action in the Anglo-French entente rather than in Morocco, expressed the general demand that "it is necessary to ask Germany what she wishes of us." No one, however, believed that Germany would question France's special position in Morocco.

Although not a voice was raised in his behalf, M. Delcassé refused to impart any new intelligence in answer to these accusations and demands. If M. Rouvier had not come to his rescue, he would have been repudiated by all parties. In defending the Foreign Minister M. Rouvier declared that not France but Germany had altered her Moroccan policy since the previous year, attributing this change to the defeat of France's ally.[19] The initiative toward conversations with Germany, he said, had already been made. "We have closed our ear to no proposal," he avowed; "anything which is in harmony with the formula . . . . : to safeguard the honor of our country and to maintain peace, ... we are ready to consider." He made the retention of M. Delcassé a cabinet question, but he assured the Chamber that in the future he would supervise the foreign policy.[20]

Upon receiving this check, M. Delcassé would have resigned had it not been for the appeals of President Loubet and of MM.

[19] As already shown, the Russian defeat at Mukden had nothing to do with the change of Germany's policy.

[20] *Journal officiel. Debats parlem.* (Chambre, April 19, 1905), pp. 1543 ff. Cf. Bertie's estimate on April 25: "The general feeling in Paris is that the chief object which the German Emperor has had in view in his recent proceedings is to show to the French people that an understanding with England is of little value to them and that they had much better come to an agreement with Germany. To this end 'il fait la guerre à l'Angleterre sur le dos de la France' and the French Public realizing that the Emperor's wrath is against England for enabling France to carry out her Morocco policy and not against France for taking advantage of her agreement with England feel that if they keep their heads nothing really serious will come of His Majesty's ill temper which they believe is not entirely shared by the German Government and still less so by the German people" (Bertie to Lansdowne, April 25, 1905, *B.D.*, III, 75, No. 93).

Paul Cambon and Barrère, both of whom were in Paris at the time.[21] His policy of treating with Germany on an equal footing was checkmated. French public opinion had forced an almost complete surrender in the face of the German menace. It remained to be seen how far M. Rouvier could yield before French desire for peace would conflict with French national honor.

II

The Emperor's injudicious assertions at Tangier compelled the German foreign office to take some positive action in Morocco instead of leaving the initiative to the Sultan. Herr von Holstein contended that "a retreat would stand on the same level with Olmütz and cause Fashoda to be forgotten."[22] By April 2 the Chancellor decided upon the following policy:[23] first, to continue denying any territorial ambitions in Morocco; second, to demand economic equality for all nations, the open door "in the widest sense"; third, and this he considered Germany's "trump card," to advocate calling an international conference like that at Madrid in 1880 for deliberating upon the entire question of Moroccan reform.[24] Of course no separate negotiations with France would be considered.

The Chancellor and Herr von Holstein believed that the pro-

[21] Mévil, pp. 257 ff.

[22] Memo. by Holstein, April 4, 1905, *G.P.*, XX, 304, No. 6601. Olmütz signified the humiliation of Prussia by Austria in 1850; Fashoda, that of France by Great Britain in 1898.

[23] Memo. by Holstein, April 3, 1905, *ibid.*, 297 ff., No. 6597.

[24] The suggestion of a conference was first made by Kühlmann in a dispatch of March 2 (*ibid.*, p. 293 n.). On March 27 Bülow still thought it possible of execution only in case Great Britain accepted it (Bülow to Kühlmann, March 27, 1905, *ibid.*, 293 f., No. 6591). After the Emperor's visit, however, he accepted the proposal. In Feb., 1904, Lascelles had reported a conversation with Bülow in which the latter had opposed calling a conference on the Macedonian question, arguing as follows: "A Congress was excellent at the end of a war when both belligerents were more or less exhausted and desired peace, but it was a most dangerous thing at any other time, and would only accentuate more strongly any difference of opinion which might exist and thus cause greater complications, unless indeed the Great Powers should have decided beforehand exactly what was to be done, and should

posal for a conference would give Germany an unassailable position. Protected by the appearance of absolute legality and disinterestedness, they hoped to break the ententes and accords between France and the other Powers, especially Great Britain, or
at least to show that Germany could force them to submit the
results of their agreements to the consideration of a general conference.[25] They did not doubt that the proposal would be accepted and that the conference would refuse to turn Morocco
over to France. For, they argued,

in case a conference meets, we are already certain of the diplomatic support
of America in favor of the open door. . . . . Austria will not quarrel with
us over Morocco . . . . Russia is busy with herself.[26] . . . . The English
Government—between Roosevelt and those English groups which think as
the *Morning Post, Manchester Guardian,* and Lord Rosebery[27]—will not
stir. Spain is of no importance, and also has a strong party in favor of the
status quo. We shall certainly be able to hold Italy in order, if necessary by
a gentle hint that while we settle with France, Austria will perhaps settle the
irredentist question. . . . . If France refuses the conference, she will put
herself in the wrong toward all the signatory Powers[28] and thereby will give
England, Spain, and Italy a probably welcome excuse to withdraw.[29]

---

have appealed to the Congress, to give the sanction of Europe to the decisions they
had already taken" (Lascelles to Lansdowne, Feb. 26, 1904, *B.D.,* V, 72). A year
later Bülow had apparently forgotten this very accurate judgment. Or possibly he
saw no other way out, and faced the facts with his usual optimism.

[25] In a memorandum by Hammann on April 7, this statement appeared: "Naturally the result would be greater if there followed from a conference a breach in
the Anglo-French accord over Morocco." Bülow's minute to that assertion was:
"We do not desire that at all, or at least we should in no instance show such an
aim. We only wish to preserve our rights in Morocco" (*ibid.,* XX, 312 f., No. 6609;
cf. Chirol, *Fifty Years in a Changing World,* p. 300).

[26] When the *Nowoje Wremja* denounced the German action Bülow, on March
27, protested strongly to Lamsdorff against this anti-German attitude. Russia was
expected to remain neutral in this affair, he declared (Bülow to Alvensleben,
March 27, *G.P.,* XX, 277 f., No. 6577).

[27] Those three had criticized the Anglo-French accord.

[28] The signatory Powers were those which had participated in the conference of
Madrid in 1880 over Moroccan affairs.

[29] Quoted from a dispatch from Bülow to William II, April 4, 1905, *ibid.,* 303,
No. 6599; and from a memo. by Holstein, April 4, 1905, *ibid.,* 304 f., No. 6601.

Immediately after the Emperor's speeches at Tangier, Herr
von Holstein proposed advocating a conference in the semiofficial
press. The Chancellor approved; but Herr Hammann, director
of the press bureau in the foreign office, objected. Inasmuch as
the Emperor and the Chancellor had both declared that Germany
would next communicate directly with the Sultan, he argued, this
abrupt change would expose German policy to the accusation of
unsteadiness. He advised preparing public opinion for a conference, for, he maintained, the government had "to combat a
much stronger aversion to a serious conflict with France and
England over Morocco in the public than in the press."[30] On
April 7 he predicted a "press storm" if the menace of war arose.[31]
So, for the time a milder note was sounded in the press. The
grievances against M. Delcassé, who was made personally responsible for Germany's action,[32] the necessity for defending
the German economic interests in Morocco, and the intimacy of
German-American relations were emphasized. Little by little
the proposal for a conference was brought to the fore.[33]

The main basis for the optimism of the German government

[30] Memo. by Hammann, April 3, 1905, *ibid.*, 300 f., No. 6598.

[31] Memo. by Hammann, April 7, 1905, *ibid.*, 311 f., No. 6609.

[32] On April 8 Bülow sent Hammann the following instructions for directing the
press: "All criticism and attacks should, under the greatest possible consideration
for the French national feeling, be directed against the systematically anti-German, insolent, and inept policy of Delcassé" (minute by Bülow to a memo. by
Hammann, April 7, 1905, *ibid.*, 313, No. 6609). On April 4 he had issued instructions to restrain the German press from war with the British press (Mühlberg to
Metternich, April 4, 1905, *ibid.*, 603 and note, No. 6839).

[33] That Holstein wished to turn loose a *Kriegsfanfare*, as Hammann later asserted, seems unlikely, for German policy at that time was not bellicose. But Holstein
did propose to exert great pressure by vigorous words and threats, and his program might very likely have had the result which Hammann foresaw. On this
controversy between the two men see Hammann, *Bilder aus der letzten Kaiserzeit*, pp. 35 f.; Otto Hammann, *Der neue Kurs. Erinnerungen* (Berlin, 1918), pp.
104 ff.; Hammann, *Zur Vorgeschichte des Weltkrieges*, pp. 210 f.; memo. by Holstein, April 3, 1905, *G.P.*, XX, 297 ff., No. 6597; memo. by Hammann, April 3,
1905, *ibid.*, 300 f., No. 6598; memo. by Holstein, April 7, 1905, *ibid.*, 308 f., No.
6606; memo. by Hammann, April 7, 1905, *ibid.*, 309 f., No. 6607.

was its friendship with President Roosevelt. Since the early part of the year both the British and the German governments had been endeavoring to win the President's support and to arouse his suspicions by accusing each other of aggressive intentions,[34] Needing the support of both to effect peace between Russia and Japan, Mr. Roosevelt had refused to believe the tales of either. He had diagnosed their trouble as a case of "jumpy nerves," and had tried in February and March, 1905, to bring them together in a new triple entente.[35] The German government had responded favorably to his suggestion; but the British government, taxing the President with being hoodwinked by the Emperor, had replied that better relations with that hostile Power were scarcely possible.[36] This lack of success with Great Britain, combined with mistrust of France, caused the President to draw closer to Germany.[37]

On April 3 the German government confidently asked Mr. Roosevelt to lend "moral support" for the maintenance of the *status quo* in Morocco and for the peaceful settlement of the Moroccan difficulty by speaking "calmly and academically," par-

[34] Durand to Lansdowne, March, 1905, quoted in Brigadier General Sir Percy Sykes, *The Right Honourable Sir Mortimer Durand: A Biography* (London, 1926), p. 280; Spring Rice to Roosevelt, undated though written in the first half of Jan., 1905, quoted in Dennett, pp. 152 f.; Sternburg to Bülow, Feb. 10, 1905, *G.P.*, XIX, 573 ff., No. 6288; Sternburg to F. O., March 7, 1905, *ibid.*, 580 f., No. 6293; Bülow to Sternburg, Feb. 21, 1905, *ibid.*, 576 ff., No. 6290; and others in *ibid.*, chap. cxxxix; Dennett, pp. 45, 73 ff.; Dennis, *Adventures in American Diplomacy*, p. 393; Joseph B. Bishop, *Theodore Roosevelt and His Times* (New York, 1920), I, 378 f., 468 f., 473; Gwynn, *The Letters and Friendships of Sir Cecil Spring Rice*, I, 406 ff., and chap. xiii.

[35] Sternburg to Bülow, Feb. 10, 1905, *G.P.*, XIX, 573 f., No. 6288; Sternburg to F. O., March 7, 1905, *ibid.*, 580 f., No. 6293.

[36] So Roosevelt asserted to Sternburg. See Sternburg to F. O., April 1, 1905, *ibid.*, 590, No. 6300; Sykes, p. 280; Dennis, pp. 397 f.; Gwynn, Vol. I, chap. xiii; Newton, *Lord Lansdowne*, p. 322.

[37] On March 21 Roosevelt declared to Sternburg: "My earnest wish is that we use as much as possible the four years which stand before me in office to improve the relations between our countries. I believe in the German people" (Sternburg to F. O., March 21, 1905, *G.P.*, XIX, 583, No. 6295).

ticularly to Great Britain, for the equal treatment of all Powers in the Sherifian Empire.[38] Ten days later it asked the President to speak to Great Britain in favor of an international conference on the Moroccan question.[39] Not delaying for a definite reply or heeding the signs of the drawing together of Great Britain and France,[40] the German government, on April 9, determined to send Count Tattenbach to Fez to combat the efforts of the French mission and to win the Sultan's approval of a conference. The Count had telegraphed that this move was essential, since the Sultan was a weakling, his advisers incompetent and venal, and since the French were otherwise likely to gain the acceptance of their plans of reform.[41]

On the same date (April 9) upon which the German government made this decision, it began to sound the other Powers concerning a conference. Austria-Hungary and Russia could be excluded from consideration although both showed disapproval of Germany's action.[42] When the Spanish government was asked on April 12 to support the proposal for a conference, the foreign minister, M. Villa-Urrutia, replied that he could accept it only if France and Great Britain did so. He suggested that the Ger-

[38] Bülow to Sternburg, April 3, 1905, *ibid.*, 592 ff., No. 6302; Bishop, I, 468 f.

[39] Bishop, I, 469.   [40] See below.

[41] In the absence of a regular minister at Tangier, Tattenbach had remained there after the Emperor's visit. See Tattenbach to F. O., April 7, 1905, *G.P.*, XX, 313 f., No. 6610; Bülow to Tattenbach, April 9, 1905, *ibid.*, 315 f., No. 6611. O'Conor, British ambassador at Constantinople, reported to Lansdowne, May 1, 1905, that Germany was trying to induce the Sultan to send a mission to Morocco with a view to establishing closer relations. The Sultan eventually refused. On Feb. 12, 1906, O'Conor was able to state why. The Sultan had sent secret emissaries to Morocco, but the Sultan of Morocco became suspicious and refused either to send a formal mission to Constantinople or to receive one thence. O'Conor also heard that the Sultan had written to Abd-el-Aziz recommending the German Emperor as the friend and protector of Islam whose advice was well worth following. See O'Conor to Grey, Feb. 12, 1906, *B.D.*, III, 248, No. 277. Tardieu states that the Sultan's letters to his Moorish colleague were written in Feb.-March, 1906 (*La Conf. d'Algés,* p. 259 n.). Nothing further is known of this affair.

[42] Radolin to F. O., April 9, 1905, *G.P.*, XX, 317, No. 6612; Bülow to Alvensleben, March 27, 1905, *ibid.*, 277 f., No. 6577.

man desires be fulfilled not by a conference but by an exchange of notes and declarations between the Powers.[43]

With Italy the German government was more brusque. While reassuring that Power that Germany had no intention of becoming a rival in the Mediterranean, Count Bülow demanded under threat of breaking the alliance that Italy support the German policy in the Moroccan affair. But on April 12 the Italian government, evading a definite position, urged a direct settlement of the Franco-German discord. Count Monts, German ambassador at Rome, reported that only in case Great Britain showed coolness toward France might Germany expect any support from her ally, who would otherwise endeavor to remain neutral.[44]

Since the German government thought that Great Britain had relinquished her Moroccan interests, it intended to ignore her and deal solely with France. On April 19 Count Metternich merely explained to Lord Lansdowne the German views in the Moroccan affair without asking for any expression of opinion. In this conversation he received the impression that the British Foreign Minister disapproved of the German action and that, against his desire, he could easily be forced to give France diplomatic support.[45]

Without waiting for either the British or the American reply, the German government, on April 18, responded to M. Delcassé's

[43] Radowitz to F. O., April 12, 1905, *ibid.*, 326 f. and note, No. 6619; Mousset, *La política exterior de España, 1873–1918*, p. 165.

[44] Bülow to Monts, April 3, 11, 12, 1905, *G.P.*, XX, 295 f., No. 6594; 318 ff., No. 6613; 322 f., No. 6616; Monts to F. O., April 12, 1905, *ibid.*, 324 ff. and notes, Nos. 6617 f. Tittoni, the Italian foreign minister, had to feel his way carefully. On April 14 he sounded the Spanish government on its attitude, and was informed that Spain would remain loyal to her agreement with France and would accept the conference only if France and Great Britain did (Nicolson to Lansdowne, April 14, 1905, *B.D.*, III, 66, No. 79).

[45] Bülow to Metternich, April 11, 1905, *G.P.*, XX, 605 ff., No. 6843; Metternich to F. O., April 19, 1905, *ibid.*, 608 f., No. 6845. On April 10, however, Radolin reported a statement by Eckardstein, which he himself seemed to think correct, to the effect that "in case of a serious Franco-German conflict England would undoubtedly stand actively on the French side and would even advance with enthusiasm against Germany" (*ibid.*, 607 f., No. 6844).

offer "to dissipate any misunderstanding" with the suggestion that "the simplest and most natural means" of settling the question of Moroccan reform would be to bring about "an exchange of ideas between all the signatory Powers" of the Convention of Madrid.[46] At the same time, through messages to the Sultan the Chancellor sought to prevent him from making any decisions before the German mission arrived, and he pressed Count Tattenbach to hasten his departure for Fez. Count Bülow realized that if the French succeeded in gaining the Sultan's acceptance of their program of reforms, the entire German action would be rendered absurd. In fact, until Count Tattenbach could persuade the Sultan to issue an invitation for a conference, the latter held the fate of Germany's policy in his hands.[47]

III

The German Emperor's visit to Tangier aroused bitter antagonism in Great Britain, where government and people believed that Germany had struck as much at Great Britain as at France in an effort to break the Entente Cordiale. Alarm over a possible German attack upon the British Isles was revived.[48] Public feeling was well expressed by King Edward who, on April 15, wrote indignantly to Lord Lansdowne:

> The Tangier incident was the most mischievous and uncalled for event which the German Emperor has ever been engaged in since he came to the throne. It was also a political theatrical fiasco, and if he thinks he has done himself good in the eyes of the world he is very much mistaken. He is no

[46] By that answer Bülow aimed to show the French government that "we do not consider separate Franco-German negotiations as adequate to the situation." See Radolin to F. O., April 14, 1905, *ibid.*, 328 ff., No. 6621; memo. by Mühlberg, April 19, 1905, *ibid.*, 332 f., No. 6623; Bülow to Tattenbach, April 18, 1905, *ibid.*, 333 f. and note, No. 6624.

[47] Bülow to Tattenbach, April 18, 1905, *ibid.*, 333 f., No. 6624; Tattenbach to F.O., April 21, 1905, *ibid.*, 335, No. 6625; Bülow to Tattenbach, April 22, 1905, *ibid.*, 336 f., No. 6626; Tattenbach to F. O., April 23, 1905, *ibid.*, 337 f., No. 6627; Bülow to Tattenbach, April 24, 1905, *ibid.*, 338, No. 6628.

[48] On April 3 Balfour repeated his denial in the House of Commons of the likelihood of a German attack.

more or less than a political "enfant terrible" and one can have no faith in any of his assurances. His own pleasure seems to wish to set every country by the ears.[49]

The Foreign Secretary's criticism was also severe.

I am afraid that we can hardly regard this Tangier ebullition [he wrote, on April 9, to Sir Frank Lascelles] as an isolated incident. There can be no doubt that the Kaiser was much annoyed by the Anglo-French Agreement, and probably even more so by our refusal to vamp up some agreement of the same kind with Germany over the Egyptian question.

We shall, I have little doubt, find that the Kaiser avails himself of every opportunity to put spokes in our wheels. . . . .[50]

This staunch pro-French sentiment was not concealed. Early in April an exchange of visits by the British and French fleets was announced for the summer. King Edward had an interview with MM. Loubet and Delcassé on April 6 while passing through Paris on his way south.[51] In Berlin at the same time Sir Frank Lascelles spoke in private "very disapprovingly" of the German action, and strongly opposed the idea of a conference.[52] And British public opinion, the true guide of the foreign policy, gave entire support to France.[53] So although the British government admitted that M. Delcassé had blundered in his handling of Germany[54] and although it knew that the secret articles of the two Moroccan accords were not in keeping with the public ones, it felt obliged both by honor and by interest to help France out of her difficulty. Its official attitude was expressed by Lord Lansdowne to the Ambassador at Berlin as follows:

My impression is that the German Government have really no cause for complaint either of us or the French in regard to the Morocco part of the

---

[49] Lee, II, 340.   [50] Newton, p. 334.

[51] Radolin to F. O., April 6, 1905, *G.P.*, XX, 311, No. 6608.

[52] Mühlberg to Metternich, April 4, 1905, *ibid.*, 604, No. 6840; Metternich to Bülow, April 6, 1905, *ibid.*, 604, No. 6841; memo. by Hammann, April 7, 1905, *ibid.*, 311, No. 6608.

[53] Metternich to Bülow, March 28, April 6, 1905, *ibid.*, 601 ff., Nos. 6837, 6841.

[54] Metternich to Bülow, March 28, 1905, *ibid.*, 602, No. 6837; Kühlmann to Bülow, March 19, 1905, *ibid.*, 261 f., No. 6562; Lascelles to Lansdowne, March 23, 1905, *B.D.*, III, 61, No. 69.

Agreement. We made no secret of its existence. It dealt exclusively with French and British interests in Morocco, and so far as the other Powers were concerned, it provided adequate security for their interests, and for the integrity of Morocco itself. What else does the Kaiser want?[55]

Particularly since British policy aimed at preventing Germany from obtaining ports anywhere in the colonial world[56] did the British government desire to keep that Power out of Morocco. And, while Sir Francis Bertie, British ambassador at Paris, reported the French government as "solid on Morocco," he added the ill-omened statement of M. Delcassé, that the German government was "turning him out."[57] Lord Lansdowne did not follow up the French suggestion of intervening in Berlin in favor of France for fear of doing more harm than good by arousing the Emperor's resentment.[58] But he did send the British Minister at Tangier to Fez to offset the effects of the German mission.[59] And on April 22 he instructed Sir Francis Bertie as follows:

It seems not unlikely that German Government may ask for a port on the Moorish coast.

You are authorized to inform Minister for Foreign Affairs that we should be prepared to join French Government in offering strong opposition to such a proposal and to beg that if question is raised French Government will afford us a full opportunity to conferring with them as to steps which might be taken in order to meet it.

German attitude in this dispute seems to me most unreasonable having regard to M. Delcassé's attitude and we desire to give him all the support we can.

On April 25 the Ambassador handed M. Delcassé the following *aide-memoire* (dated April 24):

The British Government finds that the conduct of Germany in the Moroccan question is most unreasonable in view of M. Delcassé's attitude, and it de-

[55] April 9, 1904 (Newton, p. 334).

[56] Viscount Grey of Falloden, *Twenty-five Years, 1892–1916* (New York, 1925), I, 115.

[57] Lee, II, 342.

[58] Lansdowne to Lascelles, April 23, 1905, *B.D.*, III, 67, No. 80; Lansdowne to Bertie, April 24, 1905, *ibid.*, p. 73.

[59] Tattenbach to F. O., April 27, 1905, *G.P.*, XX, 348, No. 6639.

sires to give to His Excellency all the support in its power. It seems not improbable that the German Government may ask for a port on the Moroccan coast. In that event the British Government would be willing to join the French Government in offering strong opposition to such a proposal, and it asks M. Delcassé, in case the question is raised, to give to the British Government full opportunity to concert with the French Government upon the measures which might be taken to meet that demand.[60]

By inverting the order of the sentences, the Ambassador gave to Lord Lansdowne's communication a force and a meaning which were originally lacking. He changed the emphasis from that of helping France to oppose the German acquisition of a port to that of helping her to oppose Germany in the whole Moroccan question. The one document limited the scope of the support and stressed the point of conferring beforehand as well as that of offering strong opposition. The other document began with a blanket offer of aid, and then used the present instance as one example of that offer. Moreover, the statement "to concert with the French Government upon the measures which might be taken to meet that demand" was stronger than the one used by Lord Lansdowne, "of conferring with them as to steps which might be taken in order to meet it." Sir Francis Bertie's *aide-memoire* was so colored by his own very pro-French feeling that it did not accurately reproduce his chief's proposal.

IV

M. Delcassé was "most grateful" for this support. He denied that Germany had made any such request, although he remar' ·d that some years ago Count Hatzfeldt had approached the British government on the subject. He promised to communicate with the latter if he heard of any German aspirations for a port and to warn the Sultan against giving any concession to Germany.[61] Thus, by virtue of the British offer, the French Foreign Minister was able to hold to his policy in spite of Germany's re-

[60] Lansdowne to Bertie, April 22, 1905, *B.D.*, III, 72 f., No. 90; and following documents; Spender, *Life of Campbell-Bannerman*, II, 248; Grey, I, 106 f.

[61] Bertie to Lansdowne, April 25, 1905, *B.D.*, III, 74 f., Nos. 92 f.

fusal to consider his overture and in spite of his unpopularity with the French Parliament. On May 2, he again attempted to approach the German government, offering through M. Luzzati, Italian minister of finance, to give "any satisfaction desired by Germany in order to settle the Moroccan question in a way which would not wound French honor too deeply."[62] At the same time he continued the French action at Fez. When on April 26 the Sultan, emboldened by the German intervention, requested an international guaranty of the proposed Franco-Moroccan agreement over military reforms, M. Delcassé immediately refused. "You may declare peremptorily to Ben Sliman," he instructed the French Minister on May 3, "that there can no more be intermediate Powers between France and Morocco than there are intermediate countries between Morocco and Algeria."[63]

The Foreign Minister's policy was disapproved by the French Premier, who since April 19 had assumed general control over foreign affairs. Whereas M. Delcassé, a skilled diplomat, was secretive, pro-British, and anti-German, the inexperienced M. Rouvier, a business man who sought to employ business methods in the conduct of foreign relations, suspected Great Britain of attempting to use France as a cat's-paw against Germany. Realizing that the British navy "did not have wheels," M. Rouvier favored treating Great Britain and Germany alike.[64] When the German government, instead of replying to M. Delcassé's proposal of April 13, prepared to send a mission to Fez and the German newspapers advocated an international conference on the

[62] The offer was so stated by Monts (Monts to F. O., May 2, 1905, *G.P.*, XX, 362, No. 6648).

[63] Saint-René Taillandier to Delcassé, April 26, 1905, *L.j., 1901–5*, 215, No. 248; Delcassé to Saint-René Taillandier, May 3, 1905, *ibid.*, 217, No. 251; Bourgeois et Pagès, *Les origines et les responsabilités de la grande guerre*, p. 309. Ben Sliman was Moroccan minister of foreign affairs.

[64] On Rouvier see Mévil, pp. 253 ff.; Victor Bérard, *La France et Guillaume II* (Paris, 1907), p. 296; Radolin to F. O., April 27, 1905, *G.P.*, XX, 345, No. 6635; Radolin to Bülow, May 8, 1905, *ibid.*, 373 f., No. 6657. Rouvier's policy was certainly more in keeping with French opinion.

Moroccan affair, M. Rouvier intervened personally in an effort to reach a settlement.

On April 26, while Prince Radolin's guest at dinner, the Premier brought up the Moroccan question. Protesting that the French really preferred the Germans to the English, he intimated that he appreciated Germany's defense of her Moroccan interests, and said: "We will do everything possible and will give every desired explanation and satisfaction." Denying that France was seeking to change the *status quo,* he upheld her right to suppress the anarchy in Morocco along the Algerian frontier. He offered to drop the thirty-year limitation to freedom of commerce, which, he added, was in fact already invalidated by the existing treaties between Morocco and other states. At the close of the conversation he exclaimed passionately: "It is impossible, it would be criminal for two states that are intended to agree and to approach each other to become embroiled, and especially over Morocco!" The Ambassador coldly responded that a collective settlement of the question seemed to him the simplest solution.[65]

On the following day M. Rouvier proposed indirectly to Prince Radolin a settlement of the Moroccan problem by an exchange of notes between France and the other Powers. If the majority of the Powers opposed the French program of reform, it would not be carried out. M. Rouvier had no objection to Count Tattenbach's making new commercial treaties with Morocco. But he did ask that, in case Germany were satisfied by his offer, the Emperor, on his return from the Mediterranean, should announce publicly the forthcoming settlement of the Franco-German dispute.[66]

When these offers were made, the anxiety of the German gov-

---

[65] Radolin to F. O., April 27, 1905, *ibid.,* 344 f., No. 6635. To Rouvier's assertion that "France would do everything necessary to live on the best terms with Germany" Bülow commented as follows: "Then the French Government should cease its efforts to isolate us, to break up the Triple Alliance, to incite England against us" (Bülow's minute to the foregoing dispatch).

[66] Radolin to F. O., April 27 and 28, 1905, *ibid.,* 346, No. 6636; 348 f., No. 6640.

ernment was relieved. To be sure, on April 25, Prince Radolin heard from a "usually well-informed person just returned from England" that King Edward would, on his way home from the South, declare officially to the French government that "Great Britain was ready to support the French policy in Morocco and the execution of the Anglo-French accord with her whole power."[67] But at the same time the German government learned definitely that the Sultan had made no final promises to the French and that he had agreed to postpone all decisions until the arrival of Count Tattenbach.[68] Equally satisfactory, the answer from Washington arrived.

As the President had been absent on a hunting trip in Colorado, he had not replied until April 20, when he had explained his policy to Mr. Taft, acting secretary of state, as follows:

I do not feel that as a Government we should interfere in the Morocco matter. We have other fish to fry and we have no real interest in Morocco. . . . .

At the same time if I can find out what Germany wants I shall be glad to oblige her if possible, and I am sincerely anxious to bring about a better state of feeling between England and Germany. Each nation is working itself up to a condition of desperate hatred of the other; each from sheer fear of the other. The Kaiser is dead sure that England intends to attack him. The English Government and a large share of the English people are equally sure that Germany intends to attack England. Now, in my view this action of Germany in embroiling herself with France over Morocco is positive proof that she has not the slightest intention of attacking England. . . . . I do not wish to suggest anything whatever as to England's attitude in Morocco, but if we can find out that attitude with propriety and inform the Kaiser of it, I shall be glad to do so. . . . . If we find that it will make the English suspicious—that is, will make them think we are acting as decoy ducks for Germany—why, we shall have to drop the business. . . . . I should advise your being absolutely frank with both Speck [von Sternburg] and the British people. . . . . Remember . . . . that both parties are very suspicious. You remember the King's message to me through Harry White and his earn-

[67] Radolin to Bülow, April 25, 1905, *ibid.*, 615, No. 6847.

[68] Tattenbach to F. O., April 23, 24, 25, 1905, *ibid.*, 337 f., No. 6627; 339, No. 6629; 341, No. 6632; Vassel to Tattenbach, April 21, 1905, *ibid.*, 339 ff., No. 6631.

est warning to me that I should remember that England was our real friend and that Germany was only a make-believe friend. In just the same way the Germans are always insisting that England is really on the point of entering into a general coalition which would practically be inimical to us—an act which apart from moral considerations I regard the British Government as altogether too flabby to venture upon.

In a letter to the German Ambassador on the same date, Mr. Roosevelt had reiterated that the United States had no direct interest in Morocco, had offered to serve as mediator between Germany and Great Britain and to advise the British "to arrive at an understanding over Morocco and to work in harmony" with Germany.[69]

The German Chancellor regarded this statement as "satisfactory to a high degree."[70] On April 27 he instructed Prince Radolin to uphold the project for a collective settlement and to postpone further negotiations with the French government until Count Tattenbach could send exact information from Fez concerning the actions of the French Minister.[71] In other words, he put the French off until the Count could block their efforts in Fez and secure the Sultan's acceptance of a conference. Otherwise, he feared, M. Delcassé might try to break the Moroccan resistance by intimating to the Sultan that his supposed friend, Germany, was now deserting him for a direct understanding with France.[72]

This hazardous policy was not approved by either Prince Radolin or Count Tattenbach. The former advised his chief to accept M. Delcassé's offer of April 13.[73] The Count also ex-

[69] Bishop, I, 469 ff.; Sternburg to F. O., April 25, 1905, *G.P.*, XX, 342, No. 6633.

[70] Bülow to Sternburg, April 27, 1905, *G.P.*, XX, 342, No. 6634.

[71] Bülow to Radolin, April 28, 29, 1905, *ibid.*, 346 f., No. 6637; 349 f., No. 6641.

[72] Holstein to Mühlberg, April 24, 1905, *ibid.*, 339, No. 6630; Bülow to Sternburg, April 27, 1905, *ibid.*, 342 ff., No. 6634.

[73] Radolin to Bülow, April 14, 1905, *ibid.*, 330 ff., No. 6622. Monts also regarded Delcassé's offer through Luzzati as signifying victory for Germany in her Moroccan campaign and as giving the opportunity "for a definitive friendly agreement with France" (Monts to F. O., May 2, 1905, *ibid.*, 362, No. 6648).

pressed his preference for a direct agreement with France. "In my opinion," he wrote to the Chancellor on April 29,

the condition for a separate understanding with France would first be given if the other Powers reject the idea of a conference and the Sultan also acts unreliably and declines to heed our advice and wishes,—as is to be expected. In this case we must receive Southern Morocco as our sphere of influence. . . . . We must therefore decide whether we wish . . . . to fight a long diplomatic battle of doubtful issue against France, either through supporting the Sultan with money and weapons or through relying upon the conservative, fanatically anti-French party in Morocco, or whether we wish to gain through an understanding with France a substantial pledge for a large-scale African colonial policy which aims at the acquisition of all the French African possessions.[74]

The Chancellor's reply to Count Tattenbach contained the explanation for Germany's proposal of a conference. He wrote:

Your last idea guided Germany's Moroccan policy in the past and under proper circumstances can guide it again in the future if you keep the future free. For the present, the German policy must be governed by the fact that His Majesty the Emperor . . . . declared to the King of Spain that he has enough African possessions and wishes no territory in Morocco but only the maintenance of commercial freedom. This declaration naturally does not bind us forever; but in the year which has passed since those remarks, the effect of the Southwest African events has been of a nature to increase the antagonism to colonial acquisitions by military force as well with His Majesty as with a great part of the German people. Even if, therefore, France were inclined to permit us to conquer a part of Morocco, we would for the present perhaps not be in a position to take advantage of this overture. In reality, we are confronted with the alternative either of relinquishing Morocco now to France without adequate compensation to Germany or of working for the extension of life of the Sherifian Empire in the expectation of a turn of events favorable to us. Thus, I perceive your important task to be in holding the future free for the profit of German interests. I sum it up in stating that you should bring the Sultan to declare that he could consider the French demands only if they were advised by a conference of all the

[74] Tattenbach had on the previous day talked to Lowther, British minister at Tangier, and had found him strongly opposed to a conference and in favor of a direct Franco-German settlement (Tattenbach to F. O., April 29, 1905, *ibid.*, 251 f., No. 6642).

signatory Powers. The reference to the conference I consider for the Sultan the easiest and for us the most favorable form of refusal. That the Sultan refuse the French demands is naturally the main thing.[75]

This frank document furnished the key to the German refusal of the French offers and to the persistent demands for a conference. Count Bülow's embarrassment was caused by the Emperor's renunciations at Vigo and even more by the temporary apathy if not antagonism of the German people toward further colonial acquisition. Pursuing an objective undesired by German public opinion, the Chancellor was still bent on acquiring a share in Morocco or compensation elsewhere. To delay and postpone, to "hold the future free" until public opinion veered into a more chauvinistic channel, to relieve Germany of the restrictions imposed by the Emperor's assertions, Count Bülow thought that a conference was the best means. The continuation of the crisis was a logical result of this ambition.

On the same day upon which Count Bülow penned this dispatch M. Rouvier made another offer. He was led to this move by the increasing excitement in France. The lack of response from Germany and the uncertainty about her objective, the publication of an article in the *Kreuzzeitung* on April 26 and of one in *Matin* on the next day hinting at war,[76] caused a panic on the Paris stock exchange on April 27.[77] M. Bihourd telegraphed on April 28 of the presence of "bellicose counselors" in the *entourage* of the Emperor who would have an excellent opportunity "to advocate the present time as propitious for war against France."[78] So in a conversation with Prince Radolin on April 30 M. Rouvier indorsed the Emperor's assertions at Tangier and the principles

---

[75] Bülow to Tattenbach, April 30, 1905, *ibid.*, 352, No. 6643.

[76] The article was by Professor Schiemann, who was known to be in close touch with the German government (reprinted in Schiemann, *Deutschland und die grosse Politik 1905*, pp. 110 f.).

[77] Radolin to F. O., April 27, 1905, *G.P.*, XX, 347, No. 6638; *Quest. dipl. et col.*, XIX, 576 ff.

[78] Bihourd to Delcassé, April 28, 1905, *L.j., 1901–5*, 215, No. 249.

of the Convention of Madrid, except with respect to the Algero-Moroccan frontier. He offered to "make an agreement similar to the Anglo-French one, where all doubtful points, including Morocco, would be settled." The Ambassador made no reply.[79]

The next day an intermediary explained to Prince Radolin that the Premier regarded a conference as hardly acceptable since France had engaged herself so fully in the Moroccan affair. M. Rouvier would be willing, however, to include in a general settlement such questions as those of boundaries in Africa and the Bagdad Railway. In return, the two governments should agree upon a mode of adjusting the Moroccan affair directly with the Powers. The German government refused the offer.[80]

On May 1 King Edward VII arrived in Paris where he remained for four days. Strongly supporting M. Delcassé's views, he assured the French government that Germany would not dare a war; in case of conflict, he said, France could rely on British support.[81] To the German Ambassador he praised the French for seeking a direct settlement of the Moroccan difficulty, abruptly demanding, "Why does not Berlin reply to the last French overture?"[82] His interference, however, was of no avail. In fact, French public opinion, suspecting the King and British press of

[79] Rouvier also assured Radolin that "he disapproved of much that had happened" and that he himself had taken over the general control of foreign affairs. It had cost him some effort to save Delcassé in the Chamber, he said, but he had thought it wiser to do so (Radolin to Bülow, April 30, 1905, *G.P.*, XX, 360 ff., No. 6647).

[80] Radolin to Bülow, May 1, 1905, *ibid.*, 355 ff., No. 6645; Bülow to Radolin, May 1, 1905, *ibid.*, 353 f., No. 6644.

[81] Eckardstein was informed to this effect on May 4, 1905, by Rouvier's intimate friend, Armand Levy, a Parisian financier (Eckardstein, *Lebenserinnerungen und politische Denkwürdigkeiten*, III, 106; Lee, II, 342).

[82] Radolin to Bülow, May 1, 1905, *G.P.*, XX, 616 f., No. 6848. The King may have put this question to Radolin at the desire of Delcassé, who was complaining of Germany's lack of response (Bertie to Lansdowne, April 27, 1905, *B.D.*, III, 68, No. 84). On May 11, 1905, Lansdowne wrote to Knollys, King Edward's private secretary, as follows: "The King's Mediterranean tour left matters in excellent shape so far as we are concerned" (Lee, II, 342).

attempting to estrange France and Germany, was more than ever anxious for an agreement with Germany.[83]

Distressed by refusals and silence from the German government and fearful of war, M. Rouvier sought to restore connections with Germany by sending his friend, M. Betzold, to Berlin to interview Herr von Holstein, and by persuading Baron Eckardstein, then living privately in England, to lay the French proposals directly before Count Bülow and the Emperor at Karlsruhe. These men were to inform the German officials that the French cabinet, disapproving of M. Delcassé's secretiveness, hoped to bring about the Minister's downfall over some domestic difficulty in the next three or four weeks. They were to state that while in case of war the French Government knew for a certainty that Great Britain would interfere in France's favor, the cabinet, except M. Delcassé, preferred not to seek this support. As an inducement for a direct settlement, the two emissaries were to offer Germany "a coaling station and eventually also a strip of land on the Atlantic coast of Morocco." They were especially to urge the Emperor against making any inflammatory speeches on his return from the Mediterranean.[84]

Neither M. Betzold nor Baron Eckardstein had the least success. While Herr von Holstein assured M. Betzold on May 2 of Germany's desire for good relations with France, he observed that for the time he saw no possibility of making a direct agreement with her. For, even apart from Germany's official declara-

---

[83] *Belg. Docs., 1905–14,* No. 4.

[84] Wilhelm Betzold was an international financier with wide political connections (Eckardstein, I, 243 ff.). The instructions were given to Eckardstein, May 4, by Armand Levy, like Betzold, an intimate friend of Rouvier, just after an interview between the two and the Premier, Levy had made a note of the various points which he now laid before Eckardstein, explaining that naturally Rouvier could not speak directly to him of these delicate affairs but adding that his statements were "rigorously exact" (Eckardstein, III, 100 ff.). Only Eckardstein's account of the interview with Bülow contains anything about the Moroccan proposal, but there is no reason to doubt the accuracy of his statement (see also Prince Lichnowsky, *My Mission to London, 1912–1914* [London, 1918], p. 3).

tion in favor of a collective settlement of the Moroccan question, the German government did not trust M. Delcassé sufficiently to negotiate with France. That Minister's policy toward Germany, he asserted, had been "dishonest," "hostile," "insidious," and in this affair "disrespectful." "Slow tempo, temporary truce, and removal of Delcassé would be the next," he concluded. In Karlsruhe, on May 5, Count Bülow rebuffed Baron Eckardstein with the bold assertion: "The English inciting does not impress us. In case of a conflict the game would be played between Germany and France. . . . . We are in a position to await further developments with composure." The Baron was not allowed to see William II at all.[85]

Thus every offer for a direct settlement was refused.[86] Indeed, the German government even suggested to M. Rouvier on May 7 that France take the initiative in calling a conference, arguing that "the advantage of a conference lies in that it can have no positive results. It will neither divide Morocco nor check her continuing decay. It will fulfil its object in removing the danger of an acute conflict, at the same time holding the future open.'"[87]

M. Rouvier of course would not consider the suggestion. Nor was he any longer so willing to eliminate M. Delcassé. On May 8 he informed the German government through M. Betzold that while he had been unable to convince the Foreign Minister of the faults of his policy, the latter was needed in the work of mediat-

---

[85] Memo. by Holstein, May 2, 1905, *G.P.*, XX, 357 ff., No. 6646. Paul von Schwabach's account of arranging the interview for Betzold is given in *Berliner Tageblatt*, March 21, 1922. See also Bülow to F. O., May 5 and 6, 1905, *G.P.*, XX, 368 ff., Nos. 6652 f.

[86] On May 2 the Chancellor also refused to consider Delcassé's offer through Luzzati; and when a few days later he heard that Barrère wished to be sent to Berlin to arrange affairs, he immediately advised Rouvier that he would not be received. See Bülow to Monts, May 3, 1905, *G.P.*, XX, 363 f., No. 6649; Radolin to Holstein, May 8, 1905, *ibid.*, p. 372 n.; Bülow to Radolin, May 9, 1905, *ibid.*, 372, No. 6656).

[87] Bülow to Radolin, May 4, 1905, *ibid.*, 366 f., No. 6650; Radolin to F. O., May 8, 1905, *ibid.*, 371 f., No. 6655.

ing between Russia and Japan. It might, therefore, take weeks or even months to achieve his dismissal. M. Rouvier hoped, said M. Betzold, to settle the Moroccan and other difficulties with Germany after Count Tattenbach convinced himself of the French Minister's proper conduct at Fez and after M. Delcassé had been eliminated.[88]

More unfortunate words could hardly have been chosen. The German government was opposed to an early peace between the warring Powers,[89] and its mistrust of M. Delcassé was increased by his continued justification of his policy. Since French public opinion had repudiated the Minister, since M. Rouvier, known to be weak and easily influenced, had practically offered the Minister's head, the German government determined to press the frightened and pacifically inclined French Premier until the objectionable Foreign Minister was overthrown. To that end, on May 16, Prince Radolin announced to M. Rouvier "that the prerequisite for the *rapprochement* desired by him [M. Rouvier] is for us [Germany] to have full trust in the foreign policy of France. . . . . After what has happened, this trust is lacking." The Premier replied, "I understand you fully. Leave it to me." But through M. Betzold he urged the German government to wait until he could accomplish the act by some internal crisis.[90]

Meanwhile, the German government was pressing Spain, Italy, and the United States for support. Early in May Herr von Radowitz warned the Spanish government against sending a mission to Fez at that time, and remarked that "it would be wise for Spain not to intervene in the present Moorish difficulties, and that it was to her interest to be on friendly terms with Germany, who

[88] The British and the Russian governments were also supporting Delcassé. See Radolin to Bülow, May 8, 1905, *ibid.*, 373 ff., No. 6657 f.; Betzold to Eckardstein, May 9, 1905, quoted in Eckardstein, III, 204.

[89] Sternburg to F. O., June 2, 1905, *G.P.*, XIX, 607, No. 6311, Bülow's minute.

[90] Radolin to Bülow, May 13 and 16, 1905, *ibid.*, 376 f., No. 6659; 378 f., No. 6661.

could be of greater assistance to her than any other Power."[91] At the same time Count Monts in Rome was using "menacing language," hinting at "the possibility of war."[92] In both places this talk made a deep impression.

To President Roosevelt the German government asserted that, although certain voices had been raised in France in favor of a conference, Great Britain still resisted the project. It asked the President to inform the British government that its attitude justified the suspicion that "in the accord with France they [the British] had wished to dispose not only of English rights but also of the rights of the other signatory Powers." The German government further informed Mr. Roosevelt that if the proposal for a conference became hopeless, it would then think of its interests alone and would be forced to choose "between the possibility of a conflict with France and the consideration of conditions which France might perhaps propose to avoid a conflict."[93]

Criticizing sharply the British hostility to the conference, Mr. Roosevelt promised to repeat his advice to the British government to settle its differences with Germany. Upon doing so he was again accused by the British leaders of being under German influence. He stoutly denied this accusation, writing to Senator Lodge, then in England, on May 15, as follows:

It always amuses me to find that the English think that I am under the influence of the Kaiser. The heavy witted creatures do not understand that nothing would persuade me to follow the lead of or enter into close alliance with a man who is so jumpy, so little capable of continuity of action, and therefore, so little capable of being loyal to his friends or steadfastly hostile to an enemy. Undoubtedly with Russia weakened Germany feels it can be

[91] So related by the Spanish Foreign Minister to Nicolson (Nicolson to Lansdowne, May 5, 1905, *B.D.*, III, 70 f., No. 87). Although there is no account of the conversation in *G.P.*, the language is entirely in keeping with German policy. The episode referred to the possible departure of Spain's new minister in Morocco to Fez.

[92] So reported by Egerton to Lansdowne, May 5, 1905, *ibid.*, 71, No. 88. Cf. Bülow to Monts, May 3, 1905, *G.P.*, XX, 363 f., No. 6649; Bülow to F. O., May 6, 1905, *ibid.*, 368, No. 6651.

[93] Bülow to Sternburg, April 27, May 10 and 16, 1905, *ibid.*, 342 ff., No. 6634; 620 ff., No. 6851; XIX, 600 ff., No. 6306; Bishop, I, 469 f.

fairly insolent within the borders of Europe. I intend to do my best to keep on good terms with Germany, as with all other nations, and so far as I can to keep them on good terms with one another; and I shall be friendly to the Kaiser as I am friendly to every one. But as for his having any special influence with me, the thought is absurd.[94]

Nevertheless, the British government rejected his advice. On May 19 Mr. Roosevelt had to report to Baron Sternburg that "the British Government had given him to understand that it did not wish better relations with Germany," and that "it had even hinted broadly to the secretary of state that Great Britain could take care of her affairs alone." He could not do more, he said, without exposing himself to an incivility.[95] The German government was well pleased with the result, however, for it placed Mr. Roosevelt on the German side.

On May 13 Count Tattenbach arrived in Fez. He found that the French party was still strong, with some of the Moroccan ministers bought over to that side. He accomplished his object with some difficulty. He reported immediately that the Sultan himself affirmed the accusation against the French Minister of having claimed to enjoy a mandate of Europe.[96] A few days later the Count telegraphed that upon his arrival the French Minister, under instructions from M. Delcassé, had issued a veiled threat of violence against Morocco if the Sultan agreed to a conference.[97] Upon receiving these dispatches Count Bülow imme-

---

[94] *Selections from the Correspondence of Theodore Roosevelt and Henry Cabot Lodge, 1884–1918* (New York, 1925), II, 123. See also Dennett, pp. 88 ff.

[95] The President's statements were so formulated by Sternburg. See Sternburg to F. O., May 13 and 19, 1905, *G.P.*, XX, 622 f., No. 6852; *ibid.*, XIX, 603 f., No. 6308; Dennett, pp. 184 f., 88 ff., 75 f.

[96] Tattenbach to F. O., May 15, 1905, *G.P.*, XX, 379 f., No. 6662.

[97] Tattenbach's version of the threat was as follows: "The French Government would consider it an injury to France's interests if the French proposals for reform were submitted for consideration to the signatory Powers. No Power possessed the right to intervene in the Moroccan affair, especially in the frontier question. . . . . The French Government would continue to watch sharply the affairs in Morocco, and reserved the right to act according to circumstances." See Tattenbach to F. O., May 17, 1905, *ibid.*, 380, No. 6663. Cf. with the original threat quoted above. See also Tattenbach to F. O., May 31, 1905, *ibid.*, 399 f., No. 6676.

diately warned M. Rouvier against M. Delcassé's "stormy and violent . . . . Moroccan policy."[98] As that Minister still remained in office, the Chancellor instructed Herr von Miquel, councilor at the German embassy in Paris, to inform M. Rouvier amicably but firmly that the Foreign Minister would have to go, that Franco-German relations would not improve as long as he remained in office. Indeed, if M. Delcassé's anti-German and bellicose policy became known to the German people, he was to state, it would have an effect for which Count Bülow refused to be responsible. "A change in the present situation is above all to be made possible by a change in the direction of the French foreign policy."

When Herr von Miquel carried out these instructions on May 30, the Premier realized the necessity for eliminating the Foreign Minister. In his despair he cried: "I cannot cause M. Delcassé to fall because Germany frowns. I would be reproached always . . . . always."[99] The German pressure, however, did not cease. In a telegram on May 25 Count Tattenbach reported French assertions to the Moroccans that in the face of the united action of the Mediterranean Powers, "who would never suffer an interference by Germany in Mediterranean questions," Germany would desert the Sultan. In sending this report to Rome, on May 31, the German Chancellor requested the Italian government to favor publicly the collective settlement of the Moroccan question. "No matter what turn Moroccan affairs take, Germany will follow up the consequences of the advice which His Majesty sent to the Sultan," he wrote. "Thus the possibility that the Sultan will remain isolated in this difficulty need not be considered." The Italian Foreign Minister immediately denied France's right to speak of a common policy of the Mediterranean Powers, and,

[98] Bülow to Radolin, May 22, 1905, *ibid.*, 382 f., No. 6665.

[99] Miquel was chosen for this work because he was just being transferred to St. Petersburg. See Bülow to Radolin, May 30, 1905, *ibid.*, 388 ff., No. 6669; memo. by Miquel, May 30 and 31, 1905, *ibid.*, 393 ff., Nos. 6674 f.

as Count Bülow probably intended, he passed on the German warning to the French government.[100] On May 28 Count Tattenbach telegraphed the Sultan's official rejection of the French proposals and his approval of an international conference.[101] Thereupon, through M. Betzold, the Chancellor warned the French Premier, June 1, that in as much as the Sultan had accepted the German point of view, Germany "would follow up the consequences if France continued the policy of intimidation and violence hitherto pursued by M. Delcassé."[102] On June 3 Prince Radolin described the situation to M. Dupuy, an intimate friend of M. Rouvier's, as "very serious."[103] Thus the German government struck blow after blow to force an immediate dismissal of the French Foreign Minister.[104]

On the French side, M. Delcassé remained as adamantine as

[100] Bülow to Monts, May 31, 1905, *ibid.*, 390 f., No. 6670, and note citing a dispatch from Monts of June 2, 1905; Mévil, p. 272. Egerton was informed by Barrère that Monts had said to Tittoni that "if the French Minister maintained his threat of military measures against the Sultan of Morocco, a German army would cross the French frontier" (Egerton to Lansdowne, June 13, 1905, *B.D.*, III, 95, No. 122).

[101] Tattenbach to F. O., May 28, 1905, *G.P.*, XX, 392, No. 6672.

[102] Bülow to Radolin, June 1, 1905, *ibid.*, 392 f., No. 6673; Radolin to Bülow, June 11, 1905, *ibid.*, 407, No. 6685.

[103] Radolin to F. O., June 3, 1905, *ibid.*, 401, No. 6678.

[104] The *Gaulois* published articles on June 9 and 17, 1905, asserting that Prince Henckel von Donnersmarck had also been sent by the German government to Paris about June 1 to warn Rouvier that Delcassé must be dismissed (Mévil, pp. 273 ff.; Bourgeois et Pagès, p. 310). The editors of *G.P.* state that this story is "exaggerated"; Donnersmarck was mentioned only once in the documents, they assert—in a dispatch from Radolin on June 17, 1905, describing the assertions of Donnersmarck given in *Gaulois* as apocryphal (*G.P.*, XX, 390 n.). According to Eckardstein, Rouvier declared to him on May 4 that some time previously Donnersmarck had asserted to him, apparently at Bülow's request, that there were only two possibilities, a Franco-German alliance or war. On the other hand, Eckardstein saw Donnersmarck in Berlin on June 6 and found him eager for news from London and Paris (Eckardstein, III, 103 f., 127 f.). It seems clear that Donnersmarck's assertions, whatever they were, were made on his own responsibility; that, as the editors of *G.P.* state, Bülow issued his warnings directly to Rouvier (*G.P.*, XX, 390 n.).

the Germans. Fearing an intention on the part of Germany to force his dismissal, hearing of Germany's pressure on Spain and Italy and of bellicose talk by the German Ambassador at Rome,[105] he made a bid on May 17 for British support. On that date M. Cambon apprised Lord Lansdowne of Germany's endeavor to arouse discord between Great Britain and France "all over the world." Although he did not regard the relations with Germany as "profoundly dangerous," he pictured them as serious enough to cause him "much preoccupation."

Lord Lansdowne wished to lend the pro-British Foreign Minister all possible support. Late in April, for the sake of France and the Entente Cordiale, he had run the risk of antagonizing President Roosevelt by instructing the British Ambassador in Washington not to give him an opportunity to mediate between Great Britain and Germany. He realized that the President's interference encouraged Germany and worked to the detriment of France and Great Britain. He had therefore denied to the President that there was any "subject of dispute" between Great Britain and Germany, and had expressed his inability to see "why any international complication should be created [over Morocco], unless German Gov[ernmen]t is determined to take advantage of what was at most a diplomatic oversight in order to make mischief or to disturb the *status quo*, e.g. . . . . , by demanding cession of a Moorish port."[106] But Lord Lansdowne also sought to correct any erroneous impression which Sir Fran-

[105] Nicolson to Lansdowne, May 5, 1905, *B.D.*, III, 70 f., No. 87; Egerton to Lansdowne, May 5, 1905, *ibid.*, 71, No. 88; Lansdowne to Bertie, May 3, 1905, *ibid.*, 69 f., No. 86.

[106] Durand to Lansdowne, April 26, 1905, *ibid.*, 67 f., No. 82; Lansdowne to Durand, April 27, 1905, *ibid.*, 68, No. 83. Durand did not follow that line exactly. He left the impression with Roosevelt that the Anglo-German opposition was bitter, but that nevertheless Great Britain did not want Roosevelt interfering—thus letting the latter think that Great Britain was more bellicose than she was (see above). One reason for the British government's slowness about helping Roosevelt mediate between Russia and Japan was, no doubt, that it wished to exclude all opportunity for the President to mediate between Great Britain and Germany. On April 26 Spring Rice asked Roosevelt not to support the idea of a conference (Gwynn, I, 469).

cis Bertie's *aide-memoire* of April 25 may have made. Lord Lansdowne said to M. Cambon:

> The moral . . . . seemed to me to be that our two Governments should continue to treat one another with the most absolute confidence, should keep one another fully informed of everything which came to their knowledge, and should, so far as possible, discuss in advance any contingencies by which they might in the course of events find themselves confronted. As an instance of our readiness to enter into such timely discussions, I reminded H[is] E[xcellency] of the communication which had recently been made to the French Gov[ernmen]t by you [Sir Francis Bertie] at a moment when an idea prevailed that Germany might be on the point of demanding the cession of a Moorish Port.[107]

To avoid all misunderstanding this communication was put in writing in an exchange of notes between the British Foreign Secretary and M. Cambon on May 24–25. When the former perceived that M. Cambon still interpreted the British policy in the light of Sir Francis Bertie's *aide-memoire*,[108] he reiterated his correcting statement as follows:

> I do not know that this account [of their conversation of May 17] differs from that which you have given to M. Delcassé, but I am not sure that I succeeded in making quite clear to you our desire that there should be full and confidential discussion between the two Gov[ernmen]ts, not so much in consequence of some acts of unprovoked aggression on the part of another Power, as in anticipation of any complications to be apprehended during the somewhat anxious period through which we are at present passing.[109]

[107] Lansdowne added: "I had heard fears expressed that, in order to put an end to a state of things which could not fail to be highly inconvenient to them, the French Government might be induced to purchase the acquiescence of Germany by concessions of a kind which we were not likely to regard with favour, in other parts of the world. I had myself no such misgivings, and felt convinced that each side might continue to rely upon being treated with absolute frankness by the other. His Excellency [M. Cambon] expressed his entire concurrence in what I had said." See Lansdowne to Bertie, May 17, 1905, *B.D.*, III, 76, No. 94; Spender, II, 248; *Cambridge History of British Foreign Policy*, III, 342 f.

[108] "During our last conversation about Morocco you . . . . added that . . . . if circumstances demanded it, if for example we had serious reasons to believe in an unjustified aggression on the part of a certain Power, the British Government would be entirely ready to concert with the French Government on the measures to take" (Cambon to Lansdowne, May 24, 1905, *B.D.*, III, 77, No. 95, inclosure).

[109] Lansdowne to Cambon, May 25, 1905, *ibid.*, 77 f., No. 95, and inclosure.

At some time in this crisis, the British fleet was commanded to be "in readiness to make a descent on the German coast at short notice,"[110] and conversations were begun between the French and British military and naval officers looking toward active co-operation in case of war.[111]

When news arrived of the Sultan's proposal for a conference, M. Delcassé opposed it vigorously. At his instigation the British government on June 5 ordered Mr. Lowther, who had just arrived in Fez, to advise the Sultan against the idea and to refuse the invitation.[11a] The French Minister also reported Mr. Taft's remark that the American government would probably not be favorably disposed toward a conference. Thereupon Lord Lansdowne on June 5 added his support in trying to convince the

[110] Bradford, *Life of Wilson*, p. 199. Nothing more was heard of this order, which probably came from Sir John Fisher. Fisher was in favor of "Copenhagening" the German fleet and also of landing soldiers in North Germany in case of a war (*Memories;* Newton, pp. 334 f.). In 1922, Lord Sanderson wrote as follows concerning the events of this time: "There were no doubt preparations by our military authorities for defending Belgium in case of an attack by Germany on France through Belgian territory, and these preparations must have been known to the French military attaché in London. There was also a good deal of loose talk in naval circles and some high quarters of a possible expedition to Schleswig in the possible event of war. I do not believe such a measure was ever seriously entertained, and I looked upon the report as put about for the purpose of a warning" (Sanderson to Temperley, Aug. 17, 1922, *B.D.*, III, 87, No. 105).

[111] Grey, I, 74. The British press supported the French loyally for the sake of maintaining the balance of power. See O. Eltzbacher, "The Balance of Power in Europe," *Nineteenth Century and After* (May, 1905); Steed, I, 230 ff. It is difficult to state exactly what were the British motives for supporting France so wholeheartedly in this crisis. One has to deduce them from acts, for, unlike the Germans, the directors of the British policy did not write down their reasons. As to King Edward's view of the international situation, especially of the German danger, see Spring Rice to Lansdowne, D. May 7, 1905, R. May 13, 1905, *B.D.*, IV, 77 f., No. 69, and King Edward's minute thereto. On July 10 Spring Rice, in a memo. written after talking with Lansdowne, stated that British policy aimed at maintaining the balance of power (Gwynn, I, 476).

[112] Tattenbach to F. O., May 31, June 3, 1905, *G.P.*, XX, 399, No. 6676; 400, No. 6677; Metternich to F. O., June 8, 1905, *ibid.*, 422, No. 6697; Lowther to Lansdowne, D. May 31, 1905, R. June 3, 1905, *B.D.*, III, 88, No. 106; Lansdowne to Bertie, June 1 and 5, 1905, *ibid.*, 88, No. 107; 89, No. 109; Lansdowne to Lowther, June 5, 1905, *ibid.*, 89, No. 108.

American government that "the proposal was unsound and should not be entertained."[113] To bring Spain into closer intimacy with the Entente Cordiale, the British Foreign Secretary offered early in June to effect an understanding with her over the Spanish interests in the Mediterranean and elsewhere.[114] In spite of Lord Lansdowne's correcting statements about the British policy, M. Delcassé apparently continued to interpret the British communication of May 17 in the sense of Sir Francis Bertie's *aide-memoire* of April 25. He was impressed by the practical identity of that communication with the political clauses of the Franco-Russian alliance.[115] Reassured by the British support and by the adverse attitude of the British, Spanish, and American governments toward the project of a conference, and believing with the British that Germany was bluffing, he was in no mood to recede. M. Rouvier, who was receiving all the German threats, took a different view of the situation. With some of the other members of the cabinet, he prepared for the retirement of the offending Minister.[116] During the visit of the King of Spain to Paris, May 30–June 4, little could be done. But by June 3 M. Delcassé's resignation was anticipated in parliamentary circles.[117] On June 5 the Chamber was thrown into ex-

[113] Lansdowne to Bertie, June 5, 1905, *ibid.,* 89, No. 109; Lansdowne to Durand, June 5, 1905, *ibid.,* 90, No. 110.

[114] Nicolson to Lansdowne, June 29, 1905, *ibid.,* 109, No. 136. The editors of *B.D.* promise to publish more information about this offer in a later volume.

[115] That treaty read in part as follows: "The two Governments declare that they will take counsel together upon every question of a nature to jeopardize the general peace; in case that peace should be threatened with an aggression, the two parties undertake to reach an understanding on the measures whose immediate and simultaneous adoption would be imposed upon the two Governments by the realization of this eventuality." See *Livre jaune: L'alliance franco-russe,* p. 16, No. 17, annexe; Pribram, *The Secret Treaties of Austria-Hungary,* II, 213; Bernadotte E. Schmitt, "Triple Alliance and Triple Entente, 1902–1914," *American Historical Review,* XXIX, 459 f.

[116] Thayer, *The Life and Letters of John Hay,* II, 404 f.; Eckardstein, III, 115 ff.; Radolin to Bülow, June 11, 1905, *G.P.,* XX, 497 ff., No. 6685; Bertie to Lansdowne, June 10, 1905, *B.D.,* III, 78, No. 96, recounting a conversation with Delcassé on that date.

[117] Radolin to F. O., June 3, 1905, *G.P.,* XX, 400 f., No. 6678.

citement bordering on panic by the rumor of a report from M. Barrère at Rome that if an Anglo-French alliance were concluded Germany would attack France.[118] On the same day M. Rouvier explained the gravity of the situation to President Loubet;[119] on June 6 he laid his controversy with M. Delcassé before the cabinet.

At that meeting, although well aware of his isolation, M. Delcassé valiantly defended his policy of the past seven years, a policy which he declared had been opposed by Germany alone.[120] He claimed that in a very recent exchange of notes, one of which he read, France had received from Great Britain assurance of support in case of a German attack. Asserting the possibility of a formal alliance with Great Britain, he urged acceptance of the British offer.[121] He proposed that the French, British, and Spanish governments should address identical notes to the Sultan

[118] Delcassé's formal denial of the rumor had no effect. See Mévil, pp. 284 f.; Flotow to Bülow, June 7, 1905, G.P., XX, 406, No. 6684.

[119] Radolin to Bülow, June 11, 1905, ibid., 407 ff., No. 6685; Quest. dipl. et col., XIX, 770.

[120] Delcassé informed Bertie, June 10, that the Spanish Foreign Minister "had told him that he thought that Spain, France and England, should reply to the Government of Morocco in identic terms declining the proposal" (Bertie to Lansdowne, June 10, 1905, B.D., III, 78, No. 96).

[121] The report spread in 1905 that at the French cabinet meeting on June 6 Delcassé had stated that the British government had offered an alliance to France. Lansdowne and Sanderson denied to the German government that Great Britain had ever done so. See Metternich to F. O., June 16, 1905, G.P., XX, 630 ff., No. 6858; Metternich to F. O., June 28, 1905, ibid., 635 ff., No. 6860; see also B.D., III, 87, No. 105; Metternich to F. O., Oct. 9, 1905, G.P., XX, 663 f., No. 6873. According to Mévil, the official apologist for Delcassé, just before the arrival of the King of Spain in Paris on May 30, the British government assured Delcassé that "the British military forces were ready to march with us [France] against Germany if that Power attacked us. Moreover, the principle of defensive co-operation once admitted, the English Government declared itself ready to sign in the shortest time an accord which would definitely fix that co-operation" (Mévil, p. 268). In a letter of March 20, 1922, Delcassé wrote as follows: "From the Entente it was possible for us in 1905 to proceed to a formal alliance with England. . . . . On June 6th the British offer of assistance had been only forty-eight hours in my possession" (quoted in the London Times, March 27, 1922). In connection with the Grey-Cambon correspondence of 1912, Poincaré has written: "Thus to make a joint study of the situation was the sole engagement which was made [in that

declining the conference. He assured the cabinet that Germany confronted by this Anglo-French-Spanish opposition with Italy neutral would not fight. But M. Rouvier declared that the German government had threatened war if France accepted the British offers. Turning to the ministers of war and of navy, he asked if France were prepared for that contingency. They both replied emphatically "No." As M. Delcassé was not supported by a single minister, he resigned, and M. Rouvier took over his position. Before leaving M. Delcassé prophetically warned the cabinet that after this abdication before the demands of Germany, that Power would become "more insolent and more exacting than ever"; it had not opposed his person, he said, but rather the French policy of accords. He declared that the cabinet's pusillanimity would give rise to new dangers.[122]

correspondence]. In communicating to me the result obtained, M. Paul Cambon wrote me that at the time of Lord Lansdowne an entente of that kind would have been only a beginning. Now, however, it was the last word for the Liberal cabinet. The forced resignation of M. Delcassé had perhaps made us lose in 1905, stated M. Cambon, the opportunity for a real alliance with England. All that we were able to obtain today was this engagement to confer in the presence of danger and this hypothetical approval of the programs drawn up by the general staff." See also J. A. Farrer, *England under Edward VII* (London, 1922), pp. 127 f.; Mévil, pp. 269 f.; *G.P.*, XX, 632 n., 664 n.; Raymond Poincaré, *Au service de la France. Neuf années de souvenirs: I. Le lendemain d'Agadir, 1912* (Paris, 1926), p. 221. Later Lansdowne wrote on his dispatch to Bertie of May 17, 1905, as follows: "I suppose this was the origin of the offensive and defensive alliance" *(B.D.*, III, 76, No. 94). His inference is probably correct only in part. The exchange of notes between Cambon and Lansdowne was sent to Bertie on May 31, 1905, and received by him on June 3. It is not apparent whether he communicated that exchange to the French government, although the "offer of assistance" which Delcassé has written of as having received only forty-eight hours before the cabinet meeting on June 6 may have been the notice of this exchange from Bertie. Word to Delcassé through the Governor-General of Algeria from King Edward, who was then cruising in the Mediterranean, urging the Foreign Minister not to resign also strengthened the latter's hand. The King took that step on his own initiative (Newton, p. 342).

[122] On that cabinet meeting see the following: Mévil, pp. 293 ff.; Pinon, *France et Allemagne*, pp. 164 f.; Radolin to Bülow, June 11, 1905, *G.P.*, XX, 407 ff., No. 6685; Bertie to Lansdowne, June 8, 1905, *B.D.*, III, 91, No. 114; Bertie to Lansdowne, June 10, 1905, *ibid.*, 78, No. 96, recounting a conversation with Delcassé on that date; Wolff, *Das Vorspiel*, pp. 167 ff. Cf. Bertie's explanation of Delcassé's fall (Bertie to Lansdowne, June 15, 1905, Newton, pp. 341 f.).

French public opinion was almost unanimous in its approval of M. Delcassé's downfall. This approbation was noted by Herr von Flotow, first secretary of the German embassy in Paris, who on June 7 reported to his government as follows:

> The history of the downfall of M. Delcassé shows that without a doubt there is a latent under-current in France which wishes . . . . a satisfactory understanding with Germany. It is after all significant that in the entire press of all parties there is hardly a paper which does not censure the anti-German policy of M. Delcassé. The second interesting point in the history of the past few days is the fact that in spite of the continued and almost importunate offers of English aid, ... French public opinion has never shown a real inclination to accept this support. Wherever one has opportunity here . . . . to observe public feeling, one meets the view that England is only endeavoring to engage the French power for her differences with Germany, and that in case of a crisis France would have to pull the English chestnuts out of the German fire.[123]

Great Britain was disgusted. The British government had made strenuous endeavor to save M. Delcassé, for it was certain of his loyalty to the entente, whereas it was dubious of the more pro-German M. Rouvier. It had intimated its willingness to oppose by force the German aggression;[124] but so far had met with no encouragement.

> Delcassé's dismissal or resignation under pressure from the German Government [stated Mr. Balfour to King Edward on June 8] displayed a weakness on the part of France which indicated that she could not at present be counted on as an effective force in international politics. She could no longer be trusted not to yield to threats at the crucial moment of a negotiation. If, therefore, Germany is really desirous of obtaining a port on the coast of Morocco, and if such a proceeding be a menace to our interests, it must be to other means than French assistance that we must look for our protection.[125]

---

[123] Flotow to Bülow, June 7, 1905, *G.P.*, XX, 406, No. 6684; 625, No. 6854. Cf. the report from the Belgian Minister at Paris to his government, June 8, 1905, *Zur europ. Politik*, II, 62 f. See also *Quest. dipl. et. col.*, XIX, 770 ff.

[124] Cf. *Cambridge History of British Foreign Policy*, III, 341.

[125] Quoted in Lee, II, 344. See also a letter from John Hay, who was then in London, to Henry Adams, June 7, 1905, quoted in Thayer, II, 405; Bertie to Lansdowne, June 10, 1905, *B.D.*, III, 78, No. 96. Lansdowne's reaction is expressed in Newton, p. 341.

In spite of M. Rouvier's public assertion, June 6, that his policy toward the Anglo-French understanding would remain the same as before,[126] the Entente Cordiale had received a hard blow. While expressing satisfaction that France had repudiated the anti-German Minister, the German press, under official guidance,[127] kept its discussion of the affair within the bounds of propriety. But German obtuseness to the feelings of other nations was manifested when on the day of M. Delcassé's fall the German Emperor made Count Bülow a prince.

Thus, the first period of the crisis was closed. Germany had gained her objective in winning the Sultan's acceptance of the project of a conference and in overthrowing M. Delcassé. While playing with war, the German government had had no desire to start one, and, gauging correctly French sentiment toward M. Delcassé and war, it had achieved success in Paris merely by a liberal use of threats. In the Moroccan affair the German foreign office had reached the peak of its power. But it had aroused so many complications that the crisis continued as acutely as before.

[126] Bertie to Lansdowne, June 6, 1905, B.D., III, 90, No. 111.

[127] Bülow's minute to a dispatch from Flotow, June 5, 1905, G.P., XX, 403, No. 6681.

CHAPTER XIII

THE MOROCCAN CRISIS, JUNE 6—JULY 8, 1905

The downfall of M. Delcassé was merely an incident in Germany's drive toward a conference. Prince Bülow, believing that the Minister's resignation ended the acute phase of the crisis,[1] immediately dispatched a circular note to the signatory Powers[2] informing them of Germany's acceptance of the Sultan's invitation to a conference and asking them also to accept. In this note he argued as follows: Since Article XVII of the Convention of Madrid[3] guaranteed to every Power the same treatment as the

[1] Bülow to Tattenbach, June 7, 1905, *G.P.*, XX, 418 f., No. 6692.

[2] The signatory Powers were as follows: Austria-Hungary, Italy, Spain, Great Britain, France, Russia, United States, the Netherlands, Portugal, Sweden, Belgium, and Germany.

[3] Art. XVII read as follows: "Le droit au traitement de la nation la plus favorisée est reconnu par le Maroc à toutes les Puissances representées à la Conférence de Madrid" (Leon Deloncle [ed.], *Statut international du Maroc* [Paris, 1912], p. 51). The French refused to accept this interpretation of the Convention of Madrid and of Art. XVII. Tardieu replied to the German arguments as follows: "That convention aimed to limit at the demand of Morocco the right of protection of the legations to certain Moroccan subjects which some Powers tended to abuse. It had regulated the exercise of that right, determined the conditions of naturalization for the Moroccans, those for the acquisition of landed property by foreigners, and had established the basis of the agricultural tax. Concerning general policy or stipulations about the tariff, not a word. Article XVII, which Germany invoked as the charter of international equality in Morocco, applied in reality only to the right of protection. . . . Article XVII is not a promise of the Powers among themselves never to touch the diplomatic or economic terrain. It is a promise by Morocco never to differentiate between them within the limits of 1880 and within those limits alone, that is (following the preamble of the convention) in the exercise of protection" (Tardieu, *La Conf. d'Algés*, p. 39). Lansdowne also challenged the German interpretation. "Any rights which other countries may have to most-favoured-nation treatment in Morocco would not . . . . preclude the possibility of a privileged position being in certain respects accorded to France in her dealings with the Moorish Government. Most-favoured-nation treatment is variously interpreted in different countries. But no Power has, I believe, ever contended that the obligation to give such treatment debars one country from in-

most favored nation, the Moroccan reforms had to receive the approval of all the signatory Powers. If the proposal for a conference were refused, the legal status of Morocco would remain unchanged, for the opposition of one Power alone would suffice to block the execution of any reforms proposed. But aside from these legal arguments, the conference was the best means of introducing reforms without endangering the existing political and commercial interests of the signatory Powers by concession of special rights to individual states. Moreover, since the Convention of Madrid was a compact between the Powers, France would have to obtain their sanction for a special position in Morocco. While the details of the French program of Moroccan reforms were unknown, it was evident that France sought, in violation of Article XVII, to control the land as she did Tunis. Thus, to oppose the French action was merely to defend the existing legal status of Morocco.[4]

The attitude of the Powers toward this exposé was not at all satisfactory to the German government. The Russian, Austrian, Italian, Portuguese, and Danish governments evaded a reply, leaving the initiative to the French and the British.[5] German re-

---

voking the assistance of another in improving its domestic administration, and it is obvious that such assistance can be most conveniently and effectually given when the Power which affords it is the immediate neighbour of that which receives it, nor was there any desire or intention on the part of France to deprive other Powers of the rights and privileges to which they were justly entitled under Treaty" (Lansdowne to Bertie, July 11, 1905, *B.D.*, III, 117 f., No. 150; cf. Metternich to F. O., June 6, 1905, *G.P.*, XX, 416 f., No. 6690).

The German interpretation was based upon a loose construction of that convention while the French interpretation was based upon a strict construction. Although from a legal standpoint the French view was correct, yet the precedent of an international conference over Moroccan affairs, no matter what they were, favored the German argument. Moreover, the fact remained that France had tried to change the existing status in Morocco without consulting Powers who had as much right to be considered as the three with whom she had come to terms.

[4] Bülow to Flotow, June 5, dispatched June 6, 1905, *G.P.*, 413 ff., No. 6687; *L.j., 1901–5*, 230 f., No. 268, annexe.

[5] Alvensleben to F. O., June 7, 1905, *G.P.*, XX, 419, No. 6693; Wedel to F. O., June 6, 1905, *ibid.*, 417 f., No. 6691; Monts to F. O., June 6, 9, 12, 1905, *ibid.*,

lations with Spain over the matter were complicated by reports that while M. Villa-Urrutia, the Spanish foreign minister, had been in Paris during King Alfonso's visit, he had openly aligned himself with M. Delcassé's policy. After the French Minister's downfall, the German government notified the Spanish government on June 11 that, if M. Villa-Urrutia remained in office, Germany would recall her Ambassador for an indefinite leave of absence.[6] While waiting for the Minister to be overthrown, the German government did not press Spain on the question of the conference.

The British attitude was even more adverse. When Count Metternich handed the German note to Lord Lansdowne, the latter interpreted it as meaning that "the Conference, if it were to meet, would be expected to deal not only with the introduction of reforms, but with the maintenance of the independence and integrity of Morocco, and the preservation of the open door."[7] The Ambassador's affirmative reply enhanced Lord Lansdowne's suspicion that Germany was endeavoring to break the Anglo-French understanding. While questioning strongly the propriety of a conference, the Foreign Secretary gave no definite answer. This note, however, and the passing of M. Delcassé caused the British government to recede on June 8 from its original refusal of the Sultan's invitation and to postpone its decision until it could consult with France.[8] But on June 7, Herr von Flotow reported from Paris a rumor that Great Britain had offered to France "an offensive and defensive alliance aimed at Germany"

---

415 f., No. 6688; 424 f., No. 6699; 435 ff., No. 6709; de Bunsen to Lansdowne, June 8, 1905, B.D., III, 91 f., No. 115; Smith to Lansdowne, June 24, 1905, ibid., 101, No. 129; Lansdowne to Goschen, June 21, 1905, ibid., 100, No. 127; Egerton to Lansdowne, June 9, 10, 13, 1905, ibid., 94 f., Nos. 119 ff.; Hardinge to Lansdowne, June 14, 1905, ibid., 96, No. 123.

[6] Bülow to Radowitz, June 10, 1905, G.P., XX, 425 f., No. 6701.

[7] Lansdowne to Lascelles, June 8, 1905, B.D., III, 92 f., No. 117.

[8] Metternich to F. O., June 6 and 8, 1905, G.P., XX, 416 f., No. 6690; 422 ff., No. 6697 f. King Edward also refused to permit the Prince of Wales to attend the

which the latter was still considering.[9] Hence, it was manifest to the German government that Great Britain was in complete opposition to its policy.

President Roosevelt also gave a disappointing reply. On May 25 and 30 Prince Bülow had told the President that "the decision in the question of a conference depended to a great extent upon him." He maintained that if the conference were refused as a result of Great Britain's pressure upon France, Germany would be forced to choose between a war with France and perhaps Great Britain and an agreement with the former which would serve as a prelude to a strong Continental *bloc*. Declaring that he was averse to making the choice, the Chancellor asked Mr. Roosevelt to favor the conference to the signatory Powers.[10] But the President replied on June 8 that he could hardly participate in a conference without exposing himself to the sharpest attacks, since American opinion was opposed to interfering in the Moroccan affair and inclined to approve reform by one Power.[11]

The attitude of M. Rouvier was equally unsatisfactory to the German government. The Premier expressed to the German representative through M. Betzold the hope that the fall of M. Delcassé would enable the two countries to reach a direct understanding, and promised to show the "greatest conciliation"

---

wedding of the German Crown Prince on June 6 (Lee, *King Edward VII*, II, 335 f.). Lowther had communicated the British refusal to the Sultan when on June 8 new instructions arrived for him to await further developments. See Lowther to Lansdowne, June 9, 1905, *B.D.*, III, 94, No. 118; Lansdowne to Lowther, June 8, 1905, *ibid.*, 92, No. 116.

[9] The information came from M. Bunau-Varilla, owner of *Matin* (*G.P.*, XX, 623 f., No. 6853).

[10] Bülow to Sternburg, May 25 and 30, 1905, *ibid.*, 385 f., Nos. 6667 f.; Bishop, *The Life and Times of Theodore Roosevelt*, I, 470 f.

[11] Sternburg to Bülow, June 8, 1905, *G.P.*, XX, 421, No. 6696. Durand reported that Roosevelt had said to Sternburg that "so long as the French Government object, the United States Government could not adhere to the proposal for a Conference of the Powers" (Lansdowne to Cambon, June 6, 1905, *B.D.*, III, 90 f., No. 112).

toward Germany.[12] When the German note of June 6 arrived, he immediately denied to the Powers the accusations made therein.[13] He also instructed M. Saint-René Taillandier to suspend action at Fez so as to avoid complications.[14] He endeavored to find some way by which Germany could be satisfied, France's position in Morocco be preserved and her agreements with the other Powers be upheld, and the humiliating conference be avoided. On June 7 he protested to Herr von Flotow that France could hardly accept the conference, which French public opinion rejected so completely, and remarked that Great Britain, Spain, and Italy would probably refuse it.[15] Herr von Flotow replied that Germany would not desert the Sultan. Two days later the Premier offered through an intermediary to make a general agreement with Germany not only over the Moroccan question but also over others, such as those of the Bagdad Railway and far eastern affairs.[16] In a conversation with the German Ambassador on June 10, M. Rouvier persisted, in spite of threats, in his repugnance to the conference. Why go there, he asked Prince Radolin, if Germany refused the reforms in Morocco which France considered necessary? In the course of his defense of France's previous Moroccan policy, he said: "If an understanding concerning the extension of permissible reforms could previously occur with Germany, participation in the conference might be possible." He was so discouraged that he thought seriously of resigning, for, he declared to the Prince, he could not defend before the French Chamber the German demands as then formulated.[17]

[12] Radolin to F. O., June 3, 1905, *G.P.*, XX, 402 f., No. 6680; Flotow to F. O., June 6 and 9, 1905, *ibid.*, 404, No. 6682; 425, No. 6700. In these negotiations Rouvier leaned on the advice of Révoil, who in June without holding any office was given a desk in the foreign office (Tardieu, p. 84).

[13] *L.j., 1901–5*, 230, No. 268; 231, No. 269; 233, No. 271.

[14] Rouvier to Saint-René Taillandier, June 10, 1905, *ibid.*, 230 f., No. 269.

[15] Flotow to F. O., June 7, 1905, *G.P.*, XX, 420, No. 6694.

[16] Flotow to F. O., June 9, 1905, *ibid.*, 425, No. 6700.

[17] Bülow to Radolin, June 10, 1905, *ibid.*, 427 f., No. 6702; Radolin to F. O., June 11, 1905, *ibid.*, 430 f., No. 6705; Rouvier to Bihourd, June 11, 1905, *L.j.,*

At home Prince Bülow's policy was encountering disapproval from the Emperor William II, then in a pacific mood. Toward the end of May the Emperor had rebuked the German Navy League for criticizing the naval program as inadequate.[16] On June 3 he had started the movement which culminated in the conclusion of the Russo-Japanese War and was co-operating with President Roosevelt in that work—an act which Prince Bülow would have prevented had he been aware of his master's intentions.[19] Even though the Emperor knew nothing of the French offers,[20] he was entirely willing after the fall of M. Delcassé to gratify M. Rouvier's wish for an understanding.[21] At the wedding of the German Crown Prince on June 6 he assured the French representative that there would be no war over Morocco.[22]

The beginning of Russo-Japanese negotiations for peace had no effect upon the German policy, for Russia's force was broken both by defeat and by the rapidly developing revolution.[23] But

---

1901–5, 232, No. 270. Immediately after that interview Rouvier declared to some of his friends: "They are putting a knife to my throat. I do not know where they wish to drive us" (Wolff, *Das Vorspiel*, pp. 174 f.).

[18] Schulthess, *Europäischer Geschichtskalender 1905*, p. 92.

[19] Goetz, *Briefe Wilhelms II an den Zaren 1894–1914*, pp. 370 ff.; *G.P.*, XIX, Nos. 6193, 6196 f., 6311 ff., 6318; *B.D.*, Vol. IV, chap. xxiii, Part. V.

[20] The absence of minutes by him to the dispatches during this crisis points to this fact (also see Eckardstein, *Lebenserinnerungen und politische Denkwürdigkeiten*, III, 167). The Emperor first learned of Rouvier's offer of a general colonial agreement at this time in 1907. His comment was as follows: "If I had known of that, I would have accepted it and the whole stupid conference of Algeciras would have been avoided" (Brandenburg, *Von Bismarck zum Weltkriege*, p. 215).

[21] See the Emperor's minutes, one of the very few instances in which they are to be found, to the dispatch from Radolin to Bülow, June 11, 1905 *(G.P.*, XX, 409, No. 6685).

[22] On this episode see Eckardstein, II, 139 f.; Zedlitz-Trützschler, *Zwölf Jahre am deutschen Kaiserhof*, p. 174; Bülow to Radolin, June 10, 1905, *G.P.*, XX, 429 f., No. 6704.

[23] This was General Schlieffen's opinion. Schlieffen believed that the condition of the Russian army would grow worse instead of better. See Bülow to Schlieffen, June 4, 1905, *ibid.*, XIX, 422, No. 6194; Schlieffen to Bülow, June 10, 1905, *ibid.*, 423 f., No. 6195.

the attitude of France was so uncompromising and that of the other Powers so unfavorable that Prince Bülow doubted whether he would succeed in launching the conference.[24] He endeavored to do so by a show of boldness coupled with real concessions to France.

To bring President Roosevelt back into active participation in the affair, Prince Bülow reported to him the rumor of the British offer of alliance to France and pictured the possibility of a war with France and Great Britain "not because we want too much but because we desire nothing." The Prince added that if this war did occur, a new Triple Alliance between France, Great Britain, and Japan, with which Russia might also be associated, might be formed. To preclude this event he urged the President to advise the Powers in favor of a conference or to prevent British participation in a possible Franco-German war brought on by French aggression in Morocco. By confronting the President with the choice of facing the outbreak of a new war just at the moment when he was endeavoring to stop the Russo-Japanese conflict or of supporting the proposal for a conference, Prince Bülow obtained the desired result. On June 12 Mr. Roosevelt agreed to advise the French government in favor of accepting the Sultan's invitation and against concluding an Anglo-French alliance.[25]

At the same time the German government endeavored to restrain Great Britain. Herr von Holstein asserted to the British Ambassador that "if any one had told him two years ago that a war between England and Germany was within the bounds of possibility he would have simply laughed, but now things had reached such a point that it could no longer be considered impossible." Both he and the Chancellor cited the bitterness of the British press toward Germany and the reported British offer of

---

[24] Bülow to Tattenbach, June 7, 1905, *ibid.*, 418 f., No. 6692.

[25] Bülow to Sternburg, June 9 and 10, 1905, *ibid.*, XX, 421 f. n.; 626 ff., No. 6856; Bishop, I, 476 f.; Sternburg to F. O., June 12, 1905, *G.P.*, XX, 433 f., No. 6707.

a defensive and offensive alliance to France as proofs. Neither of the two German officials believed that Great Britain would attack Germany, but they argued that the popular fear of such an aggression in their country was more plausible than that of a German invasion in Great Britain. In like manner Sir Frank Lascelles credited Germany with pacific intentions, but maintained that the British fears were more justified than the German. Herr von Holstein assured the Ambassador that "the Moroccan question would not lead to any serious complications," and Lord Lansdowne denied that Great Britain wanted war or had offered an alliance to France. As neither side believed entirely the pacific asseverations of the other, the tension in Anglo-German relations was only slightly relaxed.[26]

While making these efforts with the United States and Great Britain, Prince Bülow yielded before the French resistance. Although he explained away the Emperor's conciliatory remarks to the French government with a threat and although he warned M. Rouvier not to assume M. Delcassé's policy toward Morocco, he repeated his assurances that "the conference can have no positive results which would injure the French future." It was "merely a question of etiquette and of delay," he said, so that Germany could hold faith with the Sultan and disengage herself from the position into which M. Delcassé had forced her. Instead of demanding that all consideration of the Moroccan question be left to the conference, the Chancellor offered on June 12 to negotiate over the program for that assembly if France would first accept the Sultan's invitation. In addition, he instructed Prince Radolin to state not officially, but as his (Radolin's) personal view, that from the very nature of the affair the conference would have to adopt as fundamental "for the present no prejudice to the inde-

[26] Metternich to Bülow, June 9, 1905, *ibid.*, 625 f., No. 6855; Bülow to Metternich, June 11, 1905, *ibid.*, 628 ff., No. 6857; Metternich to F. O., June 15 and 16, 1905, *ibid.*, 441 f., No. 6712; 630 ff., No. 6858; Lascelles to Lansdowne, June 12, 1905, *B.D.*, III, 79 ff., Nos. 97 f.; Lansdowne to Lascelles, June 16, 1905, *ibid.*, 82 f., No. 99. See also Newton, *Lord Lansdowne*, pp. 335 f.

pendence of Morocco . . . . and . . . . no injury to the prospects of France." The Ambassador should state that the items to be considered by that body, as logical deductions from those two points were: police and military reforms, to be limited in time and international in character; financial reforms, likewise to be internationally executed; and the economic opening of the land in accordance with the principle of the open door. He should warn M. Rouvier against permitting Algerians to furnish the Moroccan pretender with contraband supplies; for if the Sultan should request German mediation in this affair, Germany would give it even at the risk of grave difficulties.[27]

When the Ambassador carried out these instructions two days later, he found M. Rouvier "angry, discouraged, sick" but still defending France's Moroccan policy. Nor did the Ambassador's remarks change his mood.[28] On June 16, in response to the Premier's request for further information, the Ambassador explained unofficially as further logical deductions from the two fundamental points: first, that the military reforms should be internationally ordered by a division of the mandate among the Powers in such a way that France would receive it for the area along the Algerian frontier; second, that to give an international character to the financial reforms, a state bank should be organized in which the capital and management should be divided as equally as possible among the banks representing the various Powers.[29] The Premier's apparent relief at these remarks en-

---

[27] Bülow to Radolin, June 12, 1905, *G.P.*, XX, 431 ff., No. 6706. The accusation that Algerians were helping the pretender was made by a German army officer who in June returned from the Algerian border. Governor Jonnart of Algeria denied it and asserted that the contraband came, not from Algeria but from the Riff. Although Jonnart's statement was undoubtedly correct, yet the report came in so handily that the German government used it as a weapon of intimidation against France (*ibid.*, Nos. 6724, 6746; *L.j., 1901–5*, Nos. 275 f., 281, 283 f.).

[28] Radolin to F. O., June 14, 1905, *G.P.*, XX, 438 f., No. 6710.

[29] Bülow to Radolin, June 16, 1905, *ibid.*, 439 ff., No. 6711; Radolin to Rouvier, June 16, 1905, *L.j., 1901–5*, 234 ff., No. 272.

couraged the German government to believe that a solution was near.[30]

In the meantime, in accordance with Germany's desires, President Roosevelt intervened in Paris and London. Notwithstanding his conviction that France was in the right, he advised her to avoid a war and help the Emperor "save his face" by accepting the conference. He argued that British support in case of a conflict would be of little value to France, and predicted a French victory at the conference. He promised the French government that if the United States participated, he "would treat both sides with absolute justice, and would, if necessary, take very strong grounds against any attitude of Germany which seemed . . . . unjust and unfair."[31]

In handling Great Britain the President took another line. He suspected her of wishing to make trouble. For he was receiving no support from her in his mediation between Russia and Japan; he knew that Lord Lansdowne was opposed to the conference; and, so far as he could tell from the British Ambassador at Washington, Great Britain was anxious for France to humiliate Germany by refusing the conference and was willing to face the possibility of war. He thought this sagacious on her part, but not valorous; she would be assured a victory on sea, while France would have to bear the brunt of the battle on land. So he warned Great Britain not to put difficulty in the way of a peaceful settlement between France and Germany, and otherwise ignored her.[32]

Neither Prince Radolin's conciliatory remarks nor President Roosevelt's advice won the French Premier to accept the confer-

[30] Bülow to Tattenbach, June 19, 1905, G.P., XX, 448 ff., No. 6718.

[31] Sternburg to F. O., June 17, 1905, ibid., 442 f., No. 6713; Bishop, I, 477 f.

[32] On Roosevelt and Great Britain see Bishop, I, 474 f., 481 ff., 408; Dennett, Roosevelt and the Russo-Japanese War, 37 f., 210 ff.; Sykes, The Right Honourable Sir Mortimer Durand, p. 285; Sternburg to F. O., June 12, 17, 25, 1905, G.P., XX, 433 f., No. 6707; 442 f., No. 6713; 473 ff., No. 6738; Lansdowne to Durand, June 16, July 12, 1905, B.D., IV, 89, No. 85; 91, No. 87; Spring Rice's correspondence with Roosevelt, June–July, 1905, Gwynn, The Letters and Friendships of Sir Cecil Spring Rice, I, 472 ff.

ence. While deeply impressed by reports of German threats against France in other capitols,[33] he inferred from his conversations with Prince Radolin and from an assertion of the German Ambassador in Madrid that if France agreed to the conference the German government would then be ready to commence discussions with a view to an understanding which would make the conference unnecessary.[34] M. Rouvier was also assured of the entire support of the British government. On June 16 Lord Lansdowne, in approving M. Paul Cambon's returning to Paris to advise the inexperienced Premier,[35] remarked to the Ambassador that he saw nothing to be gained

by admitting the theoretical necessity of a Conference, except perhaps to enable Germany, which had brought about M. Delcassé's downfall, to secure a further success. Our attitude must of course depend upon that of the French Government, but if they maintained their refusal, so, most certainly, should we.[36]

The French note to Germany of June 21 was therefore so composed by M. Paul Cambon as to accept the conference in principle while at the same time inviting Germany to negotiate further in order to obviate that assembly—the position which M. Rouvier had taken for two weeks. Since Prince Radolin's explanations on June 14 and 18 had been made in such an unofficial and confidential manner, the Premier did not know whether they represented the German view or not, and did not mention them in the note.[37] Hence that document of June 21 ran as follows:

[33] Threats by the German ambassadors in Paris, Rome, and Madrid (*B.D.*, III, 97, No. 126).

[34] Lansdowne to Bertie, June 16, 1905, *ibid.*, 96, No. 124; Nicolson to Lansdowne, June 17, 1905, *ibid.*, 97, No. 125.

[35] Barrère, the two Cambons, and Jusserand, all firmly in sympathy with Delcassé's policy, were holding Rouvier in line. See Egerton to Lansdowne, June 13, 1905, *ibid.*, 95, No. 122.

[36] Lansdowne to Bertie, June 16, 1905, *ibid.*, 96 f., No. 124. In Rome Egerton was working to hold Italy in line with this policy. See Egerton to Lansdowne, June 10, 1905, *ibid.*, 94, No. 120.

[37] Radolin to F. O., June 26, 1905, *G.P.*, XX, 484, No. 6745.

The Imperial Government will not fail to recognize the inconvenience which would result for it as for us from the acceptance of the Conference without a previous accord, an accord which would not infringe upon those already concluded and which would not harm in any way the interests of which the Imperial Government is solicitous. . . . . The Government of the Republic is deeply impressed by the double consideration that the Conference may be dangerous if it is not preceded by an entente, and useless if it follows one. [Nevertheless, the French government did not refuse the conference.] It desires solely to know what are, in the mind of the Imperial Government, the precise points which will be treated at the Conference and the solutions which it will offer there.

Thus they could arrive at the entente which both governments wished.[38]

The Premier acquainted the British and American governments with the contents of the note and of the German threats, and asked them to recommend this solution to Germany. He emphasized to Mr. Roosevelt especially the menace of a German attack. Declaring that the President could avert that danger, he urged him to exert influence with the Emperor in favor of peace. Mr. Roosevelt immediately agreed to do so in energetic terms.[39]

[38] Rouvier to Radolin, June 21, 1905, *L.j., 1901–5*, 235 ff., No. 273; Radolin to F. O., June 21, 1905, *G.P.*, XX, 452 f., No. 6720. The note was composed mainly by Paul Cambon. See Radolin to F. O., June 30, 1905, *ibid.*, 494, No. 6752.

[39] Lansdowne to Bertie, June 21, 1905, *B.D.*, III, 97 f., No. 126; Metternich to F. O., June 23, 1905, *G.P.*, XX, 463 f., No. 6727; Rouvier to Jusserand, June 23 and 25, 1905, quoted in Bishop, I, 478 ff. Dennis relates that while in France in May, 1926, he heard a story to the effect that Roosevelt had written to the German Emperor at this crisis warning him that "it would be a crime against civilization for Germany to declare war against France." Dennis was unable to find any such letter, and presumes that the one thought to have contained this warning was one from Roosevelt to Sternburg on June 26 [*sic*], 1905 (Dennis, *Adventures in American Diplomacy*, p. 495). The truth seems to be that Roosevelt, who had not been so schooled in diplomacy as to choose his words carefully, spoke to Jusserand as if he would use such language to the Emperor, and then softened down his words greatly when he did write to Sternburg. Cf. Jusserand's letter to Rouvier on June 25, 1905, with Roosevelt's letter to Sternburg on the same date, quoted in Bishop, I, 480 f., 483 ff. Rouvier gave Roosevelt credit for his acceptance in principle of the conference. The French Premier also asked Eckardstein to intervene again, but the latter refused since he was in such bad odor with his government (Eckardstein, III, 147 ff.).

The German reaction was hostile. As the Chancellor realized that the crisis had arisen in Franco-German relations, he endeavored by a mixture of enticements and threats to bring the impressionable and pacific M. Rouvier to accept the German terms.[40] Refusing the French request, Prince Bülow warned the Premier on June 21, 22, and 23 against resuming M. Delcassé's policy and against permitting the Algerians to aid the Moroccan pretender. While promising the French government "seriously and loyally" to work for a result satisfactory to all parties and especially for an understanding with France at the conference, the Chancellor declared to the French Ambassador: "The situation is serious. With a little good will and decision we may emerge from it." But "one should not play with fire"; "it is a dangerous game which might lead further than you and I wish." Threatening to make a defensive alliance with the Sultan if French policy forced him to, he refused the overture for negotiation and advised a quick acceptance of the conference.[41]

The German policy was not as successful as the Chancellor had

[40] "Rouvier . . . . we know does not wish a conflict with us," . . . . "the Chamber of Deputies wishes above all to avoid war" (quoted from a dispatch from Bülow to William II, June 22, 1905, *G.P.*, XX, 456, No. 6723). "The sooner we make it clear to him [Rouvier] what results the French refusal of the conference and the further support of the pretender must have, the more we diminish the dangers of the situation" (Bülow to Radolin, June 24, 1905, *ibid.*, 466, No. 6730). That the German government was playing with war but did not intend to start one is also evident from a confidential letter from Holstein to the editor of the *Kölnische Zeitung*, June 28, 1905, which expresses completely the nature of the German policy. ". . . . In brief, I consider the danger of war for Germany at the present moment vanishingly small. It will be still more diminished if a conviction of our firmness prevails. We know now for certain that in the last ministerial council Delcassé declared: 'Germany will not dare to fight, it is all bluff.' This doubt about our determination could have led to a conflict if the other ministers had shared Delcassé's views" (reprinted in *Kölnische Zeitung*, April 2, 1922).

[41] Radolin to F. O., June 22, 1905, *G.P.*, XX, 457 ff., No. 6724; memo. by Bülow, June 23, 1905, *ibid.*, 459 ff., No. 6725; Bülow to William II, June 22 and 24, 1905, *ibid.*, 455 ff., No. 6723; 464 f., No. 6729; Bülow to Radolin, June 24, 1905, *ibid.*, 465 f., No. 6730; Bihourd to Rouvier, June 23, 1905, *L.j., 1901–5*, 240 f., No. 277; Lansdowne to Lister, June 28, 1905, *B.D.*, III, 105 ff., No. 133; Whitehead to Lansdowne, June 28, 1905, *ibid.*, 108 f., No. 135.

expected. By June 21 Italy had, in spite of German pressure, accepted the conference only conditionally.[42] The British government, loyally following the lead of France, fully approved the French note (June 23).[43] In Spain, although a ministerial crisis on June 20 had eliminated M. Villa-Urrutia as Germany had demanded, the new Liberal government refused Germany's request for support; it declared on June 25 that it would remain loyal to the Franco-Spanish accord.[44] Furthermore, it was apparent that M. Rouvier would not accept the German demands in their existing form.[45] The Premier was staunchly supported by the French press, which was quickly coming to credit Germany with the intention not of making friends with France but of teaching her a lesson and of setting limits to her foreign policy.[46] More

[42] Monts to Bülow, June 21, 1905, *G.P.*, XX, 454 f., No. 6722.

[43] Metternich to F. O., June 23, 1905, *ibid.*, 463 f., No. 6727; Lee, II, 344; Lansdowne to Bertie, June 21, 1905, *B.D.*, III, 97 f., No. 126.

[44] Bülow held out prospects of aiding Spain to acquire Tangier and the surrounding territory in case of a future break-up of Morocco if Spain would uphold the German policy. The insincerity of the statement is proved by a letter from Holstein to Radolin on July 2, 1905. In regard to the Moroccan affair he wrote: "We need have no consideration for the wishes of others, at any rate not for those of Spain who has never caused other than anger or embarrassment for us." See Bülow to Radowitz, June 21, 1905, *G.P.*, XX, 453 f., No. 6721; Radowitz to F. O., June 25, 1905, *ibid.*, 473, No. 6737; Holstein to Radolin, July 2, 1905, *ibid.*, 503, No. 6757.

[45] See Rouvier's reply to the Prince of Monaco, which the latter immediately handed to the German government (William II to Bülow, June 24, 1905, *ibid.*, 464, No. 6728).

[46] Eckardstein, III, 147 ff.; report from Paris, June 18, 1905, *Zur europ. Politik*, II, 60; *Bulletin*, June, 1905, pp. 235 ff. "There appear to me to be indications that the feeling is growing in France that it is necessary to treat the Morocco question in as conciliatory a spirit as possible, but that when further demands are made by Germany they should be met by a firm refusal. . . . . The feeling of resentment against Germany on account of her present action is very strong and the spirit of the 'revanche' is reawakening; the French have pulled themselves together wonderfully after their first panic and they now seem prepared to face calmly the contingency of war in the future should the pretensions of Germany continue. "There is I think no doubt that Monsieur Rouvier could at present command a very large majority in the Chamber on any question of Foreign policy, and his efforts to preserve peace by conciliation so far as conciliation can go without loss

discouraging still, on June 24 Baron Sternburg telegraphed the following statement from President Roosevelt:

The French Government informs me unofficially . . . . that it has ceased its opposition to a conference. . . . . It seems as a matter of course that a program of the conference would be needed in advance in accordance with the usual custom in such cases. I suggest that that be arranged between France and Germany. . . . . Let me congratulate the Emperor warmly on his diplomatic triumph of the first magnitude.[47]

The German government retreated. Replying to the French government on June 24,[48] it asserted the right of the other Powers to participate in the work of Moroccan reform. It refused to negotiate a program for the conference beforehand, but admitted "that France has a very legitimate interest in maintaining order in the territory bordering on the frontier." In the verbal explanations made upon the delivery of the note, the Chancellor, denying that the conference was intended to procure for Germany a "miserable satisfaction for her *amour-propre*" or to humiliate France, declared that international reform should be attempted in Morocco first. Then if this work broke down, he said, "the future is free," and "in that future, which is perhaps not so distant, we shall again be able to become opportunists." He was profoundly surprised, he said, that the French note took no cognizance of the overtures made by the German Ambassador. He urged the acceptance of the conference so that the two countries might escape from this "perilous and dangerous situation" into "a path which leads to appeasement, conciliation, and peace."

The Chancellor also instructed Prince Radolin to inform M.

---

of dignity, will only enhance his position in the eyes of his countrymen, and assure him their unanimous support in the event of such a policy being rendered impossible" (Lister to Lansdowne, June 28, 1905, *B.D.*, III, 107 f., No. 134).

[47] Sternburg to F. O., June 24, 1905, *ibid.*, 466 f., No. 6731; Bishop, I, 482.

[48] The note was dated June 24, but was handed by Bülow to Bihourd on June 25 and by Radolin to Rouvier on June 27, 1905. See Radolin to Rouvier, June 24, 1905, *L.j., 1901–5*, 242 ff., No. 278; Bihourd to Rouvier, June 25, 1905, *ibid.*, 244 f., No. 279; Bülow to Radolin, June 25 and 26, 1905, *G.P.*, XX, 470 f., No. 6734; 472, No. 6736; Bülow to William II, June 26, 1905, *ibid.*, 476 ff., No. 6740.

Rouvier that if France accepted the conference, Germany would then be willing to work out an agreement with her on the bases mentioned previously (June 14 and 18) for a prospective program to be submitted to the Sultan.[49] If the Ambassador thought that M. Rouvier would refuse to accept the conference before the program was agreed upon, the Chancellor would permit him to propose that the French and German representatives work out a program with the Sultan in Fez. If M. Rouvier refused the conference altogether, Prince Radolin should warn him that Germany would aid the Sultan against any French aggressions. The Ambassador was to tell M. Rouvier that the Moroccan government had made offers to Germany which would insure her a leading position in that land, but that Germany would refuse them as long as the possibility of an accord with France remained.[50]

By June 27 the advantage again shifted to the German side. In Paris the more anti-British and pro-German element, led by M. Dupuy, owner of *Petit Parisien* and an intimate friend of M. Rouvier, was gaining greater influence. M. Dupuy informed the German Ambassador on June 26 that M. Rouvier, whom he represented as a rather well-meaning simpleton, now regretted having dispatched the French note and that he now sought some phrase by which the German and French views could be harmonized and the conference accepted. In fact, M. Dupuy stated that he expected the French government to make the acceptance in a day or so. Both he and M. Betzold said that the Premier still mistrusted Great Britain.[51]

Even more valuable for the German government was Mr. Roosevelt's change in attitude. When the German government explained to Mr. Roosevelt that France had not agreed to the conference except under conditions which Germany had per-

[49] However, the Sultan and the other Powers should not be precluded thereby from proposing other matters for the consideration of that body.

[50] Bülow to Radolin, June 25, dispatched June 26, 1905, *ibid.*, 470 f., No. 6734.

[51] Radolin to F. O., June 25 and 26, 1905, *ibid.*, 472, No. 6735; 479, No. 6741; Radolin to Bülow, June 26, 1905, *ibid.*, 483 f., No. 6745.

sistently refused,[52] the President immediately advised France on June 26 to accept unconditionally. He stated that the question of a program was a minor one, that the important thing was for the conference to meet. In answer, the French Ambassador protested that in view of the German Emperor's erratic temperament France could not go to the conference

without previously having drawn up a program, or at least without an understanding, indicating that which we might have reason to expect and guaranteeing in particular that solemn international undertakings, which have for a long time been public property, should not be brought into question.[53]

Thereupon Mr. Roosevelt proposed the following compromise: "Let France and Germany go into the conference without any programme or agreement; but to discuss all questions in regard to Morocco; save of course where either is in honor bound by a previous agreement with another power."[54]

In reporting to Baron Sternburg what he had done, the President said that if France and Germany agreed upon this or any other compromise, he himself would accept the invitation to the conference and would advise Great Britain to do likewise. On June 27 he offered to telegraph his greetings to the Emperor William II. He also expressed to the British Ambassador his strong hope that Great Britain would drop her objections to the conference.[55]

The President's intervention was beneficial to both the French and the German governments; it brought them into a frame of mind which permitted a compromise. The German government was elated over his action; for even though it diminished any hope of breaking the French accords over Morocco, it did seem to assure a peaceful issue of the crisis by the acceptance of the

[52] Bülow to William II, June 25, 1905, ibid., 467 ff., No. 6732; Sternburg to F. O., June 25, 1905, ibid., 473 ff., No. 6738; Bülow to Sternburg, June 26, 1905, ibid., 475 f., No. 6739; Bishop, I, 483 f.

[53] Bishop, I, 485 f.

[54] Sternburg to F. O., June 26, 27, 1905, G.P., XX, 479 ff., No. 6742 f.; Bishop, I, 485.

[55] Sternburg to F. O., June 27, 1905, G.P., XX, 480 f., No. 6743.

conference. Hence Prince Bülow telegraphed to Washington on June 27 that "if after the acceptance of the conference by France we negotiate with the French and differences arise, I shall be ready at all times to support before His Majesty the Emperor that decision which President Roosevelt recommends as practical and fair."[56]

This success, however, was offset by a report from Baron Eckardstein on June 27 that M. Delcassé had received an offer of an offensive and defensive alliance from Great Britain, but that M. Rouvier had refused to consider it. Within the past ten days, the Baron continued, the British government had informed the French Premier "that he could rely upon its diplomatic support under all circumstances, but that if he wished to make an alliance with England, the English fleet would also uphold the French policy in case of necessity."[57] After frankly repeating those statements to Lord Lansdowne on the following day, Count Metternich added that "at no moment had the German Government desired to fasten a quarrel upon France," as the British seemed to think. Lord Lansdowne replied that "the language attributed to some of the German representatives had certainly suggested the idea that it was desired to do so." He then made this important statement:

. . . . British diplomatic support was assured to the French by the Anglo-French accord. . . . . As a natural result questions which concerned that agreement would have been discussed between the two Governments and proper ways and means conferred upon to maintain intact the individual points of the accord. The question of an alliance with France has never been discussed by the British cabinet nor has an English alliance ever been of-

[56] Bülow to Sternburg, June 27, 1905, *ibid.*, 481, No. 6744. Sternburg inadvertently changed the wording of that promise to read as follows: "The Emperor has requested me [Sternburg] to tell you that if during the coming conference differences of opinion should arise between France and Germany, he, in every case, will be ready to back up the decision which you should consider to be most fair and most practical" (Sternburg to Roosevelt, June 28, 1905, quoted in Bishop, I, 487). The latter promise bound the German government more tightly than did the former, and was to cause it embarrassment later.

[57] Metternich to F. O., June 27, 1905, *G.P.*, XX, 634 f., No. 6859.

fered to France. . . . . However, he would not conceal his belief that in the event that Germany "lightheartedly" made war upon France, which he considered entirely improbable, it was not to be foreseen how far British public opinion would force the Government to support France.[58]

To this alarming information was added the report from Paris that the British were exerting all possible pressure to prevent France from accepting the conference.[59] Furthermore, when Prince Radolin carried out his instructions, June 27, M. Rouvier continued to refuse the conference without a previous understanding. To that end he offered two proposals. One, a suggestion which he took from a German newspaper, was that the French and German representatives at Fez work out a program in co-operation with the Sultan prior to French acceptance of the conference. The other was that in providing for the international regulation of the police and financial reforms France should be assured the right to execute the police reforms along the Algerian frontier while nothing definite should be stated about the organization of the police in the rest of Morocco. This agreement, M. Rouvier added, could become valid as soon as France officially accepted the conference. He also desired the recall of the three ministers from Fez so as to prevent complications.[60]

As already seen, the Chancellor was willing to accept the first proposal, although, fearing that upon further delay the Sultan might throw over the project of a conference and undermine the entire German policy, he preferred some other solution. Since he mistrusted the Sultan, he refused to recall Count Tattenbach from Fez until the conference actually met. He also held to his formula of "first acceptance, then negotiations"; but to counteract the British pressure he retreated further by agreeing on June 28 for the Premier to declare publicly that

the French Government has dropped its objections to the conference after becoming convinced from the declarations of Your Highness [Prince Ra-

[58] Metternich to F. O., June 28, 1905, *ibid.*, 636, No. 6860; Lansdowne to Whitehead, June 28, 1905, *B.D.*, III, 103, No. 132*a*.

[59] Radolin to F. O., June 26, dispatched June 27, 1905, *G.P.*, XX, 479, No. 6741.

[60] Radolin to F. O., June 27, dispatched June 28, 1905, *ibid.*, 485 f., No. 6746.

dolin] that Germany would pursue no goals at the conference which would stand in opposition to the just interests of France.

He refused, however, to permit M. Rouvier to make public anything further about the German concessions of June 14 and 18.[61] On the same day he declared to M. Bihourd that once the conference met, Germany would be freed from her obligations to the Sultan and could follow her own interests. Let international reforms first be tried in Morocco, he said; if they failed, Germany would have to consult only her own interests, among which Morocco occupied "an infinitely small place." If France, in conformity with the views of the British government, refused the conference, there would obtain a condition of *la paix armée*. If she accepted, there would be "neither victor nor vanquished."[62]

Learning that the German government regarded Prince Radolin's assertions of June 14 and 18 as official and despairing of any other solution, M. Rouvier was more inclined to accept the conference. He justified this course to the British chargé d'affaires on June 28 as follows:

He [M. Rouvier] considered that under the conditions a conference was perhaps the best way of arriving at a satisfactory solution. The Emperor had made it a point of personal honour: France would go into it with the support of England, Spain, and possibly Italy, whereas Germany would be alone; Germany was prepared to admit the preponderance of French interests on the Algerian frontier. It was absolutely necessary to arrive at some solution as the present situation was excessively dangerous. So long as the Conference was not accepted, Germany considered that she was entitled to a free hand in Morocco, and she was very very [sic] active. She would ask for all sorts of concessions, ports, cables, etc., and were the Sultan to accede to such demands the situation both for France and England would become far more critical. Monsieur Rouvier hinted that once the present difficulties had been more or less tided over at the Conference, it would be possible to see that Germany did not get too much in Morocco.[63]

[61] Bülow to Radolin, June 28, 1905, *ibid.*, 487 f., No. 6748; Bülow to William II, June 28, 1905, *ibid.*, 488 ff., No. 6749.

[62] Bülow to Radolin, July 1, 1905, *ibid.*, 495 ff., No. 6753 and Appendix; Holstein to Radolin, June 28, 1905, *ibid.*, 490 ff., No. 6750.

[63] Lister to Lansdowne, June 28, 1905, *B.D.*, III, 107 f., No. 134.

Before approving the proposal for a conference, however, M. Rouvier intended to include in the agreement with Germany some mention of France's accords with Great Britain and Spain over Morocco.[64] While M. Rouvier delayed, the German government grew apprehensive. Prince Radolin heard on June 29 that M. Paul Cambon, Sir Francis Bertie, and the British government were making every effort to prevent the French acceptance, arguing that Germany was endeavoring to nullify the Anglo-French agreement. On the next day M. Dupuy informed the Ambassador that the British "were sitting powerfully on M. Rouvier's back" to obstruct it and that Sir Francis Bertie was pressing the French Premier to make a defensive and offensive alliance with Great Britain. When M. Cambon reached Paris on June 30, M. Dupuy thought that there was grave danger of M. Rouvier's being overthrown.[65]

In this situation the German government denied on June 30 to the French government that it meant to question the Anglo-French accord. On the next day it was prepared to give way still further, but M. Rouvier accepted the conference.[66] The Premier proposed that he and the German Ambassador make an exchange of notes and sign a declaration incorporating the concessions which the German government had made to France.[67] M. Rouvier then submitted the bases of the agreement to Lord Lansdowne, who approved them.[68] After much bickering over the

---

[64] Lansdowne entirely approved of this suggestion, remarking that "it [the Anglo-French declaration] might be usefully cited for the purpose of showing that the policy of both France and Great Britain had been in favour of maintaining the independence and integrity of Morocco and preserving commercial equality" (Lansdowne to Bertie, July 1, 1905, *ibid.*, 110 f., No. 137). The rancor back of Lansdowne's statement is apparent.

[65] Radolin to F. O., June 29 and 30, 1905, *G.P.*, XX, 492 ff., Nos. 6751 f.; Lee, II, 344.

[66] Bülow to Radolin, July 1, 1905, *G.P.*, XX, 495 ff., No. 6753 and Anlage; Rouvier to Bihourd, July 9, 1905, *L.j., 1901–5*, 249, No. 285.

[67] Radolin to Bülow, July 1, 1905, *G.P.*, XX, 499, No. 6754; 501 f., No. 6756; Radolin to F. O., July 1, 1905, *ibid.*, 499 f., No. 6755.

[68] Lansdowne to Bertie, July 1, 1905, *B.D.*, III, 110 f., No. 137.

formulation of the agreement, during which a liberal repetition of German threats mixed with enticements was made, accord was finally reached on July 8.[69]

By that agreement Germany promised to pursue no goal at the conference which would compromise the "legitimate interests" of France in Morocco or

that would be contrary to the rights of France resulting from treaties or arrangements and harmonizing with the following principles: sovereignty and independence of the Sultan; integrity of his empire; economic liberty without any inequality; utility of police and financial reforms the introduction of which will be regulated for a short period by way of an international accord; recognition of the situation created for France with reference to Morocco by the contiguity, over a long stretch, of Algeria and the Sherifian empire, by the particular relations which result therefrom between the two neighboring countries, as well as by the special interest which results therefrom for France for order to obtain in the Sherifian empire.

The two governments agreed to work out a program for the conference which they would submit to the Sultan for acceptance. The French and German missions were to be recalled from Fez as soon as the conference met. Prince Radolin also stated specifically that the Anglo-French and Franco-Spanish agreements remained untouched by this understanding.[70]

The French, British, and German presses greeted this accord with relief and with the sincere hope that the crisis was past.[71] The Powers also signified their acceptances.[72]

[69] On those negotiations see *G.P.*, XX, Nos. 6754 ff.; Rouvier to Bihourd, July 9, 1905, *L.j., 1901–5*, 249, No. 285.

[70] *L.j., 1901–5*, Nos. 287 f.; *G.P.*, XX, Nos. 6767 f.; *B.D.*, III, 115 f., No. 147.

[71] See Rouvier's speech in the Chamber on July 10, 1905 (*Journal officiel. Debats parlem.* [Chambre, July 10, 1905], pp. 2825 f.). Lansdowne's speech of acceptance in the House of Lords, July 11, 1905, 4 Hansard, Vol. CIXL, col. 241. Richthofen to Radolin, July 9, 1905, *G.P.*, XX, 516 f., No. 6769. The German government prohibited Jaurès from coming to Berlin to speak before a socialist congress on July 9, but as the prohibition was based on internal reasons, it had little effect upon Franco-German relations (Schulthess, *1905*, pp. 104 f.; *L'année politique, 1905*, p. 388).

[72] The French and British governments were particularly anxious for Russia and the United States to attend. See Lansdowne to Lister, July 6, 1905, *B.D.*, III, 114, No. 143; see also *ibid.*, Nos. 149 ff., 154, 159 f., 164.

The agreement marked Germany's first reverse in her Moroccan campaign. She had been compelled to recognize France's special interest in Morocco and had failed to nullify the French ententes. Germany could have placed herself on the same basis with reference to France that Great Britain occupied, both in regard to European and to colonial affairs. Instead, however, of weakening the Entente Cordiale, instead of making a valuable colonial accord by accepting the French offers, the German government had preferred both to keep its promises to the Sultan and to free itself from those promises by forcing a conference upon an unwilling world. Caught in the toils of its own tangled policy and determined to have a share in Morocco even though the German people were uninterested, it had refused present offers of colonial gain with the hope of bringing about their renewal in the future. Its virtue, not appreciated by any other Power, was greater than its common sense.

Although the German government had receded, it had done so only after embittering the French nation and arousing it to the united defense of its national honor. As Ambassador Jusserand wrote to Mr. Roosevelt on July 11:

> I leave greatly comforted by the news concerning Morocco. The agreement arrived at is in substance the one which we had considered and the acceptation of which you did so very much to secure. Letters just received by me from Paris . . . . confirm what I guessed was the case, that is, that there was a point where more yielding would have been impossible; everybody in France felt it, and people braced up silently in view of possible great events.[73]

Germany's actions had antagonized M. Rouvier and converted him to the Entente Cordiale. M. Rouvier remarked to the British chargé d'affaires as follows:

> His Majesty [the German Emperor] had expected a complete climb-down to follow upon the change of direction of the Ministry for Foreign Affairs, but as His Excellency [M. Rouvier] said, there was no reason because he

[73] Quoted in Bishop, I, 488.

parted with Monsieur Delcassé that he should throw himself "dans les bras de l'Empereur et sur son cou."[74]

M. Cambon informed Lord Lansdowne that

after all that had happened M. Rouvier was more convinced than ever of the necessity of maintaining a close understanding with this country [Great Britain]. It was, in his view, essential that the two Governments should treat one another with the fullest confidence, and that no further steps should be taken without previous discussion between us. While holding this opinion, M. Rouvier thought it desirable to proceed with caution in dealing with the German Government and thought we should avoid parading a desire to run counter to them.

These assertions met with Lord Lansdowne's entire approval, for they signified the success of the British struggle to maintain the Entente Cordiale and to keep Germany out of Morocco. The Foreign Secretary assured M. Cambon that Great Britain had no intention of withdrawing her support. But he added: ". . . . The apparent sacrifice of M. Delcassé in the face of German pressure had created an unfavourable impression in this country, and I therefore thought there was a good deal to be said for M. Rouvier's view that it would be as well to avoid any action calculated to bring about fresh complications."[75] In other words, Lord Lansdowne intimated that British public opinion would not be so willing to support France as it had been before that display of French weakness.

In spite of this remark, signs were not lacking of close intimacy between the two countries. On July 12 *Gaulois* published the information that at the cabinet meeting on June 6 M. Delcassé had favored an alliance with Great Britain in order to hold Germany in check. Without definitely stating so, the article left

[74] Lister to Lansdowne, June 28, 1905, *B.D.*, III, 108, No. 134.

[75] Lansdowne to Bertie, July 12, 1905, *ibid.*, 118 f., No. 152. On June 28 Lowther reported a conversation with Tattenbach in which the latter gave him to understand that "what he [Tattenbach] desired the Conference should do, would be to bring about an amendment of the Anglo-French Convention of April 8th, 1904." King Edward's minute to this dispatch was, "In plain English—Germany ousts France fr[om] Morocco and puts herself in her place!" See Lowther to Lansdowne, D. June 28, 1905, R. July 10, 1905, *ibid.*, 101 f., No. 191.

the impression that the Foreign Minister had been certain of an alliance.[76] When the French and British fleets exchanged visits in July and August, the press compared the visits to that of the Russian fleet to Toulon in 1893 which had sealed the Franco-Russian alliance.[77]

The German government was thus furthering that process which it called Germany's encirclement and isolation.

[76] Schulthess, *1905*, pp. 217 f.   [77] Lee, II, 344 f.

CHAPTER XIV

THE MOROCCAN CRISIS, JULY–OCTOBER, 1905

After Germany had forced France to lay the Moroccan problem before an international conference, M. Rouvier was no longer willing to give Germany a share in Morocco. Confident of British support and heartened by the friendly assertions of the German officials, he hoped to obtain a general mandate from the conference for executing the military, police, and financial reforms.[1] Thus resuming the original French policy toward Morocco, he took steps to fulfil it by way of that assembly.

Before negotiating with Germany over a program for the conference, M. Rouvier obtained the approval of his proposals from Great Britain and Spain.[2] He also felt it necessary to affirm and supplement the Franco-Spanish agreement of 1904 in accordance with the new situation and to make certain of Spain's loyalty at the conference.

The new government formed in Madrid late in June showed immediately a more independent spirit toward France than its predecessor had done. Both M. Montero Rios, the premier, and M. Roman, the foreign minister, reiterated to the British Ambassador that "the chief aim of their foreign policy was to be on specially intimate terms with Great Britain, and to strengthen as far as possible the good understanding at present existing." But they established closer contacts with Germany, and informed the British and French governments that while Spain would abide by the Franco-Spanish Agreement she had not "abnegated her personality," and was free to take any course, in matters out-

[1] Rouvier to Bihourd, July 9, 1905, *L.j., 1901–5,* 249, No. 285.

[2] It was Lansdowne's suggestion that Spain be included. See Lansdowne to Bertie, July 12 and 13, 1905, *B.D.,* III, 118 ff., Nos. 152 f.; Cambon to Lansdowne, July 20, 1905, *ibid.,* 121 f., No. 157; Lansdowne to Manneville, July 21, 1905, *ibid.,* 122, No. 158.

side that agreement, "as might be dictated by her interests." Spanish public opinion reflected the same sentiment. Some elements even wished to use the acceptance of the conference as an excuse for withdrawing from the Franco-Spanish agreement entirely. With the help of the British government and the blunders of Germany, that antagonized Spain, M. Rouvier ironed out the differences.[3] On September 1 the French and Spanish governments signed a secret agreement.[4] Its terms were as follows:

All officers and underofficers charged with the instruction and command of the native troops in Larache and Tetouan were to be Spanish, while those in Rabat and Casablanca were to be French. The policing of Tangier should be intrusted for fifteen years to a Franco-Spanish corps commanded by a Frenchman. Contraband traffic in arms should be suppressed by France and Spain, individually in certain areas, co-operatively in others. The two governments were to work together to the end that "the participation in the capital and the works of all public enterprises will be offered to subjects of the two nations." In the state bank or in any other institution to be created the presidency should be reserved to France, while the degree of participation of Spain should be superior to that of any other Power except France.

The two Powers engage to observe this accord even in case where the stipulations of Article XVII of the Convention of Madrid of 1880 come to be extended to all economic and financial questions; they will aid each other before the Sultan . . . . to assure the loyal accomplishment of all that the present accord stipulates. Moreover, Spain being firmly resolved to act in complete accord with France . . . . and France proposing to act in the same way with Spain, it is agreed . . . . that the two Governments will

[3] Nicolson to Lansdowne, D. June 29, 1905, R. July 10, 1905, D. July 1, 1905, R. July 10, 1905, July 7 and 11, 1905, ibid., 109 f., No. 136; 111 f., No. 138; 114, No. 144; 116, No. 148; Lansdowne to Nicolson, July 8, 1905, ibid., 114 f., No. 145; Lansdowne to Bertie, July 12, 1905, ibid., 119, No. 152.

[4] Nothing is known of these negotiations. See Vidal, La politique de l'Espagne au Maroc, pp. 172 ff.; Mousset, La politica exterior de España 1873–1918, pp. 162 f.; Tardieu, Revue des deux mondes, Dec., 1912, p. 640; La Conf. d'Algés., pp. 58 ff., 156.

assist each other and will proceed in common accord in the deliberations [at the conference] in that which concerns the stipulations of the convention of October 3, 1904, in its broadest and most amicable interpretation as well as in that which concerns the different objects of the present accord. They engage to extend to each other the most complete pacific aid on all questions of a general order concerning Morocco in harmony with the cordial and friendly entente between them with reference to the affairs of the Sherifian Empire.[5]

Both governments were well pleased with the terms. The British government also readily approved them. The transaction marked another step in drawing the three Powers closer together and in handing Morocco over to the charge of France and Spain.[6]

At the same time M. Rouvier began negotiations with the German government over the program for the conference. The two were at loggerheads from the start, for the German views of what constituted a just consideration of France's interests in Morocco were different from those of the French. When, late in June, the Moroccan government offered to give various economic contracts to Germany and to appoint a few German officers for creating a small Moroccan army, Count Tattenbach was enthusiastically in favor of accepting the proposals.[7] Prince Bülow refused, and on July 11 instructed the Minister as follows:

As for your further deportment in Fez, ... keep in mind that you will soon have to co-operate with the French representative. We regard the concessions offered by the Sultan as desirable, but can accept them only if they are not in contradiction to the future decisions of the conference. Therefore . . . . delay making a decision about these offers. . . . .[8]

[5] The accord is reprinted in *Archives diplomatiques*, CXX (1911), 15 ff.

[6] Lansdowne to Lister, Aug. 30, 1905, *B.D.*, III, 131, No. 173; Cartwright to Lansdowne, Sept. 4 and 7, 1905, *ibid.*, 136, No. 175; 137 f., No. 177; Cambon to Lansdowne, Sept. 6, 1905, *ibid.*, 136 f., No. 176; Lansdowne to Cambon, Sept. 9, 1907, *ibid.*, 138, No. 179.

[7] Tattenbach to F. O., June 16, 1905, *G.P.*, XX, 444 f., Nos. 6714 f; Tattenbach to F. O., June 23 and 25, 1905, *ibid.*, pp. 524 f. n.

[8] Bülow to Tattenbach, June 19 and 20, 1905, *ibid.*, 448 ff., No. 6718 f.; Bülow to Tattenbach, July 11, 1905, *ibid.*, 524 ff., No. 6774.

Nevertheless, the Chancellor planned for the conference to divide the police and military mandate in Morocco among the Powers in such a way that France would receive the mandate for the frontier region only, while Germany would receive it for "the western coastal towns from Rabat south . . . . as suitable for a future German sphere of interest."[9] Furthermore, he expected Germany to receive her share of the economic advantages in the development of the entire land.[10]

To achieve these ends the German foreign office appointed Count Tattenbach as its representative at the conference,[11] even though he was highly objectionable to the French. It also instructed Prince Radolin on July 10 to inform M. Rouvier either directly or indirectly that "the desired understanding would be placed seriously in doubt" if he did not exclude M. Delcassé's followers, such as M. Paul Cambon and M. Georges Louis,[12] from influence upon French foreign policy, or if he should appoint M. Révoil, former governor of Algeria and a reputed Germanophobe, as a delegate to the conference.[13] Prince Radolin was also to uphold Tangier as a meeting place for the assembly; for the German government believed that the anti-French and pro-German influence of the Moroccans would be more strongly exerted there than in some European town.[14] When the Ambassador stated his government's requests to MM. Dupuy and

[9] Tattenbach to F. O., June 25, 1905, *ibid.*, p. 525 n.; Bülow to Tattenbach, June 19, July 11, 1905, *ibid.*, 450, No. 6718; 525 f., No. 6774.

[10] Tattenbach had visions of persuading the Sultan to transfer his residence from Fez to Marrakech where he would be under German influence after Morocco was divided, and where Germany could then secure the appointment of Germans as the Sultan's military instructors (Tattenbach to F. O., June 25, 1905, *ibid.*, p. 525 n.).

[11] Bülow to Tattenbach, July 11, 1905, *ibid.*, 524, No. 6774.

[12] Georges Louis was the political director of the French foreign office.

[13] Richthofen to Radolin, July 10, 1905, *ibid.*, 521 f., No. 6771; Holstein to Radolin, July 10, 1905, *ibid.*, 523, No. 6772.

[14] Mühlberg to Wedel, July 13, 1905, *ibid.*, 526 f., No. 6775; Bülow to William II, Aug. 3, 1905, *ibid.*, 537, No. 6786. This choice was also desired by the Moroccan government for its own convenience (Lowther to Lansdowne, July 24, 1905, *B.D.*, III, 123, No. 161).

Léon, both men begged him "not to put the pistol to M. Rouvier's breast too sharply." M. Rouvier was having enough difficulty with public opinion, they said.[15] The German government asked President Roosevelt to support its views about M. Révoil and about Tangier, but this time, after consulting the French government, the President refused.[16] M. Rouvier chose M. Révoil in spite of German opposition. Furthermore, asserting that Tangier was a dangerous hotbed of intrigue, he urged the choice of some European town.[17] By the end of July the German government was willing to acquiesce, although for bargaining purposes it reserved its public consent until later.[18]

It was not M. Rouvier's determined stand which induced this acquiescence, but rather the unexpected signing by the German and Russian rulers of the Björkö treaty of alliance on July 24.[19] This treaty, which provided for the later association of France in the alliance, was signed by both sovereigns under the impression that the Franco-German agreement of July 8 had settled the Moroccan affair and had cleared the way for a *rapprochement*. In view of this changed situation Prince Bülow, on July 31, instructed the foreign office as follows:

1. We must reserve the possibility of permitting France a free hand in Morocco at the moment in which she has to decide about joining the Russo-German understanding. A better use of Morocco we could hardly find and that would be by far the most favorable close of our Moroccan campaign. 2. To attain this we need not relinquish too early our general position on the Moroccan question. But the French need not believe that our aim was ultimately to set foot in Morocco. It appears to me more advisable to permit the Moroccan question to rest for a time rather than to hasten it. Pushing or threatening at this moment on account of Morocco would only press

[15] Radolin to F. O., July 14, 1905, *G.P.*, XX, 527, No. 6776.

[16] Bussche-Haddenhausen to F. O., July 25 and 30, 1905, *ibid.*, 528 f., No. 6778; 529, No. 6779; Bishop, *The Life and Times of Theodore Roosevelt*, I, 488.

[17] His view was actively supported by the British government. Lansdowne to Bertie, July 12, 1905, *B.D.*, III, 119, No. 152; Lansdowne to Lowther, July 28, 1905, *ibid.*, 123, No. 163.

[18] Bülow to William II, Aug. 3, 1905, *G.P.*, XX, 537, No. 6786.

[19] See next chapter.

France still closer to England and at the same time cause the Emperor Nicholas to suspect that directly after Björkö he is to be forced to choose between us and France.[20]

In keeping with this policy, Prince Bülow, Baron Richthofen, and Herr von Mühlberg all absented themselves from Berlin during the succeeding days, and left Count Pourtales, Prussian minister in Munich, in charge of the foreign office. As he was not in touch with the negotiations, Herr von Holstein and Dr. Kriege, the legal adviser, directed affairs. While the "Grey Eminence" approved the new direction to be given to the Moroccan policy,[21] he seemed entirely unable to relinquish a stand once taken or to sacrifice details for the achievement of a larger end. When his blunders brought him to the point of having to retreat or fight, he preferred *Machtpolitik*. Neither he nor his chief realized that some form of settlement of the Moroccan affair was necessary to allay French and British mistrust, and that their new policy of delay would prolong the period of crisis. This was particularly the case since the policy continued to lack unity. Herr von Holstein, Dr. Kriege, the Emperor, Count Tattenbach—each had his particular addition to make, whether it harmonized with the whole or not; and the gracious Prince Bülow, successor to Bismarck, accepted all contributions.

The most striking example of this lack of harmony was manifested by Count Tattenbach at Fez. Early in August the news spread that the Count had been instrumental in persuading the Moroccan government to grant to the German firm of Bourgeaud-Hansemann on July 30 a contract for building a mole in the harbor of Tangier at the price of 1,300,000 marks. It was also rumored that he was aiding negotiations between the Sultan and a group of German banks for a loan of 10,000,000 marks.[22]

[20] Bülow to F. O., July 31, 1903, *ibid.*, 531 f., No. 6782. Holstein expressed the same opinion.

[21] Holstein to Bülow, July 26, 1905, *ibid.*, XIX, 468 ff., No. 6223.

[22] The loan was proposed to the German banking house, Mendelssohn & Co., by an English firm in Tangier, Moses Pariente, in April, 1905. A syndicate of German

The French press indignantly accused the German government of double-dealing. *Le Temps* noted that Count Tattenbach had been recalled from Morocco several years before for a similar indiscretion. Germany had accused France, it said, of wishing to make a second Tunis of Morocco; but France did not intend to let Germany make a second Turkey of it. It asked that Germany again deal severely with Count Tattenbach. M. Clémenceau in *L'Aurore* spoke bluntly in an article entitled "No Dupery," and a few days later, even more strongly in one headed "C'est trop." The press also attacked M. Rouvier for permitting the Germans to hoodwink him. If Parliament had been sitting, his position might have been precarious.[23]

These criticisms were undeserved. M. Rouvier had made every effort to prevent the concessions from being given. Both he and the British government had tried to block the negotiations as soon as reports of them came through. When the definite fact of the mole concession became known, M. Rouvier, supported by Lord Lansdowne, immediately strengthened his protests to the German government against Count Tattenbach's actions. He declared that they infringed upon French rights,[24] that they were a breach of faith and a violation of the spirit of the accord

banks, among them the Bleichröder group, the Mendelssohn group, the Disconto Gesellschaft, the Berliner Handels-Gesellschaft, was formed to make it. The loan, under negotiation during the summer and early autumn of 1905, was concluded on Oct. 4, 1905 (Schulthess, *Europäischer Geschichtskalender 1905*, p. 306). It was a purely temporary one to be guaranteed by some of the Sultan's personal property in land, a fact which alarmed the French even more because it denoted a possible German design to acquire possession of territory in Morocco. On the matters of the mole and loan see the following: Chérisey to Rouvier, Aug. 1, 1905, *L.j.*, *1901–5*, 260, No. 295; Saint-Aulaire to Rouvier, Aug. 14, 1905, *ibid.*, 267 f., No. 304; note signed by the French and German representatives, Sept. 28, 1905, *ibid.*, 307 f., No. 352; Holstein to Radolin, Aug. 14, 1905, *G.P.*, XX, 540 ff., No. 6789; Pourtales to Radolin, Aug. 19, 1905, *ibid.*, 542 f., No. 6790; *Bulletin*, Aug., 1905, p. 299.

[23] Radolin to Bülow, Aug. 29, 1905, *G.P.*, XX, 549 ff., Nos. 6794 f.; Lister to Lansdowne, Aug. 2 and 15, 1905, *B.D.*, III, 126, No. 167; 128 f., No. 170.

[24] A French firm had been surveying and making estimates for some months with a view to obtaining that same contract as well as other contracts for the im-

of July 8, that they endangered the success of the conference, the harmony of Franco-German relations, and his own position as minister. It was not his fault, he said angrily, that Franco-German relations continued to be strained. He urged that the project for a loan be blocked, or if this were impossible, that the German government agree to repayment of the loan with funds from the Moroccan state bank to be established. The question whether the German or a French firm had a prior right to the contract for the mole, he asserted, should be left in abeyance until the conference should regulate the method of granting contracts for public works.[25] The Spanish government was equally angry at Germany because of Count Tattenbach's acts. On August 23 M. Montero Rios poured out his wrath to the French Ambassador over Germany's trampling on Spanish interests in Morocco. It was generally understood, he said, that Northern Morocco was reserved to Spain. Yet, he continued indignantly, Germany had acquired concessions in that area and had obtained a mortgage on the lands around Tangier.

> Under all these provocations . . . . Spain had to remain mute [so the British ambassador reported his remarks]. France was the mouthpiece of the three Powers who were working together to save the situation in Morocco and His Excellency [M. Montero Rios] expressed an earnest hope that she would not yield all along the line to German pressure and would bear in mind what were the modest but real interests of Spain in Morocco. Señor Montero Rios concluded . . . . by bringing down his fist upon the table and saying, "we shall not forget what Germany has done to us on this occasion."

When M. Jules Cambon warned the German Ambassador in Madrid on August 23 that "it might become necessary for the

---

provement of the Moroccan harbors. The French claimed that by Art. XXXIII of the contract between the Sultan and the French consortium of banks in the previous year the latter had been given a priority right to make all future loans to Morocco.

[25] Rouvier to Radolin, July 29, 1905, *L.j.*, *1901–5*, 254 f., No. 292, and following documents; Bülow to Radolin, Aug. 3, 1905, *G.P.*, XX, 533 ff., No. 6784, and following documents; Lansdowne to Whitehead, Aug. 1, 1905, *B.D.*, III, 125 f., No. 166; Lansdowne to Lowther, June 23 and 26, July 19 and 31, 1905, *ibid.*, 100, No. 128; 101, No. 130; 120 f., No. 155; 124 f., No. 165.

Powers mainly interested in Morocco to insist that all concessions recently obtained should be examined by the Conference
before they were finally ratified," M. Montero Rios heartily
approved and volunteered to speak in like manner to Herr von
Radowitz.[26]

The German government itself supported the loan in order to
strengthen its hold over the Sultan and to calm his fears about
Germany's separate negotiations with France. The contract for
the mole surprised and embarrassed Prince Bülow. He repri-
manded Count Tattenbach for having transgressed his instructions and warned him to abide by them in the future.[27] Nevertheless, he upheld both transactions against the French complaints.
He asserted to M. Rouvier that the negotiations for the contract
had been under way for several months.[28] He claimed that the
loan was not a "loan" but a harmless temporary "advance"
which could be repaid at any time. Repeating the assurances of
Germany's disinterestedness in Morocco and of friendship for
France, the German government refused M. Rouvier's suggestions for an understanding about these two affairs and was unable to comprehend the French excitement.[29] As M. Rouvier felt
that the facts spoke otherwise, the two governments reached an
impasse by the first of September.

At the same time the two governments came to a deadlock
over the choice of a meeting place and the terms of the program
for the conference. Although M. Rouvier submitted proposals

---

[26] So Cambon informed Cartwright (Cartwright to Lansdowne, Aug. 24, 1905, *ibid.*, 130, No. 172).

[27] Mühlberg to Tattenbach, Aug. 3, 1905, *G.P.*, XX, 535 f., No. 6786.

[28] Tattenbach and Kühlmann both supported the contract for the mole, which, it was found, the Emperor had also approved. See Holstein to Radolin, Aug. 18, 1905, *ibid.*, 540, No. 6789; telegram from Tattenbach, June 25, 1905, *ibid.*, p. 525 n.; Lowther to Lansdowne, June 23 and 25, July 19 and 31, 1905, *B.D.*, III, 100, No. 128; 101, No. 130; 120 f., No. 155; 124 f., No. 165.

[29] Bülow to Radolin, Aug. 3, 1905, *G.P.*, XX, 533 ff., No. 6784, and the follow-ing documents. Also Bihourd to Rouvier, Aug. 1, 1905, *L.j., 1901–5*, 260 f., No. 296; note handed by Radolin to the French government, Aug. 4, 1905, *ibid.*, 262 f., No. 298 and following documents.

about military and financial reforms on July 20 and August 1, respectively,[30] Germany did not reply until August 26. The delay was caused by the necessity of consulting Count Tattenbach, but the French government and press suspected that Germany was uneasy about possible defeat at the conference and was therefore putting France off so as to gain concessions from the Sultan.[31] In its answer the German government accepted the main lines of the French proposal, but refused to permit France to settle directly with Morocco the regulation of the police in the region of the frontier, and also declined to give way on the choice of Tangier as a meeting place. The German government planned for the conference to restrict France's interest in Morocco to this frontier region.[32] But, on August 30, M. Rouvier met rejection with rejection. To permit the conference to decide upon the reorganization of the frontier region would, he wrote in a note to Prince Radolin, mean sacrificing an advantage and a right which France had enjoyed for sixty years.[33]

On the question of a meeting place M. Rouvier urged the Spanish government early in August to propose formally to the Powers that the conference be held in Spain. Thereby he would exert pressure on Germany to relinquish Tangier. M. Montero Rios

[30] Rouvier to Radolin, July 20, Aug. 1, 1905, *L.j., 1901–5*, 253 f., No. 290; 253 f., No. 294; 256 ff., No. 294; Radolin to F. O., July 20, Aug. 2, 1905, *G.P.*, XX, 528, No. 6777; 532 f., No. 6783.

[31] Lister to Lansdowne, Aug. 15, 1905, *B.D.*, III, 128, No. 170.

[32] Bülow to F. O., Aug. 3, 1905, *G.P.*, XX, 537 f., No. 6787; Mühlberg to Tattenbach, Aug. 6, 1905, *ibid.*, 538 ff., No. 6788; Bülow to Radolin, Aug. 22, dispatched Aug. 24, 1905, *ibid.*, 544 ff., No. 6792; Radolin to Rouvier, Aug. 26, 1905, *L.j., 1901–5*, 283 ff., No. 323; memo. by Kriege, Sept. 3, 1905, *G.P.*, XX, 554 ff., No. 6798.

[33] Rouvier to Radolin, Aug. 30, 1905, *L.j., 1901–5*, 290 ff., No. 331; Radolin to Bülow, Aug. 29, 1905, *G.P.*, XX, 549 ff., No. 6794; Radolin to F. O., Aug. 31, 1905, *ibid.*, 552 ff., Nos. 6796 f.; papers communicated by M. Geoffray, Sept. 1, 1905, *B.D.*, III, 131 ff., No. 174. In one matter during August the German government had, to its embarrassment, to support France. The Moroccan government seized illegally an Algerian subject. With the approval of the Powers, the French government demanded and soon obtained his release. See *L.j., 1901–5*, Nos. 301 ff.; *G.P.*, XX, 552 n.; 559, No. 6801; *B.D.*, III, 138, No. 178.

was eager to obtain the honor for his country, but fearing a rejection of the proposal, he hesitated to make it. Under French and British persuasion, however, he dispatched a verbal note to France and Germany offering some town in Southwest Spain for the conference. As the German government made no reply, M. Montero Rios was "deeply hurt" at the "high-handed and discourteous manner" in which Germany was treating Spain.[34]

With affairs so confused, the Chancellor interfered. He sent Dr. Rosen, the future minister at Tangier, to Paris for direct negotiations. In reporting this intention to M. Bihourd on September 4, Prince Bülow expressed in general terms his desire for an entente and spoke of the mole and the loan as insignificant. But he declared that there was a line beyond which "German dignity" would not permit him to go and that if this attempt failed "we would be placed again in the situation which obtained before the accord of July 8."[35]

Dr. Rosen, who was entirely unfamiliar with the history of the negotiations when he started to Paris, soon concluded that a change of policy was necessary. In France he found that both government and people were mistrustful, fast becoming embittered, and yet strongly desirous of a speedy settlement of the controversy. On September 8 he telegraphed to the Chancellor his opinion that the German government had already given assurances to France which entitled her to expect that the regulation of the frontier region would be excluded from the deliberations of the conference, and that to move her from this view would require "the speech of cannons" and not "juristic deductions." He therefore proposed to regard this point as lost and to prevent France from spreading her influence further into Morocco by obtaining an exact definition of the limits of the frontier region. On the choice of a meeting place, he advised making

[34] Cartwright to Lansdowne, Aug. 8 and 24, 1905, *B.D.*, III, 127 f., No. 169; 130, No. 172; Leon y Castillo, *Mis Tiempos*, II, 253.

[35] Bülow to Radolin, Sept. 4, 1905, *G.P.*, XX, 557, No. 6799; 558 f., No. 6801; Bihourd to Rouvier, Sept. 4, 1905, *L.j.*, *1901–5*, 297 f., No. 339.

concessions after all else was settled; the contract for the mole
he would handle as a "bagatelle." He foresaw greater difficulty in regard to the loan, which the French considered an act of
duplicity; but he stated to Prince Bülow that he would endeavor
to uphold it even though he regarded as untenable the German
distinction between a "loan" and an "advance."[36]

Dr. Rosen's opinion, which Prince Radolin had held for some
time, turned the scales. "As it appears to me," wrote the Chancellor to Baron Richthofen on September 8, "we need above all
to extricate ourselves from this Moroccan affair, which has apparently become confused, in such a way as to maintain our prestige in the world and to preserve the German economic and financial interests intact as much as possible." He accepted Dr.
Rosen's proposals. Germany should yield on the questions of the
frontier and the meeting place, and France on those of the mole
and the loan.[37]

The ensuing negotiations, carried on by Dr. Rosen mainly
with M. Révoil, were replete with dramatic moments.[38] By September 16, the two men reached agreement on most of the points.
But when Dr. Rosen learned from M. Révoil that France expected to obtain at the conference a general mandate for the
financial and police reforms in the whole of Morocco, he made
the concession on the frontier question contingent upon an official French disclaimer of that intention.[39]

[36] Memo. by Kriege, Sept. 3, 1905, G.P., XX, 554 ff., No. 6798; Bülow to F. O.,
Sept. 8, 1905, inclosing a telegram from Rosen, ibid., 559 ff., No. 6802; Radolin to
F. O., Sept. 9, 1905, ibid., 563 f., No. 6804. Radowitz acknowledged on Sept. 7 to
Jules Cambon that Germany would defend the selection of Tangier "only for
form's sake" (Cartwright to Lansdowne, Sept. 7, 1905, B.D., III, 138, No. 178).

[37] Bülow to F. O., Sept. 8, 1905, G.P., XX, 562 f., No. 6803; Richthofen to Radolin, Sept. 10, 1905, ibid., 564 ff., No. 6805; Richthofen to Bülow, Sept. 10, 1905,
ibid., 566 f., No. 6806.

[38] On these negotiations, apart from the references cited below, see Bertie to
Lansdowne, Sept. 24, 1905, B.D., III, 140, No. 182; Lansdowne to Bertie, Sept. 27,
1905, ibid., 140 ff., No. 183.

[39] He demanded an exchange of notes to the following effect: "Neither France
nor Germany will propose exclusive candidatures to execute the military reforms

M. Rouvier rejected this demand. He offered several times to compensate Germany for her renunciation in Morocco by including other questions in the negotiations, such as those of the Bagdad and the Camerun railways.[40] Dr. Rosen declined to broaden the basis of the negotiations, however, and threatened to break them off (although in reality he had no intention of doing so) if the French persisted in their denial of his request.[41] When the French press began to attack Germany, the Chancellor warned M. Rouvier repeatedly that "if the French imagine that they can intimidate us or even publicly humiliate us, they are playing a dangerous game which can lead to war." Conditions were much as they had been three months before.[42] Then the sudden intervention of M. Witte changed the situation.

Returning from Portsmouth, where he had represented Russia in the negotiations for peace with Japan, M. Witte stopped in Paris to arrange a loan for Russia. In discussing the project with M. Rouvier, he was told that France could not consider the loan until the conflict with Germany was settled.[43] Since he was interested in a quick solution of the Moroccan difficulty and since he favored a *rapprochement* between Russia, Germany, and France against Great Britain,[44] M. Witte discussed matters with his friend Prince Radolin on the morning of September 23. Immediately after this conversation M. Witte saw the French Premier, and at the latter's request returned that afternoon to urge the French views upon the German Ambassador. M. Rouvier was willing, M. Witte said to Prince Radolin, to give verbally the most formal declaration that he would not seek a mandate for

at the conference. It is understood that for the execution of the reforms (except in the frontier region) Germany and France will remain on a basis of equality." See Radolin to Bülow, Sept. 16, 1905, *G.P.*, XX, 568 ff., No. 6808 and following documents; Radolin to F. O., Sept. 21, 1905, *ibid.*, 577, No. 6817.

[40] Radolin to F. O., Sept. 29, 1905, *ibid.*, 593 f., No. 6833.

[41] Radolin to Bülow, Sept. 16, 1905, *ibid.*, 568 ff., No. 6808.

[42] Bülow to F. O., Sept. 18 and 19, 1905, *ibid.*, 571 ff., Nos. 6810 ff.

[43] Witte, *Memoirs*, p. 416.   [44] See below.

Western Morocco at the conference, but since M. Rouvier believed that French public opinion would never accept a written one, he would rather resign than give it. Germany was sufficiently protected against that possibility in any case, the Premier had argued to M. Witte, by the requirement of unanimity in the conference. M. Rouvier had also promised, said M. Witte, to cooperate harmoniously with Germany at the assembly. M. Witte found a sympathetic listener in Prince Radolin, who was disgusted with Dr. Rosen's policy. When later in the same afternoon the Prince, Dr. Rosen, and M. Rouvier met for further discussion, the Ambassador openly supported the French side. Hence Dr. Rosen had to yield.[45]

From Paris M. Witte went to Germany. At Berlin on September 25 he persuaded the Chancellor to accept M. Rouvier's views;[46] and at Rominten on September 27–28 he was even more successful with the Emperor William II, who immediately telegraphed to Prince Bülow as follows:

> Bring Rosen to reason so that that disgusting quarreling in Paris will cease. I am completely fed up on it . . . . [*Ich habe es gründlich satt*]. France must now . . . . be shown friendship and be permitted to save her face so that she will remain without rancour and will complete the turn necessary to bring her into our alliance.[47]

As a result of M. Witte's intervention, the two Powers reached an understanding on September 28.[48] They agreed that the program for the conference should provide for police reform and the suppression of contraband traffic in arms by way of an international accord, except in the frontier region where the execution of that action should remain "the exclusive affair" of France

[45] Radolin to Bülow, Sept. 23, 1905, *G.P.*, XIX, 503 f., No. 6241; Rosen to Bülow, Sept. 22, 1905, *ibid.*, 579 ff., No. 6819 and following documents; also Witte, pp. 416 ff. Cf. Tardieu, *La Conf. d'Algés.*, p. 77.

[46] Bülow to William II, Sept. 25, 1905, *G.P.*, XIX, 505 ff., No. 6243.

[47] Bülow to F. O., Sept. 27, 1905, *ibid.*, 508, No. 6245; William II to Bülow, Sept. 27, 1905, *ibid.*, 508 ff., No. 6246; Witte, pp. 417 ff.

[48] Witte's claim in his memoirs to have prevented a Franco-German war was hardly justified. Germany did not intend war, but only intimidation (Witte, pp. 424 f.).

and Morocco. A Moroccan state bank should be created, the Moroccan monetary system be stabilized, and funds be advanced for paying the police and for carrying out certain urgent public works. Improved methods of collecting the customs and of raising revenues should be provided. The Sultan should engage not to alienate any public service to the profit of particular interests. The principle of adjudication without regard to nationality should be followed in giving contracts for the construction of public works. The conference should meet at Algeciras in Spain. In a supplementary understanding the French government acknowledged the German "loan" to be an "advance"; but, while the control of that transaction should remain in German hands, the French banks were permitted to furnish one-half the sum necessary.[49] The German government also agreed that an investigation of the relative rights of the French and German firms to the contract for the mole should be made, although it was tacitly understood that the German firm would win.[50]

To make doubly sure that, apart from this agreement, France would have her hands free at the conference, M. Rouvier made the following declaration to the German government:

Aside from the agreement to be signed between the two governments, I am not bound on any point. I renew my affirmation that I have to the same degree as the Imperial Government the desire to avoid all open discord between us at the conference and to co-operate in effecting the solutions that respect best the interests and *amours propres*, in such a way that there will be neither victor nor vanquished. . . . . The guarantee for Germany lies in the fact that, since the decisions of the conference must be unanimous, her opposition will suffice to prevent the general mandate from being given to us.[51]

[49] The German government in turn admitted that this "advance" did not place in question the right of preference of the French banking consortium to make loans to Morocco.

[50] The accord is given in *L.j., 1901–5*, 307 ff., Nos. 351 f.; *G.P.*, XX, 592, No. 6832; *B.D.*, III, 142 ff., No. 184; 146 f., No. 188.

[51] Rouvier to Bihourd, Sept. 25, 1905, *L.j., 1901–5*, 305 f., Nos. 349 f.; Radolin to F. O., Sept. 26, 1905, *G.P.*, XX, 589, No. 6828; Tardieu, *La Conf. d'Algés.*, pp. 44 f. In December, M. Louis told Bertie that the German government had replied to Rouvier's declaration by asserting that "though bound by their Agreement, they

M. Rouvier thereby changed the statement transmitted by M. Witte to Prince Radolin that France would not strive for a mandate for Western Morocco to a less binding one which would leave France free to seek a mandate if she thought that Germany could be coerced into agreeing. This ambiguity was to cause trouble later.

The Sultan's approval of this program was obtained with some difficulty. The monarch and his advisers were very diffident about reforms and feared what the outcome of the conference might be. They besieged Count Tattenbach with questions about the program, wanting to know why Morocco had been excluded from the negotiations, what the various clauses in it would result in, whether France would after all succeed in her object by way of the conference. Count Tattenbach, who was practically unsupported by the French Minister, replied that Morocco could not survive without reforms, that Germany would defend Morocco's independence and integrity. As none of the Sultan's advisers would shoulder the risk of approving the program to their master, Count Tattenbach had to do so. By October 22 he succeeded in his work. On December 1 the Sultan issued a circular letter inviting the signatory Powers to the conference.[52] The invitations were accepted.

On September 29, in reporting the conclusion of the Franco-German agreement, Dr. Rosen mentioned to his government for the first time the offers which M. Rouvier had made to include in the settlement the difficulties over the Bagdad and Camerun railways. Prince Bülow was immediately eager to open negotiations.

At the present time we must use every opportunity to create solidarity of interest between France and us [he instructed the foreign office on the next day]. Under the present circumstances every African agreement with France is useful to us. Naturally far more useful would be an understanding over

---

[Germany] reserved to themselves the faculty of supporting in the Conference any proposals made by another Government which they might consider good" (Bertie to Grey, Dec. 15, 1905, *B.D.*, III, 158, No. 195). There is no reference to this statement in *G.P.*

[52] *L.j., 1901–5*, Nos. 357 f., 362 ff., 367, 313 ff.; *G.P.*, XXI, Nos. 6889 ff., 6898; *B.D.*, III, Nos. 165, 186 ff.

the Bagdad Railway. We must always take into consideration the inclination of the English to come to terms with Russia over Asia Minor, whereby we would eventually be placed in the dilemma of suffering a defeat on the question of the Bagdad Railway or of arousing acute antagonism between Russia and us.

But, the Chancellor added, Germany must not show undue eagerness in the matter.[53]

When Prince Radolin broached the subject to the French Premier on October 18, the latter replied that he had offered "an even more far-reaching agreement" at a time when he had hoped to settle the Moroccan affair without a conference, but that under the circumstances he would consider the project only after the conference.[54] That the Chancellor could have expected any other reply showed how little understanding he had of the French state of mind.

Prince Bülow manifested the same obtuseness in an interview with M. Tardieu of *Le Temps* on October 3 as a bid for friendlier relations with France. Repeating all the German criticisms of the French policy, the Chancellor declared:

I think that the conference, far from dividing us, ought to contribute to a *rapprochement* between us. For that *rapprochement*, however, one condition is necessary: that French public opinion thoroughly recognize that the policy of isolating Germany is an object of the past. . . . . Today as yesterday, provided your colonial policy respects our commercial interests . . . . . we will not obstruct you, but in case of need will aid you in Morocco and elsewhere.

He denied that Germany sought to force upon France an anti-British policy and that Germany had any ulterior motives in her friendship with Russia. He summed up the international situation as follows:

A double system of alliances, both pacific, assures equilibrium in Europe. On those alliances we can and must superimpose friendships. You are

---

[53] Bülow to F. O., Sept. 30, 1905, *G.P.*, XX, 595, No. 6834; Richthofen to Bülow, Oct. 6, 1905, *ibid.*, XXV, 196 f., No. 8622; Bülow to F. O., Oct. 7, 1905, *ibid.*, 197, No. 8623. It was at this time that the question of including France in the alliance made at Björkö was coming to the fore (Tardieu, *La Conf. d'Algés.*, p. 136).

[54] Radolin to F. O., Oct. 18, 1905, *G.P.*, XX, 596 f., No. 6836.

friends with Italy: nothing is better. We are friends of Russia: it is perfect. But we must not give to the Franco-Italian *rapprochement* an anti-German character or to the Russo-German *rapprochement* an anti-French character.[55]

In spite of the Chancellor's attempt at conciliation, French public opinion did not like the "schoolmaster" tone of his remarks and saw therein "the proof that the Moroccan incident had been only a pretext to intervene in the direction given to France's foreign policy and to force France to modify it."[56] In fact, not a single French newspaper spoke well of the German policy.[57] Rather, *Le Matin* took occasion on October 5 to publish revelations to the effect that at the crucial French cabinet meeting of June 6 M. Delcassé had declared that

England was ready, whatever might happen, to aid France if the latter were the object of an unforeseen and improbable aggression. [It was further asserted in the article that] England, in effect, informed the Government of the Republic verbally that if France were attacked, she was ready to mobilize her fleet, to seize the Kiel Canal, and to land 100,000 men in Schleswig-Holstein. The French Government was even told later that if it so desired, that offer would be made in writing.[58]

The reports were denied by M. Delcassé and by the French and British governments.[59] But the *London Times* and the

[55] Quoted in *Quest. dipl. et col.*, XX, 497 ff., Radolin to F. O., Sept. 29, 1905, *G.P.*, XX, 593 f., No. 6833; Bülow to F. O., Sept. 30, 1905, *ibid.*, 594 f., No. 6834.

[56] Quoted from the report of the Belgian Minister at Paris to his government, Oct. 14, 1905 (*Zur europ. Politik*, II, 72). See also the article by De Caix in *Journal des debats*, quoted in *Quest. dipl. et col.*, XX, 500.

[57] *G.P.*, XXI, 16, No. 6901.

[58] Quoted in *Quest. dipl. et col.*, XX, 500 f. The revelations were made by Stéphane Lauzanne, a journalist. Lauzanne denied that he had received his information from Delcassé. He stated that he had written the articles three months ago. See Lister to Lansdowne, Oct. 11, 1905, *B.D.*, III, 83 f., No. 100; Bertie to Lansdowne, Oct. 14, 1905, *ibid.*, 84, No. 101. His assertions were in the main corroborated by two other French journalists, Eugène Lautier and Alexandre Ular, in *Figaro*, Oct. 13, 1905, and by Jaurès (*G.P.*, XX, 666 n.).

[59] *Quest. dipl. et col.*, XX, 504; Lascelles to Lansdowne, Oct. 15, 16, 20, 1905, *B.D.*, III, 84 ff., Nos. 102 ff.; Metternich to F. O., Oct. 9, 1905, *G.P.*, XX, 663 f., No. 6873.

French press believed the first part of the revelations, although the *Times* regarded the latter part as gossip.[60]

In Germany these revelations provoked an outburst of indignation. Still at odds with King Edward VII, the Emperor wanted to recall Count Metternich for an indefinite leave of absence unless the British government gave a satisfactory explanation of the disclosures.[61] But Prince Bülow knew that the Emperor's suggestion could not be carried out merely on the basis of newspaper talk. In fact, he did not believe that the revelations were accurate.[62] Still he seized the opportunity to relieve his own position with German public opinion by giving instructions for the German press to accept the revelations as true. By these means M. Delcassé should be represented as having used the Moroccan affair to bring on a war with Germany, while Great Britain should be accused of inciting the French to unleash a world-war. The press should state that Germany had never thought of attacking France, of drawing France to her by force, or of playing France against Great Britain. "It is important that the German public understand how gravé the international situation is, how necessary it is to be armed, and how wretched, in view of the seriousness of the world situation, party conflicts and the usual Philistine pettifogging appear." By so using the press, the Chancellor wrote, "we embarrass our enemies in England and bring advantage to our naval proposals."[63] Moreover, on October 26, when the Emperor dedicated a statue to Field-Marshal Count Moltke, he declared: "How we stand in the world you have seen. Therefore, the powder dry, the sword sharp, the goal known, the forces braced, and the pessimist banished, I drink to our nation in arms."[64]

[60] *Quest. dipl. et col.*, XX, 500, 503 f.; Mévil, *De la Paix de Francfort, etc.*, pp. 269 ff. n.

[61] Bülow to F. O., Oct. 14, 1905, *G.P.*, XX, 666, No. 6876.

[62] Bülow to F. O., Oct. 15, 1905, *ibid.*, 667 f., No. 6877.

[63] Bülow to F. O., Oct. 10 and 12, 1905, *ibid.*, 664 f., Nos. 6874 f.

[64] Schulthess, *1905*, p. 127.

Here were the fruits of two months and a half of tedious and irritating negotiations. Starting with the assurance that the conference would meet and that the reforms would be internationally executed, Germany ended with the same assurance, a half-share in a loan of 10,000,000 marks and a petty contract for a mole. She began with the intention of winning France for the sake of completing a continental alliance with Russia; but by her blundering mismanagement of the Moroccan affair she ruined any chance for doing so In June the victorious Germany had confronted a France fearful of war and subject to pressure. Since then Germany herself had been constantly receding before the determination of a united French nation. In June M. Rouvier had endeavored to "save France's face"; by September, Prince Bülow was trying to "save Germany's face." The tables were turned.

CHAPTER XV

THE TREATY OF BJÖRKÖ AND ITS ANNULMENT

I

By forcing France in July to submit the Moroccan question to an international conference, the German government asserted its power and restored its country's prestige; but it had had to employ means which could not often be repeated with impunity. The future of Germany's international position remained uncertain. While the Entente Cordiale had become firmer, the Triple Alliance was still unsteady and unreliable. King Edward and his nephew, the Emperor William, were having one of their numerous quarrels.[1] The German government believed positively that in case of a Franco-German war Great Britain would actively support France.[2] Although relations with President Roosevelt and with Russia remained intimate, these close friendships did not give Germany the security and power which she had enjoyed before the conclusion of the Entente Cordiale. Then suddenly, out of a clear sky, came the possibility of Germany's becoming master of the situation again. The Emperor William and Czar Nicholas arranged a meeting at Björkö, and the Emperor requested that a copy of the projected Russo-German treaty of the previous autumn be sent to him.

In the latter half of July the Emperor and the Czar were both cruising: the one in the Baltic Sea, the other in the Finnish Gulf. As it was the hope of both the Chancellor[3] and the Emperor that

---

[1] On these differences see Mühlberg to Metternich, July 18, 1905, *G.P.*, XX, 638, No. 6863 and following documents; Lee, *King Edward VII*, II, 334 ff., 346 ff.

[2] Even Lascelles, British ambassador at Berlin, admitted to Metternich that "in a Franco-German war in view of the prevailing opinion here [in England] England would be actively on the French side." See Metternich to Bülow, July 19 and 22, 1905, *G.P.*, XX, 639 f., No. 6864; 646 ff., No. 6867; Bülow to Metternich, July 22, 1905, *ibid.*, 641 ff., No. 6866.

[3] William II to Bülow, Aug. 11, 1905, *ibid.*, XXX, 497, No. 6237.

a meeting with the Czar might occur during these cruises, William II suddenly telegraphed to his cousin on July 18 that he would shortly pass the entrance to the gulf. "Should it give you any pleasure to see me . . . . , I of course am always at your disposal." Nicholas immediately replied: "Delighted with your proposal. Would it suit you meet at Bjoerkoe-sund . . . . ? . . . . Look forward with intense pleasure to seeing you." Upon receiving this answer the Emperor requested Prince Bülow to send him the draft.

The Chancellor, who was at Norderney at the time, forwarded the request to Herr von Holstein. While he was dubious about the affair, he wrote to Herr von Holstein that the meeting would at least be a useful means of keeping in close touch with Russia and finding out something about her future foreign and internal policy. Germany could not intervene in favor of Russia during the peace negotiations, he stated, but it would be advantageous to engage the Czar so far that M. Witte and Count Lamsdorff would be unable to prepare for a Franco-Russo-British entente immediately after peace was established.[4]

Herr von Holstein's long replies to the Chancellor were not very hopeful. The final draft of the treaty of the previous autumn was acceptable, he thought, if the clause added by Russia —"Their entente cordiale will also hold in the case of difficulties which may arise at the time of the negotiations of peace between Russia and Japan"—were omitted. In fact, he was willing to accept a change in Article I making the alliance valid in case of an attack by two Powers instead of by one. He no longer believed it necessary for Russia and Germany to be in complete accord before negotiations with France were begun, because M. Rouvier's cabinet would not "so absolutely oppose Germany's joining [the Dual Alliance] as Delcassé had," and because, as Russia was more dependent upon France for loans than she had been six months previously, she would take no step without the

---

[4] Bülow to F. O., July 20, 1905, *ibid.*, 435 f., No. 6206. The telegrams between the two rulers were in English.

latter's approval. Herr von Holstein expected M. Witte, Count Lamsdorff, the mother and wife of the Czar, and the French government to oppose the project and to favor an Anglo-Russo-French grouping. In his opinion almost the only reason for Russia to prefer a German alliance to the other grouping was that it could be concluded in time to be of value to Russia in the forthcoming negotiations for peace with Japan. Herr von Holstein therefore advised that if the treaty were concluded it be published immediately. Fearing rejection of the German proposal by Count Lamsdorff and an exploitation of the Russian refusal, he wished the Emperor not to take the initiative in proposing an alliance, at least until Nicholas II manifested a desire to pursue a common policy with Germany. Herr von Holstein's telegrams formed the basis for the instructions sent to the Emperor on July 22.[5]

The story of Björkö is one of drama and mystery. The two sovereigns agreed that their meeting should be kept secret until it occurred; and, although the news immediately leaked out in the Russian press, the company on the Emperor's yacht did not know where it was going or for what purpose. The rulers met, July 23–24, in Björkö Bay, far away from civilization, with only the sea and the forest-clad shore around them. The Emperor prepared himself for the interview by lifting up his hands and asking God to guide and aid him, or at least not to aid the Czar. When his yacht steamed into the bay, the Czar had already arrived. The Emperor immediately went on board the "Polar Star." After a touching exchange of embraces the two monarchs withdrew for a long conversation. "Willy" found "Nicky" feel-

[5] See the correspondence between Holstein and Bülow, July 21–24, 1905, *ibid.*, 436 ff., Nos. 6203–14. It was Holstein who determined the whole policy of the German foreign office on this question. Bülow served only as his mouthpiece. Richthofen and Metternich, and also General Moltke (who in 1906 became chief of staff), were all opposed to the project of alliance, but their opinions were either not asked or were disregarded. See Bülow to F. O., Aug. 9, 1905, *ibid.*, 488, No. 6235; Metternich to Bülow, Oct. 2, 1905, *ibid.*, XX, 659 ff., No. 6871; Eckardstein, *Lebenserinnerungen und politische Denkwürdigkeiten*, III, 167.

ing discouraged, forlorn, and friendless except for him; and Count Lamsdorff was not there to give him backbone. The gathering force of the Russian revolution, the defeat by Japan, anger at Great Britain and France, and deep appreciation for the friendly attitude of Germany and William II toward him and his country during their troubles had prepared this weak monarch to throw himself into the arms of the far stronger, confident, and brilliantly seductive Emperor. As William II asserted later, the Czar was in a mood to subscribe to almost anything.

In the first conversation between the two rulers[6] they both relieved themselves of their anger at Great Britain and King Edward VII. Nicholas II was particularly enraged at the British, whose unfriendliness toward Russia during the current war was fresh in his mind. When he described King Edward as "the greatest mischief-maker and most insincere as well as the most dangerous intriguer in the world," the Emperor agreed with him heartily. King Edward "has a passion to begin something with every Power, to make 'a little agreement,'" said William. The Czar replied as he struck the table with his fist, "Well I can only say, he shall not get one from me, and never in my life against Germany or you, my word of honor on it." When they brought up the Moroccan affair, the Czar, pleased with the Franco-German agreement, strongly seconded the Emperor's hope that out of that agreement a permanent understanding with France might develop. When the Emperor remarked that "in spite of English incitements France has absolutely refused to go to war with us [Germany], and so has shown that she will no longer fight for the sake of the lost provinces," Nicholas II replied incisively: "Yes that I saw, it is quite clear the Alsace-Lorraine question is closed once for all, thank God." As they were going on deck again the Czar once more embraced the Emperor and thanked him for coming.[7]

[6] They conversed in English. In the Emperor's account of the interview he gives the Czar's statements in that language.

[7] The Czar was also unpleasantly surprised to learn that King Edward VII was supporting the candidacy of his son-in-law, Prince Carl of Denmark, for the Nor-

That night the two groups celebrated together until daybreak. During the festivities some of the Russian officials in close touch with their master spoke openly in favor of a Continental alliance. The Emperor therefore concluded that the ground was prepared for his project. Before going to breakfast with the Czar and Grand Duke Michael the next morning, William II opened his *Losungen der Brüdergemeinde für 1905*[8] upon the following text: "Each will receive his reward according to his work." So, full of hope, he put a copy of the treaty in his pocket and set out. He found the Czar in the same mood as before. They spoke of the Anglo-French fraternization, behind which the Emperor suspected lay a "little agreement." The Czar's head drooped in dejection. "That is too bad," he grieved. "What shall I do in this disagreeable situation." "I felt that the moment had come," wrote the Emperor later to Prince Bülow, in reporting this interview.

Since the ally has preserved the policy of the free hand and of reinsurance without consulting or informing the Czar [he said to Nicholas II], it is quite permissible for him . . . . to do the same. How would it be if we also made a little agreement? We discussed one in the previous winter, but it failed because of Delcassé and tension with France. Now that is all past, we shall be good friends with the French. So does not every obstacle fall? "Oh yes to be sure, I remember well, but I forgot the contents of it, what a pity I havent got it here." I possess a copy which by chance I have in my pocket. The Czar seized me by the arm, drew me into his father's cabin, and closed all the doors. "Show it me please." The dreamy eyes sparkled. I drew the envelope from my pocket, unfolded the sheet on the writing desk of Alexander III before the pictures of the Czar's mother, between photographs from Fredensborg and Copenhagen, and laid it before the Czar. He read the text once, twice, thrice. . . . . I prayed the dear God to be with us and guide the young ruler. It was deathly still; only the sea murmured and the

---

wegian throne. Nicholas II favored Prince Waldemar, Carl's younger brother, while the Emperor favored choosing a member of the House of Bernadotte. It looked to him, said Nicholas, as if Great Britain were endeavoring thereby to get her fingers on Norway with the possible purpose of acquiring the port of Christiansund from which to block the Skaggerrack. See the references given in the succeeding footnote.

[8] "Watchwords of the Common Brethren for 1905." It was a book of proverbs.

sun shone joyfully and clear in the cozy cabin, and directly before me lay the Hohenzollern and high in the morning air waved the imperial standard. I was just reading the letters on the black cross, God with us, when the Czar said, "That is quite excellent. I quite agree!" My heart beat so loudly that I could hear it. I pulled myself together and said casually, "Should you like to sign it? It would be a very nice souvenir of our entrevue." He read it once more and replied, "Yes I will." I opened the ink-well, extending to him the pen, and he wrote with a firm hand "Nicolas." Then he passed it to me, I signed it, and as I arose he, deeply moved, folded me in his arms and said, "I thank God and I thank you, it will be of most beneficial consequences for my country and Yours; You are Russia's only real friend in the whole world, I have felt that through the whole war and I know it." Tears of joy stood in my eyes—to be sure the sweat poured from my brow and back—and I thought of Frederick William III, Queen Louise, Grandfather and Nicholas I. Were they near at that moment? At any rate they saw it all and were overjoyed.

The terms of the treaty were as follows: The Czar and the Emperor, "to assure the maintenance of peace in Europe, have agreed upon the following articles of a treaty of defensive alliance." Article I read: "In case one of the two Empires is attacked by an European Power, its ally will aid it in Europe with all its forces on land and sea." According to Article II, "The high contracting parties engage not to conclude a separate peace with a common enemy." Article III was as follows: "The present treaty becomes valid as soon as peace is concluded between Russia and Japan and will remain valid until it is denounced a year in advance." By Article IV the Czar agreed "after the coming into force of the treaty" to take "the steps necessary to initiate France into the accord and to associate herself in it as ally."[9]

[9] There is another account of the meeting written by Bülow on Aug. 18 immediately after a talk with the Emperor which does not agree in all details with this one written by the Emperor on the day after the meeting occurred. The two versions supplement each other. But the one of July 25 reproduces better the atmosphere in which the affair took place. The other version is as follows: The Czar declared that he wished to go hand in hand with the Emperor, his only friend. The latter asked why the treaty had not been signed in the previous autumn. The reply was that France had opposed it, that he (the Czar) had had to maintain the Dual Alliance, and that France and Germany had been hostile. The Emperor then

Thus the act was accomplished. How was it possible? The Emperor's explanation was simple and satisfying—God did it.[10] For he was present, as were various spirits and shades of dead and departed kinsmen. A humble and depressed Czar and an inspired Emperor with his *Losungen der Brüdergemeinde*, tears and sighs and embraces, many a dainty dish and flask of old wine, many a satisfying outburst of anger at absent enemies—no wonder the Björkö treaty was signed! The Emperor had visions of illimitable possibilities for the alliance. On July 27 he wrote to Nicholas II as follows:

In times to come it may not be impossible that even Japan may feel inclined to join it [the alliance]. This would cool down English self-assertion and impertinence, as she is her ally too. The 24th of July 1905 is a corner-

said that those relations were better, that he wished France and Germany to become friends, that the Moroccan question was to be used for that purpose, and that an understanding over it would certainly be reached. The Czar replied that if that were the case then nothing stood in the way of a Russo-German treaty. The Emperor then produced a copy of the treaty and it was signed immediately. See memo. by Bülow, Aug. 18, 1905, *G.P.*, XIX, 502 f., No. 6240. The other accounts of the Björkö interview are as follows: Tschirschky to Bülow, July 24, 1905, *ibid.*, 454 ff., No. 6218; William II to Bülow, July 25, 1905, *ibid.*, 458 ff., No. 6220; Bülow to F. O., July 24, 1905, *ibid.*, 452, No. 6215; Witte, *Memoirs*, p. 428; Savinsky, *Revue des deux mondes*, XII (1922), 798 f.; Savinsky, *Recollections of a Russian Diplomat*, p. 115; Helmuth von Moltke, *Erinnerungen, Briefe, Dokumente, 1877–1916* (Stuttgart, 1922), pp. 325 ff. The treaty was countersigned by Grand Duke Michael, Tschirschky, and Admiral Birileff, the last two apparently without reading it. The Grand Duke was asked to sign it because William II feared that Nicholas II might be deposed and Michael made czar. Naturally he did not mention his reason.

The Czar wished to consider an agreement guaranteeing to the King of Denmark the possession of his territory, so that in case of war Russia and Germany would be sure of being able to defend the Baltic Sea north of the Belt. A declaration of Danish neutrality would not suffice, Nicholas argued to the Emperor, because in case the opponent did not respect it and seized the territory as a base of operation, Germany and Russia would be in a difficult situation. But the Emperor, who together with his government was opposed to touching this important question, put Nicholas off with a promise to consider the matter with Bülow.

The Emperor also urged the Czar at this interview to grant to the Russian people a habeas corpus act which would guarantee their civil liberties, and to call a general council of state to consider the question of a constitution.

[10] *G.P.*, XIX, 459.

stone in European Politics and turns over a new leaf in the history of the
world; which will be a chapter of peace and goodwill among the great Powers of the European Continent, respecting each other in friendship, confidence and in pursuing the general Policy on the lines of a community of
interests. The moment the news of the new "groupement" will have become
known in the world, the smaller nations, Holland, Belgium, Danmark, Sweden, Norway will all be attracted to this new great centre of gravity, by quite
natural laws of the attraction of smaller bodies by the larger and compacter
ones. They will revolve in the orbit of the great block of powers (Russia,
Germany, France, Austria, Italy) and feel confidence in leaning on and re-
volving around this mass. The dual Alliance combining with the Triple
Alliance gives a Quintupel Alliance, well able to hold all unruly neighbours
in order, to impose peace even by force, if there should be a power hair-
brained enough to wish to disturb it.[11]

Notwithstanding this optimism, the treaty caused difficulty
from the start. The absence of a countersignature by the Chancellor was not considered serious.[12] But against the advice of
Herr von Tschirschky, the representative of the foreign office on
the cruise, the Emperor had without consulting the Chancellor
introduced very important changes in the draft of the treaty. In
the first article he had added the words "en Europe," while he
had re-worded the third article so that the alliance should not
become effective before the conclusion of the Russo-Japanese
War.[13] Prince Bülow was very dubious about the value of the
treaty after those changes were made, particularly the change
in Article I, "because in Europe," he wrote to Herr von Holstein, "Russia can be of no use at all to us against England." He
requested the latter's advice before acting.[14]

Herr von Holstein approved decidedly of the treaty even in its
changed form, although he regretted that the Emperor had not
obtained more while the Czar was so pliant. He said that the

[11] Goetz, *Briefe Wilhelms II an den Zaren 1894-1914*, p. 374.

[12] Bülow to F. O., July 25, 1905, *G.P.*, XIX, 453 f., No. 6217; Holstein to Bülow, July 25, 1905, *ibid.*, 457 f., No. 6219.

[13] Bülow to F. O., July 27, Aug. 9, 1905, *ibid.*, 470 f., Nos. 6224 f.; 488 ff., No.
6235.

[14] Bülow to F. O., July 26, 1905, *ibid.*, 467 f., No. 6222; 476 f., No. 6228.

treaty should be kept absolutely secret.[15] Otherwise he feared that Great Britain and perhaps also France would seek to prolong the Russo-Japanese War with the result that the Czar would be deposed, and that Great Britain, if she had aggressive plans, might hurriedly attack Germany before the alliance came into operation. He thought that the suspensive clause was especially disadvantageous to Germany in that the treaty, if effective at once, would have a calming effect upon any bellicose spirit on the part of both France and Great Britain. Moreover, he believed that France could be brought to join the alliance at the time; whereas if the action to bring her in were postponed, she would align herself more closely with Great Britain. The inclusion of the phrase "en Europe" he also regretted as being advantageous only to Russia.

In case of an Anglo-German war, Russia need not advance against India. . . . . But even with the best will Russia will not be able to help us in Europe. . . . . The only positive value from the changed treaty is the assurance that Russia can no longer enter the Quadruple Alliance.[16] The circle around Germany can no longer close. That is something. But we could have obtained more and we must expect that the publication of this treaty will cause little disquietude in England and will not be considered as a great success of German diplomacy.[17]

The Chancellor regarded the inclusion of the suspensive clause as an advantage under the circumstances; but he had grave objections to the inclusion of the phrase "en Europe."[18] When he

[15] The German government was particularly concerned lest Roosevelt become mistrustful on account of this interview and the conclusion of an alliance with Russia. It even considered imparting the terms of the treaty to him, but in view of the need for secrecy decided not to. Instead, on July 28, the Emperor wrote personally to Roosevelt making it appear that the interview dealt only with matters pertaining to the Russo-Japanese negotiations for peace (Mühlberg to Bussche-Haddenhausen, July 28, 1905, *ibid.*, 614, No. 6319). On this discussion about whether to notify Roosevelt of the accord see *ibid.*, Nos. 6203, 6206–8, 6221, 6223.

[16] He meant the one Germany feared of Russia, France, Great Britain, and Japan.

[17] Holstein to Bülow, July 26, 1905, *ibid.*, 468 ff., No. 6223; memo. by Holstein, July 28, 1905, *ibid.*, 474 ff., No. 6227.

[18] Bülow to F. O., July 28, Aug. 5, 1905, *ibid.*, 476 f., No. 6228; 482 f., No. 6231.

telegraphed these to the Emperor, the latter replied that he had made the change "after ripe deliberation" in order to prevent Germany from being obliged to aid Russia in Asia. He did not believe possible an attack by Russia on India, nor did anyone else, he stated. The advantage from the treaty lay, not in the expectation of any active help from Russia in case of a war with Great Britain but rather in the assurance that Germany would enjoy full freedom and security on her eastern frontier, that she would be able to throw all her forces against one front, that is, France, instead of against two—"naturally provided France mobilizes to help England, which is not impossible." He and General Moltke looked upon the situation in this way:

If England declares or otherwise begins war with us, you [the Chancellor] must immediately send dispatches to Brussels and Paris with a demand to state within six hours whether for or against us. We must immediately march into Belgium no matter what the reply. As to France it depends upon whether she remains neutral,—which I do not consider entirely impossible even if the probability is small;—in that case the Russian *casus foederis* does not enter into effect. If she [France] mobilizes, that is a war-threat against us in favor of England, and then the Russian regiments must march with ours. . . . . It should eventually be considered whether France could not be offered as an enticement for good behavior toward us perhaps a part of Belgium as compensation for the lost provinces.[19]

The Chancellor fully approved the Emperor's remarks concerning Belgium; but neither he nor Herr von Holstein thought that it would be possible to permit French neutrality in case of a British attack on Germany.[20] Nor was he convinced by the Emperor's other arguments. He continued to regard the inclusion of the phrase "en Europe" as "pernicious." He declared that he could not uphold the treaty before the German people unless Russia were bound to give aid in both Asia and Europe, and sought ways of bringing about a change to that effect.[21] While

[19] Bülow to F. O., July 30, Aug. 5 and 9, 1905, *ibid.*, 477 ff., No. 6229; 485 ff., No. 6233; 488 ff., No. 6235.

[20] Bülow to William II, July 30, 1905, *ibid.*, 477 ff., No. 6229; Holstein to Bülow, Aug. 5, 1905, *ibid.*, 483 f., No. 6232.

[21] Bülow to F. O., Aug. 2, 5, 9, 1905, *ibid.*, 481 ff., Nos. 6230 f.; 488 ff., No. 6235.

he had accepted the treaty at first and had congratulated the Emperor upon achieving it, and while he had thought that there was plenty of time in which to eliminate the objectionable phrase,[22] he suddenly reversed his attitude. On August 3 he stated that he could not accept the responsibility for the treaty in the present form or for bringing about the necessary changes. He therefore offered his resignation.[23]

Knowing that he had his master in a quandary, since German public opinion was already complaining about too much imperial initiative in foreign affairs, the Chancellor apparently did not expect his resignation to be accepted. He continued as before to seek means of altering the treaty without ruining it entirely.[24] And, as a matter of fact, the Emperor collapsed, agreed to anything, and on August 11 wrote a hysterical letter to his Chancellor.

I thought that I had worked and had accomplished something special for you. Then you send me a couple of cold lines and your resignation!!! Please excuse me, dear Bülow, from depicting the condition of my soul to you. To be so treated by my best, most intimate friend, without giving a single plausible reason, has been such a fearful blow to me that I have completely collapsed and fear a grave nervous sickness. You say that the situation has become so serious because of the treaty with "en Europe" that you cannot assume responsibility; before whom? And in the same breath you believe that before God you can assume responsibility of deserting your Emperor and master to whom you have sworn fidelity, who has loaded you with love and honors, your fatherland and, as I believed, your truest friend, in the situation regarded by you as critical and serious!? No, dear Bülow, that you will not do! We have both been called by God and created for each other to work for our dear German fatherland. If in your opinion a graver situation has really been made by my error—which I do not believe—, it has been done

---

[22] Bülow to William II, July 24, 27, 1905, ibid., 452, No. 6216; 471 ff., No. 6226; Bülow to F. O., July 27–29, 1905, ibid., 471, No. 6225; 476 ff., Nos. 6228 f.

[23] It is highly probable that Bülow took this step not so much because of defects in the treaty, but rather because the Emperor had disregarded his authority by making those important changes without consulting him. Under the persuasion of Richthofen he took this course in order to uphold his authority and to teach the Emperor a lesson (Eckardstein, III, 166; editor's note in G.P., XIX, 481 f., note).

[24] Bülow to F. O., Aug. 5 and 9, 1905, ibid., 482 f., No. 6231; 488 ff., No. 6235.

with the best intentions. You know me well enough to recognize that. Your person is 100,000 times more valuable to me and our country than all the treaties in the world. I have immediately taken steps with the Czar which shall weaken or eliminate those words. Do not forget that you sent me to Tangier against my will in order to achieve a success in your Moroccan policy. Read my telegrams before the visit to Tangier. You have admitted to me yourself that you were so anxious that when you received the announcement of my safe departure you had a nervous fit of weeping. For your sake because the fatherland needed it I landed, mounted a strange horse in spite of my crippled left arm, and the horse nearly caused my death—all of which was your affair! I rode through Spanish anarchists because you wished it and your policy would profit thereby! and now you want abruptly to desert me, when I have done everything—and, as I honestly believe, far more—for you, because my situation appears to you too serious. Bülow, I have not deserved that of you. No, my friend, you remain in office and with me and shall continue to work with me *ad majorem Germaniae gloriam*. You plainly owe me that because of my service this year. You can and dare not forsake me. Therewith your whole policy of this year would be disavowed by you yourself and I blamed forever. That I cannot survive. Grant me a few days to rest and collect myself before you come, for the nervous excitement caused by your letter is too great, I am now unable to argue in quiet. . . . . I appeal to your friendship for me, and let us hear no more of your intention to resign. Telegraph me "all right" after this letter; then I shall know that you will remain! For the morning after the arrival of your resignation will find the emperor no longer alive! Think of my poor wife and children![25]

How were the mighty fallen! The Chancellor had won, and of course telegraphed "All right."

In the meantime various proposals to eliminate the phrase "en Europe"[26] were being combated by Herr von Holstein, who feared that the opponents of the treaty in Russia, particularly Count Lamsdorff, might use such opportunity to propose changes on their side, to annul the treaty entirely, or at least to undermine its prestige. He wrote:

The treaty even in its present crippled form is still too valuable to risk in hazardous play. Its value lies in the crushing effect which it will have upon France and in the indirect reaction through France upon England.

[25] William II to Bülow, Aug. 11, 1905, *ibid.*, 496 ff., No. 6237.

[26] Bülow to F. O., Aug. 5 and 9, 1905, *ibid.*, 482 f., No. 6231; 485 ff., No. 6233; 488 ff., No. 6235.

. . . . Through the inclusion of "en Europe" and through the introduction of the suspensive article, the value of the treaty is lowered 50 per cent. But this 50 per cent remains to us and should not be risked.

He urged against proposal for a change until time for the treaty to come into effect or until the Emperor and the Czar had another meeting. Prince Bülow acceded to these views.[27]

II

Occurring at a crisis in world-affairs, when the Moroccan difficulty was still unsettled, when the Russo-Japanese negotiations for peace were about to begin, when the choice of a king by Norway was not yet made, the news of the unexpected and secret interview at Björkö caused a furor in the diplomatic world and in the press.[28] Especial alarm was shown by the British, jealous and mistrustful as they were of Russo-German intimacy. The English press suspected the German Emperor of seeking the Norwegian crown for a Hohenzollern and of endeavoring to close the Baltic Sea to all except the Baltic nations.[29] Sir Francis Bertie, British ambassador at Paris, was reported to have remarked that Germany seemed to harbor Napoleonic tendencies, which Great Britain would oppose as she had the original ones.[30] Mr. Spring Rice, after consulting Lord Lansdowne, wrote to President Roosevelt as follows:

The most serious aspect of the question is the general balance of power in Europe. . . . . Two of the great powers have practically disappeared so far as active intervention in European affairs is concerned, Russia and Austria. Germany is by far the most powerful of the remaining powers, and she has an old feud to settle with France. If France is attacked, there is no Russia to help her and the English Army is at present practically negligible

[27] Holstein to Bülow, Aug. 5, 6, 14, 1905, *ibid.*, 483 f., No. 6232; 487 f., No. 6234; 501, No. 6239; Mühlberg to Bülow, Aug. 10, 1905, *ibid.*, 493 ff., No. 6236; Bülow to F. O., Aug. 12, 1905, *ibid.*, 498 ff., No. 6238; memo. by Bülow, Aug. 18, 1905, *ibid.*, 502 f., No. 6240.

[28] Meyer to Roosevelt, Aug. 1, 1905, quoted in Howe, *George von Lengerke Meyer*, p. 188.

[29] Schulthess, *Europäischer Geschichtskalender 1905*, p. 195.

[30] Mühlberg to Bülow, Aug. 10, 1905, *G.P.*, XIX, 495, No. 6236.

for a continental campaign. If France is forced to accept German hegemony, England remains the only independent great power, and we are in much the same position as during the Napoleonic wars. We consider it therefore our duty to prepare for contingencies.

. . . . Of course, nobody here, except the small body of hot-heads who exist everywhere, desires to attack Germany. Our interest in peace is supreme and in fact perhaps too dominant. But we all have an uncomfortable feeling that always and everywhere we encounter the fixed and determined hostility of Germany, and that, when opportunity offers, this hostility will take an active form.[31]

Late in July, forthcoming British maneuvers in the Baltic Sea were suddenly announced in the press without any previous notification to the various governments. Following so closely after the meeting at Björkö, that announcement had a sinister significance which the Russian and the German presses interpreted as a warning to their countries that Great Britain was still mistress of the seas and that no change should occur against her will. Germany feared a British attack and, without an adequate fleet, felt herself defenseless.[32]

The British press denounced these fears as preposterous. In the House of Commons, Earl Percy, undersecretary of state for

---

[31] Memo. by Spring Rice for a letter to Roosevelt, July 10, 1905, Spring Rice to Mrs. Roosevelt, Aug. 10, 1905, quoted in Gwynn, *The Letters and Friendships of Sir Cecil Spring Rice*, I, 476, 484.

[32] Memo. by Mühlberg, Aug. 1, 1905, *G.P.*, XX, 648 f., No. 6868; Mühlberg to William II, Aug. 4, 1905, *ibid.*, 649 ff., No. 6869; Metternich to Bülow, Aug. 14, 1905, *ibid.*, 651 ff., No. 6870. The Emperor did not fear an attack at the time, but certainly at some later date. He thought that the maneuvers were meant to remind Denmark that she was an outpost for Great Britain just as Portugal was and that she must not be too familiar with Germany. And with an English princess married into the Swedish royal family and King Edward's son-in-law seeking the Norwegian throne, he feared that Norway would also become a British satellite (William II to Bülow, July 30, 1905, quoted in a dispatch from Bülow to F. O., July 30, 1905, *ibid.*, XIX, 477 ff., No. 6229). Even so sane a person as General Moltke, who in the next year became chief of staff, confided to his diary on July 30, 1905: "The visit of the Channel Fleet in the Baltic announced by England is to be regarded as a demonstration. . . . . The English are inciting in the most unbelievable fashion, they are telling the most despicable lies about us, and are representing Germany as the evil spirit in the whole world. . . . . The future lies dark before us. May Germany have the strength to bear difficult times" (Moltke, p. 331).

foreign affairs, declared on August 3 that "the situation in Europe presented no special cause for anxiety" and would present even less cause if certain "irresponsible persons were not perpetually attributing to this country Machiavellian motives of which we were quite innocent and who were always imagining that we could not enter into arrangements with one country for mutual convenience without having a hostile intent against some other country."[33] Lord Lansdowne immediately explained to the German and Russian governments that the lack of notification had been an oversight; he denied that the maneuvers were intended as a demonstration in any way.[34]

As neither side wanted trouble, this explanation cleared up the difficulty. The press became calmer and the visit of the British fleet to Swinemünde and Neufahrwasser, August 27–September 1, was used by both the British and the Germans for demonstrations of good will.[35] Yet the fact that for the first time in years the British fleet was practicing in the Baltic was not without significance. Furthermore, King Edward VII was still at odds with the German Emperor. In August and September, with the approval of his government, he refused to meet his nephew until Franco-German relations improved.[36] And at some time in August the British government learned from a member of the German Emperor's party at Björkö that at that meeting William II

[33] 4 Hansard, Vol. CLI, cols. 113, 122, 136 ff., 143.

[34] Memo. by Mühlberg, Aug. 1, 1905, *G.P.*, XX, 648 f., No. 6868; Mühlberg to William II, Aug. 4, 1905, *ibid.*, 649 ff., No. 6869. As a matter of fact, the maneuvers had been planned for some time, and to begin with had no political significance. No direct connection existed between their inception and the meeting at Björkö, but it is very probable that the British government was not at all averse to their occurring at the time (cf. Bradford, *Life of Wilson*, p. 200). Wilson was in command of the British fleet (see also *G.P.*, XIX, 478, editor's note).

[35] Schulthess, *1905*, pp. 109, 113; Bradford, p. 205.

[36] The German government learned of this fact in August but not of its approval by the British government. See Metternich to Bülow, Aug. 14, 1905, *G.P.*, XX, 658, No. 6870; Lee, II, 348, 353. On the quarrels of King Edward and his German nephew see Lee, II, 346 ff.; *G.P.*, 648 ff., Nos. 6868, 6870; Newton, *Lord Lansdowne*, p. 330.

had seemed nervous and preoccupied, that he had been seized by sudden fits of talkativeness and of silence, and that he had advocated his ideas of a coalition of Germany, Russia, and France to the exclusion of Great Britain. Lord Lansdowne's comment to that information was as follows: "The description of the Kaiser's language and demeanour fills me with disquiet. What may not a man in such a frame of mind do next?"[37]

III

When the report reached Paris on July 23 that the interview at Björkö was to occur, M. Rouvier immediately asked M. Witte, who was in Paris on his way to Portsmouth, whether it was true. M. Witte, equally in the dark, replied that he did not believe the rumor.[38] When the authentic news of the meeting came a few hours later, the French government and people were alarmed, for the Czar's meeting with the German Emperor signified a lack of regard for French feeling and seemed to belie M. Witte's assurances of Russia's devotion to the Dual Alliance.[39] Moreover, M. Witte's private advocacy of closer co-operation between the three great Continental Powers against the great naval Powers, that is, against France's friend, Great Britain, no doubt increased the concern of the French government.[40]

On July 22 M. Bompard, French ambassador in St. Petersburg, demanded an explanation from Count Lamsdorff of the report of the forthcoming meeting. The Foreign Minister assured the French government that it was a strictly private interview, devoid of any political character.[41] Nevertheless, after the

---

[37] William II to Nicholas II, Aug. 22, 1905, Goetz, p. 377; Hardinge to Lansdowne, Aug. 1, 1905, B.D., IV, 95 f., No. 91 and editor's note; Newton, pp. 337 f.

[38] Nelidow to Lamsdorff, Aug. 9, 1905, Kriegsschuldfrage, Nov., 1924, p. 477.

[39] Zur europ. Politik, II, 65 f.

[40] Nelidow to Lamsdorff, Aug. 9, Oct. 15, 1905, Kriegsschuldfrage, Nov., 1924, pp. 477, 491; Radolin to Bülow, July 25, 1905, G.P., XIX, 426 ff., No. 6198; M. Bompard states that Witte used the word "alli" (Bompard, "Le traité de Bjoerkoe," Revue de Paris, XXV [May 15, 1918], 438).

[41] Bompard, XXV, 432; Witte, p. 415; Quest. dipl. et col., XX, 174 f.

meeting occurred the French government continued to feel uneasy.[42] Although M. Bompard believed that Count Lamsdorff, faithful to the Dual Alliance, hoped that the meeting had had no significance, the Ambassador strongly suspected that the Minister had again not been consulted beforehand by his master.[43] Believing that the Emperor William II was trying through his personal relations with the Czar to destroy the Dual Alliance, he feared the results of an interview between the two sovereigns. When he learned that some sort of document had been signed by the two rulers, he surmised that it was a personal agreement of friendship by which they promised not to participate in any enterprise directed against the other and to exchange any information which came to their knowledge.[44]

Faced by the immense possibilities of the meeting at Björkö, M. Rouvier determined to forestall any Russian initiative looking toward a change in the Dual Alliance by frankly explaining his foreign policy to the Russian ambassador, M. Nelidow. On August 9, the Ambassador reported the Minister's words as follows:

The Minister assured me that the basis of his policy must remain the alliance with Russia; France needs no other. "Wherein does my policy differ from that of my predecessor?" he said to me. "Therein that I wish to establish good relations with England and Germany; but we do not intend thereby to make a closer agreement with the latter, just as on the other hand we do not desire to weaken the understanding already existing with England." Upon my remarking that several newspapers have gone so far as to speak of a German alliance, M. Rouvier replied emphatically that that would be "absolutely impossible."[45]

[42] Nelidow to Lamsdorff, Aug. 9, 1905, *Kriegsschuldfrage*, Nov., 1924, p. 477.

[43] Bompard, XXV, 432 f.; Bourgeois et Pagès, *Les origines et les responsabilités de la grande guerre*, p. 313.

[44] Bompard, XXV, 424 f. Just when Bompard learned this fact is not evident, but apparently he did so soon after the interview. Cf. Hardinge to Lansdowne, Aug. 3, 1905, *B.D.*, III, 127, No. 168.

[45] Nelidow to Lamsdorff, Aug. 9, 1905, *Kriegsschuldfrage*, Nov., 1924, pp. 477 f.

IV

The Czar, who probably felt guilty about not having consulted his Foreign Minister before signing the Björkö treaty, did not tell Count Lamsdorff of it until September 12.[46] He probably did so then because peace with Japan, signed on September 6 and soon to be officially ratified, would bring the Björkö accord into force.[47] Count Lamsdorff was horrified at the news. On October 9 he wrote to his friend M. Nelidow that the German Emperor had endeavored in the previous year to persuade "our poor monarch" to sign a treaty of defensive alliance with the obligation for France to join it. He continued:

I succeeded in preventing this crude attempt. But during the fateful meeting at Björkö, the Emperor William was able with the aid of base flattery to convince our dear Emperor that he alone was his true friend and his support, and that the only salvation for Russia and for Europe lay in a new Triple Alliance which in his opinion France would gladly join.

After informing M. Nelidow of the treaty signed at Björkö, he went on: "There you have the new mess into which we have been plunged after so many unusual adventures during the past two years. You can imagine how comforting this is."[48]

[46] There are various statements about the date upon which Lamsdorff learned of the treaty. See Iswolsky, *Recollections of a Foreign Minister*, pp. 49 f.; Savinsky, *Revue des deux mondes*, XII (1922), 798; A. Nekludow, "Autour de l'entrevue de Bjoerkoe," *Revue des deux mondes*, March 1, 1918, p. 139; Nekludow was a secretary in the Russian embassy in Paris in 1905 (Witte, p. 426; Savinsky, p. 114). The correct date is given in a dispatch from Lamsdorff to Nelidow on Oct. 9, where the Foreign Minister stated that he was first told of the treaty by the Czar just before the latter's departure for Finland on Aug. 30 (or Sept. 12, according to the new calendar). See *Kriegsschuldfrage*, Nov., 1924, p. 487. The Czar excused his delay to Lamsdorff on the grounds that he had promised William II to preserve secrecy. See *ibid.*, p. 487; Savinsky, *Revue des deux mondes*, XII (1922), 798 f.; cf. Iswolsky, pp. 49 f.

[47] There is no substantiation in *G.P.* for the assertion by Savinsky that the Czar told Lamsdorff that William II had asked him then to make known the accord to the French government (Savinsky, *Revue des deux mondes*, XII [1922], 799; Savinsky, p. 115).

[48] Savinsky, *Revue des deux mondes*, XII (1922), 799; Savinsky, pp. 115 ff.; Iswolsky, pp. 49 f.; Lamsdorff to Nelidow, Oct. 9, 1905, *Kriegsschuldfrage*, Nov., 1924, pp. 486 ff.

From the first Count Lamsdorff was determined to destroy the treaty. After comparing it with the terms of the Dual Alliance, he concluded that the one was a flagrant violation of the other.[49] In fact, he thought that in case of a Franco-German war arising out of the Moroccan affair, Russia was bound by this treaty to support Germany against her own ally. He wrote to M. Nelidow:

From long years of experience I have become convinced that the alliance with France is necessary in order to have really good relations with Germany. Otherwise we lose our independence; for I know nothing heavier than the German yoke. Without sacrificing the most intimate relations with Berlin, we have very tactfully repulsed all attempts to compromise us.

Not only did he expect France to refuse flatly to enter the new grouping, but he also considered it bad policy to give up the Dual Alliance in favor of a doubtful combination à trois. He considered the treaty to be altogether in favor of Germany, for she was bound to aid Russia only in Europe although Russia had most cause to fear Asiatic conflicts. Count Lamsdorff held that this alliance might involve Russia in the Anglo-German rivalry and might draw her into a war in which she had no interest. Preferring a policy of peace and good will with all Powers, he believed that Russia should next settle her difficulties with Great Britain, in spite of the fact that the renewal of the Anglo-Japanese Alliance in August had angered him. He was determined to extricate Russia from this situation with the least possible damage to Russo-German relations but above all without a breach in the Dual Alliance.[50]

When the Russian Foreign Minister marshaled these arguments before the Czar, the latter refused to yield. Without show-

[49] This was certainly the case. Even apart from the fact that the military clauses of the Dual Alliance provided for a war against Germany, the political clauses as revised in 1899 stated the aim of the alliance to be "the maintenance of the general peace and of the European balance of power" (Pribram, *The Secret Treaties of Austria-Hungary*, II, 206 ff.).

[50] Nekludow, *Revue des deux mondes*, March 1, 1918, pp. 137 f.; Savinsky, *ibid.*, XII (1922), 799 ff.; Witte, p. 425; Savinsky, pp. 115 ff.; Lamsdorff to Nelidow, Oct. 9, Sept. 28, 1905, *Kriegsschuldfrage*, Nov., 1924, pp. 480 f., 486 ff.; Nelidow to Lamsdorff, Oct. 5, 1905, *ibid.*, p. 483.

ing much consideration for French interest in the matter, Nicholas II replied that the alliance would be of benefit to both Russia and France and maintained that the latter would join it.[51] Although he was strongly skeptical about this possibility, the Foreign Minister was forced to inquire of M. Nelidow on September 14 whether or not France would do so.[52]

Without consulting anyone, M. Nelidow replied decidedly no. The Dual Alliance, together with the Entente Cordiale, every day becoming more intimate, he wrote, formed the foundation of the French foreign policy, whereas Franco-German relations were far from satisfactory. This new triple alliance, manifestly aimed at Great Britain, might, he continued, involve France in a war, which she wished above all to avoid, especially a war against Great Britain for the defense of German interests. Furthermore, such an alliance would mean the renunciation of all hopes of revenge for France. In fact, he thought that the slightest hint in favor of a Continental grouping would only shake France's trust in her ally. Nevertheless, he promised to investigate further.[53]

Not convinced by these arguments, the Czar clung to his plan. Just at this juncture M. Witte arrived in St. Petersburg with a letter from William II which forced a decision about the alliance.

M. Witte's ideas on foreign policy were confused. Early in May, 1905, he spoke of Germany to Mr. Spring Rice in hostile terms. In July, immediately before he left St. Petersburg for Portsmouth to negotiate peace with Japan, he was upholding among his friends and to the Czar the plan that at Portsmouth he should not only make peace but should also negotiate an "all-round arrangement" with Japan which Great Britain and France should adhere to or at least recognize.[54] A few days later at Paris

---

[51] Savinsky, *Revue des deux mondes*, XII (1922), 800 ff.; Savinsky, pp. 118 ff., 126 f.; Lamsdorff to Nelidow, Oct. 6 and 9, 1905, *Kriegsschuldfrage*, Nov., 1924, pp. 485 ff.; Witte, pp. 415 ff.; Iswolsky, pp. 44, 49.

[52] Lamsdorff to Nelidow, Sept. 14, 1905, *Kriegsschuldfrage,* Nov., 1924, p. 478.

[53] Nelidow to Lamsdorff, Sept. 21, 1905, *ibid.,* pp. 479 f.

[54] Hardinge to Lansdowne, July 25, 1905, *B.D.,* IV, 93 f., No. 89; Spring Rice to G. Balfour, July 29, 1905, and Spring Rice to Mrs. Roosevelt, Oct. 5, 1905, Gwynn, I, 481 f., 496.

he advocated the formation of a Continental grouping against the overseas Powers.[55] The renewal of the Anglo-Japanese Alliance increased his antagonism to Great Britain.[56] On his return to Paris in September, he refused an invitation from King Edward to visit England as well as an offer of British participation in the proposed Russian loan, and aided in settling the Moroccan difficulty in order to make possible a Franco-German *rapprochement*.[57]

As M. Witte had to pass through Germany on his trip home, the Emperor William obtained permission from the Czar for him to stop over and to be initiated into the secret of Björkö.[58] After a cordial interview with Prince Bülow at Berlin,[59] M. Witte journeyed to Rominten where he received an almost royal welcome from the Emperor (September 26). When William II informed him of the signing of the alliance at Björkö, the Russian statesman, according to the Emperor, wept tears of joy. M. Witte proposed that the German and the Russian ambassadors be given instructions to co-operate on all possible questions as a means of persuading France to enter the new grouping voluntarily and of preparing the world for this momentous event. In the meantime, he advised that the accord be kept closely secret. He promised to do his part in "using this foundation for the construction of a good house." Overjoyed at his success, William II accepted these suggestions. In a letter to the Czar carried by M. Witte he made

[55] Radolin to Bülow, July 22, 1905, *G.P.*, XIX, 426 ff., No. 6198. On July 26 the German government was about to inaugurate a press campaign against Witte, thinking that he was pro-British (Bülow to F. O., July 26, 1905, *G.P.*, XIX, 468, No. 6222).

[56] See Hardinge to Lansdowne, Oct. 4, 1905, *B.D.*, IV, 205, No. 195.

[57] Witte, pp. 293 f., 416 f.; Dillon, *The Eclipse of Russia*, pp. 350 f.; Radolin to Bülow, Sept. 23, 1905, *G.P.*, XIX, 503 f., No. 6241; Witte's interview in *Le Temps*, reprinted in *Quest. dipl. et col.*, XX, 439; Nelidow to Lamsdorff, Oct. 15, 1905, *Kriegsschuldfrage*, Nov., 1924, p. 491; Lee, II, 307 f.

[58] William II to Bülow, Sept. 25, 1905, *G.P.*, XIX, 505, No. 6242.

[59] At the Emperor's request Bülow said nothing to him about the Björkö treaty. See Bülow to William II, Sept. 25, 1905, *ibid.*, 505 ff., No. 6243.

this proposal for the co-operation of their foreign representatives:[60] "This common exposal of a common cause," he wrote, "will not fail to impress the world that our relations have become closer and thus slowly prepare your Allies the French for the new orientation which their policy must take for the entry into our treaty."[61]

In the conversations with M. Witte, who was not shown a copy of the treaty itself, the Emperor represented the accord as much less binding upon Franco-Russian relations than was really the case.[62] On his side, M. Witte, anxious to have the support of William II in regaining the good graces of the Czar and harboring some vague ideas about the desirability of a Continental grouping, was easily charmed by the Emperor into approval of the project. When he reached St. Petersburg, September 28, he urged upon the French Ambassador the need of a Dual Alliance–German coalition as a reply to the Anglo-Japanese Alliance. M. Bompard naturally rejected the idea.[63] When Count Witte (he had just been ennobled) protested to him the Emperor William's love for France and his attachment to the Dual Alliance, the Ambassador significantly asked, "Does not the Emperor's love for the Dual Alliance extend so far that he wished to join it?"[64] Count Lamsdorff, even less sympathetic, showed to Count Witte the actual treaty and wrathfully denounced it. The latter began to recover from the social intoxica-

[60] On the meeting at Rominten see the following: Witte, pp. 416 ff.; Iswolsky, pp. 50 ff.; Dillon, pp. 396 f.; Goetz, pp. 379 ff.; Bülow to F. O., Sept. 27, 1905, G.P., XIX, 507 f., Nos. 6244 f.; William II to Bülow, Sept. 27, 1905, ibid., 508 ff., No. 6246.

[61] William II to Nicholas II, Sept. 26, 1905, Goetz, pp. 379 ff.

[62] Bülow instructed the Emperor to that effect. See Bülow to William II, Sept. 25, 1905, G.P., XIX, 506, No. 6243. See the dispatch from the Emperor to Bülow on Sept. 27, 1905, ibid., 508 ff., No. 6246.

[63] Hardinge to Lansdowne, Oct. 1 and 4, 1905, B.D., IV, 202 f., No. 193; 205 f., No. 195.

[64] Bompard, XXV, 441 f.; Bourgeois et Pagès, pp. 318 f.

tion of his visit to Germany and to perceive that the treaty would have to be annulled.[65]

Count Lamsdorff, Count Witte, M. Nelidow, and the Grand Duke Nicholas, who was initiated into the secret, all joined forces in persuading the Czar. By appealing to their master's sense of honor and loyalty to the alliance made by his revered father, they succeeded in winning the unhappy ruler's consent to a compromise. He acknowledged that the treaty of Björkö and the terms of the Dual Alliance were in contradiction, and agreed that before the former became operative either Germany should be brought to change it in such a way that it would not affect France or that the French government should be moved to a scrutiny of the terms of the Dual Alliance "in the sense of a more or less close association with this defensive Triple Alliance." Thus, simultaneous attempts were to be made to persuade either France or Germany to change the terms of her alliance.[66]

It very soon became apparent that the French government would never accept the Björkö treaty. When M. Nelidow broached to M. Rouvier on October 4 the idea of alliance with Germany which his government claimed President Roosevelt also favored, the Premier repeated his former assertions on this question. He, in turn, stated his complete approval of an Anglo-

[65] In his memoirs Witte represented himself the dupe of the two rulers; when he read the document itself, he wrote, he was horrified. He claimed that he was largely responsible for the annulment of the treaty (Witte, pp. 425 ff.; Dillon, pp. 358 ff., 354, 413 f.; cf. Savinsky, p. 125). These accounts by him were both of a much later date, when he had been out of favor for several years and held a deep grudge against his master. Consequently he wanted to paint the latter's perfidy toward France as black as possible. That Witte thought the treaty so harmful at the time is difficult to believe. See his letter to Eulenburg, Oct. 8, 1905, *G.P.*, XIX, 519 f., No. 6250, Anlage; Witte, p. 424; Hardinge to Lansdowne, Oct. 1 and 4, 1905, *B.D.*, IV, 202 f., No. 193; 205 ff., No. 195; Spring Rice to Mrs. Roosevelt, Oct. 5, 1905, Gwynn, I, 496 f.

[66] See the following: Witte, pp. 427 ff.; Iswolsky, pp. 54 ff.; Savinsky, *Revue des deux mondes*, XII (1922), 801; Dillon, pp. 361 ff.; Lamsdorff to Nelidow, Oct. 9 and 27, 1905, *Kriegsschuldfrage*, Nov., 1924, pp. 487, 495; Bompard, XXV, 422 ff.; Savinsky, pp. 120 ff.

Russian accord.[67] Again on October 18 the Russian Ambassador reported that during a most intimate conversation with M. Rouvier he had pressed the arguments in favor of a Continental alliance against Great Britain only to receive from the Premier the following emphatic reply:

> We have aggressive intentions toward no one. We have given clear proof of our love of peace. Thirty-five years ago after a war unfortunate for us two provinces were taken away and we had to pay several billion francs for peace. Our nation submitted, and since then we have endeavored to avoid any cause for conflict or misunderstanding. To avoid difficulties which threatened to come to a head, I recently ventured to wound the pride of my country a little. But one cannot demand more of us. The nation would not tolerate a closer *rapprochement* with Germany. It cannot forget what it has suffered from her, of which suffering it has just been reminded in a careless and purposeless way. An alliance with Germany is impossible. The government is obliged to regard the feelings of the country.

As M. Nelidow commented in his dispatch, this was M. Rouvier's final reaction. It destroyed the possibility of France's entering a Continental alliance so completely that even the Czar had to acknowledge the fact.[68]

In the meantime, the Czar's letter of October 7 to William II arrived in Berlin. It read as follows:

> The great question is to draw France into our new defensive Alliance. . . . . But if France were to refuse to join us, then, not only would Art. IV drop away, but also the meaning of Art. I would change radically, because its obligations in the *present wording* point at any European Power and France too—Russia's ally. During your stay at Bjorkoe I did not have with me the documents signed by my Father. . . . . The first steps taken with the object of trying to find out, whether the French Government could be induced to join our new treaty, showed us that it is a difficult task and that

[67] Lamsdorff met with a similar response from Bompard. According to the latter, Lamsdorff suggested a combination of Russia, France, Germany, and the United States as a counterpoise to the Anglo-Japanese Alliance, "in the same manner that the political equilibrium of Europe was maintained by the Dual and Triple Alliances." See Hardinge to Lansdowne, Oct. 14, 1905, *B.D.*, IV, 211 f., No. 198; Spring Rice to Mrs. Roosevelt, Oct. 5 and 15, 1905, Gwynn, I, 497, 501 f.

[68] Nelidow to Lamsdorff, Oct. 5, 15, 18, 1905, *Kriegsschuldfrage*, Nov., 1924, pp. 481 f., 489 f.

it will take a long time to prepare to bring it over of its free will. . . . .
Therefore I think that the coming into force of the Bjorkoe treaty ought to
be *put off until* we know how France will look upon it. In case she absolutely
refuses to join our two countries, it will be necessary to change the wordings
of articles I and IV so as to bring them into full accordance with Russia's
obligations towards France, since the formation of the Triple Alliance in
1890. I shall do my best to get France to join us.[69]

Without consulting the Chancellor, William II replied on October 12 with a refusal:

I fully agree with you, that it will cost time, labour and patience to induce
France to join us both, but the reasonable people will in future make themselves heard and felt! Our Moroccan business is regulated to entire satisfaction so that the air is free for better understanding between us. Our treaty is
a very good base to build upon. We joined hands and signed *before God* who
heard our vows! I therefore think that the treaty can well come into existence. But if you wish any changes in the wording or clauses or provisions
for the future or different emergencies—as for instance the absolute refusal
of France, which is improbable—I gladly await any proposal you will think
fit to lay before me. Till these have been laid before me and are agreed
upon, the Treaty must be adhered to by us as it is.[70]

The Czar, who had expected an acquiescence,[71] was in an unhappy plight; no matter which way he turned he would be accused of breaking his word. Since France had the prior claim
and since the pressure upon him in St. Petersburg was pro-
French, he wrote to William II on November 23 that to fulfil
with equal loyalty the clauses of the Dual Alliance and those of
the treaty of Björkö he would have to add the following declaration to the latter:

In view of the difficulties in the way of an immediate adhesion by the
French Government to the treaty of defensive alliance signed at Björkö

[69] Nicholas II to William II, Oct. 7, 1905, *G.P.*, XIX, 512 f., No. 6247.

[70] William II to Nicholas II, Oct. 12, 1905, *ibid.*, 514, No. 6248; William II to
Bülow, Oct. 12 and 17, 1905, *ibid.*, 515 ff., Nos. 6249 f. The reply to Witte was
made by Eulenburg at the same time. See Bülow to Eulenburg, Oct. 18, 1905,
ibid., 520 f., No. 6251; Eulenburg to Witte, Oct., 1905, *ibid.*, 521, No. 6252. Cf.
Bompard, XXV, 443 ff. Bülow approved of the line taken by his master, for he
earnestly desired to continue the negotiations (Bülow to Eulenburg, Oct. 18, 1905,
G.P., XIX, 520, No. 6251).

[71] Lamsdorff to Nelidow, Oct. 12, 1905, *Kriegsschuldfrage*, Nov., 1924, p. 488.

. . . . it is understood that Article I of that act shall not have any application in the eventuality of a war with France and that the mutual engagements which unite the latter to Russia will be maintained in full until the establishment of an accord *à trois*.

To soften his refusal the Czar reported that Great Britain was "trying hard to get us round for an understanding about Asiatic frontier questions"; but he assured William II that he had not "the slightest intention of opening negotiations with her."[72]

This reply destroyed the entire force of the treaty; it spelled the failure of Germany's second effort to ally with Russia. The German Emperor and his government were bitterly disappointed. In the answer to the Czar on November 28, based upon a memorandum by Herr von Holstein, William II did not absolutely say yes or no, but left it to be understood that Germany still considered the treaty as binding in spite of the Czar's declaration.[73] On December 2 the Czar refused to accept the accord without the proposed declaration.[74] There the matter rested.

On January 21, 1906, the Czar wrote to William II that in keeping with "the real sense of our Bjorkoe treaty," he had ac-

[72] The letter was delivered by Osten-Sacken, Russian ambassador at Berlin, to give it full official character. See *G.P.*, XIX, 522 ff., No. 6254 and Anlage. The Czar approved this reply as early as Nov. 10. Lamsdorff to Osten-Sacken, undated though bearing the date of approval by Nicholas II of Nov. 10. See *Kriegsschuldfrage*, Nov., 1924, pp. 495 f.; Iswolsky, pp. 55 f.; Bompard, XXV, 443 ff.; Witte, p. 429; Savinsky, pp. 123 f.

[73] William II to Bülow, Nov. 26, 1905, *G.P.*, XIX, 524 f., No. 6255. The Emperor thought that Russia had shown little appreciation of German friendship during the recent war, and he declared to Bülow that the coalition of Russia, France, and Great Britain was *de facto* already existent. In the same letter he stated that Germany alone, since Russia refused her aid, must win France to the new project. For the reply to the Czar see William II to Nicholas II, Nov. 26 and 28, 1905, *ibid.*, 526 f., Nos. 6256 f. That the German government continued to hold the alliance as valid is seen from a memorandum composed by the foreign office for the Emperor just before the latter's meeting with the Czar at Swinemünde, July, 1907 (*ibid.*, p. 528 n.).

[74] *Ibid.*, 527 f., No. 6528. See also Bompard, XXV, 447; Witte, p. 429; Bourgeois et Pagès, p. 313.

cepted a proposal of President Loubet's to attach a French general to his person.

I think that this courtesy to France will bring her still closer to Russia. As long as I can hold her tight she will remain peaceful and quiet. It seems to me therefore that the continent's interests and still more so the interests of Germany can only gain from it. And with God's help some day Your right idea of forming a new "triple alliance" will become a solid reality.

In sending this letter to Prince Bülow on January 23 the Emperor wrote:[75]

I am sending you herewith another precious, bungling effort from the youthful idealist on the Russian throne! The latest phase of the Russo-Gallic Alliance borders on the ridiculous, but shows how in Paris—at London's suggestion?—a counter blow is immediately struck against every *rapprochement* between the two Emperors; every time, the little Czar by reason of the "ancient alliance" immediately falls or is won over by Lamsdorff. That he speaks on "my" idea of a triple alliance, as if I were receiving a special favor thereby, is really more than childish or naïve! . . . . And all that is served to me from behind a tear-drenched mask of eternal, most intimate friendship! How long will it be until he will have an "English general" at his side, naturally only in order to realize "my" ideal of world peace, and then a Japanese general to calm the oriental peoples, and finally an American general! His Majesty ought to be ashamed before his and my ancestors and before me to do such things, to write such letters to me, which Lamsdorff has dictated to him!

Thus the results of Björkö upon Russo-German relations were entirely different from those anticipated by the two rulers. By overreaching himself, by seeking a too-brilliant success without adequate preparation, the German Emperor alienated the Czar, who felt that he had played an ignominious rôle.[76] The consequence was that Russia again drew nearer to France[77] and began to look with more favor upon British overtures. Germany's effort to restore her dominant position in Europe and to prevent

[75] Both letters are quoted in *G.P.*, XIX, 528 n.

[76] Nekludow, *Revue des deux mondes,* March 1, 1918, pp. 142, 144. See also the correspondence between the two rulers, Jan. 21 and 29, 1906, *G.P.*, XIX, 528 n.; Goetz, p. 386.

[77] Iswolsky, p. 56.

the dreaded encirclement by means of a Russian alliance re-sulted, therefore, in preparing the ground for the very act which Germany most feared, the formation of an Anglo-Russo-French entente.

V

The German bid at Björkö for Russia's friendship and the rumors of what had happened there—approaching more and more nearly the truth by October[78]—inevitably aroused rival efforts by Great Britain. The British policy of obtaining an un-derstanding with Russia was complex. Defeat by Japan and revolution within made Russia discouraged and powerless, and broke the prestige of the chauvinistic, militaristic groups for the time being.[79] To complete the prophylactic work of fixing ade-quate restraints to the Russian expansive energy, Great Britain renewed prematurely her alliance with Japan in August, 1905, modifying the terms so that the alliance became effective in case of an attack by one Power and not only China specifically but also the "regions of Eastern Asia and of India" were included within its scope.[80] Then the British government hoped that Rus-sia, with no other alternative, would make a satisfactory settle-ment of their Asiatic differences.[81]

In the previous May, Sir Charles Hardinge, British ambassa-dor at St. Petersburg, had carried King Edward's most cordial greetings to the Russian Foreign Minister. With marked pleas-ure, Count Lamsdorff had replied that the maintenance of peace and good relations with Great Britain was *mon culte et ma re-ligion*. Remarking to the Ambassador that "interested parties" were trying to stir up discord between their countries, the Count

[78] Hardinge to Lansdowne, Oct. 1, 4, 14, 1905, *B.D.*, IV, 202 f., No. 193; 205 ff., No. 195; 211 f., No. 198; Lansdowne to Bertie, Oct. 25, 1905, *ibid.*, 217 f., No. 203.

[79] Hardinge to Lansdowne, Sept. 6, 1905, *ibid.*, 198 f., No. 191.

[80] *Ibid.*, chap. xxiv.

[81] Cf. Bertie to Lansdowne, Sept. 9, 1905, *ibid.*, 177, No. 172a; Spring Rice to Mrs. Roosevelt, Oct. 5, 1905, Gwynn, I, 498.

said that these endeavors must be frustrated. Count Lamsdorff, wrote the Ambassador to his government,

thoroughly realized the actual difficulties of the situation, but he was full of confidence that at the end of this miserable war both Governments would find a means of arriving at a satisfactory arrangement of all outstanding differences in the same manner as the Anglo-French arrangement had been made.[82]

Russia and Japan agreed upon terms of peace on September 5. Three days later, Sir Charles Hardinge notified Count Lamsdorff of the new Anglo-Japanese Alliance, and assured him most earnestly that it was one of national insurance, that Great Britain was absolutely sincere in her desire for peace and friendly relations, and that she had no wish "to interfere with the legitimate activity of Russia" or "to seek a policy of aggrandizement at her expense." Count Lamsdorff replied that he remained convinced of the value of an agreement and repeated that a third party was trying to arouse hostility between Great Britain and Russia. However, when Sir Charles Hardinge alluded to the possibility of resuming the previous negotiations at a future date, the Foreign Minister responded "that he was most anxious that they should be brought to a successful issue but that they should not be unduly hastened."[83]

This cool reply to the British sounding was caused partly by the pressing need at that time to annul the Björkö treaty, but primarily by the Anglo-Japanese Alliance, whose renewal at that moment Russia had not expected. Interpreting it as another blow to a state already humiliated by defeat, Russian public opinion denounced the treaty.[84] Thinking that the Russian animosity would pass, Lord Lansdowne proposed on October 3 a way of bringing the two countries closer together.

[82] Hardinge to Knollys, May, 1905, Lee, II, 306; Hardinge to Lansdowne, May 30, 1905, B.D., IV, 195 f., No. 189.

[83] Hardinge to Lansdowne, Sept. 9, 1905, B.D., IV, 178 f., No. 172(b); Lansdowne to Hardinge, Sept. 4, 1905, Newton, pp. 327 f.

[84] Hardinge to Lansdowne, Sept. 2, 9, 26, 1905, B.D., IV, 170 f., No. 159; 178 f., No. 172(b); 199 ff., No. 192 and following documents.

My own feeling was [he said to the Russian ambassador] that it would be a mistake to attempt too much, or to allow it to be understood that the two countries were on the eve of a comprehensive transaction analogous to that which had taken place between France and Great Britain. My idea of the procedure to be followed was rather that we should take up in detail any outstanding points as to which differences of opinion had manifested themselves and endeavour to dispose of these, and that we should then pass on to others, if we found that our work proceeded successfully.

Although the Russian Foreign Minister was gratified at the expression of British good will, he replied that

he could give no answer of a definite character, but, speaking privately, he could say that the Treaty had had a very bad effect and had left an unpleasant impression upon the mind of the Emperor, and he would recommend our Ambassador, as a friend, not to press for an answer as it might be a disagreeable one, nor to open negotiations as to a definite treaty between England and Russia as to their interests in Asia.

Count Benckendorff even remarked that "any arrangement . . . . should not be conceived in a spirit of hostility towards Germany"—an implication which the British Foreign Secretary repudiated with force.[85]

Greatly alarmed at Russian soundings about a Continental coalition against Great Britain, the French government in October tried several times to bring Russia and Great Britain together, even on any minor question.[86] In view of the Russian reserve, no definite proposals were made.[87] By October 21, however, the

[85] Lansdowne to Hardinge, Oct. 3 and 5, 1905, *ibid.*, 204 f., No. 194; 207 f., No. 196; Spring Rice to Mrs. Roosevelt, Oct. 15, 1905, Gwynn, I, 501.

[86] Hardinge to Lansdowne, Oct. 4, 8, 14, 1905, *B.D.*, IV, 205 ff., No. 195; 208 ff., Nos. 197 f.; Lansdowne to Bertie, Oct. 17 and 25, 1905, *ibid.*, 212 f., No. 199; 217 f., No. 203.

[87] See Hardinge to Lansdowne, Oct. 14, 1905, *ibid.*, 211 f., No. 198, Lansdowne's minute; *ibid.*, pp. 521 f.; report from London, Oct. 30, 1905, *Zur europ. Politik*, II, No. 22; report from St. Petersburg, Nov. 8, 1905, *ibid.*, No. 23; Metternich to Bülow, Oct. 22, 1905, *G.P.*, XIX, 663 ff., No. 6360; Metternich to F. O., Nov. 15, 1905, *ibid.*, XXV, No. 8501; Richthofen to Bülow, Oct. 24, 1905, *ibid.*, XIX, 665, No. 6361; Schoen to Bülow, Jan. 28, 1906, *ibid.*, XXV, 5 f., No. 8502; Miquel to Bülow, Oct. 24, 1905, *ibid.*, XIX, 666 ff., No. 6362; Nicholas II to William II, Nov. 23, 1905, *ibid.*, 523, No. 6254. On Oct. 21, 1905, King Edward instructed Hardinge to express to the Czar "my earnest desire that the best and most durable relations

French and British governments were certain that the danger of a Russo-German combination was past.[88] Shortly thereafter President Roosevelt, to the content of those governments, entirely denied that he favored a Continental grouping against the Anglo-Japanese Alliance.[89] When King Edward learned the truth about the Björkö affair in the autumn, he could with some relief describe his nephew, the Emperor William, as "the most brilliant failure in history."[90]

While these conversations were unsuccessful, Sir Charles Hardinge thought that "the improvement which has already shown itself in the relations between England and Russia only requires careful fostering to bear fruit in due season."[91] To that end it was necessary for the two governments to find some opportunity for disinterested co-operation—an opportunity which the Conference of Algeciras was to afford—and for Russian public opinion to reciprocate the amicable feelings of the British so that an Anglo-Russian understanding would be built upon a durable basis, like that of the Entente Cordiale. The British press was doing its share in bringing about this change of attitude. In fact, British public opinion felt more relieved than it had in months. The conclusion of the Russo-Japanese War, the renewal of the

should be established between the two countries, and that all important points should be discussed in the most amicable spirit and arranged as soon as possible" (Edward VII to Hardinge, quoted in Lee, II, 310). On Oct. 12 Lord Sydenham received a letter from Balfour stating that "the time is propitious for an understanding with Russia." Lord Sydenham, a member of the Defence Committee, wrote a draft of an agreement with Russia and sent it to the Premier, Oct. 20. On Nov. 1 he discussed Persian railways with Balfour and Sir Charles Hardinge, and, after Balfour had left, he (Sydenham) and Hardinge talked over the draft agreement. Hardinge believed that the Russians would accept it (Colonel Lord Sydenham, *My Working Life* [London, 1927], p. 182).

[88] Hardinge to Lansdowne, Oct. 21, 1905, *B.D.*, IV, 214, No. 201; Metternich to F. O., Nov. 15, 1905, *G.P.*, XIX, 521 f., No. 6253.

[89] Roosevelt to Spring Rice, Nov. 1, 1905, Gwynn, II, 8; G. Balfour to Spring Rice, Oct. 25, 1905, *ibid.*, I, 503.

[90] Eckardstein, I, 218 f.

[91] Hardinge to Lansdowne, Oct. 24, 1905, *B.D.*, IV, 216, No. 202.

Anglo-Japanese Alliance, the signing of the Franco-German agreement of September 28—all cleared the diplomatic atmosphere. The *Matin* revelations on October 5 concerning the supposed British offer of alliance to France in the previous summer placed Great Britain in a somewhat embarrassing position before the world as a disturber of peace. Moreover, it was recognized that Anglo-German animosity had almost caused a Russo-German alliance, and that, to make a settlement with Russia, Great Britain should restore better relations with Germany.[92] So British public opinion was ready to be friendly with Russia, and, in part, with Germany. During the autumn, sections of the British people, although not the government, tried to smooth over the animosities with Germany. A meeting was held in London early in December for that purpose at which eminent politicians, business men, representatives of the press, clergymen, and others were present to further the work.[93] As German public opinion responded to these efforts, a general *détente* set in.[94]

[92] Metternich to F. O., Nov. 15, 1905, *G.P.*, XIX, 521 f., No. 6253; Howe, p. 209.

[93] Report from London, Oct. 23, 1905, *Zur europ. Politik*, II, 80 f.; Bernstorff to Bülow, Sept. 8, 1905, *G.P.*, XIX, 636 ff., No. 6340. Party leaders, magazines, newspapers, and various societies in England took up the work. The *Times*, however, continued its anti-German campaign. In December, Colonel Repington published an article therein, warning the public against friendliness with Germany (Lieutenant Colonel Charles à Court Repington, *Vestigia* [London, 1919], pp. 262 f.). See also E. T. Raymond, *The Life of Lord Rosebery* (New York, 1923), p. 211; Spender, *Life of Campbell-Bannerman*, II, 208; Schulthess, *1905*, pp. 198 ff.; Metternich to Bülow, Oct. 18 and 22, Nov. 2, Dec. 3 and 20, 1905, *G.P.*, XX, 669 ff., Nos. 6879 ff.; Spender, *Life, Journalism and Politics*, I, 191 f.

[94] See Metternich to Bülow, Dec. 20, 1905, *G.P.*, XX, 690, No. 6886.

CHAPTER XVI

THE PRELIMINARIES TO THE CONFERENCE OF ALGECIRAS

I. GERMAN PRELIMINARIES TO THE CONFERENCE OF ALGECIRAS

After the Björkö treaty had been annulled by the Russian government, the Moroccan affair once more held the chief attention of the German foreign office. Already important, it became more so; for there was no longer any reason for the German government to use the Moroccan affair as a means of conciliating France and there was added need for it to justify to the German people and to the world the long diplomatic campaign over Morocco by checkmating France at the Conference.

Our chief object [wrote Prince Bülow on November 23] must be to avoid isolation at the conference. If we have the majority or all the other Powers against us on a question upon which we have engaged ourselves, boldness and threats will be of no use since after all that has occurred, our situation would be almost ludicrous.[1]

At almost the same moment the French Premier sounded the German government as to whether it would agree for France and Spain together to receive a police mandate from the Conference.[2] The inclusion of Spain, he said, would prevent the concession from appearing one-sided in favor of France and would enable the latter to keep her promise not to seek a general mandate. He added that Germany might be forced to agree to that solution. Replying doubtfully to these overtures, Herr von Flotow

[1] Memo. by Bülow, Nov. 23, 1905, *G.P.*, XXI, 14 f., No. 6900.

[2] Rouvier was apparently led astray by William II's instructions to the Prince of Monaco in October to tell Rouvier that "he would lay no hindrances whatever in the way of the French policy" (Radolin to F. O., Oct. 18, 1905, *ibid.*, XX, 596 f. and note, No. 6836). Rouvier sounded the German embassy first through a third person and then unofficially through M. Louis of the foreign office.

advised the French government to make the proposal directly in Berlin in accordance with diplomatic form. A few days later (November 30) Herr von Kühlmann reported that M. Vaffier-Pollet, representative of the Comité du Maroc in Tangier, and Count de Chérisey, former secretary of the French legation in Tangier, had proposed to him in Paris that the German and French governments make a secret agreement before the Conference to the following effect: The *status quo* in Morocco should be maintained for three or four years, after which, if conditions had not improved, Germany should not oppose the bestowal upon France of the police mandate for all of Morocco; in return, Germany should be assured of the open door and of the right for German capital to participate to the extent of 45 per cent in all governmental enterprises in Morocco, of territorial compensation in the French Congo region, and of the cession of the French right of preference to acquire the Belgian Congo.[3] Although M. Rouvier stood behind this offer, the German government did not know it and did not reply. It was much disposed to consider the overture made through Herr von Flotow; but this fact the French Premier could not know, and, misled by the German silence, he never returned to the subject.[4]

The German Chancellor's willingness to negotiate directly with France showed that he was beginning to appreciate Germany's increasingly unfavorable position in international relations. He knew that the German government faced a hard campaign and that its public opinion, which had no particular interest in Morocco and was averse to war, must be convinced of the

[3] Memo. by Mühlberg, Nov. 30, 1905, *ibid.*, XXI, 20 ff., No. 6906.

[4] On this episode see *ibid.*, Nos. 6901, 6903 ff. The editors of *G.P.* assure us that there is no indication in the documents that Rouvier followed up the subject (*ibid.*, p. 23). Joseph Caillaux states that Rouvier was back of the overture made through Vaffier-Pollet. He also asserts that in Nov., 1905, Rouvier offered the port of Mogador and its hinterland to Germany, but that the latter refused (*Agadir, ma politique extérieure* [Paris, 1919], p. 25). There is no reference to this proposal in *G.P.* Caillaux is probably referring to the offer made through Eckardstein in May, 1905.

justice of the German cause and aroused to the seriousness of the international situation. In the Reichstag on December 6 the Chancellor therefore warned the nation that while animosities had been overcome, new ones were possible, and that the British were particularly anti-German. Repeating all the German accusations against the French Moroccan policy, he justified at length Germany's defense of her interests. He avowed his strong desire for the maintenance of friendly relations with all nations. He assured his hearers that Italy remained loyal to the Triple Alliance. But he urged his country to be prepared for any emergency.[5] The speech was widely approved.[6]

The Chancellor's utterances were soon answered by M. Rouvier through the publication of a French *Livre jaune* of over three hundred pages, which was supplemented by a speech in the Chamber on December 16.[7] Therein, to the satisfaction of the French, the German accusations were denied and the national policy of France toward Morocco was exonerated.[8] According to the reports of the German representatives in Paris in December and January, France was firmly resolved not to recede further, and the French government was making military preparations[9]

These manifestations did not augur well for the German government. Nor did the terms of the Franco-Spanish agreement of September 1, 1905, which it learned of at some time before the

---

[5] Bülow, *Reden*, II, 250 ff., 272 ff.; see also Hammann, *Bilder*, pp. 43 f. At the opening of the Reichstag on Nov. 28 the Emperor declared that Germany stood with all Powers in "correct relations" and with the most of them in "good and friendly relations" (Schulthess *Europäischer Geschichtskalender 1905*, pp. 132 f.).

[6] Report from the Belgian Minister at Berlin, Dec. 2 and 11, 1905, *Zur europ. Politik*, II, 92 ff.

[7] *Journal officiel. Debats parlem.* (Chambre), pp. 4034 ff. Rouvier received a vote of confidence of 501 to 51 (*ibid.*, p. 4050).

[8] *Quest. dipl. et col.*, XX, 662 ff.

[9] William II to Bülow, Dec. 29, 1905, *G.P.*, XX, 693, No. 6887; Flotow to Bülow, Nov. 23, 1905, *ibid.*, XXI, 15 ff., No. 6901; Metternich to Bülow, Jan. 4, 1906, *ibid.*, 52, No. 6924.

314 THE FIRST MOROCCAN CRISIS, 1904–1906

Conference opened.[10] The knowledge of the terms gave a concrete basis to the mistrust of France's intentions toward Morocco, and stiffened German resistance., On December 25 the German government envisaged three ways in which the Conference
might end: first, a provisorium of about three years might be
agreed upon, at the end of which each Power would recover its
freedom of action; second, a separate agreement with France
might be made, but only in case the latter offered suitable terms;
third, a general police mandate for Western Morocco might be
given to France. This last result, equivalent to a French victory,
the German government was determined not to permit, holding a
conflict as preferable.[11] In fact, none of these solutions was very
palatable to the government. But it was determined to hold
firm,[12] and the instructions to Herr von Radowitz and Count
Tattenbach, the German delegates at the Conference, were optimistic.

The delegates were to uphold the open door and economic
equality for all. They should combat the monopoly for making
loans to Morocco claimed by the French banks. As Germany
had already recognized the legitimate interests of France by
permitting her to regulate the frontier, the mandate for police
reforms in the west should be given to a number of Powers and
should be internationally organized for a limited number of
years. If a division of mandated areas were made, Germany

[10] So Ojeda, Spanish undersecretary of state for foreign affairs, declared to Cartwright on Jan. 22, 1906 (Cartwright to Grey, Jan. 22, 1906, *B.D.*, III, 233, No.
252). There is no indication in *G.P.* that those terms were known.

[11] Memo. by Mühlberg, Dec. 25, 1905, *G.P.*, XXI, 28 f., No. 6914. It contained
the conclusions of a conference by Bülow with Richthofen, Mühlberg, and Klehmet.

[12] On Jan. 8 the government published a *Weissbuch* on Morocco of thirty-nine
pages substantiating the German accusations against the French policy. According
to Bülow it was intended to supplement the French *Livre jaune* (*G.P.*, XXI, 24 n.).
Its appearance made a painful impression in France. Rouvier found it "scarcely
courteous" and hardly indicative of the conciliatory spirit which Germany pro-
fessed to have (report from Paris, Jan. 11, 1906, *Zur europ. Politik*, II, 99 f.). It
was well received by the German press (Lascelles to Grey, Jan. 10, 1906, *B.D.*,
III, 215 f., No. 235.).

should receive her share—one with a port advantageously located for later expansion into the interior; however, Germany was ready to agree with the others not to draw any advantage for herself from this mandate. All the signatory Powers should participate equally in establishing and directing the proposed state bank, for which adequate international organization and control should be provided. Above all, the delegates should not permit themselves to be isolated or to stand alone with Morocco. Thus, in general, they were to work for the internationalization of Morocco.[13]

Prince Bülow became more and more optimistic as the Conference approached.[14] At his urging, the Sultan promised to select carefully his delegates to the assembly and to co-operate with the Powers there.[15] The Chancellor expected the neutral Powers to support Germany against the monopolistic desires of France. He particularly courted President Roosevelt; for, although he knew that Mr. White, the American delegate, would not be permitted to take the initiative at the Conference, the Chancellor thought that the President and his delegate would be able, behind the scenes, to exert a powerful influence.[16] From Russia, Prince Bülow anticipated no interference. The Austrian Foreign Minister stated his government's readiness to go hand in hand with Germany at the Conference.[17] Spanish mistrust

[13] Bülow to Radowitz, Jan. 3, 1906, *G.P.*, XXI, 38 ff., No. 6922 and Anlage.

[14] Metternich was very pessimistic about the outcome. See Metternich to Bülow, Nov. 2, 1905, *ibid.*, XX, 672 ff., No. 6881; Bülow to Metternich, Nov. 6, 1905, *ibid.*, XIX, 673, No. 6364.

[15] Tattenbach to Bülow, Nov. 4, 1905, *ibid.*, XXI, 12, No. 6898.

[16] Bülow to Sternburg, Oct. 29, 1905, *ibid.*, XIX, 641 f., No. 6341 and note; Sternburg to F. O., Nov. 3, 1905, *ibid.*, XXI, 9 f., No. 6896; Bülow to Sternburg, Nov. 7, 1905, *ibid.*, 11 f., No. 6897; memo. by Mühlberg, Dec. 11, 1905, *ibid.*, 23 f., No. 6909; Dennis, *Adventures in American Diplomacy*, pp. 398 f., 499. Mr. Choate, ambassador in London, had been selected as American delegate in August (*Roosevelt-Lodge Correspondence*, II, 172 ff.); but the final choice rested on Mr. White, ambassador at Rome.

[17] Bülow to Wedel, Dec. 22, 1905, *G.P.*, XXI, 27 n.; cf. Steed, *Through Thirty Years*, I, 234.

and jealousy of France with reference to Morocco might be aroused and used.[18] To that end the German government prevented the selection of the anti-German M. Villa-Urrutia as delegate.[19]

Toward Italy, embarrassed by her situation as Germany's ally and France's friend through an agreement over Morocco, the Chancellor modified his former tactics. He offered to support her as a candidate for the general police mandate at the Conference.[20] But the Italian government refused. Sending the aged and experienced Marquis Visconti Venosta as delegate, it gave him permission to act as he saw fit in order to keep his head out of the noose.[21] The German Chancellor approved this choice and welcomed the Marquis' statement that he would endeavor to mediate between France and Germany and to bring the Conference to a successful conclusion.[22] Prince Bülow planned to exploit Italy's position by laying down a flat *non possumus* on the question of permitting France to receive the mandate for the police, with the expectation that the Italian government would then press France to accept the German terms in order to prevent a conflict wherein it would be forced to choose sides.[23]

The Chancellor instructed Prince Radolin to impress French

[18] According to a minute by the Emperor William to a dispatch from Stumm on Feb. 20, 1906 (the only reference to this incident which *G.P.* contains), during the visit of the King of Spain to Germany in the previous November the Emperor had "proposed to the Spanish King to renew the agreement with his father and a convention regarding the common action of our armies! Whereupon the King said that he knew nothing of that matter, but would look into it upon his return." Nothing came of the matter. See *G.P.*, XXI, 191, No. 7024. See also Grey to Bertie, Dec. 20, 1905, *B.D.*, III, 160, No. 197; Nicolson to Grey, Dec. 26 and 27, 1905, *ibid.*, 165, No. 205; 167, No. 208.

[19] Nicolson to Grey, Dec. 14, 1906, *B.D.*, III, 150 f., No. 192.

[20] Bülow to Monts, Jan. 5, 1906, *G.P.*, XXI, 54, No. 6925.

[21] So expressed by San Giuliano, Italian foreign minister. (Monts to Bülow, Jan. 2, 1906, *ibid.*, 34 ff., No. 6921).

[22] Bülow to Monts, Jan. 5, 1906, *ibid.*, 53 f., No. 6925; Monts to Bülow, Jan 6, 1906, *ibid.*, 56 ff., No. 6928.

[23] Bülow to Radowitz, Jan. 8, 1906, *ibid.*, 59, No. 6929.

official circles with the fact that Germany would never permit France to obtain a general police mandate or a special position in the state bank, that if France persisted in refusing to agree to the open door in Morocco, a "very critical situation would arise" which "would lead inevitably to a grave conflict" between the two states.[24] Prince Bülow was pleased to learn that the French people were growing nervous and that M. Rouvier, M. Jules Cambon, French ambassador in Madrid, and others were asserting France's wish for a peaceful and satisfactory solution.[25]

The main reason for the Chancellor's growing optimism was the fact that in December a Liberal government had come to power in England and that British public opinion was more friendly to Germany. Prince Bülow and the Emperor both expected an improvement in Anglo-German relations, and exerted their influence in achieving it.[26] The Chancellor did not believe that the new Liberal government would stiffen the French resistance by holding out the prospect of active aid in case of war as the Unionist cabinet had done. He interpreted the overwhelming Liberal victory at the elections in January as a clear rejection of chauvinism and an equally clear expression by the nation of an earnest desire for peace and for further improvement in

[24] Bülow to Radolin, Dec. 29, 1905, *ibid.*, 30 f., No. 6916; memo. by Radolin, Dec. 29, 1905, *ibid.*, 31, No. 6917; memo. by Bülow, Dec. 30, 1905, *ibid.*, 32, No. 6918.

[25] Flotow to F. O., Dec. 20, 1905; *ibid.*, 25 f., No. 6911; Radolin to F. O., Jan. 8 and 10, 1906, *ibid.*, 60 f., No. 6931; 64 f., No. 6934; Radolin to Bülow, Jan. 16, 1906, *ibid.*, XX, 697 f., 6888; Radowitz to Bülow, Dec. 27, 1905, *ibid.*, XXI, 32 f., No. 6919 f.; Bülow also remained willing to negotiate directly with the French government over the Moroccan affair (Bülow to Radolin, Jan. 16, 1906, *ibid.*, 67, No. 6936).

[26] Report from Berlin, Dec. 24, 1905, *Zur europ. Politik*, II, 97 f.; report from Berlin, Dec. 31, 1905, *Belg. Docs., 1905–14*, No. 14; Metternich to Bülow, Nov. 2, Dec. 20, 1905, *G.P.*, XX, 672 ff., No. 6881; 685 ff., No. 6886; Bülow, II, 434; Schulthess, *1905*, p. 154. The Emperor refused twice to help before Bülow won him over. See Bülow to William II, Dec. 3, 1905, *G.P.*, XX, 679 ff., No. 6882, and the Emperor's minutes.

Anglo-German relations. He learned that Edward VII had spoken in favor of a peaceful settlement.[27] Then, just after the Conference opened, the King and the Emperor entered into personal correspondence once more.[28] The Chancellor therefore expected the British government to play the rôle of mediator instead of active French partisan, and he endeavored to impress this duty upon it.[29] In view of this situation he believed that France would accept the German solution of the Moroccan problem.[30]

Although the Chancellor knew that France was improving her defenses, he did not anticipate a war.[31] He notified General Moltke, the new chief of staff, that he need take no precautionary measures.[32] The Emperor also regarded the French fears of war

[27] So D. M. Wallace, special representative of the *London Times* at the conference, asserted to Radowitz (Radowitz to F. O., Jan. 21, 1906, *G.P.*, XXI, 95 n.).

[28] Lee, *King Edward VII*, II, 524 ff.; Edward VII to William II, Jan. 23, Feb. 5, 1906, *G.P.*, XXI, 108 f., No. 6961; 111 f., No. 6963; William II to Edward VII, Feb. 1, 1906, *ibid.*, 110 f., No. 6962.

[29] "If England restricts herself to the diplomatic support of the French claims, peace and the permanent open door are assured. But as soon as France has reason to count on the armed help of England for the conquest of Morocco and for any results therefrom, then both peace and the open door will be endangered" (Bülow to Radowitz, Jan. 17, 1906, *ibid.*, 94, No. 6950). A similar thought was expressed by Bülow to Lascelles, Jan. 24, to Sir Edgar Speyer, London banker and friend of Grey's, on Jan. 18, by Metternich to Grey, Dec. 20, Jan. 23, and was given out to the press. See *ibid.*, 96 ff., Nos. 6953 f.; 106 ff., No. 6960; 103 ff., No. 6959; *ibid.*, XX, 685 ff., No. 6886.

[30] For Bülow's reasoning see his dispatch to Moltke, Jan. 24, 1906, *ibid.*, XXI, 77 ff., No. 6943.

[31] A report of a partial French mobilization on the eastern frontier did alarm Bülow, but it was immediately proved to be untrue (*ibid.*, 71 ff., Nos. 6937 ff.).

[32] The German government had announced a new navy bill, which would have been proposed anyway, and was only hastened because the visit of the British fleet to the Baltic and the revelations in *Le Matin* insured it a favorable reception by the German public. Aside from that Germany took special pains to avoid leaving the impression that she was preparing for a conflict. Moltke, at his own suggestion, postponed his visit to Vienna to announce himself as the new chief of staff until after the conference closed so as to avoid suspicion. See Moltke to Bülow, Jan. 26, 1906, *ibid.*, 79 and note, No. 6944. See also Philip Fürst zu Eulenburg-Hertefeld, *Aus 50 Jahren. Erinnerungen, Tagebücher, und Briefe* (ed. Johannes Haller; Ber-

as "ludicrous, bordering on insanity." Late in December he roundly declared to Mr. Werner Beit, a friend of Edward VII, and to the Marquis de Laguiche, French military attaché in Berlin, that "there is absolutely no cause for any war or for any concern about an attack from us," adding, however, these more ominous words:

> Even if we had the best intentions and were loyal and wished to remain peaceful, there would be danger that in case of continued inciting of France by London, she [France] might, relying on certain aid from England, conduct herself toward us so ill-manneredly and provocatively that finally our national honor would come into question, for the sake of which we should have to resort to arms; then we would have to strike and therewith, through our "illegal attack" on France, give the occasion for England's aid. And it is monstrous perfidy [for England] to work toward such.[33]

Thus, hopeful for peace but not entirely averse to war, the German leaders saw the Conference begin.

II. FRENCH PRELIMINARIES TO THE CONFERENCE
OF ALGECIRAS

In spite of the failure of his overtures to the German government in November, the French Premier assured the *Wilhelmstrasse* on the eve of the Conference that he wished to reach an understanding at that assembly on the basis of "no victor, no vanquished." Nevertheless, both he and the French nation were determined to uphold France's ambitions and claims toward Morocco. On January 8, 1906, Prince Radolin wrote that there

---

lin, 1923), p. 311. Moltke, however, did not expect the French to recede, writing to Bülow on January 23 as follows: "In my opinion the French now consider further concession on the Moroccan question as incompatible with the honor of their land, after they have already receded once and have let Delcassé fall.

"They fear therefore that as a result of their firm stand the conference may not only end without result but may also lead to war. They themselves wish no war and do not think of attacking. But they wish to be armed against an attack from Germany" (*G.P.*, XXI, 75, No. 6942).

[33] William II to Bülow, Dec. 29, 1906, *ibid.*, XX, 690 ff., No. 6887. The account of the Emperor's conversation with Laguiche was published in *Le Temps* on Dec. 28. Richthofen spoke to a similar effect to the Belgian minister (*Belg. Docs., 1905–14*, No. 14).

prevailed in France "grave anxiety over the possibility of war-like complications. . . . . In press and public it is said that Germany wishes war, that France has receded . . . . on all points, but without satisfying Germany." At the Conference, thus Prince Radolin interpreted French opinion, "proposals would be made which would be contrary to her honor and her traditional policy in Morocco. France must defend herself and be prepared for any eventuality. . . . . Germany makes no secret of her armaments, and therefore it is imperative for France also to keep her powder dry."[34]

In this state of mind the French Parliament during the latter half of 1905 investigated French defences and put 200,000,000 francs at the disposal of the war Minister for repairing them, particularly on the eastern frontier. That work was actively begun; food and munitions were brought in; the frontier forces were increased by reserves; drilling and trial mobilizations were held.[35] As M. Delcassé had prophesied, M. Rouvier returned completely to the international policy of the fallen Minister in order to achieve victory at the Conference. The French govern-

[34] Radolin to Bülow, Jan. 8, 1906, G.P., XXI, 60 f., No. 6931; Metternich to Bülow, Jan. 4, 1906, ibid., 51 f., No. 6924; Zur europ. Politik, II, 95 f., 99; Tardieu, La Conf. d'Algés., pp. 92 ff. See also Bompard's analysis of the German policy toward France (Spring Rice to Grey, Jan. 16, 1906, Gwynn, The Letters and Friendships of Sir Cecil Spring Rice, II, 58 f.).

[35] According to Moltke, France was making military and financial preparations for defensive purposes. "The fortifications on the eastern frontier are being strengthened and put in a more defensive condition. Their provisions in munitions and food are being replenished. The forces of the frontier defence troops are apparently being brought approximately to the legal number for peace time by the addition of troops from the interior. Moreover, reserves are here and there being called up to undergo their legal drilling.

"The training of the troops on the frontier is being furthered in every way. Numerous trial mobilizations by the various garrisons and drilling of the border troops by day and night are occurring.

"But all these preparations are not to be regarded as preparations for an intended mobilization but only as precautionary measures, which are easily explained" (Moltke to Bülow, Jan. 23, 1906, G.P., XXI, 75, No. 6942).

According to the Belgian Minister at Paris, Jan. 16, 1906, the sum of 270,000,-000 francs was being devoted to the defenses (Zur europ. Politik, II, 103).

ment realized that the opposition of the French and German policies was so complete as to make retreat difficult for either party. Preparing for the worst, M. Rouvier yet hoped to exert sufficient moral pressure on Germany at the Conference to gain a French victory without precipitating a war.[36] To that end he supplemented the military measures by diplomatic work. He was certain of Russia's support because, aside from the alliance, Russia had urgent need of a French loan, which M. Rouvier would not permit until after a satisfactory conclusion of the Moroccan affair.[37] Russia's influence was restricted by the revolution and by a lack of interest in Morocco. But a promise from the Czar to exercise his personal power with Emperor William II in favor of conciliation would be of eminent value, and M. Rouvier sought to obtain it.[38] He also wished to have President Roosevelt act similarly at the proper moment. This plan was to bear fruit later; but at the time the American government replied that it had small concern in the Moroccan conference and that, while standing for the open door and exerting its influence for peace, it would interfere as little as possible in the deliberations. Mr. Root, the secretary of state, told the British Ambassador that the American delegate would "avoid any action which could tend to weaken Anglo-French entente."[39] M. Rouvier also received

[36] Meyer to Root, Jan. 9, 1906, Dennis, *Adventures in American Diplomacy*, p. 498; *Zur europ. Politik*, II, 99 f.

[37] The Russian delegate, Count Cassini, declared that in forty years he had never received such positive instructions (Tardieu, p. 88; Witte, *Memoirs*, p. 298; Spring Rice to Grey, Jan. 2, 1906, *B.D.*, III, 204, No. 223). Rouvier repeated the refusal of that loan just before the conference (Witte, pp. 295 ff., 429 f.; Nicholas II to William II, Jan. 21, 1906, *G.P.*, XXI, 125 f., and note). Concerning that loan Sir Edward Grey wrote to Bertie, Jan. 15, 1906, as follows: ". . . . Russia has demanded a loan on improper terms as the price of her support [at the conference]" (*B.D.*, III, 178, No. 216).

[38] Meyer to Root, Jan. 9, 1906, Dennis, p. 498. Witte apparently offered to obtain this promise in return for an immediate French loan, but the Czar refused to give it—at least, that was Spring Rice's inference (Spring Rice to Grey, Jan. 16, 1906, Gwynn, II, 57 f.).

[39] Dennis, pp. 498 f.; Durand to Grey, Jan. 11, 1905, *B.D.*, III, 217, No. 236.

"satisfactory assurances" from the Austro-Hungarian government; he did not expect opposition from it or from Belgium.[40] Far more important was the continuation of British aid, both for its own sake and for holding Italy and Spain in line.[41] From the new Liberal government that came in early in December, the French Premier was immediately assured of diplomatic aid by word and act.

III. BRITISH PRELIMINARIES TO THE CONFERENCE OF ALGECIRAS

When internal disputes over the question of tariff reform finally forced the resignation of the Unionist government on December 4, the Liberals, with Sir Henry Campbell-Bannerman as prime minister, entered office. In response to the popular demand they were pledged to continue the foreign policy of their predecessor, and the presence at the foreign office of Sir Edward Grey assured the fulfilment of that pledge. The Foreign Secretary was a Liberal Imperialist, a follower of Lord Rosebery. He had been one of the rebels against the leadership of Sir Henry Campbell-Bannerman, a Gladstonian Liberal, because of the latter's denunciation of the Boer War. Regretting that Lord Rosebery would not enter the cabinet, Sir Edward Grey at first refused office unless the Premier would accept a peerage and leave the leadership in the House of Commons to Mr. Asquith, another Liberal Imperialist. After much persuasion from his friends and after the influence of the Liberal Imperialists had been increased by the appointment of Mr. Haldane as secretary of war, Sir Edward receded from his demand.[42]

The new Foreign Secretary found the "mud of foreign politics" deeper than any he had ever been in; but he was soon steering himself through it as nimbly as his predecessors. Although

[40] Bertie to Grey, Dec. 22, 1905; *B.D.*, III, 165, No. 204.

[41] See Rouvier's assertion to Hardinge on Jan. 15, 1906, *ibid.*, 227 and inclosure, No. 245.

[42] Spender, *Life of Campbell-Bannerman*, II, 193 ff.; Grey, *Twenty-five Years*, I, 60 ff., Richard Burdon Haldane, *An Autobiography* (London, 1929), pp. 157 ff., 168 ff.

an idealist who hated war, he was not afraid of it, for, he wrote to Sir Francis Bertie, January 15, 1906, "We can protect ourselves . . . . for we are more supreme at sea than we have ever been."[43] He followed the ways of *Realpolitik,* playing the "grand game" of prestige politics in the ordinary way with national interest as his ultimate guide. He impressed other men with whom he had personal contact as trying to be entirely frank and honest and sympathetic. Yet his insularity, his lack of knowledge of the Continent, really prevented him from appreciating any other state's point of view. Combining the limitations of a "downright Britisher" with high moral and political rectitude, he usually believed that Great Britain was in the right and acted accordingly. Then he was unable to comprehend why other Powers misinterpreted her policy.[44]

With regard to Russia, Sir Edward Grey immediately stated to the Ambassador his hope for a settlement of the outstanding questions. Count Benckendorff thought that negotiations were impossible "while things in Russia were in their present condition." Appreciating this fact, Sir Edward Grey answered that "during this inevitable delay, it would be the policy of our Government not to do anything which would make the resumption of negotiations or a settlement more difficult later on."[45] In January of the next year, Count Witte, Russian premier, proposed to the British government that Czar Nicholas and King Edward—diplomats he distrusted as being too slow—should at a personal meeting conclude a general agreement in return for which Great Britain should make a loan to Russia. The British Ambassador soon showed him the impracticability of the idea.[46] In the same

[43] Grey to Bertie, Jan. 15, 1906, *B.D.,* III, 178, No. 216.

[44] Cf. Spender, *The Public Life* (1925), I, 112 ff.; Haldane, *An Autobiography,* pp. 215 f.; cf. Hermann Lutz, *Lord Grey und der Weltkrieg* (Berlin, 1927).

[45] Grey to Spring Rice, Dec. 13, 1905, *B.D.,* IV, 218, No. 204; Grey to Spring Rice, Dec. 22, 1905, Gwynn, II, 53 f.

[46] Spring Rice to Grey, Jan. 3 and 16, 1906, *B.D.,* IV, 219 f., No. 205; 221, No. 207; and Gwynn, II, 54 f., 57; Spring Rice to Knollys, Jan. 3 and 16, 1906, *ibid.,* pp. 22, 26.

month Count Benckendorff talked vaguely and informally with Mr. Spring Rice of the Bosphorus and the Dardanelles and of Persia—all to no object, for, as the British government perceived, Russia was indifferent to an agreement.[47] But some progress was made toward a *rapprochement*. The two governments co-operated on the Cretan and Macedonian questions.[48] Treating each other more frankly,[49] each refused to take advantage of the other early in 1906 by making a loan to Persia.[50] The British government renewed its assurances about Tibet in January.[51] British bankers agreed to participate in a forthcoming loan to Russia.[52] The Czar and King Edward were on cordial terms, the former late in January even intimated to his uncle that he would be pleased with a visit from him.[53] And the two governments were in harmony in their policy of helping France at Algeciras. So while the work of achieving the entente was slow, the British government did not let it cease.

The British Foreign Secretary also continued the previous policy toward Germany. He knew very little of that Power, did not understand it,[54] and nursed a deep suspicion of it from his experiences as undersecretary of state for foreign affairs from 1892 to 1895. He was determined not to let Great Britain fall again into that state of trouble with other Powers, which he thought had enabled Germany to treat her so high-handedly at

[47] Spring Rice to Grey, Jan. 3, 1906, Gwynn, II, 55 f.

[48] Spring Rice to Grey, Jan. 26, 1906, *B.D.*, IV, 222 ff., No. 208; Grey to Spring Rice, Dec. 22, 1905, Gwynn, II, 53 f.

[49] See Lansdowne to Hardinge, Oct. 20, 1905, *B.D.*, IV, 213 f., No. 200; Hardinge to Grey, Jan. 6, 1906, *ibid.*, pp. 622 f.

[50] *Ibid.*, chap. xxvii, Part III. Nicolson suspected that Russia acted so loyally because she had no money with which to make the loan (Nicolson to Grey, Sept. 12, 1906, *ibid.*, 242, No. 228).

[51] Grey to Spring Rice, Jan. 3, 1906, *ibid.*, 323, No. 304.

[52] Spring Rice to Grey, Jan. 3, 1906, *ibid.*, 220, No. 205.

[53] Spring Rice to Grey, Jan. 26, 1906, *ibid.*, 223, No. 208; Lee, II, 564; Spring Rice to Mallet, Jan. 31, 1906, Gwynn, II, 61 f.

[54] Haldane, *An Autobiography*, p. 215.

that time and to make demands upon her inimical to her interests.[55] His advisers in the foreign office, Sir Charles Hardinge and Mr. Eyre Crowe, were of a similar mind, lacking the balanced and comprehensive judgment characteristic of Lord Sanderson, who after years of service retired from his position as permanent undersecretary of state for foreign affairs in January, 1906.[56]

Sir Edward Grey was now confronted with the same kind of action on the part of Germany which had previously angered him. He saw a conference approaching at which the new friendship with France would be tested, at which it would be either broken or confirmed. He was resolved that if possible it should not be broken, though he did not necessarily intend that it should become stronger. "It was a matter of interest," he said on August 3, 1914, with reference to this crisis, "to preserve it [the Entente] as well as a point of honour to act up to the diplomatic obligations contained in it."[57] At the time (December 21, 1905) he expressed himself more concretely to Sir Arthur Nicolson as follows:

The Morocco Conference is going to be difficult if not critical. As far as I can discover the Germans will refuse altogether to concede to France the special position in Morocco, which we have promised France not only to concede to her but to help her by diplomatic methods to obtain.

If she can succeed in getting this with our help it will be a great success for the Anglo-French *Entente;* if she fails the prestige of the *Entente* will suffer and its vitality will be diminished.

Our main object therefore must be to help France to carry her point at the Conference.[58]

Thus for the sake of interest and honor, that invincible pair, Sir Edward Grey based British policy upon the matter of prestige. Whereas Lord Lansdowne had admitted that the Anglo-French declaration over Morocco did not bind Germany, the

---

[55] Grey, I, 100 f.

[56] Cf. memo. by Crowe, Jan. 1, 1907, *B.D.,* III, 397 ff.; memo. by Sanderson, Feb. 21, 1907, *ibid.,* pp. 420 ff.; Haldane, *An Autobiography,* p. 215.

[57] Grey, I, 100 f.   [58] *B.D.,* III, 162, No. 200.

new British Foreign Secretary was determined that Germany should formally recognize France's preponderant position in Morocco. It is to be inferred from his statement that Germany had the alternative of accepting France's monopolization of the Sherifian Empire passively or of challenging it and then being forced to accept it.

That this ominous feeling was not peculiar to Sir Edward Grey was shown early in January by a letter which Lord Ripon, one of the older members of the cabinet, wrote to Lord Fitzmaurice, parliamentary undersecretary of state for foreign affairs. It read in part as follows:

> One cannot help being anxious about this Morocco business. I am sorry though not surprised to hear that you think the Germans intend to make the Conference a failure. That a European war should arise out of the matter seems almost impossible, but when one has to deal with a potentate like the German Emperor one can feel no real security.[59]

On December 19 Count Metternich gave to Sir Edward Grey a general explanation of Germany's policy on the Moroccan question, expressing the hope that the British government would play the part of conciliator at the Conference.[60] The British Minister replied on January 3. The Conference filled him with concern, he said. After having studied the documents more thoroughly, he had found that Lord Lansdowne had stated to Count Metternich "that, in the event of war between Germany and France, public feeling in England would be such that, in his opinion, it would be impossible for England to remain neutral." This statement, he went on, he made his own; for, while the British government "wanted to avoid trouble between Germany and France," and would not "egg" France on at the Conference, yet since the entente was very popular in England he "really thought that if there was trouble, we [Great Britain] should be

[59] Lucien Wolf, *Life of the First Marquess of Ripon* (London, 1921), II, 292 f.; see also Spring Rice to Mallet, Jan. 31, 1906, Gwynn, II, 61.

[60] Metternich gives the date of the conversation as Dec. 18. See Grey to Whitehead, Dec. 20, 1905, *B.D.*, III, 160 f., No. 198; Metternich to Bülow, Dec. 20, 1905, *G.P.*, XX, 685 ff., No. 6886.

involved in it. . . . . It was not a question of the policy of the Government," he told the Ambassador; "what made a nation most likely to take part in war was not policy or interest, but sentiment, and if the circumstances arose, public feeling in England would be so strong that it would be impossible to be neutral." British opinion, he declared, would be moved not by hostility to Germany but by the wish to preserve friendship with France. He made an Anglo-German *rapprochement* contingent upon a happy outcome of the Conference, an improvement in Franco-German relations and the assurance thereby that the Entente Cordiale would not be endangered. He spoke frankly, he said, because the situation might later become such as to make openness more difficult. When Count Metternich reminded him that Lord Lansdowne had qualified his statement concerning the possibility of active British aid by the further assertion, "in case of an unprovoked attack by Germany upon France," Sir Edward Grey made no reply. But the meaning of his statement was clear to the Ambassador, who accepted it as an honest rendition of the British position.[61]

The bluntness of these remarks seemed justified immediately by the varying reports about Germany's intentions which came to the British foreign office. The German Emperor was in a friendlier mood although angry at the tone of the British press. Baron Richthofen and Herr von Radowitz both spoke of a desire

[61] On this conversation between Grey and Metternich see the following: Grey to Lascelles Jan. 9, 1906, Grey to Campbell-Bannerman, Jan. 9, 1906, quoted in Grey, I, 80 ff., 114, and in *B.D.*, III, 209 ff., No. 229; Metternich to Bülow, Jan. 3 and 4, 1906, *G.P.*, XXI, 45 ff., Nos. 6923 f. Grey repeated his statement to Metternich on Jan. 10, 1906. See Metternich to F. O., Jan. 10, 1906, *ibid.*, 64, No. 6933. See also Bülow to Sternburg, Jan. 24, 1906, quoting a dispatch from Metternich, *ibid.*, 103 ff., No. 6959. However, Van Grooten, secretary of the Belgian ministry in London, reported to his government on Jan. 14 as follows: "Of late the Minister of Foreign Affairs has repeated at various occasions to the different Ambassadors accredited in London that Great Britain has engaged herself towards France in the Moroccan question and that she will meet her obligations fully even in case of a Franco-German war and at all costs. The press and public opinion give proof of the same sentiments" (*Belg. Docs., 1905–14*, p. 19). The report is exaggerated, but it is significant that it was current.

for conciliation.[62] The British Consul in Hamburg, however, learned from Herr von Tschirschky of the German foreign office on New Year's Day that "Germany's policy always had been and would be to try to frustrate any coalition between two States which might result in damaging Germany's interests and prestige, and Germany would, if she thought that such a coalition was being formed, even if its actual results had not been carried into practical effect, not hesitate to take such steps as she thought proper to break the combination."[63] And Prince Bülow's brother, minister at Berne, remarked to his British colleague on December 31:

> No doubt the sudden intervention of Germany [in Morocco] had not been dictated by the desire to safeguard German interests in that region. The object had been a higher one. Germany was bound in self-defense to emancipate herself from the isolation with which she was threatened. First Russia, then Italy, and lastly England had been won over by France. The cordon must be broken, and the penultimate defeat of Russia had furnished the propitious moment. . . . . He thought that a *détente* would make itself felt when once the Conference was over.[64]

It was becoming more and more apparent that Anglo-German antagonism would accentuate the difficulties of the Conference. Prince Bülow informed the British government on January 11 that he advocated reforms on an international basis. Stating that M. Rouvier had promised not to seek a general police mandate for France,[65] the Chancellor made it understood that Germany could not accept that solution. In talking to the British Ambassador on the next day Herr von Holstein foresaw danger since France, relying upon British aid, might, if dissatisfied with the results of the Conference, "seek to create a *fait accompli* by invading Morocco. The Sultan would appeal to the Emperor, and war would be the result." Asseverating that France was

[62] Lascelles to Grey, Jan. 3, 1906, *B.D.*, III, 206 ff., Nos. 225 f.; Nicolson to Grey, Dec. 22, 1905, *ibid.*, 163, No. 203.

[63] Spender, *Life of Campbell-Bannerman*, II, 257 f.

[64] Acton to Grey, Dec. 31, 1905, *B.D.*, III, 167 f., No. 209.

[65] Rouvier denied that he had done so. Notes by Hardinge, Jan. 15, 1906, *ibid.*, 226 and inclosure, No. 245 (see above).

preparing for war, Herr von Holstein said that the danger could be averted if the British government would hint to the French that in the event of their invading Morocco it was doubtful whether British opinion would approve of supporting France by force of arms.

Upon being consulted, Sir Francis Bertie denied that France had any such intention, and asserted that

any communication to the French Gov[ernmen]t such as the Baron [Holstein] suggests would shake the confidence of the French Gov[ernmen]t in H[is] M[ajesty's] present Gov[ernmen]t resulting from their assurances as to policy of England (and) might lead France either to make concessions to Germany in Morocco injurious to us or bring her out of Morocco by concessions elsewhere detrimental to our interests but not greatly to those of France.

After this Sir Edward Grey telegraphed to Sir Frank Lascelles, January 15, the following curt response to Herr von Holstein's suggestion:

I hope the result of Morocco conference will prevent the contingency, which Herr von Holstein contemplates, from arising. Should it however be otherwise we cannot deprecate any action on the part of France which comes within the terms of the Anglo-French declarations of April 1904. Herr von Holstein should know this.[66]

In these negotiations the British Foreign Secretary tried to impress the German government with the fact that Great Britain placed herself squarely on the French side. This was one facet of his policy. The other had to do with France.

The British government was as eager for France to win at the conference as was the French government. To that end Sir Francis Bertie informed M. Rouvier on December 22 that his government

would loyally act up to the engagements taken by their predecessors and . . . . would give to France their unreserved support in the Conference on Morocco within the four corners of the Anglo-French Agreement and the

[66] On this episode see Lascelles to Grey, D. Jan. 3, R. Jan. 6, 1905, D. Jan. 11, R. Jan. 15; dated Jan. 12, D. Jan. 13, R. Jan. 15, 1906, *ibid.*, 207 f., No. 226; 217 ff., Nos. 237 f.; 222 f., Nos. 240 f.; Grey to Lascelles, Jan. 9 and 15, 1906, *ibid.*, 211 f., No. 230; 225, No. 243; Bertie to Grey, Jan. 14, 1905, *ibid.*, 224, No. 242; memo. by Holstein, Jan. 18, 1906, *G.P.*, XXI, 96 f., No. 6953.

programme arranged between the French and German Governments; but in order to enable them to do so effectively, and to put them in a position to act in concert with France, it would be desirable that His Majesty's Government should be made acquainted with the views of the French Government on the matters to be discussed, and as to the concessions, if any, which might be made for the satisfaction of Germany.

The British government, he said, wished to avoid the accusation of being more French than the French. Going farther still, the Ambassador assured M. Rouvier that his government was in no way associated with the friendly manifestations toward Germany then being made in England. While the British government wanted friendly relations with Germany, he stated, an improvement in those relations "would depend on the attitude of the German Government in regard to Morocco and other questions in which England was interested." The cordiality with which M. Rouvier agreed to respect this wish showed how conscious both governments were of the mutual advantages in loyal co-operation.[67]

The need therefor was manifested at once in the case of Spain. While King Alfonso was regarded as entirely loyal,[68] M. Moret, the Spanish premier who supplanted M. Montero Rios in December, was mistrusted by the British and French governments as being too friendly toward Germany and uncertain in his attitude toward the Moroccan agreements. Both governments knew of German efforts to win Spain, both learned of the German Emperor's offer in November of a military convention to the King of Spain, and both learned that at Germany's request the Spanish government had not appointed M. Villa-Urrutia as delegate to the Conference.[69] At the French initiative the two govern-

[67] Bertie to Grey, D. Dec. 22, R. Dec. 27, 1905, *B.D.*, III, 163 ff., No. 204; Grey to Nicolson, Dec. 21, 1905, *ibid.*, 162, No. 200. "Nous serons biens sûrement avec vous," Grey stated to Cambon (Grey to Bertie, Dec. 20, 1905, *ibid.*, 160, No. 197).

[68] Tardieu, pp. 81 f.

[69] Nicolson thought that he would have been "an admirable selection." King Edward's comment to the report of Germany's veto was, "a case of bullying as usual!" See Nicolson to Grey, D. Dec. 14, R. Dec. 23, 1905, *B.D.*, III, 150 f., No. 192.

ments late in December pressed M. Moret to remain loyal to them. These efforts won over the Spanish Premier. He frankly admitted that the Emperor had made the offer, but denied that he had ever considered it. He stated that Spain would support the French policy during the Conference, and hoped that the three Powers would work harmoniously together. And he told the French that "it will facilitate his support of them at the Conference if they will provide money to quiet the Spanish Opposition."[70] Nevertheless, the British government suspected that the Duke of Almodovar, the Spanish delegate and proposed president of the Conference, would be "in the hands of the German Ambassador [Herr von Radowitz]." Sir Edward Grey also feared that Spain might, to the detriment of British interests, be induced to cede a part of her possessions along the north coast of Morocco or elsewhere to Germany.[71] So Spain remained under constant observation and pressure by the Entente Cordiale.[72]

The British government put similar pressure upon Italy. In informing the Italian Ambassador on December 27 of the British policy, Sir Edward Grey remarked that the four Powers most interested in the Mediterranean were all good friends now and that he "hoped we should all come out of the Conference as good friends as we went in." The Italian government protested that it had "not only friendship but also an alliance to be considered." This item Sir Edward Grey ignored, and in Rome Sir Edwin Egerton repeatedly asserted that "a European political combina-

[70] Grey to Bertie, Jan. 15, 1906, *ibid.*, 178, No. 216.

[71] Minutes to dispatch from Nicolson to Grey, D. Jan. 5, R. Jan. 13, 1906, *ibid.*, 209, No. 227.

[72] Grey stated to the Spanish Ambassador, Jan. 3, 1906, as follows: "All the four Powers most directly interested in the Mediterranean had made arrangements with each other which were satisfactory to themselves and it was most undesirable that they should allow these arrangements to be disturbed" (Grey to Nicolson, Jan. 10, 1906, *ibid.*, 215, No. 234). On this Spanish affair see also Grey to Bertie, Dec. 20, 1905, *ibid.*, 160, No. 197; Grey to Nicolson, Dec. 14, 20, 21, 1905, *ibid.*, 151, No. 193; 161 f., Nos. 199 ff.; Nicolson to Grey, Dec. 22, 25, 27, 1905, Jan. 5 and 9, 1906, *ibid.*, 163, No. 202; 165, No. 205; 167, No. 208; 208 f., No. 227; 212, No. 231; Bertie to Grey, Dec. 22, 1905, *ibid.*, 163 ff., No. 204.

tion did not appear to regard special agreements respecting a local question, such as that of Morocco." This veiled threat and curious interpretation of the Triple Alliance were valuable aids to M. Barrère in urging Italy to the Anglo-French side. The selection as delegates of the Marquis Visconti Venosta, who had made the agreement with France in 1900, was regarded as insuring a pro-French policy. But the Italian government could make no promises of support, and Sir Edward Grey feared that the Marquis might, by trying to play the "fine" but "dangerous" rôle of mediator at the Conference, suggest some solution which would be altogether unacceptable.[73]

The Anglo-French co-operation extended to planning the procedure at the Conference and to drawing up instructions for the French delegates. Every precaution was taken for victory. The British were as sensitive to alarms as were the French. About the middle of December both governments heard that the proposed Austrian delegate thought it possible to bring matters before the Conference not mentioned in the program. M. Rouvier took immediate steps in Vienna to prevent that danger.[74] Furthermore, the two governments planned that the less difficult problems should be considered first and the police question last. M. Rouvier proposed that the published Anglo-French, Anglo-Spanish, and Franco-German agreements over Morocco should be laid before the Conference, but Sir Edward Grey objected that they might then be discussed and questioned by the Powers. The British Foreign Secretary thought that "it should appear that the Anglo-French and Franco-Spanish Agreements of 1904 were rather intended to give a formal sanction to a *de facto* state of affairs than to create a new situation." M. Rouvier accepted this suggestion. It was also in accordance with a British proposal

[73] Grey to Bertie, Jan. 15, 1906, *ibid.*, 225, No. 244; Grey to Egerton, Dec. 27, 1905, *ibid.*, 166, No. 206; Egerton to Grey, Dec. 27, 1905, Jan. 9, 1906, *ibid.*, 166 f., No. 207; 212 f., No. 232.

[74] Gorst to Bertie, Dec. 13, 1905, *ibid.*, 149 f. and inclosure, No. 191; Bertie to Grey, Dec. 15, 1905, *ibid.*, 158 f., No. 195.

that the French delegate was instructed to refuse to argue the matter of France's right in the Algero-Moroccan frontier region, since it might lead to an "embarrassing discussion."[75]

The main problem which the British and French governments had to solve was that of the police. For, as they learned from Prince Bülow,[76] Germany would propose either that Morocco be divided into sectors, each one under the police power of a different state, or that the policing be done by a lesser Power disinterested in Morocco. While the first solution could be easily rejected, the second one would be more difficult for France to combat without exposing herself to the accusation of selfishness. If the Conference broke up because of a refusal, France would be blamed. At this point the two governments received a suggestion from M. Bacheracht, Russian minister at Tangier and a delegate at the Conference, to the following effect: "All considerations of a political character and all references to 'special interests,' etc., should not be touched upon in discussion" of the police question. The problem should be considered solely from a practical point of view, of how to assure protection and safety to the foreigners. Clearly that work could be done best by France and Spain, who had had experience in handling Mohammedans, who were already policing portions of Moroccan soil, and who could employ Mohammedans from their North African territories to aid them. The policing might be regarded as experimental and temporary so as to mollify German opposition. If Germany rejected the plan, she would receive the discredit for breaking up the Conference. The British and French authorities accepted this proposal at once, for, as MM. Paul and Jules Cambon said, it would be "difficult to combat."[77]

[75] Memo. by Cambon, Jan. 15, 1906, *ibid.*, 226, No. 244 and inclosure; Nicolson to Grey, Jan. 17, 1906, *ibid.*, 228 f., No. 247.

[76] Lascelles to Grey, D. Jan. 11, R. Jan. 15, 1906, *ibid.*, 217 ff., No. 237.

[77] Nicolson to Grey, Jan. 2, 1906, *ibid.*, 205 f., No. 224; Grey to Bertie, Jan. 10, 1906, *ibid.*, 213 ff., No. 233. See also Bompard's conversation with Spring Rice as reported by the latter to Grey, Jan. 16, 1906, Gwynn, II, 59 f.

After this thorough preparatory discussion, M. Rouvier sent the following instructions to M. Révoil, a copy of which he also gave to the British government: The repression of contraband trade should be committed to France and Spain alone. A state bank should be established in which French participation in capital and in personnel should be in harmony with France's superior rights in Morocco resulting from the loan contract of June, 1904, and from the high percentage of trade (approximately 80 per cent) which France together with Great Britain and Spain had with that country as compared with that (approximately 10 per cent) of Germany. The bank should be under the French legal system and its president a Frenchman. Moroccan revenues should be augmented, but not merely by an increase in customs duties. The thirty-year limitation to commercial freedom might be extended. "In a general manner it is in the economic program that we are disposed to accord the most complete satisfaction. But you will avoid a definitive acquiescence in those solutions until you are certain that the delegates do not aim to adopt unacceptable solutions relative to the organization of the police." This question should refer solely to the policing of the coastal towns and should not concern the Moroccan army. Any internationalization of the police should be refused. The plan of dividing Morocco into sectors among the Powers, that of selecting a minor Power to accomplish the task, and that of selecting officers from neutral Powers should be absolutely refused. The policing should be conferred upon France and Spain alone.

In case the proposals conforming to our desires on that matter meet with insurmountable opposition . . . . , we would consider that, the economic questions being regulated according to our views, an accord for the maintenance of the *status quo* in that which concerns the police would be an acceptable solution, if that accord respects our rights and implies the renunciation by the other contracting parties to all action tending to reopen the question with the Sultan without previous agreement with us. . . . . In résumé . . . . no one will expect of us an adhesion to any solution of a nature to compromise the future of our national interests. Under that condition, you will show on all occasions our sincere desire to respect the rights of other countries, to open Morocco to the free competition of commercial interests, and you will affirm at the same time our desire to maintain our rights and interests only with the most formal guarantees of the sovereign rights of the Sultan, the independence and the established traditions of his Empire.[78]

A few days later, with the approval of Spain, M. Rouvier advised the French delegate to reject as "absolutely inacceptable" any plan to neutralize Morocco.[79]

These instructions denoted a determination to defeat internationalization, by all means to exclude Germany from Morocco, and to divide Morocco between France and Spain.

While these negotiations were in progress, the French government was sounding Great Britain as to a defensive agreement against Germany. Toward the middle of December Major Huguet, French military attaché in London, spoke to General Grierson, director of military operations in the British war office, about the French fears of a German attack, and questioned him about the British organization for war. When he asked whether the British general staff had ever considered operations in Belgium, General Grierson replied that "as a strategical exercise" he had worked out a plan for them last spring.[80]

On December 28 Major Huguet dined with Colonel Repington, a retired officer serving as military correspondent on the *London Times*. The conversation turned immediately to the Colonel's article of the previous day, in which he had denounced the attempts being made toward an Anglo-German *rapprochement*, expressed anxiety over the international situation, and advised full loyalty to France. The two men found themselves in entire agreement over the possibility of complications and

---

[78] Rouvier to Révoil, Jan. 12, 1906, *B.D.*, III, 220 ff., No. 239; Tardieu, pp. 101 ff., 244; Bertie to Grey, Dec. 22, 1905, *B.D.*, III, 164, No. 204. In talking to Sir Charles Hardinge on Jan. 15 Rouvier added a third alternative—"a mandate to France, Spain and a third Power to study and elaborate a scheme for submission to the Powers" (notes by Hardinge, Jan. 15, 1906, *ibid.*, 226 f., No. 245 and inclosure).

[79] Cartwright to Grey, Jan. 23, 1906, *ibid.*, 233 f., No. 253.

[80] Grierson to Sanderson, Jan. 11, 1906; *ibid.*, 172, No. 211.

over the need for France and Great Britain to be prepared for co-operation in case of a German aggression. Major Huguet said that the French embassy was worried because Sir Edward Grey, the new British foreign minister, had not renewed the assurances given by his predecessor.[81] Time was pressing, he said, for the Conference of Algeciras would open on January 16. He wished that Sir Edward Grey would broach the subject at the next diplomatic reception. The French "knew that our sympathies were with them," so Colonel Repington has recorded the military attaché's words, "but they wanted to know what we should do in case Germany confronted them with a crisis."

Colonel Repington immediately communicated the conversation to the British Foreign Secretary, who was then electioneering in Northumberland. The latter replied on December 30 as follows: "I can only say that I have not receded from anything which Lord Lansdowne said to the French, and have no hesitation in affirming it." The Colonel also reported Major Huguet's words to Sir George Clarke, secretary of the Defence Committee, and to Lord Esher, a member of that Committee. They agreed that in view of the German menace, active steps toward co-operation should be taken. As Colonel Repington was a free-lance, they suggested that he open unofficial conversations with Major Huguet and communicate the results to the British officials. The Colonel prepared a set of questions which Major Huguet took to Paris on January 7. These questions were considered by M. Rouvier, M. Etienne, minister of war, M. Thomson, minister of marine, his naval staff, General Brun, and General Brugère. On January 12 a cordial reply was returned to Colonel Repington who then imparted it to the Defence Committee.[82]

When Major Huguet related these incidents to his ambassa-

---

[81] This display of doubt about Great Britain's loyalty was one of France's best means of gaining that Power's support. See Bompard's assertions as reported by Spring Rice to Knollys, Jan. 31, 1906, Gwynn, II, 62; also see below.

[82] The story is given in Lieutenant-Colonel Charles à Court Repington, *The First World War, 1914–1918: Personal Experiences* (London, 1920), I, 2 ff.

dor, M. Cambon was so struck by the fact that British as well as French authorities were studying the problem of how quickly the British forces could be mobilized for action on the Continent that he went immediately to Paris to consult M. Rouvier.[83] The latter approved of the plan to broach Sir Edward Grey for a closer and more definite understanding.

Before returning to London, M. Cambon visited his brother in Madrid. There the two prepared the ground for later discussion by a conversation with Sir Arthur Nicolson which the latter reported (January 2) as follows:

> They [MM. Cambon] asked me, supposing, as they considered probable, that the Conference failed, what did I think would be the consequences? I replied that in my opinion it was quite possible that the Sultan would then apply to Germany to take in hand the military, financial and police administration. They remarked that that would mean war. I said that I did not consider that this would necessarily follow; but I did think that they would have to take up a very firm attitude at Fez, and prevent the Sultan from handing himself over to the Germans.[84]

This alarming forecast, together with the staunch diplomatic support which the British government was rendering France, strengthened the French authorities in their resolve. When M. Cambon reached London, he had a long conversation with Sir Edward Grey on January 10 which the latter recorded as follows:

> M. Cambon said that he did not believe that the German Emperor desired war, but that His Majesty was pursuing a very dangerous policy. He had succeeded in inciting public opinion and military opinion in Germany, and there was a risk that matters might be brought to a point in which a pacific issue would be difficult. During the previous discussions on the subject of Morocco, Lord Lansdowne had expressed his opinion that the British and French Governments should frankly discuss any eventualities that might seem possible, and by his instructions your Excellency [Sir Francis Bertie, ambassador in Paris] had communicated a Memorandum to M. Delcassé to the same effect. It had not been considered necessary at the time to discuss

---

[83] Général Huguet, *L'intervention militaire britannique en 1914* (Paris, 1928), p. 15.

[84] Nicolson to Grey, Jan. 2, 1906, *B.D.*, III, 206, No. 224.

the eventuality of war, but it now seemed desirable that this eventuality should also be considered.

M. Cambon said that he had spoken to this effect to M. Rouvier, who agreed in his view. It was not necessary, nor, indeed, expedient, that there should be any formal alliance, but it was of great importance that the French Government should know beforehand whether, in the event of aggression against France by Germany, Great Britain would be prepared to render to France armed assistance.[85]

The British statesman, embarrassed by the question, replied that he personally could give the French government no promise of active aid. He put the Ambassador off by pointing out that the Prime Minister was away, that the members of the cabinet were all electioneering, and that the verdict of the elections was doubtful. He said that he could only state as his personal opinion that "if France were to be attacked by Germany in consequence of a question arising out of the Agreement [of April 8, 1904] . . . . public opinion in England would be strongly moved in favour of France." When he added that Great Britain earnestly desired "that the conference should have a pacific issue favourable to France," M. Cambon replied that "nothing would have a more pacific influence on the Emperor of Germany than the conviction that, if Germany attacked France, she would find England allied against her." Sir Edward Grey answered that he thought that "the German Emperor did believe this, but that it was one thing that this opinion should be held in Germany and another that we should give a positive assurance to France on the subject." He could give no assurance, he said, of which he was uncertain. He "did not believe that any Minister could, in present circumstances, say more than I had done, and, however strong the sympathy of Great Britain might be with France in the case of a rupture with Germany, the expression which might be given to it and the action which might follow must depend largely upon the circumstances in which the rupture took place."[86]

[85] Grey to Bertie, Jan. 10, 1906, quoted in Spender, *Life of Campbell-Bannerman,* II, 249 ff.; Grey, I, 70 f.; *B.D.,* III, 170 f., No. 210a.

[86] This document is sufficient proof against the accusation of the editors of *G.P.* that Grey went further in his assertions to the French Ambassador in his first

As Sir Edward Grey thus postponed a definitive answer until after the elections, M. Cambon replied that he would repeat his request at that time. But he asked that in the meantime the "unofficial communications" between the British admiralty and war office and the French naval and military attachés "as to what action might advantageously be taken in case the two countries found themselves in alliance in such a war" might be permitted to continue. "They did not pledge either Government," he said.[87]

Sir Edward Grey immediately sent a report of this conversation to the Prime Minister and to Lord Ripon, and he met his friend, Mr. Haldane, at Berwick on January 12 to discuss the matter, particularly the French request concerning the military conversations.[88] He had learned that under the Unionist cabinet in the previous year such military and naval conversations had taken place, and that at the present time official conversations were going on between Admiral Sir John Fisher and the French naval attaché while the military conversations were being held unofficially between the French military attaché and Colonel Repington. When consulted on January 11, General Grierson replied that "if there is even a chance of our having to give armed assistance on land to France or to take the field on her side in Belgium in consequence of a violation of Belgian territory by the Germans, we should have as soon as possible informal communication between the military authorities of France and/or Belgium and the General Staff."[89] Neither Sir Edward Grey nor

conversation with the latter, and that afterward, apparently restrained by the more pacific Premier, he qualified his position in the interview of Jan. 31. It is apparent that Grey's statements of Jan. 10 and 31 do not differ in kind or degree, except that in the latter the Foreign Secretary expanded the conditions which he had already formulated in the earlier interview (see *G.P.*, XXI, 48 f. note; see also below).

[87] Grey to Bertie, Jan. 10, 1906, quoted in Grey, I, 70 ff., in Spender, *Life of Campbell-Bannerman*, II, 249 ff., and in *B.D.*, III, 170 f., No. 210. Cambon's account to Rouvier of the conversation is given in *ibid.*, 173 f., No. 212. Sanderson was present at that interview.

[88] Grey, I, 72, 114; Spender, *Life of Campbell-Bannerman*, II, 251 f.; Repington, I, 12 f.

[89] Grierson to Sanderson, Jan. 11, 1906, *B.D.*, III, 172, No. 211.

Mr. Haldane saw any reason why these conversations should not be carried on officially also. As the former argued:

It was quite clear that no Cabinet could undertake any obligation to go to war, but the Anglo-French Agreement was popular in Britain. It was certain that if Germany forced a quarrel on France upon the very matter of that Agreement, the pro-French feeling in Britain would be very strong, so strong probably as to justify a British Government in intervening on the side of France or even to insist on its doing so. We must, therefore, be free to go to the help of France as well as free to stand aside. But modern war may be an affair of days. If there were no military plans made beforehand we should be unable to come to the assistance of France in time, however strongly public opinion in Britain might desire it. We should in effect not have preserved our freedom to help France, but have cut ourselves off from the possibility of doing so, unless we had allowed the British and French staffs to concert plans for common action.[90]

The Prime Minister feared the interpretation that would be put upon these conversations. "I do not like the stress laid upon joint preparations," he wrote to Lord Ripon on February 2. "It comes very close to an honourable undertaking; and it will be known on both sides of the Rhine." However, he considered them to be merely "provisional and precautionary measures" not binding the government, "raising no new question of policy and therefore within the competence of the War Office." So he agreed to them.[91] It was definitely understood that these military conversations did not bind the governments.[92] On January 17 they were begun between the French military attaché and General Grierson and continued uninterrupted between the French and British general staffs until the outbreak of the World War.[93]

[90] Grey, I, 72 f.

[91] "C-B was a fine old Tory in Army matter" (Repington, I, 13). On this affair see Spender, *Life of Campbell-Bannerman*, II, 253, 256 f.; Repington, I, 12 f.; Viscount Haldane, *Before the War* (London, 1920), p. 184; Grey, I, 70 ff., 83; Haldane, *An Autobiography*, pp. 189 f.

[92] Grey, I, 70 ff.

[93] *Ibid.*, pp. 73 f.; Repington, I, 13; *B.D.*, III, 169, editor's note, 438 ff. In 1911 Grey wrote to Asquith that he never knew anything more of the course of those conversations (Grey, I, 92).

The same reasoning applied to Belgium, for both the French and the British authorities expected Germany to violate Belgian neutrality in order to strike France suddenly from the northeast.[94] On January 15 Sir Edward Grey therefore instructed General Grierson to open conversations with the Belgian military authorities "as to the manner in which, in case of need, British assistance could be most effectually afforded to Belgium for the defence of her neutrality. Such communications," he continued, "must be solely provisional and noncommittal."[95] Colonel Barnardiston, the British military attaché in Brussels, broached the subject on January 18 to General Ducarne, Belgian chief of staff, remarking that the British Minister would bring up the matter with the Belgian Foreign Minister.[96] After consulting the Minister of War, General Ducarne agreed to the conversations.[97] This decision was anticipated by Colonel Barnardiston, who had learned that the Belgian military authorities were quietly mak-

[94] Sydenham, *My Working Life*, pp. 186 f., 190; Haldane, *Before the War*, p. 45; Repington, I, 3. The British based their belief on the German construction of obviously unnecessary railroads to the Belgian frontier (*Collected Diplomatic Documents Relating to the Outbreak of the European War* [1915], pp. 365 f.).

[95] Sanderson to Grierson, Jan. 15, 1906, *B.D.*, III, 176 f., No. 214; Grierson to Barnardiston, Jan. 16, 1906, *ibid.*, 179, No. 217b.

[96] In a dispatch to Grierson on Jan. 19 Barnardiston wrote that he had told Ducarne at their first meeting that Sir C. Phipps, the British minister in Brussels, had already mentioned the matter to the Belgian Foreign Minister (*ibid.*, III, 188). In some notes by Barnardiston deposited in the war office, he stated that Phipps would speak to the Belgian Foreign Minister. The Belgian government asserts that there is no record of such a communication; rather, that the Foreign Minister learned of the military conversations from the Belgian Minister of War. There is no report of any conversation on this subject between Phipps and the Belgian Minister in the papers in the British foreign office, nor is there any record of instructions on it being sent to Phipps. On March 17 Barnardiston wrote to Grierson that both the Belgian Minister of War and the Minister of Foreign Affairs knew of the conversation (editor's note, *ibid.*, p. 203; *Collected Diplomatic Documents Relating to the Outbreak of the European War*, p. 355; Haldane, *Before the War*, pp. 201 f.). There is no doubt but that the conversations were approved by both foreign ministers.

[97] Barnardiston to Grierson, Jan. 19, 1906, *B.D.*, III, 187 f.

ing preparations for instant mobilization.[98] The Anglo-Belgian negotiations continued at least until the end of April.[99]

These conversations, both military and naval, were kept secret. The Anglo-Belgian negotiations were known to only half-a-dozen persons; the ones with France were not known to all the members of the British cabinet although reports of them leaked out in the press about the middle of 1906.[100] Sir Edward Grey wanted to prevent either these conversations or any military or naval action from being regarded as provocations. In informing Lord Tweedmouth, first lord of the admiralty, of the Anglo-French conversations, he wrote, January 16:

> Meanwhile the mood of the German Emperor is said to be pacific; the tone of German diplomacy is quiet and not aggressive. Any movement of our ships which could be interpreted as a threat to Germany would be very undesirable at this moment and most unfortunate so long as there is a prospect or even a chance that things may go smoothly at the Morocco Conference which meets today. I hope therefore that the Admiralty won't plan any special cruises or visits to Foreign ports or unusual movements of squadrons without consulting the F[oreign] O[ffice] as to the possible political effect.
>
> I assume that the present disposition of the Fleet is satisfactory as regards possibilities between Germany and France; if so the quieter we keep for the present the better.[101]

With the opening of these conversations a new military problem confronted the British which Mr. Haldane, then minister of war, has described as follows:

> It was, how to mobilize and concentrate at a place of assembly to be opposite the Belgian frontier, a force calculated as adequate (with the assistance of Russian pressure in the East) to make up for the inadequacy of the French armies for their great task of defending the entire French frontier from Dunkirk down to Belfort, or even further south, if Italy should join the Triple Alliance in an attack.[102]

[98] Barnardiston to Phipps, Jan. 17, 1906, *ibid.*, pp. 179 f.

[99] On these negotiations see the correspondence between Grierson and Barnardiston in *ibid.*, pp. 187 ff.; *Collected Diplomatic Documents Relating to the Outbreak of the European War*, pp. 350 ff.; Haldane, *Before the War*, pp. 201 ff.

[100] Spender, *Life, Journalism and Politics*, I, 193; Haldane, *An Autobiography*, p. 191.

[101] *B.D.*, III, 203.   [102] Haldane, *Before the War*, pp. 45 f.

At the time, in January, the Committee of Imperial Defence, although not all of its members knew of the military conversations then beginning, studied the question. It decided that "four Divisions and a Cavalry Division" could be landed at the nearest French port in case of a sudden outbreak of hostilities.[103] The admiralty was prepared "to bar the Channel against the German squadrons."[104] The Minister of War began a thorough reorganization of the army in order to make British aid effective at the desired moment in the future.[105]

Having settled this matter, Sir Edward Grey had the difficult problem of how to answer M. Cambon's question about a formal agreement.[106] As it was inconvenient then to hold a cabinet meeting, Sir Edward Grey talked over the reply to be given with the Premier and Mr. Haldane, who were both in London after January 26, and asked Sir Francis Bertie to write his opinion.[107]

The Ambassador wrote that France did not desire war at all, but that if a conflict did arise over Morocco either then or later she expected active British support. He warned his chief that if his answer did not assure to France

more than a continuance of diplomatic support, or of neutrality in the event of a war provoked by Germany, there is serious danger of a complete revulsion of feeling on the part of the French Government and of public opinion in France. The Government would consider that they had been deserted and might, in order to avoid the risks of a war without ally, deem it advisable to make great concessions to Germany outside Morocco in order to obtain liberty of action in that country.

[103] Statement written by Lord Sydenham, July 19, 1927, *B.D.*, III, 185, No. 221a; memo. by Brigadier General Nicholson, Nov. 6, 1911, *ibid.*, pp. 186 f.; Admiral Ottley to First Sea Lord, Jan. 13, 1906, *ibid.*, p. 186; Sydenham, p. 186.

[104] Memo. by Cambon, Jan. 31, 1906; *B.D.*, III, 193, No. 220a.

[105] Haldane, *Before the War*, chap. iv.

[106] Grey informed Cambon of the approval of the naval and military conversations on Jan. 15, but postponed answering the larger question (Grey to Bertie, Jan. 15, 1906, *B.D.*, III, 177, No. 215; 225, No. 244.

[107] Spender, *Life of Campbell-Bannerman*, II, 253, 256 ff.; Grey, I, 84. Grey's omission to consult the entire cabinet has been severely criticized. He has admitted in his memoirs that he did wrong. See especially Haldane, *An Autobiography*, p. 191; Earl Loreburn, *How the War Came* (London, 1919), pp. 80 f.; cf. Spender, *Life, Journalism and Politics*, I, 193.

Such concessions might not be very great sacrifices for France but they might well be very detrimental to the interests of the British Empire, for, in the temper in which France would then be, it could not be expected that she would give them much consideration.[108]

Sir Edward Grey's personal opinion was that "if France is let in for a war with Germany arising out of our agreement with her about Morocco, we cannot stand aside, but must take part with France." While pondering the question of an alliance, he saw the great difficulties in making one.[109] He decided to adapt the policy of his predecessor in office to the new situation created by M. Cambon's request. This policy is best explained in the long dispatch which Sir Edward Grey wrote to Sir Francis Bertie about his interview with the French Ambassador on January 31:

The French Ambassador asked me again to-day whether France would be able to count upon the assistance of England in the event of an attack upon her by Germany.

I said that I had spoken on the subject to the Prime Minister and discussed it with him, and that I had three observations to submit.

In the first place, since the Ambassador had spoken to me a good deal of progress has been made. Our military and naval authorities had been in communication with the French, and I assumed that all preparations were ready, so that, if a crisis arose, no time would have been lost for want of a formal engagement.

In the second place, a week or more before Monsieur Cambon had spoken to me, I had taken an opportunity of expressing to Count Metternich my personal opinion, which I understood Lord Lansdowne had also expressed to him as a personal opinion, that, in the event of an attack upon France by Germany arising out of our Moroccan Agreement, public feeling in England would be so strong that no British Government could remain neutral. I urged upon Monsieur Cambon that this, which I had reason to know had been correctly reported at Berlin, had produced there the moral effect which Monsieur Cambon had urged upon me as being one of the great securities of peace and the main reason for a formal engagement between England and France with regard to armed co-operation.

In the third place, I pointed out to Monsieur Cambon that at present French policy in Morocco, within the four corners of the Declaration exchanged between us, was absolutely free, that we did not question it, that

[108] Bertie to Grey, D. Jan. 13, R. Jan. 18, 1906, *B.D.*, III, 174 ff., No. 213.

[109] Grey to Bertie, Jan. 15, 1906, *ibid.*, 177 f., No. 216; Grey, I, 75.

we suggested no concessions and no alterations in it, that we left France a free hand and gave unreservedly our diplomatic support on which she could count; but that, should our promise extend beyond diplomatic support, and should we take an engagement which might involve us in a war, I was sure my colleagues would say that we must from that time be consulted with regard to French policy in Morocco, and, if need be, be free to press upon the French Government concessions or alterations of their policy which might seem to us desirable to avoid a war.

I asked Monsieur Cambon to weigh these considerations in his mind, and to consider whether the present situation as regards ourselves and France was not so satisfactory that it was unnecessary to alter it by a formal declaration as he desired.

M. Cambon replied that a war might break out over some Moroccan incident so quickly that if it were necessary for the British government "to consult, and to wait for manifestations of English public opinion, it might be too late to be of use." He repeated his request for some form of verbal assurance. Sir Edward Grey pointed out the difficulties of giving this assurance —that it would be a "solemn undertaking," that it would have to be put in writing and submitted to the cabinet and also to Parliament. He said that it would constitute the transformation of the entente into a defensive alliance, that it could not be given unconditionally, and that the conditions "would be difficult to describe." He again asked M. Cambon "whether the force of circumstances bringing England and France together was not stronger than any assurance in words which could be given at this moment." He added that German pressure "might eventually transform the 'Entente' into a defensive alliance," yet at the time he did not think that the change was needed. When M. Cambon emphasized the fact that Sir Edward Grey had expressed his personal opinion that in case of a German attack upon France, no British government could remain neutral, the latter replied that he had said this first to Count Metternich and not to him,

because, supposing it appeared that I had overestimated the strength of feeling of my countrymen, there could be no disappointment in Germany; but I could not express so decidedly my personal opinion to France, because a personal opinion was not a thing upon which, in so serious a matter, a policy could be founded. In speaking to him, therefore, I must keep well within the mark. Much depended as to the manner in which the war broke out between Germany and France.

Sir Edward Grey believed that the British people would be unwilling to fight in order to put France into possession of Morocco. But if "it appeared that the war was forced upon France by Germany to break up the Anglo-French 'Entente,' public opinion would undoubtedly be very strong on the side of France." He said, however, that British sentiment was much averse to war, and that it was not certain whether this aversion would be overcome by the desire to aid France. While he was ready to reopen the conversation at any time in the future, he did not think that the situation justified such a radical change at that time.[110] M. Cambon appeared to be satisfied with that answer.[111]

[110] Spender, *Life of Campbell-Bannerman*, II, 253 ff.; Grey, II, 76 ff.; *B.D.*, III, 180 ff., No. 219. Cambon and Grey exchanged memoranda of that conversation. According to Mr. Eyre Crowe, senior clerk in the British foreign office, Cambon's account differed from Grey's on the following points: "(A) The French note alludes to the intention of the British Admiralty in case of a conflict with Germany, to bar the Channel against the German squadrons. This passage does not occur in Sir E. Grey's draft. . . . . (B) The French note contains no allusion to the argument given in the following passage of Sir E. Grey's draft: 'I did not think people in England would be prepared to fight in order to put France in possession of Morocco. They would say that France should wait for opportunities and be content to take time, and that it was unreasonable to hurry matters to the point of war' " (Crowe's minute to the memo. by Cambon, Jan. 31, 1906, *ibid.*, 183 f., No. 220a). On Feb. 1 Sanderson talked over the two drafts with Cambon, who made some changes in his. Sanderson again emphasized the reasons why the British government could not give the desired assurance, speaking in part as follows: "I told him [Cambon] that I thought that if the Cabinet were to give a pledge which would morally bind the country to go to war in certain circumstances, and were not to mention this pledge to Parliament, and if at the expiration of some months the country suddenly found itself pledged to war in consequence of this assurance, the case would be one which would justify impeachment, and which might even result in that course unless at the time the feeling of the country were very strongly in favour of the course to which the Government was pledged" (memo. by Sanderson, Feb. 2, 1906, *ibid.*, 184 f., No. 220b).

[111] So thought Sanderson, and Grey's secretary (Grey, I, 85; Spender, *Life of Campbell-Bannerman*, II, 257; memo. by Sanderson, Feb. 2, 1906, *B.D.*, III, 185, No. 220b). Grey was absent from the foreign office for some time owing to the sudden death of his wife, Feb. 1.

Thus, Sir Edward Grey laid down the policy which he followed until the outbreak of the World War. He was open and frank with both France and Germany. To the German government he emphasized the probability of British intervention in favor of France in case of war. To the French government he gave the promise of full diplomatic support; while permitting preparations for any emergency, he refused to give to the French assurance of active aid in case of war or even to speak as firmly on that score as he did to the German government. Instead of binding Great Britain and France in an alliance—an act which would have forced him to keep a hand on France's policy toward Morocco and Germany—Sir Edward Grey kept British hands free. In giving France sufficient assurance to maintain Anglo-French intimacy and co-operation, he depended upon the uncertainty of British support in a crisis to hold France back. He relied upon the same uncertainty—this time, however, that Great Britain might enter a Franco-German conflict—to restrain Germany. By this apparently simple but really intricate policy he sought to satisfy the needs of British foreign relations.

CHAPTER XVII

THE CONFERENCE OF ALGECIRAS

The Conference of Algeciras opened formally on January 16, 1906.[1] The place was badly adapted to such a purpose. It was small, inadequately prepared to house and entertain the one hundred and fifty delegates, secretaries, and newspaper correspondents who had to remain there for over two months and a half. The delegates were quartered at one of the two hotels and the journalists at the other. They were thrown into constant contact with each other. The place swarmed with newspaper correspondents, most of them from France. There were about fifty principal ones, not to speak of the minor ones. They saw or heard or surmised about everything. They brought public opinion to the door of the Conference, and the French particularly were able at times of crisis or of important decisions to exercise a marked influence on the course of the deliberations.[2]

[1] The Conference opened later than was originally planned, the immediate cause being the marriage of the Infanta Maria Theresa, sister of King Alfonso, to Prince Ferdinand of Bavaria, on Jan. 12. The King of Spain had wanted in December to move the meeting place to Madrid, and both the French and German governments had agreed; but as the Sultan opposed, the proposal had been dropped. Bülow's opinion was that it made no difference to Germany whether the Conference met at Madrid or Algeciras or elsewhere. "It was a mistake that we originally settled ourselves on Tangier," he wrote, Dec. 25, 1905. See *G.P.,* XXI, 25 ff., Nos. 6911, 6913 ff.; *B.D.,* III, 160, No. 196; *L.j., 1901–5,* No. 368; Ministère des Affaires Etrangères, *Documents diplomatiques. Affaires du Maroc, 1906, Protocols et comptes rendus de la Conférence d'Algéciras* (1906), 5, No. 2 (hereafter referred to as *L.j., 1906).*

[2] Tardieu, *La Conf. d'Algés,* pp. 90 ff., 503 f.; Radowitz to F. O., Jan. 17, 1906, *G.P.,* XXI, 96, No. 6952. Tardieu's book contains almost an official account of the Conference from the French side. He was present as representative of *Le Temps* and had access to the fullest information, as his articles showed. His book is an excellent example of patriotic historiography carried almost to a hysterical extreme, and his interpretations have to be read with the greatest caution. Dr. Hammann criticized the work when it appeared in 1907 in two articles, one in *Grenz-*

Among the delegates there were three important groups, the German, the American-Italian-Austrian, and the British-French-Spanish-Russian. The representatives of Morocco and the smaller states took practically no part in the proceedings. In the first group Herr von Radowitz was a nonentity—old, feeble, so elusive and cautious as to be difficult to negotiate with. Count Tattenbach was the positive force, described by his British colleague as "a rasping, disagreeable man, not straightforward or truthful and evidently has to exercise much effort to control his temper."[3] He made a bad impression on the delegates by his blunt aggressiveness. Although he knew the Moroccan problem thoroughly, he was unsuited for the delicate negotiations required at the Conference. By his personality and methods he injured his country's interests. He was more influential with his government than was Herr von Radowitz, but as a rule both men merely carried out orders from Berlin. Mr. White (the American delegate), Marquis Visconti Venosta, and Count Welsersheimb (the Austrian delegate) acted as mediators. M. Révoil and Sir Arthur Nicolson were the leaders of the third group. Both had served their respective countries as minister at Tangier. M. Révoil was a supple, subtle reasoner, inclined like Herr von Holstein to lose sight of his objective in the mazes of his argument. He was oversensitive, overcautious, and very mistrustful of Germany. His obstinacy proved in the end of advantage to France, but he would have made a number of mistakes serious for his country and for the success of the Conference if he had not had the advice of Sir Arthur Nicolson. The latter was the most astute member taking an active part in the assembly, although he played his rôle so quietly that the other delegates, particularly the Germans, did not perceive his significance. A true diplomat, he carried out the difficult British policy admirably. It was primarily his work that

---

boten, 1907, p. 12, the other in the *Kölnische Zeitung,* March 30, 1907 (editor's note, *G.P.,* XXI, 92 f.). See also the masterly criticism of French policy by Dickinson, *The International Anarchy 1904–1914,* pp. 134 ff.

[3] Nicolson to Grey, Feb. 5, 1906, *B.D.,* III, 243, No. 268; Tardieu, pp. 85 f.

the Conference thrashed the fundamental problems through to a definite conclusion.

When the Conference was organized, it was decided that the formal session should be reserved for ratification of matters already agreed upon unanimously in the committee of the whole, composed of all the delegates sitting unofficially and engaging in free debate. There was also to be a special committee of formulation to draft the propositions agreed upon.[4] Naturally the work was done in these two bodies. More important were the direct negotiations between the delegates of France and Germany, which after January 25, at the urging of the other delegates, were almost constantly in progress.

The basic principles governing the work of the Conference in preparing a program of reform for Morocco were laid down by the president, the Duke of Almodovar, in his opening speech. After previous agreement with the French and German delegates,[5] he stated that everyone wished "reforms based on the triple principle of the sovereignty of the Sultan, integrity of his empire, and equality of treatment in matters commercial, that is, the open door." It was not the mission of the conference, he said, to work out a complete plan for the administrative transformation of Morocco, but rather to "study together the means of applying measures which at present appear to be the most urgent and the easiest to introduce."

The Conference, pessimistic at the beginning, took up first the questions which could be easily settled. Since these were considered primarily from the standpoint of practicality, agreement was soon reached on the following: "Regulation concerning the surveillance and repression of contraband of arms"; "declaration concerning the better collection of taxes and the creation of new revenues"; "regulation concerning the customs duties of the

[4] Tardieu, pp. 100 ff.; Radowitz to F. O., Jan. 16, 1906, *G.P.*, XXI, 92 f., No. 6949; Révoil to Rouvier, Jan. 18, 1906, *L.j., 1906,* 11, No. 4.

[5] Radowitz to F. O., Jan. 16, 1906, *G.P.*, XXI, 92 f., No. 6949; Tardieu, pp. 100 ff.; *L.j., 1906,* pp. 9 f.; Nicolson to Grey, Jan. 18, 1906, *B.D.*, III, 229, No. 248.

empire and the repression of fraud and of contraband"; "declaration relating to public services and to public works." The discussion of these matters was unimportant.[6] The troublesome problems were those of the organization of the police and the establishment of a state bank. The solution of these would determine whether France or Germany should emerge victorious. After the initial success on the minor matters, the delegates confronted these two questions with more hope.[7]

Marquis Visconti Venosta and Mr. White first tried to mediate upon the basis that Germany should make concessions on the bank, France on the police. M. Révoil was willing, being ready, so he privately informed the British delegate, to associate Italy with France and Spain on the police, but he asked for definite proposals.[8] At the instigation of the other delegates, Herr von Radowitz and M. Révoil began direct conversations on these matters on January 25.[9] Puzzled by so many reports of different German projects on the police,[10] M. Révoil assumed the defensive. But on Sir Arthur Nicolson's advice he laid his proposals frankly before the German representatives a few days later.[11] On January 29 M. Regnault, French adviser at the Conference,

[6] L.j., 1906, 264 ff., No. 37.

[7] Ibid., 5 ff., No. 3, and following documents; Radowitz to F. O., Jan. 12, 1906, G.P., XXI, 91, No. 6947; Bülow to Radowitz, Jan. 15, 1906, ibid., 92, No. 6948; Radowitz to Bülow, Jan. 26, 1906, ibid., 119 ff., No. 6967; Tardieu, pp. 100 ff.; Nicolson to Grey, Jan. 19, 1906, B.D., III, 230 f., No. 249.

[8] Nicolson to Grey, Jan. 21, 1906, B.D., III, 231 ff., Nos. 250 f.; Monts to F. O., Jan. 28, 1906, G.P., XXI, 126, No. 6970; Radowitz to F. O., Jan. 31, 1906, ibid., 130 f., No. 6975.

[9] Révoil wished to push matters into the open sessions of the Conference as much as possible, where he would have more support (Tardieu, pp. 136 ff.; Radowitz to Bülow, Jan. 26, 1906, G.P., XXI, 119 f., No. 6967).

[10] As seen below, the German government was proposing several alternative solutions of that question, and the German delegates seem also to have been discussing others on their own initiative. See Nicolson to Grey, Jan. 25 and 27, 1906, B.D., III, 235, No. 256; 239 f., Nos. 262 f.; Tardieu, pp. 144 ff.

[11] Nicolson to Grey, Jan. 24, 25, 26, 1906, B.D., III, 234, No. 254; 235 f., Nos. 256 f.; 236 ff., Nos. 259 f.; 239 f., Nos. 262 f.; Tardieu, pp. 136 ff.

outlined for Count Tattenbach the French plan on the bank as follows: The bank should be subject to French law and to the French judicial system; the capital should be so divided that France should receive 27 per cent, Spain 23 per cent, Great Britain 20 per cent, Germany 20 per cent, Italy 10 per cent; an administrative council of ten members should be chosen according to nationality by the shareholders; a directory should be named by this council; a committee of discount in Tangier selected from the resident shareholders should be established and a committee of examination should be chosen by the future subscribers; the preferential right to make loans held by the French banks should continue, but perhaps be relinquished in return for an increase in the per cent of capital given to France. M. Regnault justified the project on the grounds that "the preponderance of French economic interests in Morocco must be given expression therein," that it was a question of maintaining the open door without destroying acquired interests, and that "the open door does not signify that those who are in the house must leave it."[12]

On February 3 M. Révoil proposed to Herr von Radowitz that the mandate for the police be given to France and Spain together. "Over its form, extension and control all desirable international agreements could be made," he said, so as to prevent any other right from being deduced therefrom and to guarantee complete commercial equality. He declared that France pursued no special political aims in Morocco, but that she must demand protection in proportion to her preponderant material interests. He also informed the German delegate indirectly that France might agree to the addition of a third Power to control the execution of the mandate.[13]

In the end the German government was to accept practically

[12] Radowitz to F. O., Jan. 29, 1906, *G.P.*, XXI, 128 ff., No. 6974.; Tardieu, pp. 141 ff.

[13] Radowitz to F. O., Feb. 3, 1906, *G.P.*, XXI, 136 f., No. 6980; Tardieu, pp. 148 ff.; Nicolson to Grey, Feb. 4 and 5, 1906, *B.D.*, III, 242, No. 266; 243 f., No. 268.

these terms, but at the moment it was averse to making any concessions, believing that the Conference, "so far as grouping and general course are concerned, is turning out favorably for us."[14] Since it regarded the bank as more influential in the long run than the police, it rejected the French claim to preference for making loans on the grounds that that claim violated Article XVII of the Convention of Madrid, and proposed the use of the Egyptian mixed codes and the equal division of the capital among the Powers. Thus internationalism instead of a French preponderant control would be established in the bank.[15]

On the question of the police, which was the more important, the German government offered various plans to prevent France from obtaining military control. It endeavored particularly to interest President Roosevelt in this problem. In a long dispatch to Washington on January 20, it laid three different proposals before the President: First, the individual Powers might participate on a basis of equality in the reorganization of the police by having each one, or at least the more important ones, assume a mandate for a certain port. A time limit should be set, and the Powers should renounce any idea of giving to their occupation a permanent character. For unity of policy the Powers could come to a general agreement on various questions like those of arming and training. Second, one or several smaller Powers, such as Switzerland, Norway, Sweden, Denmark, or Holland might assume the duty. (Belgium was excluded as being too liable to French influence.) Third, no mandate should be given, but the obligation should be imposed upon the Sultan to maintain at certain points police trained and commanded by foreign officers. The choice of these officers could either be left to the Sultan completely or be confined to certain nationalities, perhaps the smaller Powers. The Chancellor offered to accept any other so-

[14] Bülow to Radowitz, Jan. 26, 1906, G.P., XXI, 114, No. 6965.

[15] Bülow to Radowitz, Jan. 30, 1906, ibid., 128, No. 6973; Radowitz to F. O., Jan. 29 and 31, 1906, ibid., 128 ff., Nos. 6974 f.; Bülow to Radowitz, Feb. 2, 1906, ibid., 132 ff., No. 6977; Tardieu, p. 142.

lution in harmony with the principle of equality and the open door.[16] On January 24 M. de Lanessan, a French writer, published in the *Siècle* a solution practically identical with No. 3. The article read in part as follows:

> There remains only one admissible solution; to charge the Sultan with the policing of his empire while determining the means over which he should have control and while instituting an international control over the organisation and employment of those means.[17]

The Chancellor immediately seized upon it with greatest favor and advocated it to President Roosevelt.

The proposal at once called forth vehement opposition in the French press. When Herr von Radowitz mentioned the article to M. Révoil on February 3, the latter replied emphatically that in view of the incompetence of the Sultan the plan was not acceptable.[18] Thus the issue was joined on the questions of both the bank and the police. In this situation, which had been anticipated by both parties, the French and German governments sought to win the Powers to their respective views.

The German government wished the Austrian, the Italian, and above all the American delegates to mediate in favor of its pro-

[16] Bülow to Sternburg, Jan. 20, 1906, *G.P.*, XXI, 99 ff., No. 6956; Tardieu, pp. 160 ff. A proposal similar to No. 1 had been made to Roosevelt by Bülow earlier in January (Bülow to Sternburg, Jan. 6, 1906, *G.P.*, XXI, 54 f., No. 6926). Bülow also offered to support Italy in seeking a general mandate on the police, manifestly in order to create antagonism between Italy and France. The offer was rejected and was soon dropped by Bülow who feared that Italy might later help France penetrate Morocco in return for French aid to Italy in Tripoli. See Bülow to Monts, Jan. 5, 1906, *G.P.*, XXI, 53 f., No. 6925; Bülow to Radowitz, Jan. 26, 1906, *ibid.*, 114 f., No. 6965; Tardieu, pp. 146 f. There is no proof in the published British and German documents of Tardieu's assertion that in January the German government also offered to support Spain in seeking this general mandate. See *ibid.*, pp. 145, 155 f. Cf. Cartwright to Grey, Jan. 22, 1906, *B.D.*, III, 233, No. 252; Nicolson to Grey, Feb. 6, 1906, *ibid.*, 244, No. 270.

[17] Tardieu, p. 146 n.; Bülow to Sternburg, Jan. 27, 1906, *G.P.*, XXI, 123 ff., No. 6968.

[18] Radowitz to F. O., Feb. 3, 1906, *G.P.*, XXI, 136 f., No. 6980; Tardieu, pp. 148 ff.

posals.[19] When on January 23 Baron Sternburg explained to Mr. Root, the American secretary of state, the German proposals on the police and asked for the American views, Mr. Root replied that the United States could not participate in any work of Moroccan police but that he personally approved most of proposal No. 3. He said that he would consult the President about the question.[20]

This reply was eminently satisfactory to Prince Bülow, who immediately urged the American government to mediate upon the basis of M. de Lanessan's proposals. On January 30 he telegraphed to Washington that the Austrian cabinet had instructed its representative at Algeciras to that effect, that the Italian Foreign Minister had spoken favorably of it, that the Czar had expressed his entire approval of the German position on the open door, that therefore the American government would run no risk in making such a proposal. The time was ripe for it, he stated.[21] He also sought to influence the President against the French proposal on the bank.[22]

[19] The German government did not desire British mediation, as it feared that Great Britain might try to pose as the protector of France and strengthen the Entente Cordiale (Bülow to Radowitz, Jan. 26, 1906, *G.P.*, XXI, 114 f., No. 6965).

[20] Sternburg to F. O., Jan. 23, 1906, *ibid.*, 102 f., No. 6958.

[21] Bülow to Sternburg, Jan. 27, 1906, *ibid.*, 123 ff., No. 6968; 127, No. 6972. On Feb. 3 Goluchowski declared to the German Ambassador that Austria would go with her ally on the questions of the police and the bank "through thick and thin" (Holstein to Wedel, Feb. 4, 1906, *ibid.*, 137, No. 6981). Dr. Kriege, of the German foreign office, was sent on a special mission to Vienna on Feb. 2 to gain the Austrian support (memo. by Kriege, Feb. 4, 1906, *ibid.*, 137 ff., No. 6982; Wedel to F. O., Feb. 5, 1906, *ibid.*, 140, No. 6983). A cabinet crisis in Italy on Feb. 1 prevented the German government from taking any immediate steps to gain Italy's active support. But Bülow expected Visconti Venosta to be willing to mediate. On Feb. 8 a new government was formed in Rome under Sonnino (Bülow to Radowitz, Feb. 7, 1906, *ibid.*, 143 ff., No. 6987).

[22] Bülow to Sternburg, Feb. 1, 1906, *ibid.*, 131, No. 6976. Bülow also instructed Sternburg to interest the American financiers in the Moroccan state bank so that they would press their government to oppose the French plan and to favor the German one. At the Chancellor's request, the German banker, Mendelssohn, who was to take charge of German interests in the Moroccan bank, endeavored to

At Algeciras, however, Herr von Radowitz found that the Italian, American, and Russian delegates all approved the French proposal of February 3 as moderate and practical.[23] When Count Tattenbach tried on February 3 to persuade Sir Arthur Nicolson to desert France and support Germany, he met with total failure.[24] As a result Herr von Radowitz again advised his government to compromise.[25] But in view of the apparently favorable attitudes of the Austrian, Italian, Spanish,[26] and American governments toward M. de Lanessan's proposal, Prince Bülow refused.[27]

Before talking with M. Révoil again, Herr von Radowitz consulted the American, Italian, and Austrian delegates concerning the chances of success of the German proposal on the police. All three declared that France would never accept it, that mediation on the basis of it would be futile. They urged Germany to agree to the French plan, with modifications, in order to prevent a

arouse the Dutch, American, and Austrian bankers in the same way. See Bülow to Radowitz, Feb. 7, 1906, *ibid.*, 145 f., No. 6987; Sternburg to F. O., Feb. 8, 1906, *ibid.*, 148, No. 6989.

[23] Radowitz to F. O., Feb. 5, 1906, *ibid.*, 140 f., No. 6984; Tardieu, pp. 152 f.; Dennis, *Adventures in American Diplomacy*, p. 500; Nicolson to Grey, Jan. 27, 1906, *B.D.*, III, 239, No. 262.

[24] Nicolson reported that Tattenbach argued as follows: "He observed that situation had completely changed since Conference had been agreed upon, and that now *vis-a-vis* to France I was exactly in the same position as the other delegates. He continued that if I urged my French colleague to make all required concessions on police question, my words would be decisive; while if I declined to say those words, I should be practically encouraging my French colleague to resist; and he hinted that if the Conference fell through a great deal of the responsibility would fall on me." See Nicolson to Grey, Feb. 4, 1906, *B.D.*, III, 241, No. 265; 242 f., No. 267; Grey to Nicolson, Feb. 13, 1906, *ibid.*, 251 f., No. 281; Tardieu, pp. 147 f.

[25] Radowitz to F. O., Feb. 6, 1906, *G.P.*, XXI, 141 f., No. 6985; Tardieu, pp. 153 f.

[26] The Spanish undersecretary of state for foreign affairs, M. Ojeda, had approved it. See Bülow to Radowitz, Feb. 7, 1906, *G.P.*, XXI, 145 and note, No. 6987. On the German attempts to win over Spain see Cartwright to Grey, Jan. 22, 1906, *B.D.*, III, 233, No. 252; Nicolson to Grey, Feb. 6, 1906, *ibid.*, 244, No. 270.

[27] Bülow to Radowitz, Feb. 7, 1906, *G.P.*, XXI, 143 ff., No. 6987.

break-up of the Conference.[28] Sir Donald Mackenzie Wallace, correspondent for the *London Times*, said the same.[29] Furthermore, Baron Sternburg reported on February 8 that Mr. Root had promised again that he would consult the President about mediating on the German proposal but that he would not undertake any move unless assured of a definite result. When the Ambassador had listed the Powers in favor of the plan, Mr. Root had asked significantly what was the attitude of Great Britain.[30]

Continuing to rely upon the mediation of the American delegate and to hope for the support of the American and Italian delegates, the German government instructed Herr von Radowitz on February 9 and 12 to hold to plan No. 3 with the two alternatives of choosing the instructors from some minor Power or of permitting the Sultan free play in the choice of them. In case the three delegates refused to mediate, Herr von Radowitz was to talk directly with M. Révoil. If the French delegate refused both the German proposals, Herr von Radowitz should request him to offer a proposal in keeping with the fundamental principle of the equality of all nations in Morocco. If M. Révoil held to his project of February 3, Herr von Radowitz should return to proposal No. 1, dividing Morocco into sectors each under the charge of a single Power.[31]

As the three delegates advised Herr von Radowitz to speak directly with the French delegate, he did so on February 13. M. Révoil grudgingly agreed to transmit the following offer to his government:

> It is proposed that the conference request the Sultan to undertake the organization of the police. He will have the duty of maintaining in the places determined upon, a troop of police which will be formed and commanded

[28] Radowitz to F. O., Feb. 9, 10, 1906, *ibid.*, 148 f., No. 6990; 155, No. 6996; Dennis, pp. 501 f.

[29] Radowitz to F. O., Feb. 9, 1906, *G.P.*, XXI, 151, No. 6992.

[30] Sternburg to F. O., Feb. 8, 1906, *ibid.*, 147 f., No. 6989.

[31] Bülow to Radowitz, Feb. 9, 12, 1906, *ibid.*, 149 ff., No. 6991; 155 f., No. 6997; Radowitz to F. O., Feb. 10, 1906, *ibid.*, 155, No. 6996; Tardieu, p. 172.

by foreign officers chosen freely by the Sultan. The funds necessary to maintain the troops will be placed at the disposal of the Sultan by the new state bank. The diplomatic corps at Tangier will exercise control over the actions of that organization; a foreign officer of one of the secondary Powers will be charged with the inspection and will report to the diplomatic corps at Tangier. This entire organization will be a tentative one to endure from three to five years.[32]

The German stand on the police was meeting with the more or less openly expressed disapproval of all the important Powers. Sir Arthur Nicolson had taken the French side from the start.[33] The pro-French attitude of Count Cassini, the Russian delegate, was confirmed by Count Lamsdorff, who on February 12 expressed to Herr von Schoen, the new German ambassador in St. Petersburg, his and the Czar's entire approval of the French proposal on the police and advised the German government to accept it.[34] Even the Austrian government urged the German government to compromise. Count Welsersheimb reported that mediation on the German project No. 3 was futile; and on February 12 Count Goluchowski, Austrian foreign minister, declared to the German Ambassador that the German proposal No. 1 was impracticable and hopeless. Regarding the situation as "rather serious," the Austrian Foreign Minister stated that "Morocco was not worth a war," and advised that in case of necessity the Conference be permitted to break up without result. Count Wedel, German ambassador at Vienna, warned the *Wilhelmstrasse* that because of domestic troubles Austria had no desire to become involved in a conflict.[35]

[32] Quoted from a memorandum given by Radowitz to Révoil on that date. See Radowitz to F. O., Feb. 13, 1906, *G.P.*, XXI, 162 f., No. 7004; Tardieu, pp. 175 f.; Nicolson to Grey, Feb. 14, 1906, *B.D.*, III, 253, No. 284.

[33] Radowitz to Bülow, Jan. 26, 1906, *G.P.*, XXI, 122, No. 6967; Radowitz to F. O., Feb. 9, 1906, *ibid.*, 151, No. 6992. See the documents in *B.D.*, III, 227 ff., Nos. 246 ff.

[34] Schoen to F. O., Feb. 12, 1906, *G.P.*, XXI, 156 f., No. 6998; Tardieu, pp. 158 f., 194 ff.; Witte, *Memoirs*, pp. 298 ff.; Nicolson to Grey, Feb. 13, 1906, *B.D.*, III, 249 f., No. 279.

[35] Wedel to F. O., Feb. 12 and 14, 1906, *G.P.*, XXI, 157 ff., No. 6999; 166 f., No. 7007.

Although in danger of becoming a minority of one, the German government hoped to win its point by a show of determination.[36] It complained vigorously to the new Italian government of the pro-French position taken by its delegate, and endeavored to persuade it to support the German views.[37] It sought to exert direct pressure upon M. Rouvier by instructing Prince Radolin to inform him that Germany had made concessions on the frontier under the expectation that France would agree to the German terms with regard to the rest of Morocco. If the Conference failed, the Ambassador was to assert, the legal status of 1880 in Morocco would again obtain. The Ambassador should also state to the Premier that if he did not stop the anti-German campaign of the French press "we [Germany] must conclude that M. Rouvier has reconciled himself to the idea of assuming the responsibility for the results of this activity."[38] On February 13 the German government, in telegrams to Rome, Washington, Vienna, London, and St. Petersburg, declared as follows:

No reason for a further retreat is evident. The principle of sacrificing one's own interests merely because they block the way for another Power could lead to such serious consequences that we consider a disruption of the conference as the lesser evil.[39]

That is, if the Powers wished to prevent a break-up of the assembly, they should persuade France to show more conciliation, for Germany would not recede. A newspaper campaign against the French views on the police accompanied these efforts.[40]

This defiance did not have the effect desired, for it was based

[36] Holstein to Radolin, Feb. 10, 1906, *ibid.*, 152 ff., No. 6994.

[37] Tardieu, pp. 198 ff.; Bülow to Monts, Feb. 10, 1906, *G.P.*, XXI, 154, No. 6995.

[38] Bülow to Radolin, Feb. 7 and 10, 1906, *G.P.*, XXI, 146 f., No. 6988; 152, No. 6993. Holstein was the inspirer of these dispatches. See Holstein to Radolin, Feb. 10, 1906, *ibid.*, 152 ff., No. 6994. On the press war see also Tardieu, pp. 167 ff.

[39] Bülow to Monts, Feb. 13, 1906, *G.P.*, XXI, 159 f. and note, No. 7000; Tardieu, p. 195. The telegram to Washington, dispatched the next day, was not of identical wording with the others but to the same effect (Bülow to Sternburg, Feb. 14, 1906, *G.P.*, XXI, 163 f., No. 7005).

[40] Tardieu, pp. 74, 163, 167, 176 f., 196; *G.P.*, XXI, 152 n.

upon an erroneous conception of the determination of France and the views of the Powers. So vehement was the opposition of the French press to the German plan, which was of course known in spite of attempts at secrecy, that the French government could not have accepted it at all. Nor did M. Rouvier have any intention of doing so. The British government, although suspecting that Germany meant to make the Conference fail, was ready to support the French proposals actively by exerting pressure upon the other Powers. On February 14 Sir Edward Grey replied to the defiant German manifesto by arguing to Count Metternich in behalf of the French views.[41]

In Russia, Count Lamsdorff, who had at the opening of the Conference anticipated a conciliatory policy from Germany, soon became disillusioned, and early in February again promised Russia's entire support to France. Several of the delegates suspected that while the German representatives realized the necessity of concessions, they were not informing their government of the gravity of the situation.[42] So Count Lamsdorff advised the French government that the only way in which to make Germany recede was by inducing the other Powers, especially Great Britain, the United States, and Italy to aid Russia in exerting moral pressure upon her and to show her that she was isolated.[43] He approached the British government with a view to co-operation in favor of France. His friendly expressions were most cordially reciprocated by Sir Edward Grey.[44] Furthermore, Mr. White

[41] Grey to Nicolson, Feb. 12, 1906, *B.D.*, III, 248 f., No. 278; Grey to Lascelles, Feb. 14, 1906, *ibid.*, 254 f., No. 285; Metternich to F. O., Feb. 14, 1906, *G.P.*, XXI, 164 ff., No. 7006.

[42] Nicolson to Grey, Feb. 6 and 7, 1906, *B.D.*, III, 244, No. 269; 245, No. 271; Tardieu, p. 154. The accusation was not deserved.

[43] Nicolson to Grey, Feb. 13, 1906, *B.D.*, III, 249 f., No. 279; Spring Rice to Grey, Feb. 13, 1906, *ibid.*, 253, No. 283; Tardieu, pp. 79 f., 158 ff., 204 f., 246 ff.; Witte, pp. 298 ff.; *G.P.*, XXI, 125 f. n.; Goetz, *Briefe Wilhelms II an den Zaren 1894-1914*, pp. 386 f.

[44] According to Bompard, the Russian government was not certain that the Liberal government in London would support France as whole-heartedly as its predecessor had done. Grey's assertions early in February reassured it entirely (Spring

and the French and British ambassadors in Washington persuaded President Roosevelt to yield to the French arguments
concerning the special interest of France in Morocco, her unique
fitness to execute the reforms, her honest desire to maintain the
open door. Considering the downfall of M. Delcassé and the acceptance of the Conference as great concessions to Germany,
Mr. Roosevelt thought that the latter should now recede in favor
of the more practical French proposal about the police. His
opinion was confirmed by expressions to the same effect from the
Italian, Russian, and even the Austrian governments. The last
two urged him to exert his influence with the Emperor for a
moderation of the German demands.[45] The President was coming to suspect Germany of wishing to divide Morocco into sectors and to regard France as the protector of Morocco's integrity.[46] He and Mr. Root both thought that Germany, believing
herself able to defeat both Great Britain and France since Russia was out of the way, was playing the "big bully"; and the
President had visions of the weak German navy's defeating the
British fleet, landing fifty thousand men in England, and taking
the island from that guileless Power.[47] Hence when M. Jusserand asked the President early in February to intervene with the
Emperor in favor of the French plan, Mr. Roosevelt agreed to
do so.[48]

With the support of Great Britain, Russia, and the United
States, the French government was almost certain of success,

Rice to Knollys, Jan. 31, 1906, and Spring Rice to Grey, Feb. 16, 1906, Gwynn, *The
Letters and Friendships of Sir Cecil Spring Rice*, II, 62 ff.; Spring Rice to Grey,
Feb. 7 and 8, 1906, *B.D.*, III, 245 f., Nos. 272 f.; Grey to Spring Rice, Feb. 8, 1906,
ibid., 246, No. 274).

[45] Sternburg to F. O., March 17 and 18, 1906, *G.P.*, XXI, 300 ff., Nos. 7112 f.;
Bishop, *The Life and Times of Theodore Roosevelt*, I, 489.

[46] Tardieu, pp. 160 ff.; Bishop, I, 489.

[47] Roosevelt to Reid, March 1, 1906, quoted in Royal Cortissoz, *The Life of
Whitelaw Reid* (New York, 1921), II, 329 f., 347; Sternburg to F. O., March 17
and 18, 1906, *G.P.*, XXI, 300 ff., Nos. 7112 f.

[48] Tardieu, pp. 161 f.; Nicolson to Grey, Feb. 11, 1906, *B.D.*, III, 246 ff., Nos.
275 f.

When on February 13 and 15 Prince Radolin complained about the tone of the French press and about the French proposal for the police, the French Premier, denying any responsibility for the press, handed the Ambassador the following memorandum:

. . . . If M. Rouvier agreed last July that the solution of the question of the Moroccan police should be international in principle, namely by conference, he was not of the opinion that it would be so in execution. As to the mandate for the police, at no moment has the French Government engaged not to ask for it. . . . . Moreover, it is not a question of organizing the police outside of the coastal towns, and it has always been understood that the principal object would be to guard the security of foreigners. . . . . The proposals ought to be examined at Algeciras, France having agreed at the demand of Germany to submit them to the conference.[49]

At the same time the French reply to the German proposal of February 13 was ready. Urged by Marquis Visconti Venosta and others, who feared a break-up of the Conference, the French government attempted to harmonize the German plan about the police with the French demands. Then Mr. White transmitted the project to President Roosevelt, who in turn would recommend it to the German government as his own, while M. Révoil would reply directly with a more general statement. Although the latter despaired of any success, this plan was carried out.[50] On February 16 M. Révoil handed the following memorandum to Herr von Radowitz:

There is no opposition to the organization of the police in the ports by the Sultan, or to the payment of the troops and officers by the Bank of State, or to the short duration of that institution, but under the condition that the foreign officers chosen by His Sherifian Majesty be French and Spanish. The point of the German proposition relative to a surveillance of the execution of

[49] Radolin to F. O., Feb. 13 and 15, 1906, *G.P.*, XXI, 160 f., No. 7001; 171 f., No. 7010; Tardieu, pp. 200 f.; Grey to Bertie, Feb. 13, 1906, *B.D.*, III, 250 f., No. 280; Nicolson to Grey, Feb. 16, 1906, *ibid.*, 259 f., No. 290.

[50] Tardieu, pp. 179 f., 249 ff. White was very critical of the German tactics in his dispatches to Washington, especially of the German attempt to negotiate directly with the Quai d'Orsay while the Conference was going on (White to Root, Feb. 11, 1905, Dennis, p. 502 and note; Nicolson to Grey, Feb. 15, 1906, *B.D.*, III, 257 f., No. 287).

that organization may be examined if the question of the nationality of the officers has been agreed upon as indicated above.[51]

On February 19 Mr. Root, declaring to the German Ambassador that Germany's persistence in her plan about the police would break up the Conference, proposed the following solution:[52]

1. That the organization and maintenance of police forces in all the ports be entrusted to the Sultan, the men and officers to be Moors.
2. That the money to maintain the force be furnished by the proposed international bank, the stock of which shall be allotted to all the powers in equal shares (except for some small preference claimed by France, which he [the President] considers immaterial).
3. That duties of instruction, discipline, pay and assisting in management and control be entrusted to French and Spanish officers and non-commissioned officers, to be appointed by the Sultan on presentation of names by their Legations.

  That the senior French and Spanish instructing officers report annually to the government of Morocco, and to the government of Italy,[53] the Mediterranean Power, which shall have the right of inspection and verification, and to demand further reports in behalf of and for the information of the Powers. The expense of such inspection, etc., etc., to be deemed a part of the cost of police maintenance.
4. That full assurances be given by France and Spain, and made obligatory upon all their officers who shall be appointed by the Sultan, for the open door, both as to trade, equal treatment and opportunity in competition for public works and concessions.

These terms, which the French government clung to notwithstanding the opposition of the French press, were unsatisfactory to the German government. At first Prince Bülow refused com-

[51] Radowitz to F. O., Feb. 16, 1906, *G.P.*, XXI, 172, No. 7011; Tardieu, p. 181; Nicolson to Grey, Feb. 17, 1906, *B.D.*, III, 260 f., No. 292. Révoil was contemplating an involved, vague reply when he talked to Nicolson. At the latter's advice it was made concise and straightforward (Nicolson to Grey, Feb. 15, 1906, *ibid.*, 256 ff., No. 287).

[52] Root to Sternburg, Feb. 19, 1906, quoted in Bishop, I, 489 ff., *G.P.*, XXI, 181 ff., No. 7019; Tardieu, pp. 249 f., 180.

[53] Italy had been chosen for obvious reasons, for she was bound to France by the accords of 1900 and 1902 and to Germany by the Triple Alliance. As such, her choice might be acceptable to both Powers (Tardieu, p. 181).

pletely the proposal of February 16, and requested the French delegate to make an offer in keeping with the fundamental principle of the equality for all nations in Morocco.[54] When the authority of President Roosevelt was added to it, however, the Chancellor receded on some points.[55] He still held that the Sultan should be permitted to choose the military instructors freely from others besides the French and Spanish nations. But he was willing to limit the nations to those participating in the bank, or, in case France feared that the Sultan might favor German officers, to at least four nationalities. In order to recognize the special rights of France in Morocco, he even agreed that the Sultan might place Tangier and perhaps some other port under the control of France alone; that in the other ports the officers of various nationalities should co-operate. Both Mr. Roosevelt and Mr. Root realized that this reply would be totally unacceptable to France, and they refused the German request to mediate on that basis.[56]

On the question of the bank, the situation was just as bad. Since early in February negotiations on it had been neglected in favor of the more important problem of the police. But to keep the Conference going, the German delegates took it up again on February 19. The next day both theirs and the French plans were submitted to the committee of the whole. The German plan provided that: an equal division of capital among the Powers should be made; the Egyptian mixed codes should be used for the bank; a mixed consular court with the addition of a Moroccan delegate to try cases involving the bank should be established at Tangier; the bank should be supervised by a Conseil de Surveillance composed of the diplomatic representatives at Tan-

[54] Bülow to Radowitz, Feb. 19, 1906, *G.P.*, XXI, 173 f., No. 7013; Tardieu, pp. 187, 249 ff.

[55] Bülow's minute to *G.P.*, XXI, 183, No. 7019; Sternburg to Roosevelt, Feb. 22, 1906, in Bishop, I, 491 ff.; Bülow to Sternburg, Feb. 21, 1906, *G.P.*, XXI, 183 f., No. 7020; Tardieu, p. 250.

[56] Bülow to Sternburg, Feb. 21, 1906, *G.P.*, XXI, 183 f., No. 7020; Sternburg to F. O., Feb. 23, 1906, *ibid.*, 213, No. 7038.

gier, and managed by a Conseil d'Administration composed of two delegates from each national group and by a director appointed by the Conseil d'Administration; statutes should be drawn up by this latter body and ratified by the Conseil de Surveillance; customs duties, perhaps with the deduction of the sums necessary for the service of the French loan, should be received by the bank; funds for the police organization and for certain needed public works should be furnished by the bank, which should also be charged with the service of the public debt, especially the French loan and the German advance, and should be the financial agent of the state and have priority right to make loans; the Conseil de Surveillance should have the right to reserve funds necessary for the police organization and for the execution of necessary public works independent of the Sultan's power, to fix the budget, and to advise the Sultan in deciding on public works.[57]

The French plan contained the following provisions: the capital should be divided into fifteen parts, of which eleven should be subscribed by financial groups in Germany, Great Britain, Austria, Belgium, Spain, the United States, France, Italy, Holland, Portugal, Russia, and Sweden, with no Power having more than one part; the other four were to be given to the French group of banks that made the Moroccan loan in 1904 in return for relinquishment of the right of preference for making loans to Morocco; the bank was to be directed by a Conseil d'Administration of fifteen members selected by the shareholders, each chosen from the nationality of the subscribing group; a high commissioner selected by the Moroccan government should watch over the bank for the Sultan; the Conseil d'Administration should select the bank officers and determine their powers; an international committee of discount chosen among the chief merchants and bankers of Tangier possessing at least twenty-

[57] The plan was drawn up with the aid of Glasenapp of the Deutsche Bank and of Mendelssohn, who was to take over the German shares in the bank. See Bülow to Radowitz, Jan. 27, 1906; *ibid.*, 115 ff., No. 6966; *L.j., 1906*, pp. 114 ff.; Tardieu, pp. 186, 221 ff.

five shares should be formed for consultative purposes on credit and discount; the bank should be subject to the French law and to the French judicial system; the statutes should be drawn up by a committee chosen from the various subscribing groups and submitted to the stockholders. France wanted the central office of the bank located at Paris, whereas Germany preferred Tangier.[58]

The main points of difference between the two projects related to the choice of the central office of the bank, the choice of legislation and jurisdiction, the surveillance of the bank, the division of the capital, and the right of preference. The one side complained that the other project would make the bank into a French institution; the other side complained that the opposing project would create, not an economic institution, but a political one aimed at France—that it disregarded recognized French rights and interests and that it was impracticable.[59] M. Regnault became indignant at the presumption of the German proposal; Count Tattenbach answered him in kind.[60] The plans were so divergent that their discussion in committee was postponed until March 3 so that time could be given for further direct negotiations.[61]

Thus, discussion on both questions reached a crisis. Fear of imminent failure pervaded the Conference. The issue was one of victory or defeat in the whole Moroccan episode. To break the deadlock the pro-French Powers again exerted moral pressure on the German government to force its retreat.[62]

[58] *L.j.*, *1906*, pp. 117 f.; Tardieu, pp. 184 f., 221 ff.

[59] *L.j.*, *1906*, pp. 113 f., 120 ff., 136 ff.; Radowitz to F. O., Feb. 20, 22, 1906, *G.P.*, XXI, 204, No. 7031; 205, No. 7033; Tardieu, pp. 186, 221 ff.; Nicolson to Grey, Feb. 20, 1906, *B.D.*, III, 265 f., No. 298.

[60] Radowitz to F. O., Feb. 19, 1906, *G.P.*, XXI, 176 f., No. 7015.

[61] *L.j.*, *1906*, pp. 113 ff.

[62] Rouvier suggested to Révoil that the representative of France, Germany, Great Britain, the United States, Spain, Russia, Italy, and Austria-Hungary meet informally and try to find a solution on the police. Nicolson and White opposed the idea as impracticable, and it was soon dropped (Nicolson to Grey, Feb. 16, 1906, *B.D.*, III, 260, No. 291).

When the French reply on the police was made to Germany, the Russian government approved it to the German authorities. Count Lamsdorff declared frankly to Herr von Schoen on February 19 his belief that Germany would be isolated in her refusal of the French proposals and that if the Conference broke up she would be blamed, particularly in Russia, for the continuation of the political and economic tension in Europe. If the Björkö ideal were to be realized, he said, France and Germany must become friends.[63]

On February 20, at French request, Count Witte urged the German government and Emperor William personally to permit a speedy settlement of the Moroccan affair. Until then, he argued, the Continental grouping could not be formed nor could Russia obtain the loan which she so greatly needed for suppressing the revolution.[64] The German government replied that if Russia wanted the loan quickly, she should advise the French government to be more conciliatory.[65] On February 23 occurred another conversation between Herr von Schoen and Count Lamsdorff, whose assertions the Ambassador reported as follows:

It is difficult to understand why we [Germany] defend so obstinately an international right on the police question at the Conference which all other Powers, in view of the practical solution offered by the French, are ready to give up. The pessimistic impression has spread throughout the Conference that we aim to frustrate an understanding.

The results of a failure would be incalculable. In France, where feelings are already very much excited and M. Rouvier would be accused of too great conciliation, a crisis with the downfall of M. Rouvier and his replacement by an intransigent person could scarcely be avoided. The continued anarchy in Morocco might bring forth bellicose complications at any moment, in which case England would certainly enter on France's side while

[63] Schoen to F. O., Feb. 19, 1906, *G.P.*, XXI, 178 f., No. 7017; Tardieu, pp. 194 f., 204 f.

[64] Tardieu, pp. 246 ff.; Schoen to F. O., Feb. 20, 1906, *G.P.*, XXI, 192, No. 7025; Eulenburg to William II, Feb. 22, 1906, *ibid.*, 194, No. 7027 and Anlage, Witte to Eulenburg, Feb. 20, 1906; Witte, p. 301.

[65] Bülow to Schoen, Feb. 21, 1906, *G.P.*, XXI, 193, No. 7026; memo. by Bülow, Feb. 23, 1906, *ibid.*, 197 f., No. 7028; Eulenburg to Witte, Feb. 27, 1906, *ibid.*, 202 ff., No. 7030; Tardieu, pp. 195, 295.

Russia would remain an inactive witness, but at the worst would be affected sympathetically. A European war would enkindle new revolutionary outbreaks which would also lead to difficult times for Germany. But the worst would be that the foundation for the peace program agreed upon by the two monarchs would be destroyed. . . . .

Denying that the outlook was so pessimistic, Herr von Schoen replied that even though the addition of the third Power to the Björkö accord might have to be postponed, that treaty would remain valid; whereupon Count Lamsdorff answered that the Dual Alliance still held good, that if France became involved in a war with Germany, the Björkö accord would collapse.[66]

When this warning had no apparent effect, Count Lamsdorff hesitated to use the Czar's influence with the German Emperor.[67] But as a final effort he had an article published on March 2 in the semiofficial journal, *L'Etat russe*, denouncing the German policy at the Conference and upholding the French.[68]

Great Britain also gave her fullest support to the French, not only in Algeciras and London, but in the various capitals of the other Powers. In upholding the French proposal to Count Metternich on February 19 the British Minister repeated his belief that British public opinion would point the way to active support of France in case of a war with Germany and would thus force the postponement of an Anglo-German *rapprochement*. The Ambassador answered that if Germany had to give in to every French pretension which arose from the Entente Cordiale in order to gain British friendship, he feared that the price was too high. The German people would come inevitably to look upon the British as their chief enemy. Sir Edward Grey assured him,

---

[66] Schoen to F. O., Feb. 23, 1906, *G.P.*, XXI, 211 ff., No. 7037; Witte, p. 301; Spring Rice to Grey, Feb. 24, 1906, *B.D.*, III, 271 f., No. 308; 273 f., No. 311.

[67] Spring Rice to Grey, Feb. 28, 1906, *B.D.*, III, 279, No. 320; Spring Rice to Knollys, March 1, 1906, Gwynn, II, 65 f.

[68] Tardieu, pp. 247, 249; Schoen to F. O., March 3, 1906, *G.P.*, XXI, 234 f., No. 7052; Schoen to Bülow, March 4, 1906, *ibid.*, 251 ff., No. 7068. The article so embittered the German government that Bülow would not show it directly to the Emperor but informed him of it personally so as to take away the sting (see the minutes to the dispatch from Schoen to F. O., March 3, 1906, *ibid.*, 235, No. 7052).

however, that if the Moroccan affair were settled permanently, he would carry out his promise to work for a *rapprochement*.[69] He also kept in close touch with the Russian government on Moroccan affairs. While refusing on February 22 Count Lamsdorff's suggestion to intervene in Berlin in favor of France, he urged Russia to do so.[70]

The British Foreign Secretary was pessimistic over the outlook for the Conference. He was especially desirous for the onus of the disruption not to rest upon France. To prevent that he was even willing for the Moroccan police to be temporarily organized under the Sultan by officers taken from a neutral minor Power with a French officer selected by the French government in general control. But he hesitated to suggest this solution to France for fear of hurting the Entente Cordiale.[71] On February 20 he recorded his reactions to the situation as follows:

If the Conference breaks up without result the situation will be very dangerous. Germany will endeavour to establish her influence in Morocco at the expense of France. France to counteract this or even simply to protect herself and a neighbour from the state of disturbance, which is now chronic in Morocco, will be driven to take action in Morocco, which Germany may make a *casus belli*.

If there is war between France and Germany it will be very difficult for us to keep out of it. The *Entente* and still more the constant and emphatic demonstrations of affection . . . . have created in France a belief that we should support her in war. . . . . If this expectation is disappointed the French will never forgive us.

There would also I think be a general feeling in every country that we

[69] A visit of the London City Council to Paris, Feb. 8, gave occasion for confirming the Entente Cordiale (*G.P.*, XXI, 185 ff. and note, No. 7021). Grey also intimated to Metternich that France would be willing to eliminate the thirty-year limitation to commercial freedom in Morocco as provided for in the Anglo-French accord. See Metternich to F. O., Feb. 19 and 20, 1906, *ibid.*, 179 ff., No. 7018; 185 ff., Nos. 7021 f.; Grey to Lascelles, Feb. 19, 1906, *B.D.*, III, 263 f., No. 296.

[70] Spring Rice to Grey, Feb. 22, 24, 28, 1906, *B.D.*, III, 269, No. 303; 271 f., No. 308; 273 f., No. 311; 278 f., No. 320; Grey to Spring Rice, Feb. 20, 22, 1906, *ibid.*, 264 f., No. 297; 270, No. 304; Grey to Spring Rice, Feb. 19, 1906, Gwynn, II, 65.

[71] Grey to Nicolson, Feb. 15, 1906, *B.D.*, III, 258, No. 288. Apparently it was not mentioned to the French at all.

had behaved meanly and left France in the lurch. The United States would despise us, Russia would not think it worth while to make a friendly arrangement with us about Asia, Japan would prepare to re-insure herself elsewhere, we should be left without a friend and without the power of making a friend and Germany would take some pleasure, after what has passed, in exploiting the whole situation to our disadvantage, very likely by stirring up trouble through the Sultan of Turkey in Egypt. As a minor matter the position of any Foreign Secretary here, who had made it an object to maintain the *entente* with France, would become intolerable.

On the other hand the prospect of a European War and of our being involved in it is horrible.

I propose therefore, if unpleasant symptoms develop after the Conference is over, to tell the French Ambassador that a great effort and if need be some sacrifice should in our opinion be made to avoid war. To do this we should have to find out what compensation Germany would ask or accept as the price of her recognition of the French claims in Morocco. There is also a point about Egypt, which might be worked in on our behalf. I should myself be in favour of allowing Germany a port or coaling station, if that would ensure peace; but it would be necessary to consult the Admiralty about this, and to find out whether the French would entertain the idea, and if so what port?

The real objection to the course proposed is that the French may think it pusillanimous and a poor result of the *Entente*. I should have to risk this. I hope the French would recognize that in a war with Germany our liabilities would be much less than theirs. We should risk little or nothing on land, and at sea we might shut the German fleet up in Kiel and keep it there without losing a ship or a man or even firing a shot. The French would have a life and death struggle and that expenditure of blood and treasure with a doubtful issue. They ought therefore not to think it pusillanimous on our part to wish to avoid a war in which our danger was so much less than theirs.

I have also a further point of view. The door is being kept open by us for a *rapprochement* with Russia; there is at least a prospect that when Russia is re-established we shall find ourselves on good terms with her. An *entente* between Russia, France and ourselves would be absolutely secure. If it is necessary to check Germany it could then be done. The present is the most unfavourable moment for attempting to check her. Is it not a grave mistake, if there must be a quarrel with Germany for France or ourselves to let Germany choose the moment, which best suits her.

There is a possibility that war may come before these suggestions of mine can be developed in diplomacy. If so it will only be because Germany has made up her mind that she wants war and intends to have it anyhow, which

I do not believe is the case. But I think we ought in our minds to face the question now, whether we can keep out of war, if war breaks out between France and Germany. The more I review the situation the more it appears to me that we cannot, without losing our good name and our friends and wrecking our policy and position in the world.[72]

Thus Sir Edward Grey intended to do his utmost to preserve peace even at the risk of antagonizing France. He desired to postpone the Moroccan settlement if necessary until the Anglo-Russian entente could be consummated, believing that then France would be in a far stronger position with reference to Germany. But if war did arise, he was determined to throw his entire influence in favor of active participation.[73]

In Rome, M. Barrère, loyally seconded by Sir Edwin Egerton, endeavored to interpret the Franco-Italian accords in such a way as to induce the Italian government to take the French side openly in case of a vote at the Conference. The Italian government refused. It also refused to support Germany, and left matters in the hands of its delegate.[74]

[72] Memo. by Grey, Feb. 20, 1906, *ibid.*, 266 f., No. 299.

[73] Sir Charles Hardinge, permanent undersecretary of state for foreign affairs, believed that the way to prevent Germany from attacking France because of some French action in Morocco was for Great Britain to inform Germany that she is "absolutely 'solidaire' with France as far as the Moroccan question is concerned." He feared that if Great Britain did leave France in the lurch, "an agreement or alliance between France, Germany and Russia in the near future is certain" (memo. by Grey, Feb. 20, 1906, and Hardinge's minute, *ibid.*, 266 ff., No. 299). Mr. Eyre Crowe, senior clerk in the British foreign office, a prejudiced, bitter opponent of Germany, suspected that Germany might demand and seize a port in Morocco or obtain a lease as she had done at Kiaouchau in China. He advised warning the Sultan against Germany. Sir Edward Grey regarded the proposal as premature so long as the Conference was sitting, but said that the eventualities referred to should be kept in mind (minutes to dispatch from Spring Rice to Grey, Feb. 24, 1906, *ibid.*, 272, No. 308).

[74] Monts to Bülow, Feb. 13, 1906, *G.P.*, XXI, 168 f., No. 7008; Monts to F. O., Feb. 13, 1906, *ibid.*, 161 f., No. 7002; Bülow to Monts, Feb. 14, 1906, *ibid.*, 162 and note, No. 7003; Monts to Bülow, Feb. 27, 1906, *ibid.*, 230 ff., No. 7050; Monts to Bülow, March 11, 1906, *ibid.*, 286 ff., No. 7103; Monts to Bülow, Feb. 24, 1906, *ibid.*, 216 f., No. 7043; Tardieu, pp. 198 f., 205 f.; Grey to Egerton, Feb. 19, 1906, *B.D.*, III, 262, No. 295; Egerton to Grey, March 3, 1906, *ibid.*, 283, No. 325.

Similarly, the French and British representatives co-operated to prevent Spain, somewhat disgruntled over the Moroccan accords, from refusing to live up to its obligations. The Spanish government promised complete loyalty. But when it appeared that the conference would fail, the Spanish government felt that as host it should endeavor to prevent that issue. On February 19 the Duke of Almodovar read to Mr. Révoil a note in which he said that for the sake of a settlement Spain was willing to accept the following plan as a sort of truce: The police should be organized by the Sultan under the control of the diplomatic corps for three years; the instructors should be exclusively Moroccan except at Tetouan, where they should be Spanish, and at Oudjda, where they should be French; France and Spain might renew their claims after the three years if they saw fit.[75]

Horrified at the idea, the Anglo-French combination immediately busied itself to bring Spain back into line. At Madrid the British and French representatives informed the foreign office that if Spain deserted her friends the Anglo-French opposition to the German projects would continue anyway. They argued that a break-up of the Conference with the maintenance of the Franco-Spanish accords was preferable to the success of the Conference through the ruin of those accords, in which lay their sole guaranty for the morrow. M. Ojeda, acting minister of foreign affairs, acknowledged to the British representative that "he hated France and French influence in Morocco, and that he had no confidence in and personal dislike for French Ambassador," but he added that "he would act faithfully in accordance with Spain's engagements, although he disliked them." M. Moret, the Spanish premier, also protested his loyalty to the accords. The Duke of Almodovar was instructed to abstain in the future from all initiative not previously concerted with his French col-

---

[75] "C'est la pire des solutions," wrote Tardieu, p. 155 and elsewhere. See the conversation between Ojeda and Stumm reported by the latter on Feb. 20, 1906, *G.P.*, XXI, 189 ff., No. 7024; Tardieu, pp. 155 ff., 199 f.; Cartwright to Grey, Jan. 22 and 26, 1906, *B.D.*, III, 233, No. 252; 236, No. 258.

league.[76] To prevent any bad feelings from this episode, the British and French governments thanked Spain for her loyalty. Thus the danger from Spain was averted.[77]

M. Rouvier consulted the smaller governments represented at the Conference with a view to obtaining their open support in case matters were forced to a vote. But they remained neutral.[78]

The French government, again sustained by Great Britain,[79] even sought to influence Austria in its favor, and with some success. Finding Count Goluchowski of the opinion that after France's concessions on February 3 and 16 Germany should show moderation, the French Ambassador hinted discreetly that the Foreign Minister speak to the German government to that effect.[80] Count Goluchowski, who on February 14 had suggested

[76] Tardieu writes that the instructions were "all that France wished" (Tardieu, pp. 207 f., 255).

[77] Tardieu has a long story about German threats and intimidations toward Spain between Feb. 11 and 20. The King of Spain, he writes, was angry, but Ojeda listened to the siren voice of Stumm, first secretary of the German embassy in Madrid. According to the German documents, Stumm had at least two conversations with Ojeda during February, one on Feb. 20, trying without success to influence Spain to support the German proposals (G.P., XXI, 145, 189 ff.). On the Spanish proposal see Tardieu, pp. 199 f., 188 ff., 207 ff.; Grey to Cartwright, Feb. 19, 1906, B.D., III, 262 n., No. 295; 271, No. 307; Cartwright to Grey, Feb. 21, 22, 24, 1906, ibid., 268 f., No. 301; 270 f., No. 305; 273, No. 310; Grey to Nicolson, Feb. 22, 1906, ibid., 269, No. 302; Nicolson to Grey, Feb. 23, 1906, ibid., 271, No. 306.

[78] The Belgian government informed him that its delegate had orders to abstain from voting in case of a conflict, and to participate actively in the Conference only when the commercial interests of Belgium were involved. The Dutch government said that its delegate would vote with the majority. Sweden replied that she would abstain from voting in case of disagreement (Tardieu, p. 257).

[79] As Sir Edward Grey knew how interested Austria was in keeping Great Britain and Germany friendly, he impressed upon the Austrian government, Feb. 26, "how unfortunate" was the German stand on the police, and "how impossible it was to improve the relations between England and Germany as long as there was this dispute between Germany and France about a matter on which we had an Agreement with France which was publicly known to the whole world, and which had been the very beginning of our friendship with France" (Grey to Goschen, Feb. 26, 1906, B.D., III, 276 f., No. 316).

[80] Tardieu, pp. 202 f.

a compromise to the German government very similar to the French offer of February 16, urged it to accept the offer and to seek compensation in the settlement of the bank question. Both the American and the Italian delegates approved it, he argued, and he predicted that if the Conference broke up Germany would be blamed.[81] On February 23 Emperor Francis Joseph himself intervened. Calling the German Ambassador to him, he said that Austria would act with Germany at the Conference, but that according to all reports from Algeciras they would be isolated in case of a vote. Such an isolation would be unpleasant for both Powers, but far graver, he said, was the possibility that out of a failure of the Conference might develop a new grouping of the Powers separating Russia from the two monarchies and associating her with Great Britain and France. He declared that it was necessary to avoid that turn.[82]

The French party at the Conference knew that Germany was isolated, that even her ally, Austria, opposed her policy.[83] On February 26 M. Révoil, refusing to make any further proposal, asserted to the German delegates: "If the Conference recognizes the utility of new guarantees, we will not refuse to examine them. It belongs to the Conference . . . . to determine the solution." In other words, he told Germany that, having demanded the Conference, she might permit it to settle the matter.[84] He and Sir Arthur Nicolson were devising some means by which a rupture of the Conference should not occur over the bank question and by which the responsibility for a rupture should not fall on France and Great Britain. The issue on the bank was not as clear

[81] Wedel to F. O., Feb. 14 and 18, 1906, *G.P.*, XXI, 166 f., No. 7007; 175 f., No. 7014. To the Italian and American governments Goluchowski openly censured the German attitude (Tardieu, p. 203, and above; Goschen to Grey, Feb. 24, 1906, *B.D.*, III, 273, No. 309).

[82] Memo. by Bülow, Feb. 24, 1906, *G.P.*, XXI, 213 f., No. 7039; Tardieu, pp. 257 ff.; Spring Rice to Grey, Feb. 28, 1906, *B.D.*, III, 279, No. 320.

[83] Spring Rice to Grey, Feb. 28, 1906, *ibid.*, 278, No. 318; 279, No. 320.

[84] Radowitz to F. O., Feb. 26, 1906, *G.P.*, XXI, 177 f., No. 7016; Tardieu, pp. 187, 266 f.; Nicolson to Grey, Feb. 26, 1906, *B.D.*, III, 276, No. 315.

cut as on the police, and public opinion would not understand why financial differences could not be harmonized. So the two men planned to bring the police question up first for decision. They did not favor taking a formal vote on that matter, as Count Lamsdorff suggested,[85] for they perceived that the American, Italian, Dutch, Belgian, and Swedish delegates would very probably not vote. But they intended in some way to make plain to Germany the preference of the Conference for the French police proposal. Then if Germany remained adamantine, she would receive the blame for the break-up of the assembly.[86]

The opportunity came on March 3. During the discussion of the bank in the official session of the Conference, Germany's views were supported solely by Austria and Morocco and were opposed, for the first time, by a firm British-French-Spanish-Russian group.[87] That same day, on the motion of Sir Arthur Nicolson and with the aid of the Duke of Almodovar, the Conference voted to take up the question of the police on February 5 instead of that of the bank. The German and Austrian delegates alone opposed the motion, even the Italian representative siding openly against them.[88] At the session on March 5 Germany was again isolated. Her policy in regard to the police was not even defended by Austria, while the French plan was openly approved by Great Britain, Russia, Spain, and Portugal.[89]

[85] Spring Rice to Grey, Feb. 24, 1906, *B.D.*, III, 274, No. 311.

[86] Nicolson to Grey, Feb. 25 and 26, 1906, *ibid.*, 274 ff., Nos. 312 f.; Tardieu, Part III, chap. ii, *passim*, pp. 268 ff.

[87] Radowitz to F. O., Feb. 21, March 3, 1906, *G.P.*, XXI, 204 f., No. 7032; 233 f., No. 7051; Tardieu, pp. 143 ff., 227, 223 ff.

[88] Tardieu, pp. 275 ff.; *L.j., 1906*, pp. 159 ff.; Radowitz to F. O., March 3 and 9, 1906, *G.P.*, XXI, 233 f. and note, No. 7051; Nicolson to Grey, March 3, 1906, *B.D.*, III, 282, No. 323; 283 f., No. 326. The French press played up that vote as a great victory; the German press and government took the opposite view. Nevertheless, the German delegates complained to the Italian, Belgian, Spanish, and even the Austrian delegates about their actions; and the vote undoubtedly helped to accomplish the object of Nicolson and Révoil.

[89] *L.j., 1906*, pp. 168 ff.; Nicolson to Grey, March 7, 1906, *B.D.*, III, 285 ff., No. 330; Tardieu, pp. 283 ff.

All the delegates were pessimistic. As direct negotiations had proved futile, M. Révoil and Sir Arthur Nicolson both expected that the antagonism would come to a head at the next session and the Conference would break up.[90] Herr von Radowitz reported to his government that agreement was impossible if Germany held to her present terms, for France would not recede, and that the other representatives, anxious to conclude the Conference, were in favor of the French police proposal. Even Count Tattenbach thought that his government was too obstinate.[91] In Berlin, however, Herr von Holstein, misjudging the French feeling, planned to meet the crisis by disregarding the Conference and making a direct temporary agreement with the French government. The visit to Berlin of Baron de Courcel, former ambassador at Berlin, on February 20–22, afforded him the opportunity to propose the following terms: In regard to the police the two governments should make a temporary settlement for four or five years; France, in consideration of her special interests in Morocco, should be given one port to police alone, while officers in equal numbers of the various nationalities, including French and German, should co-operate in each of the other seven ports; in the bank France should also be given a slight advantage. Let France accept this internationalization for the time being, he said, and in a few years she and Germany could come to a direct permanent settlement of the Moroccan question by which Germany, in return for concessions elsewhere, would leave the land entirely to France. These concessions he declared to be the ut-

[90] Nicolson to Grey, March 3 and 7, 1906, *B.D.*, III, 282 f., No. 324; 285, No. 328. On March 7 Grey again advised the Spanish government to stand firmly with France and Great Britain (Grey to de Bunsen, March 7, 1906, *ibid.*, 285, No. 329).

[91] Tardieu states that on March 5 Tattenbach openly said so to several of the delegates (p. 291). Bülow also found it necessary to bolster up the courage of the German delegates. See memo. by Bülow, March 7, 1906, *G.P.*, XXI, 256, No. 7069. See also Metternich to F. O., Feb. 20, 1906, *ibid.*, 188, No. 7023; Radowitz to Bülow, Feb. 26, 1906, *ibid.*, 217 ff., No. 7044; Radowitz to F. O., Feb. 27, March 5, 1906, *ibid.*, 226, No. 7048; 243 ff., Nos. 7061 f. King Edward's visit to Paris, March 4–5, at which time he showed special favor to Delcassé, was also a significant sign to the Germans (Lee, *King Edward VII*, II, 510; Bertie to Grey, March 5, 1906, *B.D.*, III, 284, No. 327).

most that Germany would make; she preferred to let the Conference disband rather than recede further. Baron de Courcel seemed favorable to the plan; but, on March 6, M. Rouvier refused to consider it or any other direct negotiations with Germany.[92] So that channel was definitely closed.

While this effort was being made, Prince Bülow took personal charge of all the details concerning the Moroccan affair.[93] The Chancellor had no idea of permitting a disruption of the Conference,[94] and began to consider a proposal suggested by the Austrian delegate on February 26 for a way out. In its final form this project provided that the organization of police in Tangier, Saffi, Rabat, and Tetouan should be intrusted to the French; in Mogador, Larache, and Mazagan to the Spanish; in Casablanca to the command of a Swiss or Dutch officer with powers of inspection over all the police. It further proposed that this inspector should report to the diplomatic corps at Tangier, which should exercise general control over the reorganization of the police. Herr von Radowitz, Count Welsersheimb, and Marquis Visconti Venosta all declared this to be the least that the French would accept.[95] The German government endeavored first to have Austria and Italy mediate on the basis of the plan outlined

[92] On this episode see Tardieu, pp. 241 ff., 296; Grey to Bertie, Feb. 28, 1906, *B.D.*, III, 278, No. 319; Bertie to Grey, March 5, 1906, *ibid.*, 284, No. 327; Nicolson to Grey, March 8, 1906, *ibid.*, 288, No. 331; memos. by Holstein, Feb. 22, 1906, *G.P.*, XXI, 206 ff., and note, Nos. 7034 f.; Holstein to Radolin, March 4, 1906, *ibid.*, 237, No. 7055; Radolin to F. O., Feb. 27, March 5 and 6, 1906, *ibid.*, 225, No. 7047; 240 f., No. 7059; 250 f., No. 7067; Bülow to Radolin, March 5, 1906, *ibid.*, 240, No. 7058. Courcel spoke to Louis, of the French foreign office, about the project on March 5. On the next day Rouvier mentioned it to Radolin, only to refuse it. On Holstein's views see also Lascelles to Grey, March 1, 1906, *B.D.*, III, 280 f. and inclosure, No. 321.

[93] Hammann, *Bilder*, pp. 37 f.; memo. by Holstein, Feb. 22, 1906, *G.P.*, XXI, 208 f., No. 7035; Holstein to Radolin, March 4, 1906, *ibid.*, 237, No. 7055; *ibid.* p. 338, editor's note.

[94] See the conversation with Tschirschky on March 16 recorded by Zedlitz-Trützschler, *Zwölf Jahre am deutschen Kaiserhof*, pp. 146 f.

[95] Radowitz to F. O., Feb. 26, March 8, 1906, *G.P.*, XXI, 233 f., No. 7045; 262 f., No. 7077; *L.j., 1906*, pp. 187 f.

to Baron de Courcel;[96] but on March 4 Count Goluchowski, the Austrian foreign minister, regarding the step as futile, refused to do so. Instead he urged that either Count Welsersheimb's project be accepted *in toto* or that the selection of officers be left to the Sultan with the understanding that he choose only French and Spanish ones.[97] From Italy also came a negative response.[98] When Count Tattenbach himself favored the Austrian plan, the Chancellor accepted it on March 6 with the proviso that the commander at Casablanca choose his officers from other nationalities than French and Spanish, and also that France accede to the German demands on the bank. Then the Chancellor sought to obtain a combined Austro-Italian mediation for the plan.[99]

On March 8 Count Welsersheimb's project and the French plan of February 16 were formally introduced in the Conference.[100] On March 10 both were referred to the committee for formulation on a motion by Herr von Radowitz, who said:

[96] Bülow to Radowitz, Feb. 28, 1906, *G.P.*, XXI, 224 f., No. 7046.

[97] Goluchowski reluctantly agreed to mediate on that basis at first, but after learning of the vote of March 3 and after consulting Welsersheimb he changed his mind (Wedel to F. O. March 1 and 4, 1906, *ibid.*, 228 ff., No. 7049; 238 f., No. 7056).

[98] Monts to Bülow, Feb. 27, 1906, *ibid.*, 230 ff., No. 7050; Radowitz to F. O., March 3, 1906, *ibid.*, 235 f., No. 7053.

[99] Bülow to Radowitz, March 6 and 7, 1906, *ibid.*, 245 f. and note, No. 7063; Bülow to Wedel, Bülow to Monts, March 6, 1906, *ibid.*, XXI, 248 f. and note, No. 7065.

[100] *L.j., 1906*, pp. 183 ff.; Radowitz to F. O., March 8, 1906, *G.P.*, XXI, 261 ff., Nos. 7076 ff., Nicolson to Grey, March 8 and 9, 1906, *B.D.*, III, 288, No. 331; 289 ff., No. 334. Visconti Venosta, informed at the last minute of the proposed Austrian mediation, refused angrily to co-operate in it. Why he did so is difficult to see. He claimed that the Austrian project was not in keeping with the German view which he represented. This, however, seems a poor excuse, for he had approved the project when it was first suggested. It seems more likely that Visconti Venosta was seeking to avoid taking the Austro-German side publicly against France. The Austrian government was more alarmed at his refusal than was the German government, which consoled itself with the fact that the Italian delegate was performing useful work under cover. See Wedel to F. O., March 9 and 11, 1906, *G.P.*, XXI, 269, No. 7083; 271 f., No. 7087; Monts to F. O., March 7, 1906, *ibid.*, 257, No. 7070; Radowitz to F. O., March 11, 1906, *ibid.*, 272 and note, No. 7088.

It seems to me that accord ought to be reached on the basis of the two projects. . . . . That of the French delegation certainly contains proposals which deserve the most serious examination. They ought to be completed by those of the Austro-Hungarian project.[101]

The Austro-German proposal was a welcome surprise to the Conference, which recognized it as a great concession. Sir Arthur Nicolson found that "members of the Conference, with the exception of French and Spanish, are unanimous in favour of" it. He as well as the other delegates did not hesitate to inform M. Révoil frankly of this view. In Algeciras, London, and Paris the British government on March 9–10 stated to the French authorities that Germany's concessions "had brought an agreement so near that it would not do to let the Conference break up now without a settlement." "I would," said Sir Arthur Nicolson to M. Révoil, "support him [M. Révoil] to the best of my ability in whatever course he might take, but I must tell him that in the event of the Conference ending in a failure we should be placed in an exceedingly false position with all the public feeling of Europe against us."[102] Sir Edward Grey thought that "Germany has conceded the substance and it would be a great pity, if France sacrificed the substance to the shadow."[103]

M. Révoil, whose views were also valid for the Spanish delegates, was totally unwilling to accept the Austrian proposal. He was handicapped by the unexpected fall of the French government on March 7 over a minor question concerning relations with the church. A week before the French Premier would have accepted the Spanish proposal of February 19 as a means of last

[101] *L.j., 1906,* pp. 189 ff.; Radowitz to F. O., March 10, 1906, *G.P.,* XXI, 270, No. 7085; Tardieu, p. 293; Nicolson to Grey, March 10, 1906, *B.D.,* III, 292 f., No. 337. By these words Radowitz did not mean that Germany would accept the French terms, as Tardieu imagines (Tardieu, pp. 308 ff., 313).

[102] Nicolson to Grey, March 9 and 10, 1906, *B.D.,* III, 288 f., No. 332; 294, No. 338; Grey to Bertie, March 9, 1906, *ibid.,* 289, No. 333; Bertie to Grey, March 10, 1906, *ibid.,* 292, No. 336; Radowitz to F. O., March 8 and 10, 1906, *G.P.,* XXI, 261, No. 7075; 264 f., No. 7079; 269 f., No. 7084; Dennis, p. 503. Cf. Tardieu, pp. 297 f., 308 f.

[103] Grey to Nicolson, March 10, 1906, *B.D.,* III, 292, No. 335.

resort.[104] Now out of power, though remaining at the foreign office until the new government was formed, M. Rouvier of course could not make concessions even had he so desired. Staunchly supported by the French press, which on March 13 published the instructions to M. Révoil,[105] he and the French delegate demanded the following modifications in the Austrian plan:

The police instructors at Casa Blanca to be, like at the other seven ports, French or Spanish.

Distribution of ports to French or Spanish instructors to be a matter for agreement between French and Spanish Gov[ernmen]ts. The Inspector General to be a subject of neutral state and to have powers of inspection at all eight ports without right to command or give orders to French and Spanish instructors, and to make his reports to the Sultan of Morocco and not to the diplomatic body at Tangier.

He also preferred as inspector a Swiss or, even better, a Dane to a Dutchman for fear the latter might be too much under German influence.[106]

Both MM. Rouvier and Révoil believed that Germany would recede on these points, for on about March 8 the Prince of Monaco arrived in Paris from Berlin with a message for M. Rouvier from Prince Bülow to the effect that Germany would accept a French and Spanish police "under the most discreet control of an officer from a lesser Power."[107] The message was undoubtedly misleading and the French hope unjustified.[108] When Marquis

[104] Bertie to Grey, March 2, 1906, *ibid.*, 281 f., No. 322.

[105] Tardieu, pp. 299 f., 309 f., 321, 328; Grey, *Twenty-five Years*, I, 103.

[106] Nicolson to Grey, March 9, 1906, *B.D.*, III, 288 f., No. 322; Bertie to Grey, March 10, 1906, *ibid.*, 292, No. 336.

[107] Radolin to F. O., March 8, 1906, *G.P.*, XXI, 265 f., No. 7080.

[108] On March 5, 6, and 7, Bülow showed no inclination to accept the French plan, but held firmly to the Austrian one. See Bülow to Wedel, March 5 and 6, 1906, *ibid.*, 239, No. 7057; 248 f., No. 7065; memo. by Bülow, March 7, 1906, *ibid.*, 256, No. 7069. He may, however, have made this statement to the Prince of Monaco without explaining that by "the most discreet control of an officer from a lesser Power" he really meant the Austrian plan and did not intend an acceptance

Visconti Venosta, Mr. White, and Sir Arthur Nicolson, at M. Révoil's request, asked the German delegates March 9, 10, whether they would give way, the latter assured them that Germany had spoken her last word, that "the establishment of the inspector at a port as instructor was a *sine qua non* condition."[109]

M. Révoil was "greatly disappointed" and "a little unstrung." He told Sir Arthur Nicolson that his government would not accept such a solution. "He said with much bitterness that the Germans had internationalized the finances, and they now intended to introduce the principle throughout Morocco. France would leave the Conference having yielded everything and gained nothing." His chief concern was that if France were forced to accept the Austrian plan, "the outcry which would be raised against it in France might be utilized to weaken the Anglo-French understanding." Sir Arthur Nicolson replied that he "would always support him [M. Révoil], but I had given warnings as a friend should." And Sir Arthur added "that he must face the situation as it stood, and that there could be no question of breaking down the Conference on that point, and at a moment when a favourable end was so nearly reached."[110]

In Paris, M. Rouvier

rather demurred [to the British Ambassador] to the supposition that the conference was so favourably impressed by the Austrian scheme. He said that France still counted on her side Spain, England, Russia, Portugal, and others had only been gained over by the German Delegates having persuaded them that Germany would make no further concessions.[111]

---

of the French plan. Tardieu's assumption that Bülow made the surrender and then receded from his concession after the fall of the French government on March 7, hoping to exploit this embarrassing situation, is, so far as we can tell, devoid of foundation (Tardieu, pp. 293 ff., 314 f.).

[109] Germany also refused to recede on the police in return for French concessions on the bank (Nicolson to Grey, March 10 and 11, 1906, *B.D.*, III, 294 f., Nos. 338 f.).

[110] Nicolson to Grey, March 11 and 12, 1906, *ibid.*, 295 f., No. 339; 297 ff., Nos. 341 f.

[111] Bertie to Grey, March 11, 1906, *ibid.*, 296 f., No. 340.

Mr. Eyre Crowe was alarmed for the Entente Cordiale; he urged the greatest caution in advising France to recede. But Sir Edward Grey on March 12 repeated to M. Cambon that in his opinion France "should accept the Swiss at Casa Blanca rather than let the Conference break up."[112]

As the pressure of the delegates was so strong, M. Révoil and the Duke of Almodovar began on March 11 to consider tentatively the plan of associating actively a Swiss inspector with the French and Spanish in the policing of Tangier.[113] Nothing could be decided until the new French government was formed. Meanwhile, the opposition of views became public in the Conference session of March 11 when two matters remaining unsolved on the question of the bank were taken up. In a previous sitting Sir Arthur Nicolson, in agreement with M. Révoil, had proposed that three censors be chosen to oversee the bank. In accepting this proposal Herr von Radowitz stipulated that in order to preserve the principle of internationality the censors should be chosen by the respective governments from the personnel of the banks interested in the Moroccan state bank and that a copy of the censors' reports should be sent to the governments of the signatory Powers. The French delegates, however, desired that the first censors be selected by the committee drawing up the statutes of the bank and should thereafter be chosen by co-optation and that their reports should be sent to the council of administrators of the bank. The French continued to demand four shares, while Germany was willing to concede them only three.[114] At the session on the next day M. Révoil refused the Austrian

[112] Crowe's minutes to the dispatch from Nicolson to Grey, March 12, 1906, *ibid.*, 299, No. 342; Grey to Nicolson, March 12, 1906, *ibid.*, 300, No. 344.

[113] Nicolson to Grey, March 11, 12, 14, 1906, *ibid.*, 295, No. 339; 298, No. 341; 303, No. 349. Rouvier also approved this plan. See Hardinge to Nicolson, March 15, 1906, *ibid.*, 305, No. 354.

[114] The number of censors was later increased to four, one each from Great Britain, Spain, France, and Germany. See Radowitz to F. O., March 8 and 11, 1906, *G.P.*, XXI, 263 f., No. 7078; 272 f., No. 7089; *L.j.*, *1906*, pp. 152 f., 182, 189 ff.; Tardieu, pp. 291 f.

proposal to give the command in Casablanca to an officer of a third Power, but agreed to the inspection by one, preferably a Swiss.[115]

In reporting M. Révoil's pertinacity to Berlin on March 11, Herr von Radowitz stated: "I have been told by all my colleagues, even the English, that after our action they would no longer consider justified the French adherence to the points declared inacceptable by us and they have so expressed themselves to M. Révoil."[116] On the next day Marquis Visconti Venosta said in confidence to Herr von Radowitz that the latter would "not be able to come to an arrangement with M. Révoil without a positive intervention of the government at Paris. . . . ."[117] The same day the *Lokalanzeiger* published an exaggerated report from its correspondent at Algeciras in which the "complete isolation" of France in the committee was spoken of; Italy, Russia, the United States, and even Great Britain, the article read, had put themselves on the German side.[118]

Instead of maintaining a dignified silence while public opinion and the persuasion of the Powers compelled France to give way or break up the Conference, Prince Bülow tried to increase the pressure by beginning a diplomatic and press campaign against France. With German thoroughness he overdid the thing. On March 12 he sent telegrams to the German ambassadors at Vienna, London, St. Petersburg, Rome, Washington, and Paris in which he stated that the generous concessions granted by Germany on March 10 had made agreement seem possible. Then all had been placed in doubt again by sudden and unexpected opposition from the French delegates. The other delegates, including the British, he continued, had expressed to Herr von Radowitz and to M. Révoil their opinion that France should now recede; and, after repeating Marquis Visconti Venosta's

[115] Radowitz to F. O., March 12, 1906, *G.P.*, XXI, 279, No. 7094.

[116] Radowitz to F. O., March 11, 1906, *ibid.*, 273, No. 7089.

[117] Radowitz to F. O., March 12, 1906, *ibid.*, 274, No. 7090.

[118] Quoted in *ibid.*, p. 274 n.; and in Tardieu, p. 316.

statement, he asked the various governments to intervene at Paris "so that the voice of reason will again rule there and further opposition be given up."[119]

The Russian, Italian, and Austrian governments agreed to advise France to accept the Austrian compromise. Sir Edward Grey, whom Count Metternich did not ask to intercede in behalf of the plan as he believed that the British Minister would refuse, welcomed the German concessions but loyally upheld the French proposals.[120] Mr. Roosevelt unexpectedly replied most adversely.

In a letter on March 7 the President advised the Emperor to accept his proposal of February 19. He justified his interference by quoting a passage from Baron Sternburg's letter to him on June 28, 1905, to the effect that "the Emperor has requested me to tell you that in case, during the coming conference, differences of opinion should arise between France and Germany, he, in every case, will be ready to back up the decision which you should consider to be most fair and most practical." He warned the German government that it would lose "credit" and "moral power" in the world if the Conference failed.[121] In his reply on March 12 the Emperor announced his acceptance of the Austrian plan, and urged the President to support it.[122]

---

[119] G.P., XXI, 274 ff., Nos. 7091 ff.; Tardieu, p. 318; Bishop, I, 495 ff. Bülow also sent a condensed telegram to the German banker, Mendelssohn, then in St. Petersburg negotiating a loan with Witte.

[120] Schoen to F. O., March 13, 1906, G.P., XXI, 279 f., No. 7095; Monts to F. O., March 13, 1906, ibid., 280 f., No. 7097; Wedel to F. O., March 13, 1906, ibid., 281 f., No. 7099; Metternich to F. O., March 13, 1906, ibid., 282 ff., No. 7100; Grey to Lascelles, March 13, 1906, B.D., III, 301 f., Nos. 347 f.

[121] Sternburg to F. O., March 7, 1906, G.P., XXI, 259 ff., No. 7074; Bishop, I, 493 ff.; Tardieu, pp. 251 f., 297.

[122] Bülow to Sternburg, March 12, 1906, G.P., XXI, No. 7093; Bishop, I, 495 ff.; Tardieu, p. 335. The President's intervention was extremely embarrassing to Bülow, who, after calling Sternburg's attention to the difference between the original wording of the promise to Roosevelt sent from Berlin in the previous June and that sent to the President by Sternburg, threatened to disavow the Ambassador (G.P., XXI, 277 f., No. 7093). However, he did not do so.

Upon receiving that reply Mr. Roosevelt on March 14 denounced the Austrian project to Baron Sternburg as "absurd because it favors the very ideas the conference has been trying to eliminate namely partition and spheres of influence," and also because it was impracticable. On the other hand, "placing French and Spanish officers in the same ports gives according to my view a safer guarantee than placing them separately in single ports," he said. In spite of that reply, however, Prince Bülow regarded the German position as "at present not at all unfavorable."[123]

Meanwhile, the French were restoring their front. In Paris a new government was formed by M. Sarrien on March 14 with M. Bourgeois at the foreign office. M. Bourgeois, with whom Prince Radolin was on cordial terms, was known to be a conciliatory statesman interested in harmonizing international differences. But he could hardly begin his career in office with an unpopular concession on the Moroccan question. He renewed M. Révoil's instructions, refusing to compromise on the police in any manner whatever.

It was a bold act. The French government knew that the Russian, Italian, British, and Austrian governments disapproved. Several influential members of the French Parliament tried to persuade M. Bourgeois that the British government, influenced by Sir Henry Campbell-Bannerman, would withdraw its support from France. The new cabinet was alarmed by the British advice to accept a neutral police in Casablanca rather than break up the Conference, and some of the ministers suspected that Great Britain and Germany were about to come to an arrangement leaving France in the lurch. In a French cabinet meeting M. Clémenceau was at first the only minister to combat these doubts.[124]

But the move succeeded. M. Bourgeois quickly repulsed the

[123] Sternburg to F. O., March 14, 1906, *ibid.*, 285 f., No. 7102.

[124] Bertie to Grey, March 15, 16, 17, 1906, *B.D.*, III, 306, Nos. 355 f.; 307 f., No. 358; 309 f., No. 361; Grey, I, 102 ff.

intervention, half-hearted as it was, of the Russian, Italian, and Austrian ambassadors in Paris in favor of the Austrian plan; he even gathered from his conversation with the Austrian representative that the latter's government would try to persuade Germany to relinquish her stand on the policing of Casablanca.[125] In addition, as soon as the French instructions were published, Sir Edward Grey immediately informed the French government that Great Britain would "of course" support it.[126]

When he learned of the French doubts about the continuation of British aid, he rather indignantly replied that the French leaders, MM. Bourgeois, Etienne, and Clémenceau,

should be told that there has never been any question here of discontinuing our support to France. We have given it throughout at Algeciras and in every capital in Europe where required and shall continue this so long as the French wish it and trust us. Cordial co-operation with France in all parts of the world remains a cardinal point of British policy and in some respects we have carried it further than the late Government here were required to do.

Any advice Nicolson has given to Révoil has been on the understanding that this support would be continued, and if he has given advice freely it has

[125] Tardieu, pp. 327 f., 343; Radolin to F. O., March 14 and 15, 1906, *G.P.*, XXI, 291 f., No. 7104; 295 ff., No. 7107; Bertie to Grey, March 16, 1906, *B.D.*, III, 307 f., No. 358.

[126] Grey to Bertie, March 14, 1906, *B.D.*, III, 303, No. 350; 304, No. 352. In private both Sir Edward Grey and Sir Charles Hardinge greatly deplored the French refusal. On March 15 the former wrote to Sir Francis Bertie as follows: "I think the French made a great mistake in not closing at once with the German concession at Algeciras; they could have made it appear to be a diplomatic victory for themselves. . . . . Even the *Times* correspondent of Algeciras thinks France ought not to break off on such a wretched point as Casa Blanca, which I believe is a useless hole. However, if she does, we shall back her up" (*ibid.*, 304 f., No. 353). And on the same day Sir Charles Hardinge wrote to Sir Arthur Nicolson as follows: ". . . . If the Conference breaks up over such an absurd point as the Casablanca proposal *we* shall be in a disagreeable position, as I remember well your opinion that the French position will not be difficult for Germany to undermine in Morocco and we shall then be exposed to any violent action which the French may take to retrieve their losses and shall find ourselves compelled to support France in a war against Germany. If the Conference is broken off I shall not like the outlook. I felt very strong about telling Cambon that in our opinion the Austrian proposal should be accepted rather than allow the Conference to fall through" (*ibid.*, 305, No. 354).

been because of his complete confidence that this was understood by his French colleague. The same is true of my conversations with Cambon. . . . . The Prime Minister has been cognizant of all I have said and has cordially approved of it.

Sir Arthur Nicolson denied that either directly or indirectly had he ever said to the German delegates that France ought to give way on any point.[127] Sir Edward Grey informed the other governments that the British fidelity to France would continue as before. And on March 18 *Le Temps* published the instructions to Sir Arthur Nicolson so that public opinion could see how complete that support was.[128]

If the French leaders intended to bring Great Britain back unreservedly into line by expressing these doubts about British support, they succeeded. M. Bourgeois could with more assurance inform the German Ambassador that France had receded as far as she would. On March 17 Prince Radolin reported his words as follows:

The Minister added that he stood on the defensive, that he supported entirely the previous policy of Rouvier and Révoil, ... that he had agreed in principle with the appointment of a general inspector from some lesser state "subject to agreement on details" but that under no circumstances would he permit the inspector to exercise a command or a collaboration. That is a question of principle, a vital question for France and her prestige in Algeria. Moreover in case the conference ends without result, the *status quo* is no disadvantage for France. Germany, not France, had demanded the conference. "It is your turn now to speak, but not of the police. It is lost effort."

He accused the German government of being responsible for the pressure of the other Powers on France. According to instructions, Prince Radolin replied in a serious tone but without threat that the steps taken by those governments were caused by Ger-

---

[127] Grey to Bertie, March 15, 1905, *ibid.*, 307, No. 357; Grey to Nicolson, March 14, 1906, *ibid.*, 304, No. 351; Nicolson to Grey, March 15, 1906, *ibid.*, 304 n., No. 351; Spring Rice to Lamsdorff, March 17, 1906, quoted in Grey, I, 107 f.; Tardieu, pp. 311 f.

[128] Grey, I, 107 f.; Tardieu, pp. 329 f., 347.

many's great concessions of March 10.[129] But the vote of confidence given without debate to the new cabinet by the Chamber on March 19 showed that M. Bourgeois interpreted French feeling correctly.[130]

There were signs at Paris and Algeciras as early as March 17 that Austria was seeking some new way out of the deadlock, and that Germany might accept the French view about Casablanca.[131] Before the Austrian mediation had time to materialize, however, the renewed intervention of the American government turned the scales in favor of France. On March 16 Prince Bülow had replied to Mr. Roosevelt with arguments showing that the Austrian plan would preserve the unity and integrity of Morocco whereas the French plan would divide the country into spheres of influence.[132] The President remained unconvinced. Thinking that the whole German action was intended to humiliate France, he and American public opinion took the French side. While he no longer believed that Germany aimed at war with her western neighbor, he and his advisers did suspect her of intending by the Austrian proposal to gain a port and a sphere of influence in the Mediterranean. Germany's extreme demands were arousing dissatisfaction among the other delegates at Algeciras, he told Baron Sternburg, and Austria and Russia had already asked him to advise Germany to moderate them. So, while he declared that he would not hold out if the other Powers accepted the Austrian plan, he remained hostile to it. He threatened to publish the entire correspondence on the subject if the Conference failed.

[129] Radolin to F. O., March 17, 1906, *G.P.*, XXI, 303 f., No. 7114; Tardieu, pp. 343 f.; Nicolson to Grey, March 18, 1906, *B.D.*, III, 311, No. 363.

[130] *Journal officiel. Debats parlem.* (Chambre, March 14 and 19, 1906), pp. 1290, 1438 f.

[131] The conversation on March 15 between Bourgeois and the Austrian Ambassador also pointed in this direction. See Bertie to Grey, March 16, 1906, *B.D.*, III, 307 f., No. 358. See also Nicolson to Grey, March 17, 18, 21, 1906, *ibid.*, 308, No. 359; 310 f., No. 362; 311 f., No. 364; 314 f., No. 368; Grey to Bertie, March 17, 1906, *ibid.*, 308 f., No. 360.

[132] Bülow to Sternburg, March 16, 1906, *G.P.*, XXI, 293 ff., No. 7106.

Baron Sternburg learned that Mr. Root had said privately that Germany's attitude at the Conference was "petty and unworthy of a great nation," that she was fast losing the confidence of the world. In reiterating the American stand, Mr. Root wrote to the Ambassador: "If we had sufficient interest in Morocco to make it worth our while, we should seriously object, on our own account, to the adoption of any such arrangement [as the Austrian plan]."[133]

With the net drawing tighter around Germany, Prince Bülow notified President Roosevelt on March 19 that Germany would accept the American plan of having French and Spanish officers in about equal numbers co-operate in each of the ports, supervised by a general inspector from another nation.[134] President Roosevelt was jubilant over Germany's acceptance of his plan. He immediately proposed it to the French government and asked the British to support him.[135]

From this side the President met with strenuous opposition. France and Spain would have nothing to do with the idea of mixed police, except if necessary in Tangier and Casablanca. Complaining of too many peacemakers,[136] Sir Edward Grey supported the Franco-Spanish view. Mr. Roosevelt suddenly grew timid and refused to defend his project before the Conference.[137]

---

[133] Sternburg to F. O., March 17 and 18, 1906, *ibid.*, 300 ff., Nos. 7112 f.; 305 ff., No. 7115; Bishop, I, 497 ff.

[134] Bülow to Radowitz, March 16, 19, 22, 1906, *G.P.*, XXI, 298 f., No. 7110; 307 ff., No. 7117; 311, No. 7120; Radowitz to F. O., March 17, 18, 21, 1906, *ibid.*, 299 f., No. 7111; 306 f., No. 7116; 310 f., No. 7119; Tardieu, pp. 344 ff.; Bülow to Sternburg, March 19, 1906, *G.P.*, XXI, 309 f., No. 7118.

[135] Dennis, pp. 505 f.; Grey to Durand, March 22, 1906, *B.D.*, III, 317, No. 374.

[136] Grey to Goschen, March 21, 1906, *B.D.*, III, 315 f., No. 371.

[137] On this episode see Nicolson to Grey, March 19, 21, 23, 1906, *ibid.*, 312 ff., Nos. 365 ff.; 315, No. 370; 318, No. 376; 319 f., No. 379; Grey to de Bunsen, March 21, 1906, *ibid.*, 316, No. 372; Bertie to Grey, March 22, 1906, *ibid.*, 317 f., No. 375; Grey to Durand, March 22 and 23, 1906, *ibid.*, 317, No. 374; 318, No. 377; Durand to Grey, March 24, 1906, *ibid.*, 320 f., Nos. 380 f.; de Bunsen to Grey, March 27, 1906, *ibid.*, 325 f., No. 385; Tardieu, pp. 385 ff.; Sternburg to F. O., March 21 and 22, 1906, *G.P.*, XXI, 311 f., No. 7121; 321, No. 7126; Radowitz to F. O., March 21, 1906, *ibid.*, 310 f., No. 7119.

The German government was therefore forced to fall back on Austrian mediation.[138]

In a private conversation on March 23 Count Welsersheimb informed M. Révoil that Germany might sacrifice her demand for a neutral police at Casablanca if France would make reciprocal concessions. M. Révoil was willing to limit the number of French shares in the bank to three. But for the other unsettled problems of determining how much international control should be established over the police and bank and how the police should be divided among the various ports, the two men failed to find a solution. On the first question the German government demanded as a *conditio sine qua non* that the inspector should be made responsible to the diplomatic corps at Tangier, which should exercise a general supervision over the police. M. Révoil, on the other hand, supported by the British and Spanish delegates, desired that the diplomatic corps be excluded from intervening in this matter at all. On the question of the bank the Germans wanted the various governments and the diplomatic corps at Tangier to have some authority over the censors while the French did not. As to the division of ports the French formally requested that the settlement of this problem and of other details should be left for France and Spain to determine later with the Sultan; the Germans preferred to have the Conference itself divide the ports between these two Powers.[139]

At that point the Conference again reached a deadlock. With

---

[138] The Austrian government was opposed to trying to mediate upon the basis of Roosevelt's proposal (unsigned and undated memoir handed by Szogyeny to the German government, March 23, 1906, *G.P.*, XXI, 321, No. 7127).

[139] France could afford to make the concession on the bank because she had assured herself of the votes of Italy, Great Britain, Spain, Belgium, and the United States, which with her own three votes would constitute a majority. On this discussion see Tardieu, pp. 297, 342, 347 ff.; *L.j., 1906,* pp. 196 ff.; Bülow to Radowitz, March 24, 1906, *G.P.*, XXI, 322 f., No. 7129; Radowitz to F. O., March 16, 23, 25, 26, 1906, *ibid.*, 297, No. 7109; 322, No. 7128; 324 ff., No. 7131; 326 f., Nos. 7132 f.; Nicolson to Grey, March 23, 1906, *B.D.*, III, 319 f., No. 379.

victory in view the French, on March 26, refused to give way;[140] while the Germans, who had already made the great concession, sought to save as much as they could. They felt compelled to be firmer because the publication in *Le Temps* on March 21 of the very pro-French instructions to the Russian delegate at Algeciras, succeeding the publication of the French and British instructions, made it appear as if the German government were being coerced into retreat.[141] With one or two exceptions, the delegates, anxious to conclude the Conference and attributing little importance to these matters, were inclined to think that

[140] Tardieu, pp. 362, 365 ff.; Radowitz to F. O., March 26, 1906, *G.P.*, XXI, Nos. 7132 f.; Nicolson to Grey, March 26, 27, 1906, *B.D.*, III, 321, No. 382; 322 ff., No. 383.

[141] This publication, which was another answer to the exaggerated article in the *Lokalanzeiger* on March 12, angered the German government. A short time previously Bülow had asked the Russian government to use its influence in moderating the anti-German campaign of the French press, especially of Tardieu in *Le Temps*. Instead of doing so, the Russian government issued this denial that it had ever advised France to accept the Austrian police proposal and asserted that Russia had never ceased and would not cease from acting toward France as a faithful ally. The German government complained to the Russian government against its so manifestly taking the French side, and threatened to refuse German participation in the forthcoming Russian loan. Both Lamsdorff and Witte were impressed by the vigor of the complaints, and tried to explain the affair away. Nelidow had endeavored to influence Tardieu, they said, and had spoken to him in general terms of the instructions which he had just received. To the Ambassador's amazement, he had discovered an entirely false account of these instructions published in *Le Temps*. On demanding an explanation from Tardieu, the latter said that he had obtained his information in the French foreign office. Both ministers as well as the Ambassador expressed their regrets over the affair, and Lamsdorff published a correct version of the instructions. But as Schoen said, the latter version did not change the previous one much. Osten-Sacken weakened the Russian explanation by admitting to Tschirschky that Nelidow himself had given an "excerpt" of the instructions to the offending journalist. So the German government was not appeased by the excuses (see Bülow to Schoen, March 22, 1906, *G.P.*, XXI, 312 f., No. 7122, and following documents. As a matter of fact, those instructions were published on purpose to impress upon Germany that Russia held to the Dual Alliance and did not regard the Björkö accord as binding. See Witte, pp. 298 ff.; Iswolsky, *Recollections of a Foreign Minister*, pp. 23 f.; Tardieu, pp. 330 ff.; Nicolson to Grey, March 21, 1906, *B.D.*, III, 315, No. 369; Spring Rice to Grey, March 21, 1906, *ibid.*, 316 f., No. 373.

France ought to recede on the question of the responsibility of the inspector.[142] President Roosevelt was once more urging that both France and Spain be given a joint mandate and that they accept from the Conference a joint responsibility for every port no matter how the ports were divided.[143] After the session on March 26, the mediators again set to work. Germany agreed for France and Spain to divide the ports as they wished and to submit their decision to the Conference for approval. Both Powers made concessions on the question of the control of the bank. On the most difficult problem of the responsibility of the police inspector, the French, British, Spanish, Russian, and Italian first delegates met privately at M. Révoil's suggestion and worked out a formula. Then Mr. White submitted it to the German delegates, and the latter accepted it (March 27).[144] The difficulties were thereby settled.

In the meantime trouble, which did not come to the surface, had arisen between France and Spain. The Franco-Spanish accord of 1905 had provided for the policing of only five ports, whereas the Conference had dealt with all eight. France wanted the other three left to her; but Spain refused. On March 18 she requested that Tangier be given to her, but the French government rejected the suggestion, offering instead to agree that Casablanca as well as Tangier should be policed by French and Spanish together. This offer was refused by Spain, who on about March 25 made the additional request that she should be given an extra share in the bank by the Conference instead of receiving it later from France according to agreement. The French would not accede to this, but by March 31 the two Powers decided that

[142] Even the Russian and Spanish delegates considered this matter of no importance. See Tardieu, pp. 361 ff.; Radowitz to Bülow, March 28, 1906, *G.P.*, XXI, 330 f., No. 7137.

[143] Sternburg to F. O., March 24, 1906, *G.P.*, XXI, 324, No. 7130.

[144] Radowitz to F. O., March 26 and 27, 1906, *ibid.*, 326 ff., Nos. 7132 ff.; Radowitz to Bülow, March 28, 1906, *ibid.*, 330 f., No. 7137; Nicolson to Grey, March 27, 1906, *B.D.*, 324 f., No. 384; Tardieu, pp. 371 ff.

the officers should be Spanish in Tetouan and Larache, French and Spanish in Casablanca and Tangier, and French in the other four ports.[145]

The Conference accepted this division, together with the following terms on the police: They should function for five years; they should be inspected at least once a year by a Swiss officer stationed at Tangier[146] who should report to the Sultan; this officer was also empowered to make as many special reports as he saw fit; he should likewise send a copy of these reports to the dean of the diplomatic corps in order that that body might

confirm that the Moroccan police is functioning in conformity with the decisions taken by the Conference and that it may see whether it guarantees in an efficacious manner and in conformity with the treaties the security of persons and of the property of foreigners as well as that of commercial transactions; . . . . in case of demand before it by an interested legation the diplomatic corps may, after advising the representatives of the Sultan of its action, request the inspector to make an inquiry and draw up a report on the complaint made.

On the question of the bank it was stipulated that the censors should be chosen with the approval of their governments by the various state banks of the countries involved. Instead of using the expression that the censors should exercise "the supervision of the administration of the Bank in the name of the signatory Powers," a phrase to which the French objected as smacking of internationalization again, the delegates substituted the less colorful one that the censors should exercise "the supervision of which they are invested by the present Act in that which concerns the administration of the bank."[147]

Thus, formulas were found. Details were cleared up; minor

[145] On these negotiations see Tardieu, pp. 378 ff. Almodovar tried to reopen the question of Tangier with the French on April 1 but had no success (*ibid.*, pp. 394 ff.; see also *L.j., 1906*, p. 239).

[146] A Swiss was selected at France's wish because Switzerland was so little interested in Morocco. See Nicolson to Grey, March 28, 1906, *B.D.*, III, 326 f., No. 386.

[147] Tardieu, pp. 396 ff.; *L.j., 1906*, p. 210; Lee, II, 362.

points settled. On April 7 the delegates signed the general act. The Conference of Algeciras was ended.[148]

The conclusions of the Conference were determined by the exigencies of international relations and the interests of European Powers, not by the needs of Morocco. The less interested Powers had aimed chiefly at preserving peace in Europe. France and her satellite, Spain, had been concerned with maintaining their interests in Morocco and with preventing any other Power from gaining a foothold there. Germany alone had endeavored to defend Moroccan rights, and she had done so only because that policy had been in accord with her interests. The Moroccan delegates had in general been disregarded by the Conference, which assumed that the Sultan would under pressure accept its decisions. Although the assembly had formally acknowledged the independence and integrity of Morocco and the sovereignty of the Sultan, it had shown little more regard for them than had the Anglo-French and Franco-Spanish agreements of 1904–5. While the open door had been allowed, the French and Spanish military control in Morocco assured to those two Powers the main economic advantages. In view of the terms of the Franco-Spanish accord of 1905, it was certain that those Powers would not preserve equality of economic treatment. France and Spain had both fought internationalization so effectively that the international supervision established was entirely inadequate to command respect. The idea that a Power might be charged by the other Powers with the exercise of a mandate for the sake of the "backward people" had not as yet been seriously considered by any government. In February and March President Roosevelt and the German government had discussed the proposal of granting to France and Spain a mandate in Morocco "from all the Powers, under responsibility to all of them for the

[148] *L.j., 1906*, pp. 196 ff.; Radowitz to F. O., March 27 and 31, 1906, *G.P.*, XXI, 328 ff., Nos. 7134 ff.; 331 f., No. 7138; Radowitz to Bülow, March 28, 1906, *ibid.*, 330 f., No. 7137; Tardieu, pp. 396 ff. The final act is found in *L.j., 1906*, pp. 262 ff.

maintenance of equal rights and opportunities"[149]—that is, for the advantage of the Western Powers not for that of Morocco—but the trouble lay in the absence of any existing machinery which would have enabled it to be put into effect.

The reforms provided for were hardly more than a beginning. They were unsatisfactory both to the Moroccans and to the French and the Spanish. The Moroccan government was surprised at the outcome of the Conference, having expected that France would be arraigned before that body as before a tribunal. The mass of the Moroccan people remained hostile to reform; they were turning their homage more to the pretender and to Raisouli. Even those ministers who recognized the necessity for change denounced the Conference proposals as benefiting the Europeans and European trade in Morocco but not the Moroccan government. "The conference has turned Morocco over to the French," said El Tores, a delegate to that assembly, to Dr. Rosen. He thought that either acceptance or rejection of the Conference act by the Sultan would be a misfortune.[150] Ben Sliman, the Moroccan foreign minister, was equally despondent.

He regarded the outlook after the decision of the Conference as simply hopeless [so Mr. Lowther reported his assertions]. If the Makhzen assented to the Conference's decision there was an end to the Moorish Government, as a Government. The ports were thereby practically handed over for ever to the Powers. These were of importance to Europeans and of a certain financial value to the Sultan although they were but a small part of the country and their populations a mere handful of those of the Sultan's subjects, who, in normal times, had acknowledged His Majesty's rule, and paid taxes. But the decisions of the Conference Ben Sliman considered, in practice if not in theory, left the Sultan no means or hopes of doing anything to re-establish order and restore prosperity to the vast mass of his people, to whose needs at large the proposed reforms were totally inadequate and he was deeply disappointed with them.

His Excellency would therefore infinitely have preferred the reforms to have been so framed that the Powers would have exercised some kind of direction, assistance and advice at the Court itself, the influence of which

[149] Bishop, I, 492, 494, 496 ff.
[150] Rosen to Bülow, May 17, 1906, *G.P.*, XXI, 601 f., No. 7276.

would have been, in course of time, felt throughout the country to the great advantage of all concerned. As it was, the Makhzen seemed to be left in as impotent and ridiculous a position as ever in the eyes of its subjects.[151]

Opinion at court was divided upon whether to accept the decisions of the Conference or not. When the dean of the diplomatic corps in Tangier officially communicated the Conference act to the Sultan, the latter tried to delay a decision and to discuss certain points. But on June 18 he reluctantly signed the act with reservations. All indications pointed to the opposition of the Moroccan government to any serious efforts at reforms.[152]

The Conference had made inadequate provisions for coping with Moroccan opposition. There could be no half-measures in handling Morocco. Europe had to leave her alone entirely or give the mandatory Powers complete freedom to "shoot" reforms into the land. The right to police eight towns would just suffice to involve France and Spain in a series of petty, indecisive clashes with the natives. If they wished to employ more military authority, they would have either to obtain the permission of the Powers or to risk another international crisis by taking an unauthorized initiative. As soon as the execution of the reforms should begin, the inadequacy of all this diplomatic activity would become evident. The Moroccan problem had not been solved.

[151] Lowther to Grey, April 22, 1906, *B.D.*, III, 338, No. 402.

[152] Grey to Nicolson, March 12, 1906, *ibid.*, 299 f., No. 343; Nicolson to Grey, March 13, April 3, 1906, *ibid.*, 301, No. 346; 330, No. 392; Lowther to Grey, April 17 and 22, 1906, *ibid.*, 337 ff., Nos. 401 f.; 346 f. and inclosure, No. 412; memo. by Geoffray, Aug. 31, 1906, *ibid.*, 341 ff., No. 405; Tardieu, pp. 425 ff.

CHAPTER XVIII

CONCLUSION

The conclusion of the Conference relaxed the tension in Europe and cleared the way for a gradual improvement in the relations of the Powers. Both sides expressed satisfaction with the results, which, according to official interpretation, left behind neither victor nor vanquished.[1] None the less it was evident that Germany had been defeated. She had tried to obtain a material interest in Morocco; she had endeavored to break the Entente Cordiale and therewith the other French ententes; she had sought to disrupt or to modify the Dual Alliance. And she had failed in every effort. In attempting to restore her dominating position of the time before the formation of the Entente Cordiale, Germany had only driven France, Great Britain, and Russia into closer intimacy and had furthered the very alignment of the Powers which she had feared. By defending an international

---

[1] On April 5 Bülow declared in the Reichstag as follows: "A time of alarm lies behind us. There were weeks when the thought of armed complications occupied our minds. . . . . We wished to show that Germany does not let herself be handled as a *quantité negligeable*. . . . . We may now look into the future with more calmness. The Conference of Algeciras has, I believe, had a result equally satisfactory to Germany and France and useful to all nations" (*Reden*, II, 303 ff.). On April 12 Bourgeois spoke in the French Chamber in a similar vein: ". . . . All the work of the conference has aimed to harmonize the three essential conditions of Moroccan reform [the sovereignty of the Sultan, the integrity of his empire, and commercial liberty] with the rights and the special interests that France has the duty of defending. . . . . That result has been obtained, thanks to the reciprocal concessions seriously weighed and loyally consented to in terms absolutely honorable for all and without the abandonment of the fruits of our country's past efforts, of the dignity of its present situation, or of the safeguards of its future. . . . . France has been able to put to the test the solidarity of her alliance and friendships to which precious sympathies have been joined" (quoted in *L.j., 1906*, pp. 290 ff.). The act was accepted by the French Parliament and by the German Reichstag in Dec., 1906 (Schulthess, *Europäischer Geschichtskalender 1906*, pp. 219, 328 ff.; Tardieu, *La Conf. d'Algés*, pp. 415 ff.).

right which no one else valued she had permitted her isolation, except for the support of Austria, to be exposed to all the world. At the Conference she had forced Russia, Italy, and even the United States reluctantly to take the French side. Germany had entirely miscalculated the situation.[2]

The German statesmen realized that their international position had grown more serious. Italy's meager support at the Conference was further proof that Germany could not rely upon that ally.[3] The increased importance of Austria to Germany was tacitly admitted when, on April 13, the Emperor William thanked Count Goluchowski for playing the "brilliant second" at the Conference and promised him: "You can also be certain of similar service from me in a similar case."[4] Prince Bülow, whom his master had not consulted beforehand, warned him, however, "(1) that our relations with Austria have now become

[2] Cf. Stuart, *French Foreign Policy from Fashoda to Serajevo*, pp. 221 ff.; Tardieu, *La France et les alliances*, pp. 239 ff. Schoen reported that his French colleague, Bompard, had expressed his opinion as follows: "What has resulted . . . . from the Conference of Algeciras? First, a welding together of France and England which the former did not at all wish in this measure. Then an almost complete isolation of Germany and probably no small amount of ill-humor among all the Powers, who saw themselves compelled to take an open stand on questions in which they really had little interest. Finally, apparent discord between Russia and Germany. True, the Conference has left behind neither victor nor vanquished; Germany has achieved internationalization; France, a certain recognition of her special position. But the existing sources of friction do not appear to have been destroyed, but rather new ones to have been created. . . . . The Conference, together with its previous history, has left in the French nation a certain mistrust which may not disappear quickly and which will for years stand in the way of a genuine friendly *rapprochement*, which is desired on both sides and which was so near" (Schoen to Bülow, April 7, 1906, *G.P.*, XXI, 341, No. 7144).

[3] Monts was so disgusted with Italy that he wished the terms of the Triple Alliance to be radically modified at the next renewal (Monts to Tschirschky, June 8, 1906, *G.P.*, XXI, 364 ff., No. 7156). The Austrian Ambassador reported that the German Emperor said that "it would give him great satisfaction for us at a suitable moment, which in view of the unreliable policy of the kingdom is not impossible, to teach the latter [Italy] a wholesome lesson, even by arms" (Pribram, *The Secret Treaties of Austria-Hungary*, II, 138).

[4] Schulthess, *1906*, p. 92.

more important than ever, since that state is our only reliable ally; (2) that we must let our relative political isolation be noticed by the Austrians as little as possible."[5] And in September the Emperor commented sarcastically: "Fine prospects! In the future we can count on the Franco-Russian Alliance, Anglo-French Entente Cordiale and Anglo-Russian Entente, with Spain, Italy, and Portugal as appendages thereto in the second line!"[6]

To counteract this isolation the German government could do little for the time being except remain quiet.[7] It permitted relations with Italy to continue as before.[8] It assumed a "correct but reserved attitude toward France."[9] It refused to sanction German participation in the Russian loan, but otherwise remained on friendly terms with that Power.[10] Its main desire was to reach some kind of an understanding with Great Britain so as to share in the entente movement.[11] Anglo-German relations did improve, but the British government replied to German soundings that more time should elapse before the two governments

[5] Bülow to William II, May 31, 1906, *G.P.*, XXI, 360, No. 7154.

[6] Minute by William II to a dispatch from Miquel to Bülow, Sept. 19, 1906, *ibid.*, XXV, 23, No. 8518.

[7] Tschirschky to William II, May 12, 1906, *ibid.*, XXI, 433 f., No. 7184; Bülow to F. O., Aug. 13, 1906, *ibid.*, 449, No. 7193. The resignation of Holstein from the foreign office in April was also considered as significant of a change of policy. On that episode see *ibid.*, pp. 338 f., editor's note.

[8] Bülow to Monts, Nov. 16, 1906, *ibid.*, 387 f., No. 7165, and others in chap. cliv.

[9] Tschirschky to Metternich, July 7, 1906, *ibid.*, 439, No. 7188.

[10] Schoen to Bülow, May 14, 1906, *ibid.*, XXII, 21 ff., No. 7355, and other documents in chap. clx. On the question of the loan see the report from the Belgian Minister at Berlin, April 11, 1906, *Zur europ. Politik*, II, pp. 110 ff.; Witte, *Memoirs*, pp. 304 ff.

[11] "Our relations with England have for a long time been of a very delicate nature. It is the object of my serious care to bring about an improvement herein." See Tschirschky to General von Einem, July 9, 1906, *G.P.*, XXI, 440, No. 7190. See also the Emperor's remark to a similar effect in a memorandum by him, Aug. 15, 1906, *ibid.*, XXIII, 84, No. 7815.

should attempt any concerted efforts to bring their countries closer together.[12]

German public opinion was dissatisfied with the way in which its foreign affairs were being conducted; its alarm over the international situation increased as the year progressed. When the debate in the Reichstag on that subject, delayed because of the Chancellor's illness, was held on November 14, Herr Bassermann of the National Liberal party remarked as follows:

Today the Triple Alliance has no further practical utility. The Italian press and population lean more and more towards France. Austria has been too much praised for this rôle of "brilliant second" which she herself declined. The Franco-Russian Alliance remains intact, and the disposition of France towards us is less friendly than formerly. The explanations at Cronberg between the English and German sovereigns does not prevent England from pursuing her old policy of isolating us. We live in an era of alliances between other nations. . . . . Our policy lacks tranquillity and consistency, and we see brutal hands derange well prepared plans.[13]

As these criticisms were widespread, Prince Bülow replied in a long and carefully prepared speech. Admitting the deep hostility of France to Germany, he expressed the hope that the two nations would live peacefully together. As to Anglo-German relations he declared: "A long period of misunderstanding lies behind us. The needle of the political barometer has happily gone from rain and wind to changing." He denied that any deep antagonisms

[12] The improvement in Anglo-German relations was manifested by visits of German burgomasters in May, of German journalists to England in June, by a visit of Edward VII to his nephew at Cronberg in August, and by the presence of Mr. Haldane at the German maneuvers later in the same month. See Lee, *King Edward VII*, II, 528 ff.; Haldane, *Before the War*, pp. 37 ff., 57 ff.; Metternich to Bülow, May 8, 1906, *G.P.*, XXI, 427 ff., No. 7181; Mühlberg to Radolin, June 27, 1906, *ibid.*, 437 f., No. 7187; Bülow to F. O., Aug. 13, 1906, *ibid.*, 449, No. 7193 and following documents; memo. by William II, Aug. 15, 1906, *ibid.*, XXIII, 84 ff., No. 7815; Tschirschky to Metternich, Sept. 4, 1906, *ibid.*, 86 f., No. 7816. See also the documents in *B.D.*, Vol. III, chap. xxii; Grey, *Twenty-five Years*, I, 110 ff. During Grey's absence the foreign office at first opposed Haldane's visit for fear of alienating the French (Haldane, *An Autobiography*, p. 202; Spender, *Life of Campbell-Bannerman*, II, 260).

[13] *Stenogr. Berichte*, Reichtag (1906), p. 4238; Tardieu, *La France et les alliances*, pp. 243 f.

divided the two countries and that the German fleet was a menace to Great Britain. He suggested that time should be allowed for the two nations to approach each other. "We have no thought," he said, "of wishing to push ourselves in between France and Russia or France and England." He announced that "for some time negotiations between Russia and England have been under way which promise that an understanding will be reached over certain Central Asiatic regions. . . . ." He added: "We have no reason at all to disturb these negotiations or to regard their probable result with mistrustful eyes." But he issued the following warning: "The Entente Cordiale without good relations between the Powers and Germany would be a danger to European peace. . . . . Such an encirclement is not possible without the exercise of a certain pressure. Pressure produces counter-pressure, from pressure and counter-pressure explosions may finally arise." He denied that Germany was isolated and testified to the loyalty of her two allies; but he declared that Germany was strong enough to defend herself alone. Urging the nation not to be uneasy, he said: "More than once we have been in situations where the danger of a general grouping against us lay nearer than today. . . . . The political world is still agitated by a certain excitement which calls for carefulness and prudence, but gives no cause for pusillanimity." He concluded with a vigorous defense of his own and the Emperor's methods of conducting foreign affairs. His words were widely applauded, even though they did not assuage German fears or stop criticism.[14]

The satisfaction of the French and British governments with the results of the Conference was real. Although France had had to recognize the international character of Moroccan reforms, she had practically asserted her position in that land. She had also preserved her ententes and alliance against Germany's attacks, and had herself shown a determined spirit hitherto lacking

---

[14] Bülow's speech is given in Bülow, II, 306 ff.; see also Hammann, *Bilder aus der letzten Kaiserzeit*, pp. 45 ff.

in the Third Republic. The British government had had no direct interest in the Moroccan crisis except from the point of view of general policy, but it was well pleased that the Entente Cordiale had stood the test, that it had grown firmer than before.[15]

Out of this crisis the Entente Cordiale emerged as a lasting dynamic combination for checking Germany. As Sir Edward Grey remarked to the French Ambassador, July 9, 1906, "If we [Great Britain] were called on to take sides [between France and Germany], we must take sides with France as at Algeciras. As long, however, as Germany kept quiet, there was no reason for trouble, and things would go on quietly."[16] The British Foreign Secretary did not thereby give France a blank check against Germany, nor had he done so during the crisis. He had cautioned the French that British support would in last analysis depend upon public opinion. But as the crisis at the Conference in March had shown, he could be forced to take the French side even though he disapproved of it.

The Entente Cordiale was so necessary to both Powers and yet so loose in form that it acquired a peculiar character. Dependent not upon the written word but upon feeling, it had constantly to be kept warm. It partook more of the nature of a jealous engagement than of a trustworthy and tolerant marriage. Each party was particularly mistrustful of any playing by the other with Germany. Still other causes divided them from Germany. They regarded the latter's interference in the Moroccan affair as gratuitous and unjustified. "All that is necessary," wrote Sir Edward Grey in May, 1906, "is for the Germans to realize that they have got nothing to complain of."[17] France and Great Britain feared that Germany might attempt another aggression. As the

[15] Bertie to Grey, April 4, 1906, *B.D.*, III, 330 f., No. 395; Grey to Bertie, April 4, 1906, *ibid.*, 331, No. 396; Grey to Spring Rice, Feb. 19, 1906, Gwynn, *The Letters and Friendships of Sir Cecil Spring Rice*, II, 65.

[16] Grey to Bertie, July 9, 1906, *B.D.*, III, 361, No. 420.

[17] Grey's minute to a dispatch from Lascelles to Grey, May 24, 1906, *ibid.*, 358, No. 416.

British Foreign Secretary stated in June, 1906, implying an accusation in doing so, "The Germans do not realize that England has always drifted or deliberately gone into opposition to any Power which establishes a hegemony in Europe."[18] The French and English believed so firmly that German diplomacy called for the arousing of discord between Powers at every opportunity that they were almost reluctant to have any dealings with the *Wilhelmstrasse*. They saw German intrigues everywhere—in Persia, in Abyssinia,[19] in Paris, in London. When the German Ambassador in Paris spoke in July of a detente in Anglo-German relations, the French and British governments suspected therein an attempt to weaken the Entente Cordiale.[20] Each government, therefore, was cool toward the renegade Power. "When one recovers from a year's sickness," stated the semiofficial *Le Temps* with reference to Franco-German relations, "the convalescence cannot be immediate."[21] Sir Edward Grey appeared friendlier; in July he described Anglo-German relations as again normal. But he refused Germany's bid for an understanding because public opinion was not prepared and especially because France would object. Count Metternich remarked to him on July 31 that M. Delcassé's policy had been to encircle Germany and that at present the British and French press also asserted that this aim should be accomplished with the help of Russia. The Count warned Sir Edward Grey that that dangerous game

[18] Minute by Grey, June 9, 1906, *ibid.*, 359, No. 418.

[19] *Ibid.*, p. 356; IV, 381 f., No. 328.

[20] The German instructions to Radolin used *detente*. Bourgeois used *rapprochement* in his memorandum of the conversation with the German Ambassador. In talking to Grey, Cambon spoke of *entente*. There may have been point to this change, for Grey, who was sensitive about Anglo-French relations, immediately assured the French that Anglo-German relations were not and would not become too intimate, and that an entente did not exist. See Grey to Bertie, July 9, 1906, *ibid.*, III, 361 f., No. 420; Bertie to Grey, July 12, 1906, *ibid.*, 362 f., No. 421; Mühlberg to Radolin, June 27, 1906, *G.P.*, XXI, 438, No. 7187; Tschirschky to Metternich, July 7, 1906, *ibid.*, 438 f., No. 7188.

[21] Bertie to Grey, March 31, 1906, *B.D.*, III, 328, No. 387.

might call forth a situation which would make it necessary for Germany to break the circle.

> A peaceful policy on the other hand is [he said] to extend the hand to Germany and to draw her into the circle of the others. . . . . But so long as in England the German attempts at *rapprochement* are repulsed through fear of arousing displeasure among the French, it appears to me that the policy of creating a balance of power is preferred here to that of drawing Germany into the circle of friendship.

The Foreign Secretary denied that the policy of agreement with Russia was directed in any way against Germany. But when the Ambassador asked "Are, openly avowed, friendly relations with Germany compatible with England's friendship with France?" he replied, "That depends on German politics." The Ambassador immediately countered, "No, it rather seems to depend on French interpretation of German politics."[22] The British Foreign Secretary, however, was not to be moved by German criticisms. The British as well as the French put Germany on her good behavior.

Notwithstanding Sir Edward Grey's denial, this mistrust of the Central Power was an important inducement for Great Britain and France to complete the Entente Cordiale by an entente between Great Britain and Russia.[23] Conditions were more favorable for success than they had ever been. The Moroccan affair no longer occupied international attention. The domestic situation in Russia was more stable with the calling of the Duma. And M. Iswolsky, who succeeded Count Lamsdorff in the Russian foreign office in 1906, brought new vigor into the Russian policy. As a partisan of an agreement with Great Britain, he took up the negotiations, and after an intermittent pursuit of

[22] Metternich to Bülow, July 31, 1906, *G.P.*, XXI, 441 ff., No. 7191; Grey to Lascelles, July 31, 1906, *B.D.*, III, 363 f., No. 422.

[23] On Feb. 20, 1906, Grey wrote: "The door is being kept open by us for a *rapprochement* with Russia; there is at least a prospect that when Russia is re-established we shall find ourselves on good terms with her. An *entente* between Russia, France and ourselves would be absolutely secure. If it is necessary to check Germany it could then be done" (*B.D.*, III, 267, No. 299).

them, brought them to completion in the next year.[24] Thus the work of insuring against Germany was continued.

What the entente Powers regarded as insurance, Germany called encirclement. Both sides had been playing the game of the balance of power. France had tried to abandon this game in the previous year, but Germany's refusal of her offers had driven her back into the play. Neither side appreciated the other's point of view; neither heeded the other's warnings. Each side accused the other of aiming at its defeat, of being a menace. Each scoffed at the other's fears, but each continued to arm and to broaden and tighten the policy which each warned the other was leading to trouble. Neither side had learned anything from this episode except to be more cautious. Neither changed its method.

The motives that caused this crisis still obtained as guiding forces. Prestige and national interests were at stake on both sides. Having become deeply engaged in the Moroccan affair, Germany, France, and Great Britain could not easily back out of it, especially since the Conference of Algeciras had given a better sanction than ever to both sides. That France and Spain would give Germany opportunities for intervening was, in view of the difficulty which they would encounter in reforming Morocco, just as certain as that Germany would take advantage of those opportunities. The Moroccan problem both in its local and in its international aspects left behind plenty of raw material from which future conflicts could arise. The crisis was only the first of these episodes born of the clashings of mutual fears and ambitions, nurtured on hazardous playing with war and on diplomatic blunderings. The road to Armageddon lay open.

[24] *Ibid.*, Vol. IV, chap. xxv, Part IV; Gwynn, Vol. II, chaps. xiv ff.; William L. Langer, "Russia, the Straits Question, and the European Powers, 1904-8," *English History Review,* Jan., 1929; and others.

INDEX

INDEX

INDEX